Talents Unfolding

Talents Unfolding

COGNITION AND DEVELOPMENT

edited by

Reva C. Friedman

Bruce M. Shore

AMERICAN PSYCHOLOGICAL ASSOCIATION • WASHINGTON DC

Published by
American Psychological Association
750 First Street, NE
Washington, DC 20002

Copies may be ordered from
APA Order Department
P.O. Box 92984
Washington, DC 20090-2984

In the U.K., Europe, Africa, and the Middle East, copies may be ordered from
American Psychological Association
3 Henrietta Street
Covent Garden, London
WC2E 8LU England

Typeset in Century Schoolbook by EPS Group Inc., Easton, MD

Printer: United Book Press, Inc., Baltimore, MD
Cover Designer: Berg Design, Albany, NY
Technical/Production Editor: Jennifer Powers

The opinions and statements published are the responsibility of the authors, and such opinions and statements do not necessarily represent the policies of the APA.

Library of Congress Cataloging-in-Publication Data
Talents unfolding : cognition and development / edited by Reva C. Friedman and Bruce M. Shore.
    p. cm.
  Includes bibliographical references and index.
  ISBN 1-55798-643-6 (alk. paper)
    1. Gifted children. 2. Gifted persons. I. Friedman, Reva C.
II. Shore, Bruce M.
BF723.G5 T35 2000
155.45′5—dc21
                                                      99-049344

British Library Cataloguing-in-Publication Data
A CIP record is available from the British Library.

Printed in the United States of America
First Edition

Contents

Contributors

John Colombo, Department of Human Development, University of Kansas, Lawrence

David Henry Feldman, Eliot-Person Department of Child Development, Tufts University, Medford, MA

Reva C. Friedman, Department of Teaching and Leadership, University of Kansas, Lawrence

Howard Gardner, Graduate School of Education, Harvard University, Cambridge, MA

Lynn T. Goldsmith, Education Development Center, Inc., Newton, MA

Nancy Ewald Jackson, College of Education, University of Iowa, Iowa City

Sandra I. Kay, Monroe-Woodbury Central School District, Central Valley, NY, and visiting scholar, Columbia University, New York, NY

Martha J. Morelock, Department of Psychology and Human Development, Peabody College of Vanderbilt University, Nashville, TN

Marion Porath, Department of Educational and Counselling Psychology and Department of Special Education, University of British Columbia, Vancouver, British Columbia, Canada

W. Allen Richman, Department of Human Development, University of Kansas, Lawrence

Nancy M. Robinson, Halbert Robinson Center for the Study of Capable Youth, University of Washington, Seattle

D. Jill Shaddy, Department of Human Development, University of Kansas, Lawrence

Bruce M. Shore, Department of Educational and Counselling Psychology, McGill University, Montreal, Quebec, Canada

Alane J. Starko, Department of Teacher Education, Eastern Michigan University, Ypsilanti

MaryLou Fair Worthen, School of Human Development, University of Texas at Dallas

Foreword

This book about psychological issues in the development of gifted individuals is the product of a precious legacy from the estate of Esther Katz Rosen, PhD (1896–1973). Rosen was a clinical psychologist and a Fellow of American Psychological Association (APA) Divisions 7, 12, and 13. She received her doctorate in 1925 from Columbia University's Teachers College and practiced for the next 40 years in Philadelphia.

We know little about Rosen except that she was married to a judge and had no children. From the fact that she graduated from Goucher College at age 20, however, we can surmise that she had been a gifted child herself. Whatever the source of her knowledge, Rosen understood giftedness as an unrecognized area of special need and special potential for children. When she left the bulk of her estate to the American Psychological Foundation with the directive that the funds be used "for the advancement and application of knowledge about gifted children" she made a significant and continuing impact on the field. Her legacy has provided exciting opportunities for developmentalists of many theoretical persuasions to turn their attention to psychological issues of giftedness.

Our hope is that this book, like its predecessor, *Talent in Context: Historical and Social Perspectives on Giftedness* (APA, 1998), will inspire a new group of psychologists to become involved in this field and, as they encounter gifted individuals, put these insights to work and extend them in new directions. Giftedness withers and disappears without encouragement and challenge; tomorrow's leaders, even its rare geniuses, may be lost if we are heedless of what creates and nourishes talent and achievement. Please join the writers of these thoughtful, careful, and enlightened chapters in rising to the opportunities made possible by Rosen's legacy.

NANCY M. ROBINSON, PhD
Trustee, American Psychological Foundation

Preface

Intellectual activity anywhere is the same, whether at the frontier of knowledge or in a third-grade classroom. What a scientist does at his desk or in his laboratory, what a literary critic does in reading a poem, are of the same order as what anybody else does when he is engaged in like activities—if he is to achieve understanding. The difference is in degree, not in kind.

Jerome S. Bruner, 1963/1960, p. 14

Is intellectual activity the same anywhere and across ages and levels of expertise, different only in degree and not kind? Is this true even for high-level intellectual activity such as that engaged in by scientists, philosophers, persons of letters, professionals, or experts in various fields? Is this true even for children who demonstrate remarkably capable thinking and performance? The research addressed by the chapters of this book casts light on these and related questions. How does the third-grade child's thinking compare to the adult expert's? What do we know about the child who has the understanding to which Bruner (1960/1963) referred?

This book was preceded by *Talent in Context: Historical and Social Perspectives* (Friedman & Rogers, 1998), which introduced the context of giftedness and talent at two social psychological levels: (a) at a societal level, wherein broad influences of culture and gender, for example, shape the understanding and evolution of valued abilities, and (b) at the level of individuals known through personal encounter in the family or school or through reputation as a result of their fame. *Talent in Context* also pointed toward some of the influences in the reconceptualization of giftedness or abilities in general, particularly in terms of creativity, the cognitive psychology of expertise, and the breadth of human endeavor, wherein talent may be sought and nurtured.

This book, *Talents Unfolding: Cognition and Development*, focuses sharply on the individual child's intellectual activity and finds its voice primarily in cognitive development of the individual. Although children spend a major part of their waking hours in school, this book does not uniquely or primarily focus on school learning, although continuing dependence on IQ and measures of scholastic success in many studies demonstrate the existence of several links to it. The goals of this book are to advance the baseline of understanding of the development of exceptional intellectual achievements and potential in individuals from infancy through adulthood and to sharpen scientists' research skills in the continued investigation of these phenomena. The intended audience includes developmental, cognitive, and professional psychologists; educators; and scholars from other disciplines who are especially interested in high ability and talent in children as well as adults, especially those who are curious to explore the poorly charted path between the exceptional thinking of children and that of adults.

These chapters, like those in *Talent in Context* (Friedman & Rogers, 1998), are from the Esther Katz Rosen Symposia on the Development of Gifted Children held at the University of Kansas in 1997. This project is supported by the American Psychological Foundation and the University of Kansas, honoring Rosen's long-standing commitment to enhancing the conceptual foundation supporting theory, research, and practice related to giftedness in children and arising from the vision of the Board of Trustees of the Rosen Fund. The authors whose work was selected for this book fill in numerous details about the many faces of giftedness, how these faces change with age or development, and ways in which more effective research may be conducted. Contributors are primarily developmental psychologists focused on early childhood and educational and cognitive psychologists with particular interest in giftedness and creativity as expressed during school ages. They take as a premise that giftedness has many meanings and add that these different meanings are partly expressed in the development of high ability and the potential for outstanding performance in different domains from infancy to adulthood. Even though the history of the field began and to some extent remains with the psychology of individual differences and the examination of differences in achievement or measured abilities between or among individuals, this book is less focused than *Talent in Context* on the problem of defining giftedness and instead celebrates as a whole the kaleidoscope of intellectual potential within individuals.

This book is clearly not concerned with comparing groups in terms of achievement or potential or the development thereof. That largely unidimensional argument, typically IQ or performance based, is rather distasteful, both socially and intellectually, for psychologists, educators, and others whose intellectual curiosity addresses the development of talent. This does not preclude a continuing interest in IQ or achievement; rather, it is a matter of the purpose to which these measures are put (e.g., comparing individuals or groups or understanding the development of the abilities of individuals and the factors that enhance or hinder that development). Whether applied to ability differences noted among cultural groups or differentiated school services, these books cast light on what scientists and educators can learn for general benefit from individuals and groups of individuals whose intellectual performance differs in reliable and systematic ways, perhaps at specific times of their lives or in particular domains of socially valued or other activity. It becomes abundantly clear in these chapters that intellectual ability is neither unidimensional nor stagnant for long periods of a person's lifetime. The chapters present both theoretical reviews and empirical studies. Some also focus explicitly on the methodology of research, especially case studies. In all cases, we hope that readers will find relevance not only to the study of individuals of high ability or potential but also in examining the full spectrum of human ability. Has the relative neglect of highly able children and adolescents in the developmental literature created an unnecessarily low ceiling of educational expectations and tolerance or respect for diversity? If this book succeeds, perhaps one outcome will be to see the word *normal* disappear from the literature addressing children's accomplishments. An astoundingly wide range of intellectual performance is normal in growing human beings. This book presents a glimpse of some of it.

Our profound appreciation goes to Frances Degan Horowitz, president of the City University of New York's Graduate School, whose commitment, vision, and energy fueled this project, and to Nancy M. Robinson, professor and director, Center for Capable Youth at the University of Washington, for her wise guidance and unconditional support of the symposia and particularly for the resulting books. Richard L. Schiefelbusch, director emeritus of the Life Span Institute, Stephen R. Schroeder, its current director, and Mabel L. Rice, director of the Merrill Advanced Studies Center, provided much appreciated support and a home for the project. Fred and Virginia Merrill, along with their daughter Melinda Merrill, contributed their vision of excellence to bringing the symposia series to fruition. The chairs and staff of the University of Kansas Departments of Teaching and Leadership, Psychology, Research in Education, and Special Education contributed resources to the operation of the project. Over the 6 years of the symposia, Frances Degan Horowitz; John C. Wright, professor at the University of Texas; and Stephen R. Schroeder added their considerable expertise to codirecting the symposia. Our appreciation also goes to the Symposium Advisory Committee at the University of Kansas for their collective creativity, wisdom, and energy: John A. Colombo, Human Development and Family Life; Thomas O. Erb, Teaching and Leadership; Paul G. Friedman, Communication Studies; E. Peter Johnsen, Psychology and Research in Education; Kathleen McCluskey-Fawcett, professor of human development and family life and associate vice-chancellor; Douglas L. Murphy, evaluation specialist at the University of Texas Health Center; and Nona A. Tollefson, Psychology and Research in Education. We would also like to acknowledge the many students and professional colleagues in gifted education who contributed their time to carry out the many tasks that made the symposia personally welcoming to participants.

Meredith V. Porter, symposia coordinator, shaped the environment leading to these chapters with her careful attention to critical details that kept the project on course, and her unfailing good humor made even the most mundane aspects of the symposia and book projects workable. Lisa Straus at the American Psychological Foundation and Mary Lynn Skutley, Margaret Schlegel, Chris Davis, and Jennifer Powers at APA Books made possible the transformation of symposia papers into text.

Bruce thanks his wife Bettina for her patience and support, including a winter drive from Montreal to Kansas to work on the book, and also their children Darren and Monica for everything, including just being there.

To the symposia plenary speakers, discussants, roundtable presenters, and participants, we extend our heartfelt thanks. Their commitment to the topic and to exploring new ideas and forging new connections across disciplines were critical to the success of this project. Their feedback shaped the symposia and this book, and we hope they will continue to mold the field into the next millennium.

References

Bruner, J. S. (1963). *The process of education*. New York: Vintage. (Original work published 1960)

Friedman, R. C., & Rogers, K. B. (Eds.). (1998). *Talent in context: Historical and social perspectives*. Washington, DC: American Psychological Association.

Introduction

No matter what the initial characteristics (or gifts) of the individuals, unless there is a long and intensive process of encouragement, nurturance, education, and training, the individuals will not attain extreme levels of capability in these particular fields.

Benjamin S. Bloom, 1985b, p. 3

Exceptional performance attracts a wide general audience as well as the attention of specialists. Witness, for example, the world-record number of television viewers for the Olympic games or the high ticket prices that spectators will pay to attend top arts or professional sporting events. Similarly, corporations will pay highly to recruit top executives, marketing staff, lawyers, and creative personnel.

Such exemplary performance has a history in each individual, and all persons and society as a whole stand to benefit from any action that can bring out the best in all people, especially those whose potential is exceptionally high. Surprisingly, however, there has been relatively little formal study of the long and intensive period of nurturance that lies behind such accomplishments or of the intellectual and creative elements that are nurtured. For nearly a century, researchers and educators have been actively interested in the quality labeled *giftedness* and children who exhibit this quality, commonly called *gifted*. The word *gifted* tends to make people uncomfortable, especially when it applies to themselves or their own child. It is also psychologically problematic because it has been closely associated with a single conceptualization of high ability, namely a high score on an IQ test. Scholarship in the field is moving away from the term, and practice is beginning to respond with multiple views of high ability, some of them linked to the domain of activity, some to creativity, and all to the realization that the nurturance of high potential in a human being involves both unfettering potential that is within the person and adding knowledge and skills that were not there before. In other words, the nature *versus* nurture question has become a nature *and* nurture question, both having much to offer to the development of human talent.

In this book, we invite the professional or academic psychologist with an interest in the development of human potential to explore some of the latest research on high ability and its development across the life span. We place special emphasis on high ability in childhood, but this is done within the context of trying to develop theories of high ability that also can be used to explain high-level intellectual and creative accomplishments in adulthood. At the beginning of the 20th century, Alfred Binet (Binet & Simon, 1905) focused entirely on children in his practical investigation of the intellectual skills of children who experienced difficulty in school. More contemporary work has embraced the language and constructs of the cognitive sciences, with expert adult behavior as the starting point. This book examines the thinking of children, adolescents, and adults in these terms.

We hope this book will stimulate dialogue among researchers and between practitioners and researchers across traditional discipline boundaries and also serve as a springboard for a new wave of research that will affect the understanding of talent, policies related to talent identification and development, and practices pertinent to the emergence and nurturing of talent as a dynamic, developmental, and systemic phenomenon.

New Meanings to High Ability

An important paradigm shift is occurring in the study of high ability, especially in children. This area of study and practice has sometimes been given the unsatisfactory but conveniently short label *gifted education* to refer to the provision of educational services to children who demonstrate exceptionally capable performance or achievement, or in some way the potential to do so. Part of the shift may be occurring in the label, away from the notion that some children have an endowment (*gift*) that others do not, that this endowment somehow marks them advantageously for life, and that this predetermination is irrevocably determined very early in life. This shift is occurring because the theoretical base of the education of highly able children and the study of giftedness is rapidly expanding. Its dependence on differential psychology, and particularly on psychometric traditions with weak links to curriculum, is diminishing. For two decades or more, the influences of Piaget, neo-Piagetian scholars, Vygotsky, Bruner, and applied cognitive science have been increasingly apparent. Tomlinson and Callahan (1992) asserted with considerable justification that the education of highly able children provides possibly the best examples of educational applications of applied cognitive science.

The direction in which the education of highly able children is moving is best described as "talent development" (cf. Bloom, 1985a; Feldhusen, 1992). There are several important presumptions in this shift. First, psychologists and educators are addressing a lifelong process, not a selection that occurs once and forever in early childhood or preadolescence at the latest. Second, there is a dual focus, both on the individual and on the domain in which the talent or talents develop, and these interact. Third, intervention and opportunity are central to the success of the enterprise. Athletic talent involves a coach, organizational leadership a mentor, and musical and academic talents a teacher. Coach, mentor, model, teacher, counselor, psychologist, and parent—all who play a role in talent development—share a special characteristic of the teaching profession and its scholars and practitioners. Education is an optimistic profession and science. Fully capitalizing on the gifts and talents of every individual requires a broad definition of giftedness such as provided in *Talent in Context: Historical and Social Perspectives on Giftedness* (Friedman & Rogers, 1998) and seeing giftedness not as the privilege of a select few but as a set of maximal expectations toward which (not necessarily always up to which) efforts can be focused. When the potential accomplishments of extremely capable children and adults are ignored, an artificially lowered ceiling is imposed on general educational expectations. Reis (1992) has documented, for example, that the average reading level of regular school texts in the United States has declined by two full years in the past few decades. Lowered expectations may affect the educational accomplishments of a whole society.

The study of giftedness and the education of highly able children are not the magic solution to this problem, but attention to giftedness in mainstream psychology is an important part of the foundation of educational theory that helps to shape good curricula; teaching; remedial practice; and therapeutic services for children, adolescents, and young adults. The goals of this book, to advance the understanding of the development of exceptional intellectual achievements and to sharpen research of these phenomena, are consistent with this paradigm shift, and, we hope, fuel it effectively.

Scope and Organization of the Book

There are 12 chapters in this book, arranged in 3 sections. The sections address specific contributions to developmental psychology arising from the study of high ability and intellectual potential across the life span:

- developmental perspectives on giftedness,
- giftedness and cognition, and
- domain-related talent.

The book is organized around these three themes. Within each section we have attempted to do the following:

- follow a pattern from attention to the very young to the older child,
- present a variety of theoretical perspectives, and
- include general conceptual material as well as empirical data.

Sometimes these all occur within single chapters. In several cases, specific advice is given on how to improve research on these topics. A detailed introduction to the chapters is provided at the beginning of each of the three sections.

Taking a broader overview of this book as a whole, our attention is particularly drawn to the issues of the provision of instructive opportunity as a prerequisite for exceptional intellectual accomplishment; domain or task specificity in tracing the development of high ability across years of development; the continuity or discontinuity of this development, and whether or not one can affix common templates to questions about the development of high ability at different ages; and the role of studies of very young children, even infants.

It may be fair to suggest that gifted children complicate the lives of developmental psychologists. Some behavior progresses rapidly to high levels of achievement, and whereas personal and contextual readiness likely play a role in exceptional performance in these areas, it also appears to be strongly related to domain or task specificity and to be characterized by discontinuity of development. It may be measurable and notable at one time during a lifetime but not at others. Other learning seems to unfold more slowly and continuously and to be dependent on personal development. The extent to which either is dependent on opportunity and expert teaching has not been well mapped. It is not even clear if the pairing of discontinuity and task or domain specificity in the last statement, for example, is a valid hypothesis to raise at this point. What is clear is that highly capable young people do not always persist with a domain of activity, and this could be as much a matter of interest or motivation as anything else; many very able people have multiple interests that might be explored in turn (Rysiew, Shore, & Carson, 1994; Rysiew, Shore, & Leeb, 1999). Such multipotentiality is hardly addressed in these chapters.

We are also faced with expansion if not change in the defining variables of giftedness from IQ and demonstrated achievements to the antecedents of adult expertise and the concerns of cognitive science and intelligent tutoring (sometimes referred to as *artificial intelligence*). There is a clear developmental story in the examination of childhood cognition and adult expertise. A major constraint in these studies is that most of the younger participants do not have the experience of the adults, so similar intellectual potential may not be realized because of a weaker base. However, a much more positive view can be taken. There is considerable and probably seriously underestimated potential among very able youngsters to engage in the adult intellectual world, a world distinguished by learning. And this potential may extend much farther than anticipated.

An Invitation to Further Consideration

In many ways, the intellectual activity of gifted children can indeed be connected to that of highly able adults. The evidence is constrained by much of it being the product of cross-sectional or retrospective research. In terms of the general objectives of this book, however, we are hopeful that we have raised the baseline of understanding of the development of exceptional intellectual achievements and potential in individuals from infancy through adulthood and provided both substantive and methodological guidance to those interested in investigating these phenomena. We remain the optimistic professions and sciences, invigorated by the educational challenges these studies reveal but alerted to the scope of the missed opportunity if the teaching needed to bring out the giftedness and develop the accomplished adult is not widely available. We hope our colleagues in psychology, education, and related fields will share the challenge of better understanding the development of exceptional abilities as a part of the core of our science and profession.

References

Binet, A., & Simon, T. (1905). Méthodes nouvelles pour le diagnostic du niveau intellectuel des anormaux. *L'Année Psychologique, 11,* 191–244.

Bloom, B. S. (Ed.). (1985a). *Developing talent in young people.* New York: Ballantine.

Bloom, B. S. (1985b). The nature of the study and why it was done. In B. S. Bloom (Ed.), *Developing talent in young people* (pp. 3–18). New York: Ballantine.

Feldhusen, J. F. (1992). The response of gifted education to school reform: "Physician, heal thyself." *Gifted Child Quarterly, 36,* 3.

Friedman, R. C., & Rogers, K. B. (1998). *Talent in context: Historical and social perspectives.* Washington, DC: American Psychological Association.

Reis, S. M. (1992). *The dumbing down of textbooks and how it affects high ability students.* Storrs, CT: National Research Center on the Gifted and Talented.

Rysiew, K. J., Shore, B. M., & Carson, A. D. (1994). Multipotentiality and overchoice syndrome: Clarifying common usage. *Gifted and Talented International, 9*(2), 41–46.

Rysiew, K. J., Shore, B. M., & Leeb, R. T. (1999). Multipotentiality, giftedness, and career choice: A review. *Journal of Counselling and Development, 77,* 423–430.

Tomlinson, C. A., & Callahan, C. M. (1992). Contributions of gifted education to general education in a time of change. *Gifted Child Quarterly, 36,* 183–189.

Part I

Developmental Perspectives on Giftedness

The five chapters of this part begin with an overview by Nancy M. Robinson, "Giftedness in Very Young Children: How Seriously Should It Be Taken?" Robinson starts with the basic observation that most studies of high ability have ignored very young children. Perhaps the reason is that these children are difficult to study. However, the benefits are important, as discussed by Robinson and illustrated well by John Colombo, D. Jill Shaddy, and W. Allen Richman in chapter 6 in Part II. Robinson outlines three general reasons for the importance of young gifted children to developmental psychology: (a) What works well for gifted children may also help others, (b) increasing the variance in groups studied may highlight relations otherwise masked by constrained range on measures used, and (c) it often is possible to examine domain-specific development not observable in other children. Robinson's chapter also raises the topic of domain specificity, an issue that provides one of the more lively debates in applied cognitive science (cf. Keating, 1990; It is interesting that Keating began his research career in the study of mathematical precocity and later concentrated on cognitive development in general.). Robinson sets the stage for links to the contributions of parents by Lynn T. Goldsmith in chapter 5 and others in this book and to the chapter by Sidney M. Moon, Joan A. Jurich, and John F. Feldhusen (1998) in *Talent in Context: Historical and Social Perspectives on Giftedness* (Friedman & Rogers, 1998). Robinson concludes with suggestions for developmental research questions that invite inquiry with populations of young gifted children.

In chapter 2, "Strategies for Modeling the Development of Giftedness in Children," Nancy Ewald Jackson complements Robinson's suggested research topics with several specific methodological improvements for future studies. In particular, Jackson advocates prospective studies that test specific relationships between present and future performance. Both Robinson's and Jackson's chapters are strongly linked to IQ as a measure of giftedness. However, both are sensitive to the greater breadth of the concept of giftedness, and both are strongly interactionist in their conceptualizations. One of the outcomes of Jackson's focus is the conclusion that the nature of giftedness changes with age. Howard Gardner (chapter 4) and Goldsmith (chapter 5) echo this, but Colombo, Shaddy, and Richman (chapter 6) disagree. Jackson also creates links to cognitive psychology and the issue of domain specificity and proposes a conceptual model for the development of high ability.

Martha J. Morelock presents a detailed case study of exceptionally high ability in chapter 3, "A Sociohistorical Perspective on Exceptionally High-IQ in Children." This chapter is unique in linking the study of high ability to Lev S. Vygotsky's work on sociolinguistic development and the social influence on development; it appears that only one other researcher (Kanevsky, 1992) has taken this perspective. This approach is fascinating because it helps to operationalize Vygotsky's pedagogically attractive notion of a *zone of proximal development*, one of whose elements is the centrality of interaction with an adult. Vygotsky's theory therefore strongly supports efforts to define the teaching and learning environment at home, school, or elsewhere to facilitate the development of exceptional talent.

The role of the teacher, mentor, or coach is to take the learner beyond what he or she can do on his or her own and explore what can be undertaken only with the help of someone more competent. The constantly changing educational challenge is to define that zone for a learner at a particular time on a particular class of tasks and to ensure that teachers with appropriate knowledge and pedagogical skills are available.

In chapter 4, "The Giftedness Matrix: A Developmental Perspective," Howard Gardner presents a conceptual chapter that goes beyond the application of his well-known construct of multiple intelligences to giftedness on several points. Gardner sharpens the precision of several terms, including *intelligence, giftedness, prodigiousness, precocity, expertise*, and *creativity*. For example, a prodigy is proposed to be a child or adolescent distinguished by capable performance in domains or on tasks that are not usually noted in the individual's particular age group, not only by faster or more accurate performance on age-relevant tasks (i.e., higher IQ). Intelligence, however, is a capacity valued within a culture (cf. Friedman & Rogers, 1998) which means that intelligence is related to context. Gardner stresses that most past work on high ability has concentrated on individuals and given insufficient attention to the task or domain. Links to other chapters in this book include the observation that giftedness can be different at different ages. For examples, see the Jackson (chapter 2) and Goldsmith (chapter 5) chapters and the fascinating study of Wolfgang Amadeus Mozart as a popular example of child prodigy elaborated in considerable detail by David Henry Feldman in the final chapter (chapter 12).

Goldsmith concludes part I with preliminary results of the first follow-up of a longitudinal study of prodigious youths in chapter 5, "Tracking Trajectories of Talent: Child Prodigies Growing Up." Her six cases, initially preteenagers or young adolescents, were contacted again when they approached age 20. Especially detailed data were available for two of the six. The baseline data were collected and described with Feldman (1986). Goldsmith made the fascinating observation that most of the participants she observed as young prodigies—young people performing at high levels in domains not normally associated with their age group—did not persist to early adulthood in the same domain as first characterized their prodigiousness. She also reported two sets of parents living vicariously through the successes of their children. The numbers are too small to link these phenomena. Even though most of the children changed their domain of exceptional achievement between childhood and young adulthood, they were still successful at the latter stage. This research does not directly inform us what underlying ability has persisted, but it is clear that the study of abilities cannot be separated from the development of affective skills, including the ability to cultivate an interest in a topic, and cognitive skills, such as being able to master new domains rapidly. Adult high performance is built on some kind of foundation, but it may not be the same in every domain or for every individual. This question needs further study across domains, as there is considerable evidence that an early start is at least a considerable advantage in some endeavors (e.g., playing the violin), but it may be much less essential in others (e.g., rarely is the detailed study of the law undertaken before well past adolescence).

References

Feldman, D. H. (with Goldsmith L. T.). (1986). *Nature's gambit: Child prodigies and the development of human potential*. New York: Basic Books.

Friedman, R. C., & Rogers, K. B. (1998). *Talent in context: Historical and social perspectives*. Washington, DC: American Psychological Association.

Kanevsky, L. S. (1992). The learning game. In P. S. Klein & A. J. Tannenbaum (Eds.), *To be young and gifted* (pp. 204–241). Norwood, NJ: Ablex.

Keating, D. P. (1990). Charting pathways to the development of expertise. *Educational Psychologist, 25*, 243–267.

Moon, S. M., Jurich, J. A., & Feldhusen, J. F. (1998). In R. C. Friedman & K. B. Rogers (Eds.), *Talent in context: Historical and social perspectives* (pp. 81–99). Washington, DC: American Psychological Association.

1

Giftedness in Very Young Children: How Seriously Should It Be Taken?

Nancy M. Robinson

Research with very young gifted children can open special windows on both developmental processes in general and the life-span trajectory of giftedness itself. This chapter examines what is known and unknown about early development and parenting young gifted children. The answer to the question posed in the chapter title is that giftedness in very young children can be taken seriously indeed.

From a number of theoretical perspectives, not the least of them Freud's and Piaget's, we have learned to view the early years as critically formative. Yet, even among the community devoted to research with gifted children, remarkably little attention has been paid to very young children (Gallagher, 1988; Horowitz, 1992; Karnes, 1983). The father of life span research, Lewis Terman, himself ignored the earliest years. Furthermore, the mainstream developmental psychology research community has paid practically no attention to early giftedness, despite the fact that, for many years, infancy and the preschool years have constituted a strong research focus. In fact, in research with "normal" children of any age, attention has focused primarily on measures of central tendency and not on individual differences. To the extent that outliers are noted at all, only the bottom of the distribution has received much attention. This tunnel vision needs correction.

There are understandable reasons for having neglected young children in previous research on giftedness. First, the reliability of developmental assessment is notoriously low during early childhood (McCall, Appelbaum, & Hogarty, 1973). Probably of greater importance, it is only after public school entry in this country that communities really begin to share responsibility for their children and therefore pay attention, theoretically at least, to the special needs that gifted and talented children may have. But these children do not catapult into school without histories, and some of the lessons they have to teach us may become buried if we begin our research too late.

Most of the focus of this chapter will be on children who are intellectually or academically precocious, recognizing that intelligence represents but a part of the spectrum of abilities. Only scattered case reports are available of very young children who are precocious in other domains. We use the term *precocity*, which means earlier-than-expected development, interchangeably with the terms *giftedness* or *advanced development*. Among the children referred to are those whose development varies from mildly advanced to astonishing. Some are advanced in many and some only in one or a few cognitive domains, and they also differ widely in many other characteristics (McGuffog, Feiring, & Lewis, 1987). Let us try to remember these individual differences when reflecting upon what very young gifted children can teach us.

A Scientific Mandate for Developmental Psychology

There are three major reasons for studying talented preschoolers. First, heritability issues aside, what has been working well for young gifted children may also be beneficial to others. A second reason for investigators to attend to gifted children is not so obvious: Increasing the variance in the groups we study can highlight subtle relationships likely to be overlooked when subject groups are more homogeneous for ability. Furthermore, gifted young children can help to answer questions about domain-specific development that average groups usually cannot.

Propitious Developmental Influences

Children with advanced development are likely to have benefited from favorable developmental supports. Looking at gifted children who are thriving, we can ask

- What conditions of early childhood are especially favorable to optimal development? Do parents of precocious children behave differently from other parents, have different sets of expectations, provide different resources, conduct family battles in different ways? Or do they simply do well what we already know to be good parenting practices?
- What are the origins of the critical motivational concomitants of high achievement? Are they persistence, commitment, high standards for one's performance, intellectual risk taking? Can we distinguish the eventual creative spirits from more typical preoperational, intuitive early childhood "creative thinkers"?
- Conversely, what do capable young children do to elicit resources, mold their own environments, and set their own trajectories?

Enhanced Variance, Domain-Specific Precocity, and Their Research Possibilities

As mentioned above, there are several ways in which the inclusion of gifted children in developmental research can make distinctive contributions. First, simply increasing the heterogeneity of samples may highlight subtle relationships that would otherwise escape notice. Including more children at the lower end of the spectrum picks up unspecified problems and anomalies of development that may confuse matters, while including more children at higher levels is, in this sense, more likely to clarify them. We can increase the variance by raising the top of the distribution, by including children whose development is uneven, or by contrasting gifted and average groups.

Furthermore, few children in the average range will show marked within-subject differences; otherwise, they would be labeled as precocious or delayed in one or more domains. Some gifted children are, to be sure, evenly advanced across the board but many—if not most—are not (Achter, Lubinski, & Benbow, 1996). It may be useful to reconceptualize precocious children as representing not simply advancement but differential patterns of talents.

Domain-specific precocity, when present, permits us to address questions such as the following:

- How early do distinctive patterns of ability appear?
- What are the driving forces behind such patterns—in the children's biology, their environments, their personal resources, the strategies they use to deal with the world?
- Do precocious children resemble older children in their areas of competence, as a mental-age or developmental model would imply; are they just more efficient "learning machines" than their age-matched peers; or is their thinking qualitatively different from that of one or both of these groups?
- Are there a few paths to precocity, or many? For example, do early talkers tend to be alike in the way they master their domain? Do precocious arithmeticians resemble one another in their skills?
- How does precocity in one domain relate to other domains? For example, does precocity in spatial reasoning accompany advancement in mathematical reasoning? Does precocity in verbal reasoning or memory accelerate self-regulation?
- How stable are early patterns? For example, are early talkers and precocious counters recognizable as advanced within their own domains later on, or is their precocity expressed in different form, showing what Kagan (1971) has called *heterotypic continuity*? (Do early talkers persist in the gift of gab, or do they instead become primarily advanced readers, authors, or social leaders as they grow older?)

In the following discussion of existing information about young gifted children, it may be helpful to keep this list of questions in mind. There is much to be learned from the wedding of developmental research to research about giftedness.

Early Development of Young Gifted Children

Retrospective Studies

Since the days of Galton (1869), numerous authors (e.g., Albert, 1980; Cox, 1926; Goertzel, Goertzel, & Goertzel, 1978; McCurdy, 1960; Ochse, 1990; Radford, 1990; Simonton, 1998; West, 1960) have examined the fascinating, although probably biased and surely fractionated, information available about the very early lives of people (mostly men) who later became famous. Some findings will give us pause. Few of these eminent men had attended common school prior to entering a university, and none attended a preschool. Even more unsettling, despite the economic and cultural advantages and the warm affection to which most of these boys were exposed, there were a significant number of contrasting histories—people who grew up in abusive circumstances and many who experienced significantly early losses. Actually, Bloom's (1985) study of world-class achieving young adults did not find that they had been either abused or home schooled. Indeed, it was typically only in middle childhood that the children were introduced to disciplined study in their domain and that their own deep and passionate commitments emerged. What was true in the past may not be true today, or perhaps few of Bloom's world-class achieving young people will enter the history books.

Prodigies

Prodigies are children who are distinguished by performance that is not only promising but also impressive by adult standards (e.g., Feldman, 1986; Goldsmith, 1990; Radford, 1990). Rare are the very young children who can therefore be rightly called prodigies. There is an interesting set of very young pianists, many of them blind or otherwise disabled, who are sufficiently talented to be judged by adult standards, albeit usually not classical standards (Miller, 1991). The monkeys sketched beginning at ages 2 and 3 by the Chinese girl Yani (Ho, 1989; Zhensun & Low, 1991) are truly remarkable. Prodigies are so rare before age 6 that even most experts will never see a preschool-age prodigy in vivo. Yet, their existence defines one end of a continuum of individual differences and demonstrates that expected age norms can in fact be seriously violated.

Early Signs of Precocity

How early can advanced development be recognized? There are numerous anecdotal accounts for unusual alertness and focus in babies who later are seen as precocious, but this evidence is relatively ephemeral. There are more empirical reports of high newborn cry counts (Abroms, 1982b), rapidity of visual habituation during the first few months (McCall & Carriger, 1993; Rose, Slater, & Perry, 1986), advanced visual recognition memory as shown by preference for the novel over the familiar (Fagan & McGrath, 1981; McCall & Carriger, 1993; Rose, Feldman, & Wallace, 1992), cross-modal transfer (Rose et al., 1992), and early attention and information processing (Bornstein, 1989), all of which apparently correlate with later cognitive development, especially verbal ability.

Cognitive skills make themselves known in diverse ways in gifted pre-school-age children. Many have fears typical of older children, for example (Klene, 1988), and encounter troubling concepts such as death, failure, and infinity at tender ages. Although, on average, they are not particularly advanced in motor skills (Krinsky, Jackson, & Robinson, 1977; Robinson, Dale, & Landesman, 1990), their skills at complex as opposed to simple motor tasks tend to reflect their mental abilities (Leithwood, 1971). Their perspective-taking (Tucker & Hafenstein, 1998) and social cognition as seen, for example, in stated solutions to social conflicts tend to be advanced (Kitano, 1985; Roedell, Jackson, & Robinson, 1980), whereas their actual social behavior is thought by most investigators (Abroms & Golin, 1980; Barnett & Fiscella, 1985; Kitano, 1985) but not all (Roedell et al., 1980) to be more sophisticated, cooperative, and independent than that of non-gifted children. Those without mental-age peers as playmates may become quite discouraged (e.g., Abroms, 1982a; Gross, 1992, 1993).

Identifying Children

When parents are given behavioral criteria or checklists, they are rather good at identifying giftedness in their children (Hanson, 1984; Klein, 1992; Louis & Lewis, 1992; Silverman, Chitwood, & Waters, 1986). For example, in a longitudinal study undertaken by H. Robinson, Roedell, and Jackson (cited in Robinson & Robinson, 1992), half the 550 children nominated at ages 2–5 years attained initial IQs of 132 or higher; even among those with IQs lower than 132, many showed genuine precocity in specific domains. Similarly, in a study of mathematically precocious young children, questionnaire responses of parents of 100 kindergartners clearly correlated with their children's assessed behavior (Pletan, Robinson, Berninger, & Abbott, 1995), and nearly half of the 778 children nominated scored two standard deviations or more above the mean for their age on tests of mathematical reasoning (Robinson, Abbott, Berninger, & Busse, 1996).

Other investigators (Louis & Lewis, 1992; Silverman et al., 1986) have found similar or even higher mean scores in parent-nominated groups. Parents tend to be best at identifying precocity in domains in which there are distinctive milestones and clear normative expectations, as there are, for example, in early language, reading, and mathematical reasoning, and to be less accurate in identifying precocity in areas such as short-term memory and spatial reasoning (Robinson et al., 1990; Robinson & Robinson, 1992). When checklists or testing are used, the most reliable characteristics to emerge in the younger children is excellence in memory, both immediate and long-term, followed by long attention span, extensive vocabulary, older playmates, and personal maturity (Klein, 1992; Lewis &

Louis, 1991; Louis & Lewis, 1992; Robinson et al., 1990; Silverman et al., 1986).

Parents are much better than test scores alone at initially identifying gifted young children. There are plenty of appropriate psychometric measures to use with young children, but early scores and high scores tend to be discouragingly unstable (McCall et al., 1973). Indeed, when investigators have followed infants and preschool children identified solely by exceptionally high test scores (Shapiro et al., 1989; Willerman & Fiedler, 1974, 1977), the children's later development does not seem remarkable. There is, however, some possibility that a shift to using measures of infant visual memory might be more predictive (McCall & Carriger, 1993).

In contrast, when parents identify giftedness in children, test scores tend to confirm the parents' observations and, for the children as a group, to remain as high or even higher over time (Robinson, Abbott, Berninger, Busse, & Mukhopadhyay, 1997; Robinson & Robinson, 1992). Such findings suggest that, on average, advanced ability does tend to maintain its rapid pace of development. Even though, within the group, individual children's comparative status may change, the continuing high mean scores suggest that real and somewhat stable advancement is being identified. Such findings in very young children—whose base of knowledge and skills is quite small in toddlerhood relative to subsequent developmental increments—contradict the position that interage correlations are the result of adding unpredictable and uncorrelated increments to scores that started out far ahead, as suggested by theorists such as Anderson (1940) and Humphreys (Humphreys & Davey, 1988).

Emergence of Domain-Specific Abilities

Despite the folklore that developmental domains are undifferentiated during the early years of childhood, young gifted children can and do yield evidence for the early emergence of differentiated ability patterns. Three such salient skill areas during the early years are language, reading, and mathematical reasoning.

One example of such research was conducted by this author and colleagues Dale, Crain-Thoreson, and Landesman, who studied 25 verbally precocious toddlers, 21 of whom were followed from age 18 months to 6½ years. Not only did verbal precocity, including verbal memory, emerge as a coherent domain observable across situations and persistent over time, but it contrasted with other domains in which the children were not particularly advanced, such as spatial reasoning and motor skills (Robinson et al., 1990). The children were not early readers (Crain-Thoreson & Dale, 1992), but once they began, their verbal ability and their ability to analyze phonemic structure were clear assets in producing superior reading (Dale, Crain-Thoreson, & Robinson, 1995). Interestingly, as toddlers the children showed a variety of language preferences, some being more social and imitative while others were more analytic, demonstrating that there may be several paths to outstanding performance within a single domain.

Children who enter school as competent readers can also be found with relative ease and have been the object of considerable research. As Jackson (1992) reported, not all who read early are especially bright, and not all bright children read early but, on average, early readers do tend to attain relatively high IQs, tending toward a mean of about 130. Jackson's review of work in this area demonstrates that, like early talking, there are a variety of avenues to early reading, especially obvious when the children are attacking single words. Most young readers prefer to read prose quickly to get the gist of the story. Over time, precocious readers tend to retain considerable advantage over classmates in reading skills, word attack giving way to advanced comprehension as the most distinguishing feature of their competence. How dreary are the early school years, however, for many of these children who must endure their classmates' struggles to acquire skills they may have learned years before!

Advanced mathematical reasoning in young children can also be identified with reasonable accuracy, at least as early as ages 4–5 (Pletan et al., 1995; Robinson et al., 1996). The identified children were also advanced in visual–spatial reasoning and verbal reasoning, although not as advanced as they were in math. Spatial and quantitative factors were highly correlated; the verbal factor correlated more weakly with the others. Two years later, the children's mathematical reasoning remained at least as advanced and the relationships among the factors remained stable, although a group randomly assigned to "Saturday math clubs" showed an increased correlation among verbal and quantitative factors (Robinson et al., 1997).

Cognitive Studies

How do bright young children actually learn and problem solve, and how do they resemble and differ from their chronological-age (CA) mates and mental-age (MA) mates? Very few investigators (Kanevsky, 1992; Lempers, Block, Scott, & Draper, 1987; McClelland, 1982; Moss, 1992; Planche, 1985; Porath, 1992; Shigaki & Wolf, 1982) have asked the "MA–CA" question. Young gifted children learn faster, reason with advanced logic, show advanced verbal reasoning, and generalize more readily than not-so-bright children of their chronological age; this is hardly news. These cognitive skills are a central part of what it means to be bright. What we need to know is precisely how their management of cognitive tasks resembles or differs from older, normally developing children who reason at the same overall level of competence, that is, are of comparable mental age. Especially because of the richness of critical shifts seen in most children between ages 4 and 6 or 7, preschool children with mental ages in this latter range should be able to shed considerable light on the underlying processes involved.

Some things are known, and about others there are conflicting data. McClelland (1982), for example, demonstrated that preschool children with high Stanford–Binet IQs solved more verbal problems but fewer performance problems on that test than did MA-matched older children. In contrast, Lempers et al. (1987), comparing very bright preschoolers with both a CA-matched group and an MA-matched group on a spatial projective task, a cognitive perspective-taking task, and an affective perspective-taking task, found that the bright younger children resembled MA mates in all three. In France, Planche (1985) found that bright preschoolers actually exceeded the problem-solving skills shown by MA-matched older children of average IQ. Using CA norms rather than experimental groups, Zha (1984) similarly found advancement in analogical reasoning in very bright Chinese preschoolers.

Numerous studies in the Piagetian mode were reported in the 1970s (see Spitz, 1985; Tannenbaum, 1992), and even Piaget, little as was his interest in individual differences, is quoted by Spitz as having described bright children as able to problem solve at a level above that expected for their age. Taking as the criterion attainment of concrete operations such as conservation of number and quantity, the evidence points to moderate advancement. Bright 4-year-olds tend not to succeed (Brown, 1973; Moore, Nelson-Piercy, Abel, & Frye, 1984), possibly because of limited experience (Spitz, 1985), whereas bright 5-year-olds do (DeVries, 1974; Little, 1972). Furthermore, once young gifted children catch on to an idea, it is theirs with minimal further practice (Porath, 1992). In "Vygotskian" terms (Vygotsky, 1978), once performance expectations fall within the zone of proximal development, these children master the task with impressive efficiency and transfer their insights easily to new problems.

Piagetian measures and standard intelligence measures tend, not surprisingly, to be correlated (Kaufman, 1971; Zigler & Trickett, 1978). Spitz (1985) argued that IQ is "at least twice as valuable for making predictions of performance on Piagetian tasks than is knowing only the CA, even with unexceptional children" (p. 120). Indeed, problems that call upon logic and conceptual analysis as well as generalization and executive control are more difficult for children with mental retardation and easier for gifted children than their MAs would predict.

Research on the metacognitive competence of preschool gifted children suggests, intriguingly, that these children are more accurate observers of their own behavior and utilizers of a greater variety of learning strategies than are other children (Moss, 1990, 1992; Moss & Strayer, 1990). Kanevsky (1992; Kanevsky & Rapagna, 1990) used the MA–CA match design to study average-IQ and high-IQ children at ages 4–5 and 7–8 years. The Tower of Hanoi and two similar (transfer) problems, one of them computerized, were the tasks to be solved. Although the scores of high-IQ younger children were like those of the older average-IQ children, their behavior was more like that of the older high-IQ children. Both the high-IQ groups wanted help on their own terms, not necessarily when it was offered; they verbalized the underlying similarities in the nature of the games; they saw errors as learning opportunities. Once they had solved the tasks, they made them more difficult and monitored the situation to optimize both level of challenge and level of effort or, as Csikszentmihalyi (1982) has described it, to "maintain flow." Kanevsky also noted, however, that once the younger children had reached the limit of their energy reservoirs, they collapsed into small-child crankiness.

Differences in domains of precocity, styles of learning, areas of precocity, personal approaches to dealing with other children and adults, energy levels, emotional maturity, and life experiences, to say nothing of biological equipment, make every child unique. And yet, here focusing on children whose precocity is in cognitive domains, we have described not only similarities to older, normally developing children in cognitive skills but behavior that resembles older, bright children. None of these is revolutionary or unexpected. The developmental continuum of giftedness begins very early.

Parenting the Gifted Young Child

Children with the characteristics described earlier need parenting and other environmental supports that are appropriate to their individual and often fluctuating maturity levels. Parenting not only has important causal effects on precocity, but also constitutes a response to it.

Reciprocal Contributions: The Child as an Active Partner

Children growing up in the same family shape different environments, and gifted children, by virtue of their curiosity and passions, advanced skills, perseverance, and adept recruitment of assistance from adults, are probably even more effective at this than are nongifted children. In behavioral genetics terminology, precocity contributes to nonshared environments even within families (Plomin, 1994).

To cite one example of children's shaping their environments, in the study of early talkers mentioned earlier (Crain-Thoreson & Dale, 1992; Dale et al., 1995), the children who knew most about reading at age 4½ and were the best readers at age 6½ had shown the greatest interest in being read to when observed at age 2. Although these reading-oriented children later also tended to be those who subsequently received—and had perhaps elicited—early reading instruction, the two effects were additive in predicting emerging literacy. Similarly, Thomas (1984) found that early readers had shown strong early preference for reading-readiness toys over fantasy toys.

There are a few interesting studies linking early personal characteristics and subsequent performance on intelligence tests. At all ages, gifted individuals are seen as more curious, explorative, and risk-taking than others (Carter, 1958; Cooperative Research Group on Supernormal Children, 1981; Hunt & Randhawa, 1980; Miles, 1954; Terman, 1926). Within unselected populations, more positive outcomes during elementary school have been found for children who, during preschool or at school entry, are more active and energetic (Sontag, Baker, & Nelson, 1958); are more curious, assertive, and socially skilled (Kohn & Rosman, 1972); and show a relative preference for teacher over child interaction (Harper & Huie, 1987). Gifted children clearly contribute to their own developmental trajectories through temperament, style, and use of resources.

Parental Contributions to Cognitive Development

Gifted children tend to come from homes where parental educational level is higher, learning opportunities are greater, and expectations are higher than in the homes of nongifted children, although the correlation is far from perfect. Biographers of eminent persons have repeatedly documented the richness of resources and stimulation and the high level of demands in homes of the to-be-eminent (Bloom, 1985; Cox, 1926; Galton, 1869; Goertzel et al., 1978; McCurdy, 1960; Terman, 1926). Today's gifted children tend to come from more advantaged homes (Gottfried, Gottfried, Bathurst, & Guerin, 1994); they have even attended better quality early day care than those not gifted (Field, 1991). Even within low-income (post-Head Start) groups, greater personal and tangible family resources as well as more effective parenting practices are associated with high attainment (Robinson, Weinberg, Redden, Ramey, & Ramey, 1998). If Terman's study were to be repeated today, no doubt there would be diligent efforts to find children from more varied backgrounds, but the reality is that many children are truly disadvantaged from the moment of conception because of the stresses and restricted resources experienced by their families. This unwelcome but undeniable fact is, indirectly, the most potent threat to public school programs for gifted children, which are often criticized and vulnerable to being dropped because their composition is unrepresentative of the school population as a whole.

Parental education is a distal factor; we must look to more proximal factors, such as the day-to-day interactions of parents and children, to understand the processes that impinge on development. Responsive and stimulating parenting is effective parenting of the gifted child, just as it is for other children (Clarke-Stewart, 1973; Robinson et al., 1998), but effective parenting of gifted children takes extra time as well as skill at activities that promote development. Karnes, Shwedel, and Steinberg (1984) found that parents of gifted preschoolers spent much more time in crucial activities with children such as reading, playing, making up rhymes and songs, and going to interesting places than did their comparison group. Unexpectedly, Thomas (1984) found that fathers of early readers worked, on average, 10 fewer hours a week than did fathers of nonreaders.

In conjunction with the research on metacognition mentioned previously, Moss (1990, 1992; Moss & Strayer, 1990) demonstrated not only that gifted preschoolers are more effective problem solvers and use more metacognitive strategies, but that to a significant degree they pick up cues from their mothers. Reminiscent of the research in the 1960s that compared lower- and middle-class mothers (e.g., Hess & Shipman, 1969), Moss found that mothers of brighter children encouraged metacognitive strategies by structuring problems while letting the children define their own problems and develop their own solutions, rather than providing the tasks or direct solutions or talking about children's nontask behavior.

In one of the few studies to observe competent toddler and preschool children's interactions with their mothers at home, White and Watts (1973) reported that mothers of the competent, as opposed to average, children not only talked a great deal to the children but "performed excellently the functions of designer and consultant . . . they design a physical world . . . beautifully suited to nurturing . . . burgeoning curiosity. . . . These mothers . . . get an enormous amount (in terms of frequency) of teaching in 'on the fly,' and usually at the child's instigation" (pp. 243–244).

There are, of course, individual differences in the strategies used by parents of bright children. Fowler (1981), studying highly precocious children, described two parenting styles, one which involved a deliberate, planful, structured, and rather demanding instructional approach, and another that was more responsive and incidental. Both sets of parents were, however, stimulating, playful, child-centered, and sensitive about when to move to new concepts. Fowler (1990) elsewhere described remarkable results of early intervention in mother–child language.

No investigator has found parents of gifted children engaging in developmentally inappropriate tactics such as those promulgated by Doman (e.g., 1979) or his coworkers. The prescribed subject matter suggested by those authors is often foreign to the experience of the young child; furthermore, teaching methods are adult driven, directed at rote memory, and repetitive rather than assisting children to set their own problems and derive their own solutions. In my study of children with precocious language (Robinson et al., 1990), only one child was being brought up by adults who were using such deliberate strategies to teach language, and this child had, in fact, a broad vocabulary but was lowest in the group on language complexity. What seem to count are sensitive guidance and participation in the child's exploration and scaffolding problem solving in the broad sense.

Parental Contributions to Personality Development

For a trajectory of high accomplishment, accompanying characteristics such as high aspirations, commitment, persistence, and the willingness to take intellectual risks are essential. Some investigators, indeed, include such characteristics in their definitions of giftedness (Renzulli, 1978). Only a little is known about the role of parenting in the early years in these respects.

Achievement motivation. The urge to master is an essential ingredient of ultimate achievement, with precursors observable in early childhood (Freeburg & Payne, 1967; Geppert & Kuster, 1983; White, 1983). Theories about the development of achievement motivation (Dweck & Elliott, 1983;

McClelland, Atkinson, Clark, & Lowell, 1953) clarify the finding that children who seek achievement have mothers who valued early independence (Winterbottom, 1958), and that parents who encourage independence expose their children to opportunities to master challenges autonomously (Trudewind, 1982). Karnes et al. (1984) found that parents of gifted preschoolers were more likely than parents of nongifted preschoolers to value independence in children. In a study examining gifted preschoolers' perceptions of their own competence, Windecker-Nelson, Melson, and Moon (1997) similarly discovered these self-perceptions to be related to mothers' attitudes toward independence and strictness.

Similarly, Terman and Oden (1947) observed that the parents of the most successful men in their study had encouraged initiative and independence. Moreover, looking at the early childhoods of world-class achievers, Bloom (1985) described the parents during the early years as child-centered and involving the children informally in areas of family interest, but also as instilling in them the "value of achievement": self-discipline, the importance of doing one's best, and the satisfaction of accomplishment.

Viewing the dismal academic achievement of many older gifted children who later adopt an *entity* (something given) theory of intelligence as opposed to an *incremental* (acquired through learning) theory (Dweck & Elliott, 1983), we may speculate that the roots of this trap may well be laid in early childhood, although subject to heavy reinforcement as the child enters school. When things always come too easily, with little reason or reinforcement for trying hard things, how can a very bright child conclude other than that high ability is indeed a gift? As Csikszentmihalyi, Rathunde, and Whalen (1993) discovered with adolescents, it is those families with high expectations as well as high support that produce children who fulfill their promise.

Aspirations and perfectionism. Young gifted children are identified frequently in case studies as perfectionistic and self-critical; they often set high standards for their own performance and monitor their attainment according to what others think (Strang, 1951; Whitmore, 1980). What is good and necessary for ultimate high achievement, that is, setting high but not unattainable goals for oneself, can be either a positive or a negative force in one's life. A delight in mastering more difficult, challenging tasks may well be essential to success. Even in young infants, pleasure in test-taking can be more predictive of later high ability than actual test scores (Birns & Golden, 1972). Similarly, Gottfried et al. (1994) reported that infant test-taking pleasure had been significantly higher in children identified as gifted or nongifted at school age.

While parents can help to support expectations, internalization of the goals at some point is essential, certainly by middle childhood. Indeed, Hewitt and Flett (1990) found that the depressive features that can accompany perfectionism in adults are the product not of setting one's own standards too high, but of feeling unable to measure up to the standards of others.

Creativity and risk taking. Most investigators hold some notion of creativity (Sternberg, 1988), or intellectual risk taking, as essential to realization of the promise of giftedness. Even in early childhood, there are marked individual differences in the cautiousness with which children approach problems. The essence of being willing to take some risks is that one will make mistakes. Even among our verbally precocious toddlers, there were distinct differences in risk taking, the children producing more pronoun reversals being those who also used more pronouns correctly, courageously willing to use complex language, right or wrong (Dale & Crain-Thoreson, 1993).

Very few studies address original thinking, or cognitive risk taking, in young children, although its roots very likely begin in early childhood (Freeman, 1996). In one of the few exceptions, Moore and Sawyers (1987) found moderate stability over a 4-year period in measures of original thinking in children who, when seen at age 4, differed on this dimension, independently of IQ (Moran, Milgram, Sawyers, & Fu, 1983).

Negative criticism can be destructive of such spirit. Lovecky (1992) suggested focusing on the idea that each attempt can lead to another. This was the model used successfully by the young artist Yani's father, who was also her teacher (Zhensun & Low, 1991).

Unasked Questions

Research findings dealing with the few questions raised earlier are sketchy indeed. There does exist an additional literature on early educational programs for gifted children (Robinson, 1993), but most of it is free of data and is at best descriptive. We have therefore elected not to include it here.

Let us, then, close with a list of some of the many remaining questions about which there is no evidence at all. Many of these questions relate to topics currently of central interest to developmental psychologists and are meant to illustrate the possibilities that inclusion of gifted children can introduce to mainstream research:

- Can verbally precocious very young children introspect and report about their own internal processes, such as self-regulation, social comparisons, or the building of self-esteem? Children who have the verbal tools may be able to describe subjective processes unavailable to observers.
- Does high intelligence in young children serve as a protective factor to enhance resilience against adversity, biological as well as social, as it does for older children? Are the negative effects of physical abuse, poverty, or divorcing parents, for example, attenuated by high capability?
- Does high intelligence lend itself to secure attachments, possibly because of advanced object permanence and the ability to retain an image of the parent's return? Conversely, does stranger anxiety

arise earlier in bright children because of earlier recognition of unfamiliarity? Do infants with superior memory establish earlier multiple attachments with support figures, such as grandparents, who are seen infrequently?

- Do bright toddlers and preschoolers develop different, or more effective, ideas about how they and other people think (theories of mind) than do average children? Does their understanding translate into more empathic or emotionally competent behavior?
- What are the effects of advanced cognition on real-life behavior? For example, is a child with many verbal solutions to conflict better able to resolve quarrels on the preschool playground than the child with few? Is the child with precocious worries about war, death, or infinity exceptionally vulnerable to anxieties that older children find easier to handle?
- Do young gifted children tend to be advanced in self-help skills and regulation of emotions? Such matters have important implications for educational decisions such as placing a 3-year-old in preschool with 4-year-olds, or encouraging early entrance to kindergarten.
- Do the parenting styles effective with older talented students (Csikszentmihalyi et al., 1993) help to minimize asynchronies between cognitive and personal–social maturity? For example, are authoritative parents (Baumrind, 1971) able to manage verbal negotiations with their gifted young children in more growth-enhancing ways than are either authoritarian or permissive parents? Do they produce children with incremental as opposed to entity theories of intelligence (Dweck & Elliott, 1983)?
- Are gender differences minimized or enhanced in bright children? Do some emerge earlier than expected? We (Robinson et al., 1996, 1997) have reported some evidence for an advantage in favor of young, math-gifted boys, but such research is only a beginning.
- With the advent of noninvasive neuro-imaging techniques, can we detect early differences in brain structures or functional patterns and efficiencies when gifted and average young children are compared?

Conclusion

To summarize, our argument is that life-span research with gifted children can profitably start very early indeed, both to contribute to knowledge about normal development and to understand the origins and enhancement of high competence. We have reviewed several ways in which the inclusion of gifted children can contribute to research in developmental psychology by identifying optimal conditions of development, the origins of achievement motivation and creativity, and the contributions children make to molding their own experiences. Including young children with domain-specific advancement opens a number of other windows that are otherwise closed.

Lest this emphasis on research lead the reader to believe that young gifted children are interesting mainly for the light they shed on others, let us also reflect that what they tell us has implications for the quality of their lives as they are living them in the present. Children who are different need adapted environments. They need friends who are interesting and fun to talk, play, and learn with; they need to hear exciting stories; they need challenges; they need answers to their complicated questions. Early childhood is not just a way station on the road to the future; it is a part of life itself.

References

Abroms, K. I. (1982a). Classroom interactions of gifted preschoolers. *Teaching Exceptional Children, 14,* 223–225.

Abroms, K. I. (1982b). The gifted infant: Tantalizing behaviors and provocative correlates. *Journal of the Division for Early Childhood, 5,* 3–18.

Abroms, K. I., & Golin, J. (1980). Developmental study of gifted preschool children and measures of psychosocial giftedness. *Exceptional Children, 46,* 334–341.

Achter, J. A., Lubinski, D., & Benbow, C. P. (1996). Multipotentiality among the intellectually gifted: It was never there and already it's vanishing. *Journal of Counseling Psychology, 43,* 65–76.

Albert, R. S. (1980). Family positions and the attainment of eminence: A study of special family positions and special family experiences. *Gifted Child Quarterly, 24,* 87–95.

Anderson, J. E. (1940). The prediction of terminal intelligence from infant and preschool tests. *Yearbook of the National Society for the Study of Education, 39(I),* 385–403.

Barnett, L., & Fiscella, J. (1985). A child by any other name: A comparison of the playfulness of gifted and nongifted children. *Gifted Child Quarterly, 29,* 61–66.

Baumrind, D. (1971). Current patterns of parental authority. *Developmental Psychology Monographs, 4*(1, Pt. 2).

Birns, B., & Golden, M. (1972). Prediction of intellectual performance at 3 years from infant tests and personality measures. *Merrill–Palmer Quarterly, 18,* 53–58.

Bloom, B. S. (Ed.). (1985). *Developing talent in young people.* New York: Ballantine.

Bornstein, M. H. (1989). Stability in early mental development: From attention and information processing in infancy to language and cognition in childhood. In M. H. Bornstein & N. A. Krasnegor (Eds.), *Stability and continuity in mental development: Behavioral and biological perspectives* (pp. 147–170). Hillsdale, NJ: Erlbaum.

Brown, A. L. (1973). Conservation of number and continuous quantity in normal, bright, and retarded children. *Child Development, 44,* 376–379.

Carter, T. M. (1958). The play problems of gifted children. *School and Society, 86,* 224–225.

Clarke-Stewart, K. A. (1973). Interactions between mothers and their young children: Characteristics and consequences. *Monographs of the Society for Research in Child Development, 38* (6–7, Serial No. 153).

Cooperative Research Group on Supernormal Children. (1981). Summary of a year's research on supernormal children. *Acta Psychologica Sinica, 13*(1), 35–41.

Cox, C. M. (1926). *Genetic studies of genius: Vol. 2. The early mental traits of three hundred geniuses.* Stanford, CA: Stanford University Press.

Crain-Thoreson, C., & Dale, P. S. (1992). Do early talkers become early readers? Linguistic precocity, preschool language, and emergent literacy. *Developmental Psychology, 28,* 421–429.

Csikszentmihalyi, M. (1982). Learning, "flow," and happiness. In R. Gross (Ed.), *Invitation to lifelong learning* (pp. 167–187). Chicago: Follett.

Csikszentmihalyi, M., Rathunde, K., & Whalen, S. (1993). *Talented teenagers: The roots of success and failure.* New York: Cambridge University Press.

Dale, P. S., & Crain-Thoreson, C. (1993). Pronoun reversals: Who, when, and why? *Journal of Child Language, 20,* 573–589.

Dale, P. S., Crain-Thoreson, C., & Robinson, N. M. (1995). Linguistic precocity and the development of reading: The role of extralinguistic factors. *Applied Psycholinguistics, 16,* 173–187.

DeVries, R. (1974). Relationships among Piagetian, IQ, and achievement assessments. *Child Development, 43,* 746–756.

Doman, G. (1979). *Teach your baby math.* New York: Pocket Books.

Dweck, C. S., & Elliott, E. S. (1983). Achievement motivation. In E. M. Hetherington (Ed.), *Handbook of child psychology: Socialization, personality, and social development* (4th ed., Vol. 4, pp. 343–391). New York: Wiley.

Fagan, J. F., III, & McGrath, S. K. (1981). Infant recognition memory and later intelligence. *Intelligence, 5,* 121–130.

Falbo, T., & Cooper, C. (1980). Young children's time and intellectual ability. *Journal of Genetic Psychology, 137,* 299–300.

Feldman, D. H. (with Goldsmith, L.). (1986). *Nature's gambit: Child prodigies and the development of human potential.* New York: Basic Books.

Field, T. M. (1991). Quality infant day-care and grade school behavior and performance. *Child Development, 62,* 863–870.

Fowler, W. (1981). Case studies of cognitive precocity: The role of exogenous and endogenous stimulation in early mental development. *Journal of Applied Psychology, 2,* 319–367.

Fowler, W. (1990). *Talking from infancy: How to nurture and cultivate early language development.* Cambridge, MA: Brookline.

Freeburg, N. E., & Payne, D. T. (1967). Parental influence on cognitive development in early childhood. *Child Development, 38,* 65–87.

Freeman, J. (1996). The early development and education of highly able young children. In A. J. Cropley & D. Dehn (Eds.), *Fostering the growth of high ability: European perspectives* (pp. 75–85). Norwood, NJ: Ablex.

Gallagher, J. J. (1988). National agenda for educating gifted students: Statement of priorities. *Exceptional Children, 55,* 107–114.

Galton, F. (1869). *Hereditary genius: An inquiry into its laws and consequences.* London: Macmillan.

Geppert, U., & Kuster, U. (1983). The emergence of "wanting to do it oneself": A precursor of achievement motivation. *International Journal of Behavioral Development, 6,* 355–365.

Goertzel, M., Goertzel, V., & Goertzel, T. (1978). *300 eminent personalities.* San Francisco: Jossey-Bass.

Goldsmith, L. (1990). The timing of talent: The facilitation of early prodigious achievement. In M. J. A. Howe (Ed.), *Encouraging the development of exceptional skills and talents* (pp. 17–31). Leicester, England: British Psychological Society.

Gottfried, A. W., Gottfried, A. E., Bathurst, K., & Guerin, D. W. (1994). *Gifted IQ: Early developmental aspects.* New York: Plenum.

Gross, M. U. M. (1992). The early development of three profoundly gifted children of IQ 200. In P. S. Klein & A. Tannenbaum (Eds.), *To be young and gifted* (pp. 94–138). Norwood, NJ: Ablex.

Gross, M. U. M. (1993). *Exceptionally gifted children.* London: Routledge.

Hanson, I. (1984). A comparison between parent identification of young bright children and subsequent testing. *Roeper Review, 7,* 44–45.

Harper, L. V., & Huie, K. S. (1987). Relations among preschool children's adult and peer contacts and later academic achievement. *Child Development, 58,* 1051–1065.

Hess, R. D., & Shipman, V. C. (1969). Early experience and the socialization of cognitive modes in children. *Child Development, 36,* 869–886.

Hewitt, P. L., & Flett, G. L. (1990). Perfectionism and depression: A multidimensional analysis. *Journal of Social Behavior and Personality, 5,* 423–438.

Ho, W.-C. (Ed.). (1989). *Yani: The brush of innocence.* New York: Hudson Hills.

Horowitz, F. D. (1992). A developmental view in the early identification of the gifted. In P. S. Klein & A. Tannenbaum (Eds.), *To be young and gifted* (pp. 73–93). Norwood, NJ: Ablex.

Humphreys, L. G., & Davey, T. C. (1988). Continuity in intellectual growth from 12 months to 9 years. *Intelligence, 12,* 183–198.

Hunt, D., & Randhawa, B. (1980). Personality factors and ability groups. *Perceptual and Motor Skills, 50,* 902.

Jackson, N. E. (1992). Precocious reading of English: Origins, structure, and predictive significance. In P. S. Klein & A. Tannenbaum (Eds.), *To be young and gifted* (pp. 171–203). Norwood, NJ: Ablex.

Kagan, J. (1971). *Change and continuity in infancy.* New York: Wiley.

Kanevsky, L. (1992). The learning game. In P. S. Klein & A. Tannenbaum (Eds.), *To be young and gifted* (pp. 204–241). Norwood, NJ: Ablex.

Kanevsky, L., & Rapagna, S. O. (1990). Dynamic analysis of problem solving by average and high ability children. *Canadian Journal of Special Education, 6,* 15–30.

Karnes, M. B. (Ed.). (1983). *The underserved: Our young gifted children.* Reston, VA: Council for Exceptional Children.

Karnes, M. B., Shwedel, A. M., & Steinberg, D. (1984). Styles of parenting among parents of young gifted children. *Roeper Review, 6,* 232–235.

Kaufman, A. S. (1971). Piaget and Gesell: A psychometric analysis of tests built from their tasks. *Child Development, 42,* 1341–1360.

Kitano, M. K. (1985). Ethnography of a preschool for the gifted: What gifted young children actually do. *Gifted Child Quarterly, 29,* 67–71.

Klein, P. S. (1992). Mediating the cognitive, social, and aesthetic development of precocious young children. In P. S. Klein & A. Tannenbaum (Eds.), *To be young and gifted* (pp. 245–277). Norwood, NJ: Ablex.

Klene, R. (1988, August). *The occurrence of fears in gifted children.* Paper presented at the Annual Meeting of the American Psychological Association, Atlanta.

Kohn, M., & Rosman, B. L. (1972). Relationship of preschool social–emotional functioning to later intellectual achievement. *Developmental Psychology, 6,* 445–452.

Krinsky, R., Jackson, N. E., & Robinson, H. B. (1977). Analysis of parent information on the identification of precocious intellectual development in young children. In H. B. Robinson, W. Roedell, & N. Jackson (Eds.), *Identification and nurturance of extraordinarily precocious young children: Annual report to the Spencer Foundation* (pp. B31–B44). Seattle: University of Washington, Child Development Research Group. (ERIC Document Reproduction Service No. ED 151 095)

Leithwood, K. A. (1971). Motor, cognitive and affective relationships among advantaged preschool children. *Research Quarterly, 42,* 47–53.

Lempers, J., Block, L., Scott, M., & Draper, D. (1987). The relationship between psychometric brightness and cognitive–developmental precocity in gifted preschoolers. *Merrill Palmer Quarterly, 33,* 489–503.

Lewis, M., & Louis, B. (1991). Young gifted children. In N. Colangelo & G. A. Davis (Eds.), *Handbook of gifted education* (pp. 365–381). Boston: Allyn & Bacon.

Little, A. (1972). A longitudinal study of cognitive development in young children. *Child Development, 43,* 1024–1034.

Louis, B., & Lewis, M. (1992). Parental beliefs about giftedness in young children and their relation to actual ability level. *Gifted Child Quarterly, 36,* 27–31.

Lovecky, D. V. (1992). Exploring social and emotional aspects of giftedness in children. *Roeper Review, 15,* 18–25.

McCall, R. B., Appelbaum, M. I., & Hogarty, P. S. (1973). Developmental changes in mental performance. *Monographs of the Society for Research in Child Development, 38*(3, Serial No. 150).

McCall, R. B., & Carriger, M. S. (1993). A meta-analysis of infant habituation and recognition memory performance as predictors of later IQ. *Child Development, 64,* 57–79.

McClelland, D., Atkinson, J., Clark, R., & Lowell, E. (1953). *The achievement motive.* New York: Appleton-Century-Crofts.

McClelland, S. E. (1982). *A verbal/performance analysis of the Stanford–Binet Intelligence Scale and the development of high-IQ preschoolers.* Unpublished doctoral dissertation, University of Washington, Seattle, WA.

McCurdy, H. (1960). The childhood patterns of genius. *Horizon, 2*(5), 33–38.

McGuffog, C., Feiring, C., & Lewis, M. (1987). The diverse profile of the extremely gifted child. *Roeper Review, 10,* 82–89.

Miles, C. D. (1954). Gifted children. In L. Carmichael (Ed.), *Manual of child psychology* (2nd ed., pp. 984–1063). New York: Wiley.

Miller, L. K. (1991, April). *Development of musical "monosavant" skill.* Paper presented at the convention of the Society for Research in Child Development, Seattle.

Moore, C., Nelson-Piercy, C., Abel, M., & Frye, D. (1984). Precocious conservation in context: The solution of quantity tasks by nonquantitative strategies. *Journal of Experimental Child Psychology, 38,* 1–6.

Moore, L. C., & Sawyers, J. K. (1987). The stability of original thinking in young children. *Gifted Child Quarterly, 31,* 126–129.

Moran, J. D., III, Milgram, R. M., Sawyers, J. K., & Fu, V. R. (1983). Original thinking in preschool children. *Child Development, 54,* 921–926.

Moss, E. (1990). Social interaction and metacognitive development in gifted preschoolers. *Gifted Child Quarterly, 34,* 16–20.

Moss, E. (1992). Early interactions and metacognitive development of gifted preschoolers. In P. S. Klein & A. Tannenbaum (Eds.), *To be young and gifted* (pp. 278–318). Norwood, NJ: Ablex.

Moss, E., & Strayer, F. F. (1990). Interactive problem-solving of gifted and non-gifted preschoolers with their mothers. *International Journal of Behavioral Development, 13,* 177–197.

Ochse, R. (1990). *Before the gates of excellence: The determinants of creative genius.* Cambridge, England: Cambridge University Press.

Planche, P. (1985). Modalites fonctionelles et conduites de resolution de problemes chez des enfants precoces de cinq, six et sept ans d'age chronologique [Functional modalities and problem solving in precocious children five, six, and seven years old]. *Archives de Psychologie, 53,* 411–415.

Pletan, M. D., Robinson, N. M., Berninger, V. W., & Abbott, R. D. (1995). Parents' observations of kindergartners who are advanced in mathematical reasoning. *Journal for the Education of the Gifted, 19,* 30–44.

Plomin, R. (1994). *Genetics and experience: The interplay between nature and nurture.* Thousand Oaks, CA: Sage.

Porath, M. (1992). Stage and structure in the development of children with various types of "giftedness." In R. Case (Ed.), *The mind's staircase: Exploring the conceptual underpinnings of children's thought and knowledge* (pp. 303–317). Hillsdale, NJ: Erlbaum.

Radford, J. (1990). *Child prodigies and exceptional early achievers.* New York: Free Press.

Renzulli, J. S. (1978). What makes giftedness? Reexamining a definition. *Phi Delta Kappan, 60,* 18–24.

Robinson, N. M. (1993). Identifying and nurturing gifted, very young children. In K. A. Heller, F. J. Mönks, & A. H. Passow (Eds.), *International handbook for research on giftedness and talent* (pp. 507–524). Oxford, England: Pergamon.

Robinson, N. M., Abbott, R. D., Berninger, V. W., & Busse, J. (1996). The structure of abilities in math-precocious young children: Gender similarities and differences. *Journal of Educational Psychology, 88,* 341–352.

Robinson, N. M., Abbott, R. D., Berninger, V. W., Busse, J., & Mukhopadhyay, S. (1997). Developmental changes in mathematically precocious young children: Longitudinal and gender effects. *Gifted Child Quarterly, 41,* 145–158.

Robinson, N. M., Dale, P. S., & Landesman, S. (1990). Validity of Stanford–Binet IV with linguistically precocious toddlers. *Intelligence, 14,* 173–186.

Robinson, N. M., & Robinson, H. B. (1992). The use of standardized tests with young gifted children. In P. S. Klein & A. Tannenbaum (Eds.), *To be young and gifted* (pp. 141–170). Norwood, NJ: Ablex.

Robinson, N. M., Weinberg, R. A., Redden, D., Ramey, S. L., & Ramey, C. T. (1998). Family factors associated with high academic competence among former Head Start children. *Gifted Child Quarterly, 42,* 148–156.

Roedell, W. C., Jackson, N. E., & Robinson, H. B. (1980). *Gifted young children.* New York: Teachers College Press.

Rose, D., Slater, A., & Perry, H. (1986). Prediction of childhood intelligence from habituation in infancy. *Intelligence, 10,* 251–263.

Rose, S. A., Feldman, J. F., & Wallace, I. F. (1992). Infant information processing in relation to six-year cognitive outcomes. *Child Development, 63,* 1126–1141.

Shapiro, B. K., Palmer, F. B., Antell, S. E., Bilker, S., Ross, A., & Capute, A. J. (1989). Giftedness: Can it be predicted in infancy? *Clinical Pediatrics, 28,* 205–209.

Shigaki, I. S., & Wolf, W. (1982). Comparison of class and conditional logic abilities of gifted and normal children. *Child Study Journal, 12,* 161–170.

Silverman, L. K., Chitwood, D. G., & Waters, J. L. (1986). Young gifted children: Can parents identify giftedness? *Topics in Early Childhood Special Education, 6*(1), 23–38.

Simonton, D. K. (1998). Gifted child—genius adult: Three life-span developmental perspectives. In R. Friedman & K. B. Rogers (Eds.), *Talent in context: Historical and social perspectives on giftedness* (pp. 151–175). Washington, DC: American Psychological Association.

Sontag, L. W., Baker, C. T., & Nelson, V. L. (1958). Mental growth and personality development: A longitudinal study. *Monographs of the Society for Research in Child Development, 23*(2, Serial No. 68).

Spitz, H. H. (1985). Extreme décalage: The task by intelligence interaction. In E. D. Neimark, R. De Lisi, & J. L. Newman (Eds.), *Moderators of competence* (pp. 117–145). Hillsdale, NJ: Erlbaum.

Sternberg, R. J. (Ed.). (1988). *The nature of creativity.* Cambridge, England: Cambridge University Press.

Strang, R. (1951). Mental hygiene of gifted children. In P. Witty (Ed.), *The gifted child* (pp. 131–162). Lexington, MA: Heath.

Tannenbaum, A. (1992). Early signs of giftedness: Research and commentary. *Journal for the Education of the Gifted, 15,* 104–133.

Terman, L. M. (1926). *Genetic studies of genius: Vol. I. Mental and physical traits of a thousand gifted children* (2nd ed.). Stanford, CA: Stanford University Press.

Terman, L. M., & Oden, M. H. (1947). *Genetic studies of genius: Vol. IV. The gifted child grows up.* Stanford, CA: Stanford University Press.

Thomas, B. (1984). Early toy preferences of four-year-old readers and nonreaders. *Child Development, 55,* 424–430.

Trudewind, C. (1982). The development of achievement motivation and individual differences: Ecological determinants. In W. W. Hartup (Ed.), *Review of child development research* (Vol. 6, pp. 669–703). Chicago: University of Chicago Press.

Tucker, B. W., & Hafenstein, N. L. (1998, May). *Perspective taking in young gifted children.* Paper presented at the Fourth Biennial Henry B. & Jocelyn Wallace National Research Symposium on Talent Development, University of Iowa, Iowa City, IA.

Vygotsky, L. S. (1978). *Mind in society: The development of higher psychological processes.* Cambridge, MA: Harvard University Press.

West, S. S. (1960). Sibling configuration of scientists. *American Journal of Sociology, 66,* 268–271.

White, B. L. (1983). The origins of competence. In B. M. Shore, F. Gagné, S. Larivee, R. H. Tali, & R. E. Tremblay (Eds.), *Face to face with giftedness* (pp. 3–26). New York: Trillium.

White, B. L., & Watts, J. C. (Eds.). (1973). *Experience and environment: Major influences on the development of the young child* (Vol. I). Englewood Cliffs, NJ: Prentice Hall.

Whitmore, J. R. (1980). *Giftedness, conflict, and underachievement.* Boston: Allyn & Bacon.

Willerman, L., & Fiedler, M. F. (1974). Infant performance and intellectual precocity. *Child Development, 45,* 483–486.

Willerman, L., & Fiedler, M. F. (1977). Intellectually precocious preschool children: Early development and later intellectual accomplishments. *Journal of Genetic Psychology, 131,* 13–20.

Windecker-Nelson, E., Melson, G. F., & Moon, S. M. (1997). Intellectually gifted preschoolers' perceived competence: Relations to maternal attitudes, concerns, and support. *Gifted Child Quarterly, 41,* 133–144.

Winterbottom, M. (1958). The relation of need for achievement in learning experiences in independence and mastery. In J. Atkinson (Ed.), *Motives in fantasy, action and society* (pp. 437–453). Princeton, NJ: Van Nostrand.

Zha, Z. (1984). A comparative study of the analogical reasoning of 3- to 6-year-old super-normal and normal children. *Acta Psychologica Sinica, 16,* 373–382.

Zhensun, Z., & Low, A. (1991). *A young painter: The life and paintings of Wang Yani. China's extraordinary young artist.* New York: Scholastic.

Zigler, E., & Trickett, P. K. (1978). IQ, social consequence, and evaluation of early childhood intervention programs. *American Psychologist, 33,* 789–796.

2

Strategies for Modeling the Development of Giftedness in Children

Nancy Ewald Jackson

A central argument of this chapter is that methods used for studying the development of giftedness in children have not caught up with recent changes in how we understand development and giftedness. Unless theory and method are reconciled, we have little hope of advancing understanding of how giftedness develops and how it can be nurtured. However, we can bring methods for studying giftedness in line with developmental theory by studying how different kinds of gifted performances emerge and change as children grow older. An example developed in detail from joint consideration of the literature on giftedness and cognitive development shows how precocious reading, a kind of gifted performance that is relatively common in early childhood, can indicate underlying abilities that may be expressed in different domains later.

Since the 1970s, conceptualizations of development and of giftedness in childhood have changed dramatically. Most of us no longer think of individual differences in intellectual ability or personality as stable traits to be estimated as a fixed product of the interaction of genetic and environmental factors. As attempts to explain the mechanisms of development have become more sophisticated, many theorists now view individual differences in developing behaviors as reflections of complex, cumulative, and bidirectional interplay between the child's unfolding characteristics and changing environmental contexts (Plomin, 1997; Scarr, 1992). Similarly, conceptions of giftedness in childhood have evolved beyond Terman's (1925) and Hollingworth's (1942) early conclusions that general intelligence was a stable trait strongly influenced by native endowment and that childhood IQ indicated the upper limit of a child's potential for exceptional intellectual accomplishment in adulthood. Nonetheless, most of the designs currently used to study the development of giftedness are remarkably similar to those adopted by Terman (1925) and Hollingworth (1942). Working within the framework of these designs makes it impossible to

The author thanks her colleague David Lohman and the editors for their helpful comments on preliminary drafts of this chapter.

test important hypotheses that can be derived from current conceptions of development and giftedness.

In the following sections I review the implications of current conceptions of individual differences in development and of giftedness for generating hypotheses about the development of giftedness in childhood. I then describe the research designs that dominate current longitudinal study of the development of giftedness and note their limitations for testing new hypotheses. Finally, I present examples from my own research and other studies that suggest a better strategy for designing developmental studies of giftedness.

Current Conceptions of Individual Differences in Development

Those of us who study individual differences in development face a complex problem. We seek to describe and explain not just average patterns of change with age, but systematic individual differences in those changes. If an individual-differences researcher finds no continuity in patterns of individual differences across age, he or she faces all the usual problems of interpreting null findings. Therefore, developmentalists who want to understand individual differences must find some kind of predictable intraindividual continuity across time and developmental change.

Some radical critics have rejected the goal of understanding and predicting individual differences in development as incompatible with the complexity of developmental processes (Kessen, 1991). However, our responsibility to provide the best empirical base possible for formulating social policy and designing systems for early identification and remediation of developmental difficulties requires us to study individual differences as sensibly as we can, even though our conclusions will be imperfect (Horowitz & O'Brien, 1989; Scarr, 1985). Furthermore, the study of individual differences provides strong tests of and should contribute to theories that describe development in terms of universal characteristics for each age group (Scarr, 1992; Siegler, 1996; Underwood, 1975).

Notwithstanding the worthiness of the goal of modeling individual differences in development, the more we understand about how children change across development, the harder it may seem to find continuity within that change (e.g., Scarr, 1985, 1992). Success in doing so will depend on our ability to recognize and model a complex, dynamic process in which almost nothing is as straightforward as it once seemed.

Development Is a Sequence of Bidirectional Transactions

Developmentalists have begun to recognize the limits of static conceptualizations of organism–environment interactions and clear distinctions between nature and nurture (Bevan, 1991; Gottlieb, 1991; Lerner, 1991; Turkheimer & Gottesman, 1991). For example, Gottlieb (1991) proposed that an individual's development should not be described as the result of a unidirectional flow of influence from genetic activity to structural maturation and hence to the organism's activity or experience. Rather, he suggested that effects within the developing systems are bidirectional, such that experience can influence structural maturation and structure can influence genetic activity.

Just as the activity of genes must be considered in the context of environmental effects that occur across the life span, the development of the individual is considered by many current theorists to be intimately tied to the social context in which that development is embedded. Lerner (1991) has argued that changing interactions between the developing individual and the social context "are the core of what human development is all about" (p. 31). Scarr (1992; Scarr & McCartney, 1983) and Plomin (1997) have expressed an aspect of this idea that may be especially important for understanding the development of giftedness in childhood—the hypothesis that genotypic predispositions become progressively more important as children mature and have more opportunities to shape their own environments. This principle is well documented for intelligence (e.g., Plomin, 1997), but it remains to be tested for more elaborate or domain-specific definitions of gifted performance.

A related behavior genetics principle with strong implications for the study of giftedness is that genotypic influences on development are likely to be strongest in environments that provide solid support for basic developmental needs and abundant, equal opportunities for the pursuit of individuals' emerging interests (Plomin, 1997; Scarr, 1992). When every child has equal opportunities to develop his or her full potential, those individual differences in potential that are influenced by genotype become apparent. In a society in which some children never have a fair chance to develop their talents fully, we cannot tell who could have been the most outstanding performers.

The Meaning of Behaviors and Experiences Changes Across Development

Many years ago, Kagan (1971) argued that continuity in individual differences across development is likely to be heterotypic, that a trait such as intelligence is likely to be expressed in different forms as a child matures. The utility of this principle has been evident in work that links an infant's rapid development of a preference for novel stimuli to verbal intelligence later in childhood (Fagan, 1985; Rose & Feldman, 1995, 1997).

Developmentalists also now recognize that measures that appear comparable except in level of difficulty may tap qualitatively different processes at different ages. More fundamentally, a construct such as reading or mathematics ability must be defined and measured differently as skill develops. Individual differences in component skills such as word identification in reading or computation in mathematics are important sources of variation among beginners, but exceptional fluency in word identification or efficiency in arithmetic computation are not appropriate indices of mature literary or mathematical achievement.

The Meaning of Behaviors and Experiences Varies Across Contexts

Since the early 1980s, developmentalists have become more circumspect about generalizing their conclusions across populations and across behavioral contexts. We have learned that good parenting may take different forms depending on how parents perceive the environment in which their children need to survive (Ogbu, 1981) and that intelligence may be manifest in different ways in different cultures (Gardner, 1983; Sternberg, 1985). We also have learned that our assessments of children's competencies and of the factors that contribute to good performance can change radically depending on aspects of context such as familiarity of the setting and specific task demands (e.g., Ceci & Bronfenbrenner, 1985; Saxe, 1988). A constructivist, relativistic perspective on development suggests the need for similarly constructivist and relativistic conceptions of giftedness. However, the field still struggles with the conflicts inherent in attempting to reconcile a traditional, absolutist conception of giftedness with more relativistic conceptions (Coleman, Sanders, & Cross, 1997).

Current Conceptions of Giftedness in Childhood

Current conceptions of giftedness in children are compatible with current conceptions of development in their emphases on change with age, on the bidirectional interaction of multiple forces, and on the culture-specificity of any definition.

Although child prodigies have been an object of fascination for hundreds of years (Hollingworth, 1942; Shavinina, 1999), children are not likely to produce creative work that is remarkable by absolute standards. Therefore, our current conceptions of childhood giftedness were strongly influenced by the development of intelligence tests and the associated idea that childhood IQ indicated a stable, innate ability. Terman (1925) established the tradition of defining giftedness in childhood in terms of high general intelligence, which he regarded as an indicator of potential for adult achievement.

The Terman tradition lingers in some recent conceptions of giftedness. For example, Tannenbaum (1986) defined giftedness in children as potential for adult achievement, noting that the idea of special education for the gifted "would be irrelevant if there were no developmental connection between early promise and later fulfillment" (p. 28). Defining childhood giftedness in terms of potential for adult achievement is tempting for practitioners because this conceptualization, however tenuous its empirical base, can be used to argue for gifted education in terms of future benefits to society from the eventual realization of young students' potential. However, Tannenbaum's suggestion that potential is the only basis for special education of gifted children overlooks the critical issue of the school's responsibility to provide education well matched to a child's current achievement and interests. The principle that each child deserves to be educated in the least restrictive environment possible applies to exceptionally able children as well as to those who have disabilities (Jackson & Doellinger, 2000).

Giftedness Changes With Age

Many contemporary psychologists and educators have moved toward conceptualizations of giftedness in which age is an intrinsic element of the conception. For example, Humphreys (1985) has observed that "there is no diagnostic category of giftedness that is independent of a given stage of development" (p. 336). Similarly, Renzulli (1986) has argued for a dynamic conceptualization of giftedness as "a condition that can be developed" (p. 60) and expressed a preference, which I share, for focusing on the development of gifted behaviors rather than gifted persons (Jackson & Butterfield, 1986). Dynamic conceptions of giftedness also have been proposed by Feldman (1986a) and Gruber (1986), although Gruber, whose own studies have been retrospective analyses of the lives of eminent adults, shared Tannenbaum's inclination to think of childhood giftedness only as a potential.

Csikszentmihalyi and Robinson (1986) have offered a conceptualization of the development of giftedness across the life span that is fully consistent with other dynamic views but goes beyond them to specify what kinds of changes in the expression of giftedness we might expect as an individual matures through successive stages of cognitive development, meets a succession of psychosocial challenges, and is faced with qualitatively different creative and professional tasks. Their theory offers a framework that suggests why prodigious childhood achievement is more common in some fields than in others. For example, music (at least at the level of technical competence) is described as a field conducive to early mastery because, unlike fields such as the graphic arts, it has a closed symbol system that offers learners a clear structure and standards of excellence that are relatively stable and accessible. Csikszentmihalyi and Robinson also suggested several paths that may lead child prodigies away from eminence in the field of their earliest achievement, such as the social pressures of adolescence or the stress of public competition.

Csikszentmihalyi and Robinson were not the first to observe that the requirements for success differ for beginners and mature professionals in creative fields, but the scope and coherence of their developmental account makes it a good starting point for thinking about how the development of giftedness should be studied. From that perspective, the major limitation of Csikszentmihalyi and Robinson's theory is that it does not address the possibility, which is strongly suggested by the case study literature (e.g., Feldman, 1986b; Jackson & Klein, 1997), that giftedness in an individual may not just wax and wane but can appear in different domains at successive points in development (Jackson, 1992).

More recently, Shavinina (1999) has considered child prodigies from an age-dependent perspective that emphasizes a developmental progression through sensitive periods. In these periods, children "actualize their cognitive potential and accelerate their mental development" (p. 34). The developmental view of giftedness proposed here differs from Shavinina's in specifics and explanatory style, but I share her interest in the ways in which prodigies and other young gifted performers shift from one domain of interest to another as they grow older.

Giftedness Is Complexly Determined

Since Terman's (1925) early work, conceptions of giftedness in childhood have become broader and more complex as well as more dynamic. In addition to emphasizing the temporal specificity and context dependence of gifted behaviors, most current conceptualizations of giftedness in children stress the dependence of creative–productive giftedness at any age on the fortunate coincidence or interaction of multiple factors (Eccles & Harold, 1992; Feldman, 1986b; Renzulli, 1986; Sternberg & Lubart, 1992). For example, exceptional achievement in mathematics may occur only if an individual has developed an aptitude for mathematical reasoning, has access to stimulating instruction, is willing to study for long hours and persist in working on problems despite repeated failures, and has no greater preference for similarly time-consuming activities in other domains (Eccles & Harold, 1992). Theorists sometimes specify minimum threshold levels or curvilinear relations between a given factor and gifted performance (e.g., Simonton, 1997; Sternberg & Lubart, 1992) rather than linear relations. Often, the absence of any critical factor is hypothesized to be sufficient to block the development of creative–productive giftedness (e.g., Renzulli, 1986).

Theorists differ in whether they choose to deal with the complexity of giftedness by packing complexity into the construct of giftedness itself or unpacking (i.e., simplifying) the construct of giftedness and allowing it to be complexly determined. The former approach is exemplified in the work of Renzulli (1986), who has regarded above-average ability, task commitment, and creativity as converging aspects internal to the construct. To be gifted, an individual must, by definition, have all three qualities. In contrast, one can pare the construct of giftedness to a minimum in order to make it conceptually and empirically narrower and then propose correlates or determinants for that construct. This is the approach that a colleague and I took when we proposed that

> gifted performances are instances of excellent performance on any task that has practical value or theoretical interest . . . the term *performance* [should] be construed broadly and dynamically. Thus learning a new skill with unusual speed or ease would qualify as an instance of gifted performance. (Jackson & Butterfield, 1986, p. 155)

The advantage of defining giftedness itself in terms of performance alone is that measuring the construct becomes more manageable. One then can devise separate measures of quality of performance, degree of task commitment, cultural and personal meaning of the task, and so on, relating each of these constructs, separately and jointly, to both current and future performance. The disadvantage of this analytic approach is that the richness of a more complex construct of giftedness is dispersed across a network that may be difficult to gather up when a situation calls for considering the phenomenon in an integrated way.

Childhood Giftedness Is Multifaceted and May Be Domain Specific

Most current conceptions of giftedness are sufficiently broad and flexible to include remarkable achievements in diverse domains, even when those achievements do not require high levels of general intelligence. Some even allow for the possibility that a child with below-average general intelligence may be gifted within a narrow realm, as in the remarkable cases of musical and artistic savants (Miller, 1989; Morelock & Feldman, 1993, 1997; Treffert, 1989).

When childhood and adult giftedness are conceptualized as exceptional achievement within a specific domain (Feldman, 1986a, 1986b; Jackson, 1992; Jackson & Butterfield, 1986; Shavinina, 1999; Sternberg, 1987), the counterproductive division between schoolhouse giftedness in childhood and creative–productive giftedness in adulthood (Siegler & Kotovsky, 1986) is minimized. One can define giftedness in childhood as domain-specific achievement without requiring that a child's achievements be creative or remarkable by adult standards (Jackson & Klein, 1997). Doing so brings conceptualizations of giftedness in line with modular and situated theories of cognition (Stanovich, 1990). However, conceptualizing giftedness as something more complex and specific than IQ raises new questions about appropriate frames of reference and standards of excellence in various domains (e.g., Feldman, 1986a; Sternberg & Zhang, 1995) as well as the more fundamental problem of defining domains and contexts in which childhood giftedness may be expressed.

Some theorists have suggested that specific intellectual abilities are not likely to be differentiated in young children (Humphreys, 1985). However, both specialized skills and specialized deficits have been identified in children of preschool age (Nation, 1999; Scarborough, 1990). Cognitive abilities may be more differentiated in individuals high in general intelligence (Detterman & Daniel, 1989). Therefore, even though skills are likely to become progressively more modularized and differentiated as a child's expertise develops, it is reasonable to consider the possibility of domain-specific giftedness even during the preschool years (Jackson & Klein, 1997).

Giftedness and Development Can Be Integrated

Current conceptions of development and giftedness in childhood are consistent with one another in acknowledging the complexity of developmental processes and the value of regarding the individual as constructing a life in continuing transactions with an ever-changing environment. To understand either concept, we must consider how nature and nurture inter-act across the life span and how continuities in individuals' lives can be understood in the context of developmental change. Unfortunately, the methods that most investigators have been using to study the development of giftedness in childhood are not suited to testing the kinds of hypotheses that come from such elaborate conceptualizations.

Current Methods for Studying the Development of Giftedness

Reading the current literature on the development of giftedness in child-hood as it appears in the field's journals and books yields two strong im-pressions. First, designs have changed little since Terman (1925; Terman & Oden, 1947) and Hollingworth (1942). We still are doing two basic kinds of research: (a) large-sample prospective longitudinal studies à la Terman (Subotnik & Arnold, 1994) or (b) prospective or retrospective case studies à la Hollingworth and the biographers of eminent individuals (e.g., Gross, 1993; Shavinina, 1999). Second, the Hollingworth-type case studies seem to reveal more about the nature of giftedness in early childhood, even to a reader like me who usually favors traditional large-sample designs and quantitative analyses.

Large-Sample Prospective Longitudinal Studies

The designs used to study giftedness have been influenced by a central challenge. Giftedness, no matter how it is defined, is a rare event. There-fore all researchers who want to study the development of giftedness must use a sampling strategy that will guarantee the inclusion of sufficient numbers of the rare individuals of interest.

Some investigators have done longitudinal studies of giftedness by identifying high-performing cases within very large national databases (e.g., Willerman & Fiedler, 1977). This approach enables investigators to look both forward and backward at development, recording both the extent to which high early achievement is maintained and the extent to which mature high achievers would be missed by various selection criteria ap-plied earlier in development. For researchers interested in the develop-ment of giftedness, the major limitation of the databases available for sec-ondary analysis is that they may not contain key data: Constructs of interest to the investigator may not have been measured, or the measures used may not have had sufficient ceiling to detect individual differences in high-level performance.

Most large-sample longitudinal studies of childhood giftedness have been follow-ups of children selected for their performance on an index of general ability such as an intelligence test (Tomlinson-Keasey & Little, 1990). These prospective longitudinal studies often have involved children who were selected initially as a result of participation in an educational or competitive program such as the Study of Mathematically Precocious

Youth Mathematics Talent Search (e.g., Benbow & Arjmand, 1990). The focus of these program-based investigations typically has been on the participants' continued achievement within the same or apparently related domains.

Program-based longitudinal studies can generate useful models of the factors associated with the extent to which initial achievement on the selection criterion measure is followed by later success in the same realm. They are especially useful if the questions relate to the effectiveness of the educational program in which the study participants have taken part. In the absence of program effects (Humphreys, 1985), the performance of the selected group will decline in degree of exceptionality over time, usually to a great extent if the study extends for more than a few years (Humphreys, 1985; Mills & Jackson, 1990).

Because piggy-backing developmental research on educational programs is a cost-effective way to support basic scientific inquiry, most recent longitudinal studies of gifted children with samples large enough to permit path analyses of individual differences in development have been tied to talent searches or educational programs (Subotnik & Arnold, 1994; Subotnik, Kassan, Summers, & Wasser, 1994). Sample bias and the effects of program participation may limit the generalizability of findings from these studies, but their most serious limitation is that they start too late. Longitudinal studies of children whose first contact with investigators is concomitant with their participation in some educational program are not likely to provide prospective data on the development of giftedness in the preschool and early elementary school years, when change is likely to be most dramatic and important questions need to be addressed (Tomlinson-Keasey, 1990).

In any prospective study of giftedness that goes beyond analysis of full-population databases, success depends heavily on the extent to which the initial selection criterion is reliable and related to the outcomes of interest. Measures of general ability may not be efficient or theoretically informative as selection criteria, in part because the composition and meaning of those measures changes drastically across the first years of life (Lewis & Michalson, 1985). Domain-specific selection criteria may not work any better. For example, Crain-Thoreson and Dale (1992) identified a sample of two-year olds who were precocious in the development of their oral language. The investigators hypothesized that precocity in oral language would be associated with subsequent precocity in the development of literacy. However, when the children reached age $4\frac{1}{2}$ years, the group was not remarkably precocious in reading. This problem is not limited to studies of development during the preschool years. Mills and Jackson (1990) found that individual differences in reading achievement at the age of 11 or 12 years were only moderately related to individual differences in the extent to which the children had been precocious in their postkindergarten reading achievement. Longitudinal studies like these, focused on the development of giftedness within a single domain, will pick up homotypic, but not heterotypic, continuities (Kagan, 1971).

In general, recent large-sample prospective longitudinal studies of giftedness have provided little information of any sort about development during early childhood. Because their samples are limited to children who already have achieved well at the time of selection, these studies also cannot tell us about the ways in which giftedness might emerge in children who were not identified early. For that information, we must look to other designs.

Case Studies

Case studies that present qualitative interpretations of the development of individual children or small groups (e.g., Feldman, 1986b; Miller, 1989; Shavinina, 1999) also appear frequently in the literature, as do retrospective analyses of the childhoods of eminent individuals derived from personal reports or historical records (e.g., Gruber, 1986). In case study research, sampling problems usually are circumvented by abandoning any claims about representativeness of the participants. Cases are selected because they have come to the investigators' attention and aroused their interest or because they meet a criterion such as extremely high IQ (e.g., Gross, 1993).

Case studies have been a long-favored hypothesis generation tool for developmentalists, and recent interest in identifying the mechanisms underlying change with age has made the intensive, qualitative analysis of observations of small groups of children more widely accepted (Siegler & Crowley, 1991). Reading a good case study engenders an intuitive sense that one understands the child being described and that patterns perceived in that child's development might be generalized to other, apparently similar, cases. For example, Feldman (1986b) described a chess prodigy's unexpected transformation into whiz-kid stock market entrepreneur and speculated that this shift of interest may have been related to the low status of chess (and the high status of money making) in American society, coupled with the young man's self-professed love of mastering new domains of expertise.

The richness of the data available in case studies is well matched to the complexity of current conceptualizations of development and giftedness. The typical case study includes a wealth of information about diverse aspects of a child's behavior and experience. Therefore, the odds that previously unrecognized but developmentally important patterns will be detectable within that individual's history may be greater than the odds that similarly important patterns and connections will be apparent in a large-sample survey in which observations of each case must be limited and standardized.

Retrospective case histories of the development of eminent individuals (e.g., Gruber, 1986) have a special place in the literature because they offer an opportunity to search for early signs of promise in individuals who may appear to have been unremarkable as children. Some signs presaging eminence often can be found, and retrospective case studies can suggest hypotheses about continuities in development that might not otherwise be evident. However, the advantages of hindsight are notoriously hard to translate into effective prediction. This same caution applies to the retrospective information about early childhood often included in case studies of prodigies identified in middle childhood or adolescence (Feldman, 1986b).

In general, post hoc analyses of rich case study data can be plausible, fascinating, and useful as sources of ideas about why childhood giftedness may wax, wane, or change form, beginning in the earliest years. However, a scientific field whose primary database is a collection of case studies is not likely to progress rapidly toward the generation of new knowledge or offer an empirical base for practice. Case studies offer little opportunity to disconfirm most kinds of hypotheses about development. Furthermore, case studies tell us nothing about the prospective odds that children who have been identified as chess masters before the age of 10 years will become stock market analysts or about the odds that a particular prodigy will choose one path over another.

Quantitative predictions of this sort cannot be done without information from large-sample longitudinal research. Developmental researchers need to design longitudinal studies of the development of giftedness in children so that choices of what, who, and when to observe are consistent with the best predictive models that we can generate from current conceptualizations of development and giftedness.

Designing Prospective Studies of the Development of Giftedness in Childhood

In 1986, Siegler and Kotovsky proposed that researchers should build formal models of giftedness and its development. They observed that

> modeling gifted performance would require detailed specification of the processes involved and of the knowledge base on which such processes operate. Modeling the development of gifted performance would require specification of an initial state of a potentially gifted person, a set of transition processes, a set of experiences on which the transition processes would operate, and the end state that would be embodied in the model of performance. (pp. 434–435)

No one has yet proposed such a formal model of the development of giftedness in childhood. However, considering this recommendation in terms of what already is known about giftedness and development suggests some ways in which a useful program of research might evolve. In the remainder of this chapter, examples from my own research and other related studies are used to suggest some new approaches for studying the development of giftedness. The focus of these examples is on children who are, at one point in their development, distinguished by their precocious mastery of reading. Steps that might be taken in the study of such children are listed and then illustrated with examples from our research program.

Although the focus is on the development of precocious readers, a similar approach could be implemented in the study of other forms of domain-specific giftedness.

Step 1: Define Giftedness in a Manageable Way

For the purpose of studying the development of giftedness in childhood, a performance-focused definition such as the one proposed in a previous section seems most manageable. By defining giftedness simply as exceptional performance or exceptionally rapid learning, we create opportunities to see how other factors such as motivation and creativity might be related to changes in performance across age.

Step 2: Working Backward, Consider What Forms of Precocity Are Most Common in Creative–Productive Adults

What forms of giftedness in early childhood are most likely to be precursors of creative–productive giftedness in adults? As Gruber (1986) has suggested, looking backward at the early years of eminent adults may suggest some likely candidates in the form of behaviors that might appear quite different from those for which an individual ultimately attains recognition. Precocious achievement in reading is one accomplishment that fares well from this perspective.

Early reading is mentioned in case studies of many eminent adults (Cox, 1926); in retrospective reports from the parents of children later identified as being extraordinarily high in intelligence or as earning high scores at an early age on the Scholastic Aptitude Test (Hollingworth, 1942; Terman & Oden, 1947; VanTassel-Baska, 1989); and in case studies of children identified as prodigies in mathematics, chess, music, literature, and other fields (Feldman, 1986b; Shavinina, 1999). The prospective odds that a precocious reader will become a creatively gifted performer in later childhood or adulthood are not known, but these retrospective data suggest that this early achievement is worth studying further.

Prospective longitudinal studies of precocious readers are feasible because this form of gifted performance is relatively common in young children (both boys and girls) and likely to be noticed by parents and teachers (Jackson, 1992). In the United States, where exposure to print on signs, labels, and television is almost universal even for children growing up in households bare of books, precocious reading occurs in children from all socioeconomic backgrounds (Durkin, 1984). Other forms of precocity that also are likely to emerge in the preschool or earliest elementary school years, such as remarkable achievement in music, mathematics, or writing and drawing (Feldman, 1986b; Shavinina, 1999), may be less common or less readily noticed in our culture, but also are worth considering in a comprehensive search for early manifestations of giftedness.

Step 3: Develop Cognitive Process Models of Gifted Performance

Understanding of developmental transitions in gifted performance is most likely to grow out of analysis of the tasks and performances in which a developing child is likely to demonstrate a remarkable level of achievement. If we want to predict which children are most likely to be exceptionally skilled at something, we first must determine what is involved in that skill. Therefore, we should focus our attempts to understand developing giftedness in well-analyzed skill domains such as reading.

Step 4: Consider the Child's Motivation for Becoming a Gifted Performer

Cognitive developmentalists tend to focus on developmentally prior cognitive precursors of or prerequisites for achievement. This is one way to look at the how and why of becoming a gifted performer. However, these questions also can be addressed in terms of opportunity and motivation. Issues of opportunity are subsumed in Step 5 and cognition in Steps 6 and 7, but motivation deserves special attention.

The creative–productive giftedness of adulthood is characterized by intrinsic motivation to resolve creative tensions and by interest in finding and solving important new problems (Csikszentmihalyi & Robinson, 1986; Gruber, 1986). From adolescence to adulthood, the best predictor of this kind of performance is earlier behavior that was similar in kind, if not in scale (Csikszentmihalyi & Robinson, 1986; Wallach, 1985). Given all the ways in which the experiences of middle childhood can affect interests and motivational patterns, it may not be possible to enhance the prediction of adult giftedness by considering information about how and why a child has become a gifted performer in early childhood. However, this early motivation may foretell something about patterns of development in at least the next few years. Furthermore, motivation is a special contributor to gifted performance because it appears to be influenced relatively little by genotype (Plomin, 1997).

Children's reasons for mastering a domain may be domain-specific or generalizable, transient or stable, and extrinsic or intrinsic. For example, some precocious readers are described by their parents as having learned to read because they wanted independent access to information such as the latest baseball scores or because their other play opportunities were restricted by chronic illness. It is hard to know what one would expect children to do in later years if their precocious reading acquisition has been motivated by such domain-specific and potentially transient needs. The fact that a child has made considerable effort to solve a self-defined problem bodes well for the child's future as a problem solver, but one cannot make any predictions about the domains toward which the child's interests eventually might turn. However, the child who learns to read early because of a fascination with the diverse real and imaginary worlds accessible through literature might be a good candidate for continued literary achievement. Yet another child, whose precocity during early childhood is the product of intensive home or school instruction and social reinforcement, may pursue intellectual activities with less commitment if he or she discovers other means of earning the attention of parents, teachers, and peers.

Whatever the domain, achieving or maintaining a gifted level of performance is likely to require increasing amounts of time and effort as a child matures and standards of excellence become more stringent. A child whose early achievements suggest considerable persistence might be more likely to keep up with these increasing demands. However, priorities can change, and children whose diverse skills and interests create conflicts may become increasingly likely to choose activities in which the immediate rewards are generous relative to the investment required (Eccles & Harold, 1992; Sternberg & Lubart, 1992).

Step 5: Consider How Universals of Cognitive Development and Culturally Determined Tasks Contribute to the Development of Gifted Performance

As Csikszentmihalyi and Robinson (1986) have observed, the ways in which children show precocious achievements that are remarkable by adult standards are likely to reflect universal sequences of cognitive development (Case, 1992) and the ways in which particular cultures elaborate those sequences with culture-specific developmental tasks. Combining this principle with Sternberg's (1987) suggestion that specific forms of intellectual giftedness reflect the operation of knowledge acquisition components leads to the hypothesis that gifted performance should be most evident in skill domains in which new forms of competence are emerging as a result of a universal or culturally imposed timetable.

Following this reasoning, intellectual giftedness in infants would most likely be manifest as exceptionally efficient processing of basic perceptual features of their environments. Infants whose attentional patterns suggest rapid assimilation of and memory for new experiences are more likely than others to be highly intelligent in early childhood (Fagan, 1985; Rose & Feldman, 1995, 1997; Sternberg, 1981), although differences in experience during and beyond infancy also will influence development. Borkowski and Peck (1986) have suggested that such infants are likely to inspire their caregivers to interact with them in ways that will encourage the development of strong problem-solving skills. Results consistent with this hypothesis have been reported by Plomin (1997).

Gifted two- or three-year-olds are likely to demonstrate skills that are readily observed by outsiders as well as a caregiver and that can be evaluated using well-established developmental norms. This may be the first age at which it is feasible to identify children for longitudinal studies of giftedness. During the early preschool years, children face the universal developmental task of mastering their native language. They also may encounter culture-specific symbol systems such as pictures and written language. At this age, gifted performers in our culture might best be defined as those children who are exceptionally advanced in their mastery of oral language, reading or writing, or the comprehension or production of nonverbal symbols such as drawings. The information-processing efficiency first detectable in infancy now may be transformed into performances such as the demonstrations of very rapid letter-naming speed. This measure begins to be a good longitudinal predictor of precocious reading achievement by the age of 2 or 3 years (Jackson & Myers, 1982; Mills & Jackson, 1990; Wolf, 1991).

Skills in areas such as oral language, reading, music, and drawing differ from the skills at which an infant might excel in that their development is more likely to be related to between- and within-family variation in availability of appropriate stimulation and to the amount of time a child devotes to practicing the skill. There appears to be relatively little generality in precocious mastery of these systems. As noted earlier, precocious talkers are not very likely to become precocious readers, and precocious readers may not be precocious drawers or writers (Crain-Thoreson & Dale, 1992; Henderson, Jackson, & Mukamal, 1993). However, reports of precocious drawing and precocious musical talent are prominent in case studies of precocious readers, with musical precocity often appearing soon after a child's first mastery of letters (Durkin, 1966; Feldman, 1986b; Gross, 1993; Jackson, 1992; Shavinina, 1999).

Precocious drawing skill is not likely to be an early sign of artistic talent. Precocity in the graphic arts seems to be rare, perhaps because becoming a creative artist involves mastering complex and ill-defined skills within a rapidly changing field (Csikszentmihalyi & Robinson, 1986; Morelock & Feldman, 1993). However, a young child who precociously masters the conventions of two-dimensional representation of the visual world may be manifesting cognitive abilities that will emerge again in other domains in which nonverbal representations can be important, such as the physical sciences and mathematics (Case, 1992) or field biology (Shavinina, 1999).

As children grow, the dramatic changes in thinking that typically occur between the ages of 5 and 7 years may occur earlier in gifted performers (Jackson & Butterfield, 1986). As reasoning powers expand, there are new, more complex symbol systems to master and manipulate. At age 4 or 5 years, a child who already has mastered the code of an alphabetic writing system might become passionately absorbed in a more complex system, such as arithmetic. In some children or some cultures, a transition from precocious literacy to precocious mastery of numbers may occur even earlier. Very early mathematical precocity was evident in several of the case reports of Russian prodigies summarized by Shavinina (1999).

During and beyond the elementary school years, progression through the universal sequences of cognitive development would be expected to lead children toward gifted performance in increasingly complex and abstract domains, such as computer programming, chess, and higher mathematics. During these years, children whose initial manifestations of giftedness were in areas such as reading or drawing might switch their allegiance to domains that offer more advanced analytical challenges (e.g., Feldman, 1986b; Gross, 1992, 1993). For example, one prodigy described by Shavinina (1999) progressed from enthusiasm for reading, writing, and arithmetic at age 3 years to a passion for categorizing and ordering all sorts of information and then to learning foreign languages with different alphabets.

Step 6: Consider How Domain Characteristics Interact With the Child's Development

The notion that some domains are more accessible than others to young children, given their cognitive limits, has already been introduced. However, the nature of the symbol system a child must learn and manipulate to become a gifted performer in a domain may vary greatly depending on the aspect of performance one considers and the level of proficiency at which the child is performing.

As suggested earlier, children may be more likely to demonstrate remarkable precocity in closed rather than open symbol systems. Systems such as oral language, reading, and writing can be considered relatively closed if one focuses on aspects of the system for which there is a limited set of elements and combination of rules whose use requires retention and manipulation of order information. Thus, mastery of the phonemes, grammatical morphemes, and syntax of oral language or the grapheme–phoneme correspondences of an alphabetic written language would be the kind of closed-system learning that is conducive to precocity. Learning these systems requires exposure to a database from which the rules or patterns can be abstracted, but precocity of this sort is not as likely to be as dependent upon quality of experience as learning oral vocabulary or reading comprehension might be.

At the lower end of the individual-differences continuum, closed-system aspects of learning oral language and reading tend to be closely related to one another (Scarborough, 1990) and show variation that has a substantial genotypic contribution (Olson, Forsberg, & Wise, 1994).

The most striking aspect of the oral language of one two-year-old reader was the length and grammatical complexity of his sentences. His language also showed his awareness of and attraction to rhyme and other sound patterns (Henderson et al., 1993). Although precocious readers are usually well above average in verbal intelligence, precocious reading achievement is not as strongly associated with verbal intelligence or oral vocabulary as one might expect (Jackson, 1992; Jackson, Donaldson, & Cleland, 1988; Jackson, Donaldson, & Mills, 1993). Indeed, some precocious readers are substantially delayed in their oral language development but highly skilled at pronouncing printed words. This phenomenon—hyperlexia—may be related to other forms of savant syndrome (Nation, 1999).

As a child progresses toward higher levels of skill mastery within a domain, the nature of the skills required for excellent performance may change. As Feldman (1986b), Gruber (1986), Csikszentmihalyi and Robinson (1986), and Bamberger (1986) all have observed, children may be called on to represent information in new ways, to develop a personal creative voice, or deal with a task that requires new kinds of skills. As the requirements for excellent performance in a domain change, precocious achievers may lose their pre-eminence or transfer their application of elementary information-processing skills and well-developed learning strategies to an accessible new domain. A child whose precocious achievement in reading rested in a skill for breaking the alphabetic code might not be a strong candidate for a literary career or even for exceptionally high reading achievement beyond the primary grades (Curtis, 1980; Mills & Jackson, 1990). However, some such children may transform themselves into mathematics or computer science prodigies during their elementary school years (Jackson, 1988a; Jackson & Kearney, 1999; Mills & Jackson, 1990). Similar transitions may occur across other sets of domains, and one tragic fictional example is depicted by Aldous Huxley (1924) in his short story "Young Archimedes." In this story, a young boy's attempt to make a transition from prodigious achievement in musical performance to fascination with mathematics is frustrated by a sponsor who wants to continue exploiting the boy's more immediately marketable talent for music.

Step 7: Consider the Extent to Which Gifted Performance Requires General Intelligence

Although giftedness in childhood can be either general or domain specific, the latter form is linked more closely with adult creative–productive giftedness and therefore may be of greater interest to developmentalists. However, the long-term implications of early giftedness in a domain are likely to vary with the extent to which that achievement requires or is accompanied by high general intelligence. For example, mastery of higher mathematics is more likely to be associated with a high level of general intelligence than is excellence in musical performance (Shuter-Dyson, 1982). Therefore, one might expect children who are good code learners at the age of 4 or 5 years to become gifted adult mathematicians only if they are high in general intelligence; less generally intelligent code learners might gravitate to music or various technical fields.

The extent to which general verbal intelligence is involved in the emergence of domain-specific precocious achievement may vary depending on how extremely precocious that achievement is. For example, a review of the literature suggests that children who are exceptionally high in verbal intelligence often begin reading at the age of 4 or 5 years. However, children who begin reading even earlier, at the age of 2 or 3, seem more likely to be superior in specific reading-related abilities (Jackson, 1992).

Why not return to Terman's approach and base the study of giftedness in childhood entirely on measures of general intelligence (Zigler & Farber, 1985)? This approach has several empirical and theoretical disadvantages. Intelligence test scores are unstable in the preschool years, are only moderately stable in middle childhood, and, taken as wholes, are not good predictors of early achievement in specific domains (Lewis & Michalson, 1985; McCall, Appelbaum, & Hogarty, 1973). Many extremely successful individuals have earned intelligence test scores that are only modestly above average, so any stringent IQ criterion for identifying gifted performers in childhood inevitably would miss many highly productive adults (Humphreys, 1985).

One could argue that measures of domain-specific abilities cannot be more stable than a general ability measure such as the IQ and that regression effects in long-term prediction should be larger if one uses less broadly based predictors (Humphreys, 1985). However, the relative stability of the IQ is no advantage if this score does not draw heavily on abilities essential to the gifted performances of interest. As Sternberg (1987) has hypothesized, gifted performances in specific domains may depend heavily on exceptional ability to rapidly automatize the processing of new information. Intelligence tests reflect this kind of ability to some extent, but it should be captured better by more direct measures of performance within the domains of interest.

Identifying young children who are gifted performers in specific domains probably is an inefficient exercise if one's only goal is early identification of potentially creative–productive adults. However, studying the emergence and transformation of specific kinds of gifted performance in childhood, such as precocious reading, offers the researcher opportunities to work within a framework of intrinsically important and well-understood cognitive tasks. Within this complex and solid framework, identifying a good model of development across even a span of a few years is likely to enhance our understanding of gifted performance and general principles of development.

A Conceptual Model of the Development of Precocious Achievement in Literacy, Mathematics, and Music

The seven principles summarized earlier in this chapter were used to generate a first-approximation conceptual model of the development of precocious achievement in literacy, mathematics, and music during childhood. This model reflects the author's own studies of precocious reading as well as the broader literatures on individual differences in development of skills in these domains.

Already committed to defining giftedness in terms of exceptional performance (Step 1) and aware that precocity in reading is often reported in the life histories of eminent adults (Step 2), my colleagues and I focused on developing a cognitive process model of precocious reading (Step 3). We analyzed the reading and related cognitive skills of several large samples of children who were reading at exceptionally advanced levels before they began first grade. We chose these post-kindergarten readers to study because they were at an age when precocious achievement in reading is common enough to study using large-sample techniques and because, at this age, reading is especially important in the child's everyday life. Consistent with Step 4 in the proposed plan for model development, we were aware that being able to read as well as the average child who is in the third or fourth grade is an unusual and dramatic accomplishment for a five- or six-year-old.

The results of this program of studies provided a sketch of the component skills and cognitive profiles of precocious readers. These children vary widely in verbal intelligence around a mean of about 130 (Jackson, 1992). Degree of reading advancement within a group of precocious readers is only moderately related to verbal intelligence (Jackson et al., 1988, 1993). Degree of precocity in reading also is moderately related to the speed with which a precocious post-kindergartner names individual letters (Jackson & Biemiller, 1985; Jackson et al., 1988, 1993).

These findings suggest that very young children who will be precocious readers by the time they have finished kindergarten are at least as likely to be identified by rapid letter-naming speed as by high verbal intelligence. Letter-naming speed is an interesting correlate of reading precocity because this task taps a more general ability to name familiar visual stimuli that has come to be known as rapid automatized naming, or RAN. Several investigators have identified slow RAN as a distinct deficit among many poor readers (Torgesen & Burgess, 1998; Wolf, 1991). Therefore, it makes sense that this ability should be especially well developed in precocious readers. The reflectivity of precocious readers is worth examining further as a potentially stable characteristic of extremely high achievers.

Analyses of precocious readers' skills also suggest that individuals differ in their skill patterns or reading styles as well as in overall degree of advancement (Backman, 1983; Jackson, 1988a, 1988b; Jackson et al., 1988, 1993). On the average, precocious readers are advanced in performance on tasks involving identification or manipulation of sounds within words (Backman, 1983; Blachman, 1984). However, variation within the group is sufficient to dismiss the possibility that advanced performance on phonological analysis tasks is prerequisite for precocious success in reading (Backman, 1983; Fletcher-Flinn & Thompson, in press). Some children seem to make considerable progress by relying heavily on recognizing words from their visual form (Backman, 1983; Jackson, 1988b). Perhaps precocious readers differ in the extent to which their rapid advancement reflects especially well-developed auditory or visual processing skills (Francis, Fletcher, Maxwell, & Satz, 1989). A related possibility is that some precocious readers may be especially well able to draw inferences about component letter-sound patterns from mastery of a whole-word reading vocabulary. Their inferences about the structure of English words could be sufficient for them to read new words but not explicit enough for them to perform well on formal tests of letter-sound knowledge (Fletcher-Flinn & Thompson, in press).

Despite individual differences in their skill patterns, precocious readers' rapid progress reflects very solid mastery of word-identification skills. These children are not identifying words by guessing from context (Jackson & Donaldson, 1989). They are extremely fluent readers of text, whether they are reading aloud or silently, and some also read isolated words very rapidly (Breznitz, 1987; Fletcher-Flinn & Thompson, in press; Jackson & Biemiller, 1985; Jackson & Donaldson, 1989; Jackson et al., 1993).

Precocious readers seem to have diverse reading interests (Step 4) as well as varied skill patterns. Their reasons for reading may remain stable over time and influence how precocious reading might develop during the elementary school years. In one longitudinal study, individual differences in the reading and related academic interests of precocious readers remained moderately stable from post-kindergarten to fifth or sixth grade; at both ages, boys' interests were more technical and girls' interests were more literary (Mills & Jackson, 1990).

Children in the United States and many other Western societies are expected to begin to learn to read at about the age of 6 years. Considering Step 5 of the model development plan, one notes that mastering this developmental task at an unusually early age is noteworthy and qualifies as a culturally relevant gifted performance (Jackson & Klein, 1997; Sternberg, 1993). However, as precocious readers grow older, achievements in other domains may draw greater attention. For example, the mother of one 3-year-old boy was most aware of and concerned about the educational implications of his precocious reading, although she also noticed that he had mastered some basic mathematics concepts and could recite the numerals to 100. However, when this boy had turned 5, his mother appeared more interested in his recent accomplishments in mathematical reasoning. At this time, she told me that her son had engaged her in the following dialogue:

> *Son:* "Do you know how much 3×8 is?"
> *Mother:* "I think I do. Do you?"
> *Son:* "Yes. It's 24. Do you know how I know? It's because 3×4 is 12."

At 5, this boy's reading had continued to progress and was still advanced for his age, but his precocious understanding of mathematics was beginning to stand out more clearly relative to what children in kindergarten are expected to know.

Given the diversity of precocious readers' skill patterns, one would not expect their reading to have a single set of cognitive precursors or always to lead to subsequent achievements in the same domain. However, there may be some common threads or identifiable alternative patterns leading to and from precocious reading. Some of these have been described earlier. The prevalence of particular patterns is unknown. However, in one study of the subsequent academic achievement test performance of children identified initially as post-kindergarten readers, the children's scores on fourth-grade mathematics tests were almost as high as their scores in reading on the same tests. The precocious readers who were highest in verbal intelligence and who were reported to have started reading at the earliest ages earned the highest mathematics test scores (Jackson & Kearney, 1999).

Predictions about what is likely to become of a child whose first demonstration of giftedness has been as a precocious reader reflect questions about development in the context of the motivational, cultural, domain-specific, and general intellectual factors identified and discussed in Steps 4 through 7 of the model development plan. These predictions are summarized in the model of development depicted in Figure 2.1. The model is a conceptual one because it is too complex and too incompletely specified to be testable as expressed here. However, the diagram gives an overall picture of the kinds of gifted performance that might be important at different ages and of how achievements and skills in one age period may influence development in the next. The primary purpose of the model is to suggest how heterotypic as well as homotypic continuities in the development of giftedness may emerge as elementary information-processing components are used in mastering a succession of different skills as children mature, face new developmental challenges, and encounter new learning opportunities. This model is proposed to encourage the formulation of alternative testable developmental models. It does not represent conclusions about how gifted performance develops. Some omissions or placements within the model represent close judgment calls. Indeed, the current model differs in some respects from a predecessor (Jackson & Klein, 1997) because some of my judgments have changed as new theory and data have emerged.

The kinds of achievement included in the model represent forms of precocity that have been observed in children (Feldman, 1986b; Goldsmith, 1987; Gross, 1992, 1993; Shavinina, 1999). Except for literary production and verbal intelligence, all rest heavily in the mastery of closed symbol systems (Csikszentmihalyi & Robinson, 1986). Forms of precocious achievement are placed in the model according to their most likely age of emergence, and most of the specified causal paths have been documented as correlations in the individual-differences literature.

The developmental model recapitulates and elaborates ideas introduced earlier in this chapter. For example, precocious reading is seen as a skill that emerges in the preschool years, initially in the form of advanced word reading. Whether a precocious reader is likely to continue to be precocious in reading comprehension and literary production or in some other area, such as mathematics or music, is influenced by the child's other abilities and changing environmental influences, including factors such as gender stereotypes and opportunities for study.

High verbal intelligence is included as a type of gifted performance in the age range of 4 to 7 years because the kinds of behaviors reflected in verbal intelligence test scores have become relatively stable and observable by that age and because verbal intelligence mediates the development of more specific forms of precocity then and later. Verbal intelligence also could be listed as a kind of gifted performance during the 7–12-year age period. However, the importance of verbal intelligence as a distinct form of gifted performance diminishes as children mature and have more opportunities for extended involvement and achievement in specific domains of knowledge.

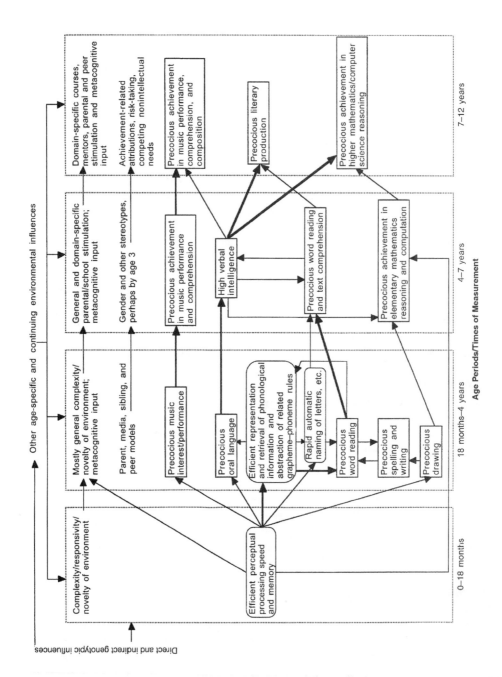

Precocious talents in the physical sciences and foreign language acquisition also could have been included in the model at the 7–12-year level. Case studies (e.g., Gross, 1993; Jackson & Kearney, 1999; Shavinina, 1999) have suggested that the precursors of precocity in these domains may be similar to those for precocity in mathematical reasoning. However, scientific and foreign language precocity are omitted because the theoretical and empirical links to support their inclusion in the model remain largely undetermined.

Environmental influences and motivational and other mediators of achievement are underspecified in the figure, but the current representation does suggest some issues that merit further consideration. For example, how should one represent and test for the ways in which a child's early achievements in a domain infuence his or her subsequent experiences? If precocious reading is associated with mathematical precocity, is this relation attributable to the ways in which parents and teachers react to precocious readers as well as to the common process origins and direct path we have specified? Do motivational influences related to competing time commitments become increasingly strong as children mature and their continued gifted performance within any discipline requires increasing investment (Eccles & Harold, 1992)? Are passive genotype → environment effects of parents on children most important early in childhood, as suggested by Scarr and McCartney's (1983) and Plomin's (1997) behavior genetics models? Alternatively, do the parental aptitudes and interests that convey these effects have sustained or increasing impacts on the development of gifted performance as the family commitment required to help a child develop expertise increases with the child's age and mastery of the discipline? The present model does not answer questions like these, but at least it raises them.

Conclusions

Comprehensive and powerful predictive models of the development of gifted performance in childhood may yet be formulated if we propose models, and designs for testing the models, that are consistent with the best

---

Figure 2.1. (opposite page) A conceptual model of continuity and change across childhood in the development of gifted performance in reading, mathematics, language, and music. The four large boxes indicate a breakdown of childhood into age periods that coincide roughly with Piaget's stages and with major transitions in a child's everyday experience. Influences on development are indicated by free-standing text within and outside these boxes; these influences are hypothesized to affect all of the behaviors in a box. Aspects of behavior that can be observed and measured easily in everyday situations are named in small rectangular boxes; behaviors that may be evident only in a formal testing situation are named in small rounded boxes. Arrows indicate hypothesized causal influences, with heavier arrows suggesting stronger relations.

current thinking about the nature of development and the nature of gift-edness. Such models are likely to be most useful if they begin with anal-yses of domain-specific forms of childhood giftedness that appear fre-quently in retrospective accounts of the development of eminent adults and that can be described in cognitive process models.

The model proposed here focuses on developmental transitions across the knowledge and skill domains of literacy, mathematics, and music. The code systems children must learn and automatize to perform well in these superficially different domains may place similar demands on the child's developing information-processing abilities. Both the case study literature and consideration of the nature of the domains suggest that a frequent pattern of developmental transitions in childhood giftedness may begin with precocious reading acquisition and during the preschool years and progress to precocious achievement in mathematics. Precocious interest and achievement in music may be another thread in development during this period.

Any prospective longitudinal study that involves selection of a sample for high performance on some Time 1 criterion measure inevitably will overlook many children who eventually will become gifted performers by Time 2 or Time n. However, it may not be feasible to study the develop-ment of giftedness in unbiased samples that represent children at all lev-els of ability without selection for any particular attributes, especially if one is interested in the development of giftedness in early childhood. Therefore, longitudinal studies should be designed to allow for the possi-bility of predictable developmental transitions in forms of giftedness, such as those hypothesized here. Coordinated consideration of the patterns of a child's domain-specific and generalizable cognitive skills, the child's mo-tivation for precocious achievement, and the environmental support avail-able to nurture the child's gifts should enhance the accuracy of longitu-dinal predictions.

References

Backman, J. (1983). Psycholinguistic skills and reading acquisition: A look at early readers. *Reading Research Quarterly, 18,* 466–479.

Bamberger, J. (1986). Cognitive issues in the development of musically gifted children. In R. J. Sternberg & J. E. Davidson (Eds.), *Conceptions of giftedness* (pp. 388–416). Cam-bridge, England: Cambridge University Press.

Benbow, C. P., & Arjmand, O. (1990). Predictors of high academic achievement in mathe-matics and science by mathematically talented students: A longitudinal study. *Journal of Educational Psychology, 82,* 430–441.

Bevan, W. (1991). Contemporary psychology: A tour inside the onion. *American Psychologist, 46,* 475–483.

Blachman, B. A. (1984). Relationship of rapid naming ability and language analysis skills to kindergarten and first grade reading achievement. *Journal of Educational Psychol-ogy, 76,* 610–622.

Borkowski, J. G., & Peck, V. A. (1986). Causes and consequences of metamemory in gifted children. In R. J. Sternberg & J. E. Davidson (Eds.), *Conceptions of giftedness* (pp. 182–200). Cambridge, England: Cambridge University Press.

Breznitz, Z. (1987). Increasing first graders' reading accuracy and comprehension by accelerating their reading rates. *Journal of Educational Psychology, 79,* 236–242.

Case, R. (1992). *The mind's staircase: Exploring the conceptual underpinnings of children's thought and knowledge.* Hillsdale, NJ: Erlbaum.

Ceci, S. J., & Bronfenbrenner, U. (1985). "Don't forget to take the cupcakes out of the oven": Prospective memory, strategic time-monitoring, and context. *Child Development, 56,* 152–164.

Coleman, L. J., Sanders, M. D., & Cross, T. L. (1997). Perennial debates and tacit assumptions in the education of gifted children. *Gifted Child Quarterly, 41,* 105–111.

Cox, C. M. (1926). *Genetic studies of genius: Vol. 2. The early mental traits of three hundred geniuses.* Palo Alto, CA: Stanford University Press.

Crain-Thoreson, C., & Dale, P. S. (1992). Linguistic precocity, preschool language, and emergent literacy. *Developmental Psychology, 28,* 421–429.

Csikszentmihalyi, M., & Robinson, R. E. (1986). Culture, time, and the development of talent. In R. J. Sternberg & J. E. Davidson (Eds.), *Conceptions of giftedness* (pp. 264–284). Cambridge, England: Cambridge University Press.

Curtis, M. E. (1980). Development of components of reading skill. *Journal of Educational Psychology, 72,* 656–669.

Detterman, D. K., & Daniel, M. H. (1989). Correlations of mental tests with each other and with cognitive variables are highest for low IQ groups. *Intelligence, 13,* 349–359.

Durkin, D. (1966). *Children who read early.* New York: Teachers College Press.

Durkin, D. (1984). Poor black children who are successful readers. *Urban Education, 19*(1), 53–76.

Eccles, J., & Harold, R. D. (1992). Gender differences in educational and occupational patterns among the gifted. In N. Colangelo, S. G. Assouline, & D. L. Ambroson (Eds.), *Talent development: Proceedings from the 1991 Henry B. and Jocelyn Wallace National Research Symposium on Talent Development* (pp. 2–30). Unionville, NY: Trillium.

Fagan, J. F., III. (1985). A new look at infant intelligence. In D. K. Detterman (Ed.), *Current topics in human intelligence: Vol. 1. Research methodology* (pp. 223–246). Norwood, NJ: Ablex.

Feldman, D. H. (with Benjamin, A. C.). (1986a). Giftedness as a developmentalist sees it. In R. J. Sternberg & J. E. Davidson (Eds.), *Conceptions of giftedness* (pp. 285–305). Cambridge, England: Cambridge University Press.

Feldman, D. H. (with Goldsmith, L.). (1986b). *Nature's gambit: Child prodigies and the development of human potential.* New York: Basic Books.

Fletcher-Flinn, C., & Thompson, G. B. (in press). Learning to read with underdeveloped phonemic awareness but lexicalized phonological recording. A case study of a 3-year-old. *Cognition.*

Francis, D. J., Fletcher, J. M., Maxwell, S., & Satz, P. (1989). A structural model for developmental changes in the determinants of reading achievement. *Journal of Child Clinical Psychology, 18,* 44–51.

Gardner, H. (1983). *Frames of mind.* New York: Basic Books.

Goldsmith, L. T. (1987). Girl prodigies: Some evidence and some speculations. *Roeper Review, 10,* 74–82.

Gottlieb, G. (1991). Experiential canalization of behavioral development: Theory. *Developmental Psychology, 27,* 4–13.

Gross, M. U. M. (1992). The early development of three profoundly gifted children of IQ 200. In P. Klein & A. J. Tannenbaum (Eds.), *To be young and gifted* (pp. 94–140). Norwood, NJ: Ablex.

Gross, M. U. M. (1993). Nurturing the talents of exceptionally gifted individuals. In K. A. Heller, F. J. Monks, & A. H. Passow (Eds.), *International handbook of research and development of giftedness and talent* (pp. 473–490). Oxford, England: Pergamon.

Gruber, H. E. (1986). The self-construction of the extraordinary. In R. J. Sternberg & J. E. Davidson (Eds.), *Conceptions of giftedness* (pp. 247–265). Cambridge, MA: Cambridge University Press.

Henderson, S., Jackson, N. E., & Mukamal, R. A. (1993). Early language and literacy skills of a precocious reader. *Gifted Child Quarterly, 37,* 46–50.

Hollingworth, L. S. (1942). *Children above 180Q.* New York: World Book.

Horowitz, F. D., & O'Brien, M. (1989). In the interest of the nation: A reflective essay on the state of our knowledge and the challenges before us. *American Psychologist, 44,* 441–445.

Humphreys, L. G. (1985). A conceptualization of intellectual giftedness. In F. D. Horowitz & F. O'Brien (Eds.), *The gifted and talented: Developmental perspectives* (pp. 331–360). Washington, DC: American Psychological Association.

Huxley, A. (1924). *Young Archimedes and other stories.* New York: George Doran.

Jackson, N. E. (1988a). Case study of Bruce: A child with advanced intellectual abilities. In J. M. Sattler (Ed.), *Assessment of children* (3rd ed., pp. 676–678). San Diego: Author.

Jackson, N. E. (1988b). Precocious reading ability: What does it mean? *Gifted Child Quarterly, 32,* 200–204.

Jackson, N. E. (1992). Precocious reading in English: Sources, structure, and predictive significance. In P. Klein & A. J. Tannenbaum (Eds.), *To be young and gifted* (pp. 171–203). Norwood, NJ: Ablex.

Jackson, N. E., & Biemiller, A. J. (1985). Letter, word, and text reading time of precocious and average readers. *Child Development, 56,* 196–206.

Jackson, N. E., & Butterfield, E. C. (1986). A conception of giftedness designed to promote research. In R. J. Sternberg & J. E. Davidson (Eds.), *Conceptions of giftedness* (pp. 151–181). Cambridge, England: Cambridge University Press.

Jackson, N. E., & Doellinger, H. (2000). Policy implications of continuing controversies in gifted education. In W. Wraga & P. Hlebowitsh (Eds.), *Research review for school leaders* (Vol. 3). Mahwah, NJ: Erlbaum.

Jackson, N. E., & Donaldson, G. (1989). Precocious and second-grade readers' use of context in word identification. *Learning and Individual Differences, 1,* 255–281.

Jackson, N. E., Donaldson, G., & Cleland, L. N. (1988). The structure of precocious reading ability. *Journal of Educational Psychology, 80,* 234–243.

Jackson, N. E., Donaldson, G., & Mills, J. R. (1993). Components of reading skill in postkindergarten precocious readers and level-match second graders. *Journal of Reading Behavior, 25,* 181–208.

Jackson, N. E., & Kearney, J. (1999). Achievement of precocious readers in middle childhood and young adulthood. In N. Colangelo & S. G. Assouline (Eds.), *Talent development III. Proceedings from the 1995 Henry B. and Jocelyn Wallace national research symposium on talent development* (pp. 203–217). Scottsdale, AZ: Gifted Psychology Press.

Jackson, N. E., & Klein, E. J. (1997). Gifted performance in young children. In N. Colangelo & G. Davis (Eds.), *Handbook of gifted education* (2nd ed., pp. 460–474). Boston: Allyn & Bacon.

Jackson, N. E., & Myers, M. G. (1982). Letter naming time, digit span, and precocious reading achievement. *Intelligence, 6,* 311–329.

Kagan, J. (1971). *Continuity and change in infancy.* New York: Wiley.

Kessen, W. (1991). Directions: Where do we turn now? *SRCD Newsletter,* pp. 2, 12, 14.

Lerner, R. M. (1991). Changing organism-context relations as the basic process of development: A developmental contextual perspective. *Developmental Psychology, 27,* 27–32.

Lewis, M., & Michalson, L. (1985). The gifted infant. In J. Freeman (Ed.), *The psychology of gifted children* (pp. 35–58). Chichester, England: Wiley.

McCall, R. B., Appelbaum, M. I., & Hogarty, P. S. (1973). Developmental changes in mental test performance. *Monographs of the Society for Research in Child Development, 38*(3, Serial No. 150), 83.

Miller, L. (1989). *Musical savants: Exceptional skill in the mentally retarded.* Hillsdale, NJ: Erlbaum.

Mills, J. R., & Jackson, N. E. (1990). Predictive significance of early giftedness: The case of precocious reading. *Journal of Educational Psychology, 82,* 410–419.

Morelock, M. J., & Feldman, D. H. (1993). Prodigies and savants: What they have to tell us about giftedness and human cognition. In K. A. Heller, F. J. Monks, & A. H. Passow (Eds.), *International handbook of research and development of giftedness and talent* (pp. 161–184). Oxford, England: Pergamon.

Morelock, M. J., & Feldman, D. H. (1997). High-IQ children, extreme precocity, and savant syndrome. In N. Colangelo & G. A. Davis (Eds.), *Handbook of gifted education* (2nd ed., pp. 439–459). Boston: Allyn & Bacon.

Nation, K. (1999). Reading skills in hyperlexia. A developmental perspective. *Psychological Bulletin, 125*(3), 338–355.

Ogbu, J. (1981). Origins of human competence: A cultural–ecological perspective. *Child Development, 52,* 413–429.

Olson, R. K., Forsberg, H., & Wise, B. W. (1994). Genes, environment, and the development of orthographic skills. In V. W. Berninger (Ed.), *The varieties of orthographic knowledge. I. Theoretical and developmental issues* (pp. 27–72). Dordrecht, The Netherlands: Kluwer.

Plomin, R. (1997). Genetics and intelligence. In N. Colangelo & G. A. Davis (Eds.), *Handbook of gifted education* (2nd ed., pp. 67–74). Boston: Allyn & Bacon.

Renzulli, J. S. (1986). The three-ring conception of giftedness: A developmental model for creative productivity. In R. J. Sternberg & J. E. Davidson (Eds.), *Conceptions of giftedness* (pp. 53–92). Cambridge, England: Cambridge University Press.

Rose, S. A., & Feldman, J. F. (1995). Prediction of IQ and specific cognitive abilities at 11 years from infancy measures. *Developmental Psychology, 31,* 685–696.

Rose, S. A., & Feldman, J. F. (1997). Memory and speed: Their role in the relation of infant information processing to later IQ. *Child Development, 68,* 630–641.

Saxe, G. B. (1988). Candy selling and math learning. *Educational Researcher, 17*(6), 14–21.

Scarborough, H. (1990). Very early language deficits in dyslexic children. *Child Development, 61,* 1728–1743.

Scarr, S. (1985). Constructing psychology. Making facts and fables for our times. *American Psychologist, 40,* 499–512.

Scarr, S. (1992). Developmental theories for the 1990's: Development and individual differences. *Child Development, 63,* 1–19.

Scarr, S., & McCartney, K. (1983). How people make their own environments: A theory of genotype → environment effects. *Child Development, 54,* 424–435.

Shavinina, L. V. (1999). The psychological essence of the child prodigy phenomenon: Sensitive periods and cognitive experience. *Gifted Child Quarterly, 43,* 25–38.

Shuter-Dyson, R. (1982). Musical ability. In D. Deutsch (Ed.), *The psychology of music* (pp. 404–412). New York: Academic Press.

Siegler, R. S. (1996). *Emerging minds: The process of change in children's thinking.* New York: Oxford University Press.

Siegler, R. S., & Crowley, K. (1991). The microgenetic method: A direct means for studying cognitive development. *American Psychologist, 46,* 606–620.

Siegler, R. S., & Kotovsky, K. (1986). Two levels of giftedness: Shall ever the twain meet? In R. J. Sternberg & J. E. Davidson (Eds.), *Conceptions of giftedness* (pp. 417–436). Cambridge, MA: Cambridge University Press.

Simonton, D. K. (1997). When giftedness becomes genius: How does talent achieve eminence? In N. Colangelo & G. A. Davis (Eds.), *Handbook of gifted education* (2nd ed., pp. 335–350). Boston: Allyn & Bacon.

Stanovich, K. E. (1990). Concepts in developmental theories of reading skill: Cognitive resources, automaticity, and modularity. *Developmental Review, 10,* 72–100.

Sternberg, R. J. (1981). Novelty-seeking, novelty-finding, and the developmental continuity of intelligence. *Intelligence, 5,* 149–155.

Sternberg, R. J. (1985). *Beyond IQ: A triarchic theory of human intelligence.* Cambridge, England: Cambridge University Press.

Sternberg, R. J. (1987). A unified theory of intellectual exceptionality. In J. D. Day & J. G. Borkowski (Eds.), *Intelligence and exceptionality: New directions for theory, assessment, and instructional practices* (pp. 135–172). Norwood, NJ: Ablex.

Sternberg, R. J. (1993). Procedures for identifying intellectual potential in the gifted: A perspective on alternative "metaphors of mind." In K. A. Heller, F. J. Monks, & A. H. Passow (Eds.), *International handbook of research and development of giftedness and talent* (pp. 185–208). Oxford, England: Pergamon.

Sternberg, R. J., & Lubart, T. I. (1992). Creative giftedness. In N. Colangelo, S. G. Assouline, & D. L. Ambroson (Eds.), *Talent development: Proceedings from the 1991 Henry B. and Jocelyn Wallace National Research Symposium on Talent Development* (pp. 66–88). Unionville, NY: Trillium.

Sternberg, R. J., & Zhang, L.-F. (1995). What do we mean by giftedness? A pentagonal implicit theory. *Gifted Child Quarterly, 39,* 88–94.

Subotnik, R. F., & Arnold, K. D. (Eds.). (1994). *Beyond Terman: Contemporary longitudinal studies of giftedness and talent.* Norwood, NJ: Ablex.

Subotnik, R. F., Kassan, L. D., Summers, E. S., & Wasser, A. B. (1994). *Genius revisited: High IQ children grow up.* Norwood, NJ: Ablex.

Tannenbaum, A. J. (1986). Giftedness: A psychosocial approach. In R. J. Sternberg & J. E. Davidson (Eds.), *Conceptions of giftedness* (pp. 21–52). Cambridge, England: Cambridge University Press.

Terman, L. M. (1925). *Genetic studies of genius. Mental and physical traits of a thousand gifted children* (Vol. 1). Stanford, CA: Stanford University Press.

Terman, L. M., & Oden, M. H. (1947). *The gifted child grows up. Genetic studies of genius* (Vol. 4). Palo Alto, CA: Stanford University Press.

Tomlinson-Keasey, C. (1990). Developing our intellectual resources for the 21st century: Educating the gifted. *Journal of Educational Psychology, 82,* 399–403.

Tomlinson-Keasey, C., & Little, T. D. (1990). Predicting educational attainment, occupational achievement, intellectual skill, and personal adjustment among gifted men and women. *Journal of Educational Psychology, 82,* 442–455.

Torgesen, J. K., & Burgess, S. R. (1998). Consistency of reading-related phonological processes throughout early childhood: Evidence from longitudinal–correlational and instructional studies. In J. L. Metsala & L. C. Ehri (Eds.), *Word recognition in beginning literacy* (pp. 161–188). Mahwah, NJ: Erlbaum.

Treffert, D. A. (1989). *Extraordinary people: Redefining the "idiot savant."* New York: Harper & Row.

Turkheimer, E., & Gottesman, I. I. (1991). Individual differences and the canalization of human behavior. *Developmental Psychology, 27,* 18–22.

Underwood, B. J. (1975). Individual differences as a crucible in theory construction. *American Psychologist, 30,* 128–134.

VanTassel-Baska, J. (1989). Profiles of precocity: A three-year study of talented adolescents. In J. L. VanTassel-Baska & P. Olszewski-Kubilius (Eds.), *Patterns of influence on gifted learners* (pp. 29–39). New York: Teachers College.

Wallach, M. A. (1985). Creativity testing and giftedness. In F. D. Horowitz & M. O'Brien (Eds.), *The gifted and talented: Developmental perspectives* (pp. 99–124). Washington, DC: American Psychological Association.

Willerman, L., & Fiedler, M. F. (1977). Intellectually precocious preschool children: Early development and later intellectual accomplishments. *Journal of Genetic Psychology, 141,* 13–20.

Wolf, M. (1991). Naming speed and reading. *Reading Research Quarterly, 26,* 123–141.

Zigler, E., & Farber, E. A. (1985). Commonalities between the intellectual extremes: Giftedness and mental retardation. In F. D. Horowitz & M. O'Brien (Eds.), *The gifted and talented: Developmental perspectives* (pp. 387–408). Washington, DC: American Psychological Association.

3

A Sociohistorical Perspective on Exceptionally High-IQ Children

Martha J. Morelock

Over the past three decades, developmental psychologists have been directing increased attention toward the work of the Russian cognitive developmentalist Lev S. Vygotsky (1896–1934). Vygotskian theory focuses on the development of verbal–conceptual abstract thought and the primary role language plays in mediating thought and behavior as well as in interpreting experience. I posit in this chapter that because of this focus, Vygotskian theory offers an excellent theoretical framework for understanding the development of extraordinarily high-IQ children, because they are characterized by the precocious emergence of high-level verbal–conceptual thought.

In this chapter I use Vygotskian theory as an explanatory framework for interpreting the development of one extraordinarily high-IQ child, Jennie Cartwright (a pseudonym) (Morelock, 1991).[1] Somewhere between the ages of 3 years, 8 months and 4 years, 6 months Jennie experienced a cognitive leap in her capacity for abstract thought, as was inadvertently documented through successive Stanford–Binet L–M testings at those two ages. Accompanying the cognitive changes was a period of intense existential questioning and marked emotional turmoil.

The chapter begins with a brief overview of some of the essential elements of Vygotsky's sociohistorical developmental theory. This is followed by sections in which excerpts from Jennie's developmental history are used to illustrate Vygotskian theoretical elements and in which implications for future research are explored. The chapter concludes with a discussion of the implications of this case study for conceptualizations of giftedness.

Vygotskian Theory: A Synopsis of Essentials

A major focus of Vygotsky's work is the examination of how mental functions such as memory, attention, perception, and thinking first appear in an elementary form in the child and then, over the process of development,

---

[1]In the interest of confidentiality, Jennie Cartwright, all names of members of her family, and Dr. London are pseudonyms.

are transformed into higher psychological processes such as voluntary attention, logical memory, and abstract thought. Vygotsky (1978) characterized *elementary functions* as mental functions that are totally and directly determined by stimulation from the natural environment. Elementary functions are found not only in human beings, but also in animals lower in the phylogenetic scale. *Higher functions*, on the other hand, are uniquely human and result from the creation and use of socioculturally evolved stimuli: tools (i.e., "technical" tools) and signs (i.e., "psychological" tools, such as language).[2] Through such socioculturally evolved stimuli, an immediate situation and the reaction linked to it are altered by active human intervention. Thus, Vygotsky maintained, these artificially produced stimuli become mediators of thought and behavior (Vygotsky, 1978).

Language as a Psychological Tool

Kozulin (1990) pointed out that Vygotsky's notion of mediation of thought allows for three large classes of mediators: (a) signs and symbols (i.e., psychological tools), (b) individual activities, and (c) interpersonal relations. Even so, Vygotsky never veered from regarding language as the primary psychological tool mediating thought.[3] In Vygotsky's framework, language used in the service of other higher mental functions is the chief instrument of integration and order in human mental life (Bruner, 1987).

A Sociohistorical Theory

Vygotsky's strong emphasis on the major importance of language—and other mediational instruments—in shaping human mental functioning is clear. Equally as clear is the historical role of culture in producing mediational tools. Because of this, Vygotskian theory has been referred to as a *sociohistorical theory* (Wertsch, 1991) or *cultural–historical theory* (Van Der Veer & Valsiner, 1991).

Wertsch (1985, 1991) noted that, ultimately, three themes form the core of Vygotsky's theoretical framework: (a) a reliance on a genetic or developmental method, (b) the assertion that higher mental processes have their origin in social processes, and (c) the claim that mental functioning and human action are mediated by tools and signs. As would be expected, these same themes were reflected in Vygotsky's approach to the study of child development.

---

[2]Although Vygotsky regarded language as the primary psychological tool, he also recognized the existence of others. Examples are "various systems for counting, mnemonic techniques, algebraic symbol systems, works of art, writing, schemes, diagrams, maps, and mechanical drawings, all sorts of conventional signs, etc." (Vygotsky, 1981b, p. 137).

[3]Some research in the fields of linguistics and neurology appears to support Vygotsky's emphasis on the primary importance of language—not only for the development of conceptual thought, but also for the normal cerebral hemispheric specialization important for both linguistic and nonlinguistic mental functioning (see Curtiss, 1977; Gazzaniga & Smylie, 1984; Sacks, 1989).

Vygotskian Paedology

When Vygotsky became actively involved in paedology (the Soviet discipline of child study in Vygotsky's era) in the 1920s, it was approaching its second decade of existence (Van Der Veer & Valsiner, 1991). It was, as Vygotsky saw it, a "symptomatic science," studying external features of child development and describing when this or that feature generally emerged in the developing child. Explaining the emergence of the described features lay beyond its capacity. Vygotsky sought to differentiate paedology from other disciplines dealing with children (e.g., child psychology or pedagogics) by defining it as the science of children's development. His goal for the discipline was for it to go beyond external symptomatology and reconstruct the causal system leading to psychological development.

Vygotsky designated the case study in its longitudinal version as the appropriate methodology for paedology, noting that the most sensible control condition for studying a developing child is that of the previous organizational state of the same child rather than of any other child. To make generalizations more feasible, Vygotsky suggested pairing primary within-case longitudinal analysis with secondary between-cases longitudinal comparison (Van Der Veer & Valsiner, 1991).

The Vygotskian Child

Vygotsky's view of the developing child grows out of his sociohistorical framework, with the concept of mediation taking center stage. Again, he emphasized that although cognitive capacities are first introduced on a social, or interpsychological, level, they gradually become internalized and begin to operate on the intrapsychological level. In describing this process of internalization, Vygotsky formulated his "general genetic law of cultural development":

> Any function in the child's cultural development appears twice, or on two planes. First it appears on the social plane, and then on the psychological plane.
>
> First it appears between people as an interpsychological category, and then within the child as an intrapsychological category. This is equally true with regard to voluntary attention, logical memory, the formation of concepts, and the development of volition . . . it goes without saying that internalization transforms the process itself and changes its structure and functions. Social relations or relations among people generally underlie all higher functions and their relationships. (Vygotsky, 1960/1981a, p. 163)

In tracing the internalization and cerebralization of language, Vygotsky (1934/1986) noted that the child goes through three stages in the acquisition of language. At first, as stated earlier, language is appropriated as a communicative tool and used only socially in the interpsychological

circumstance. Later, the child develops "egocentric speech," an interme-
diate stage of language development where the child uses externally au-
dible speech as an instrument for assisting in problem solving or in play
situations when he or she is alone. The final stage is that of "inner speech,"
when language becomes useable as a private and internal instrument of
thought. The advent of inner speech marks the point at which language
has become completely internalized, cerebralized, and dialectically interrelated with thought.

The logicalization of thought. Vygotsky (1978) also spoke of the "logicalization" of thought that takes place in the course of development. During the early stages of children's development, words are not an organizing
factor in thought. The typical thought of older preschool and elementary
school children lacks the verbal–logical quality of mature thinking. It is
based on practical experience and visual–graphic memory. By the time
children reach adolescence, however, the logical operations they use to
reflect reality and the psychological processes that govern their thinking
have undergone a marked change. Graphic thinking processes are transformed into a scheme of semantic and logical operations in which words
become the principal tool for abstraction and generalization (Luria, 1976).

The dialectical interrelationship of emotion and cognition. One problem of developmental theory as Vygotsky saw it was to give a meaningful
account of the relation between children's lower emotions and adults'
higher emotions (Van Der Veer & Valsiner, 1991). The concept of the dialectical interrelationship of mature mental functions provided such an
account. According to Vygotsky, the most elementary function of emotion
is the facilitation or priming of appropriate instinctive action. In human
beings, however, emotion recedes from its original links with instinctive
action and takes on new functions stemming from its interpenetration and
interfunctioning with cognition. Rather than existing as independent functions, emotions and cognition are mutually interdependent and unified in
a dynamic, meaningful system. Emotions are constituted by the cognitive
appraisal of events, whereas, conversely, cognition is permeated and affected by emotion. Human emotion changes its nature, becoming more
complex as cognitive capacities develop. Mature human emotion involves
cognitive interpretations based on moral and other values absent in infants (Ratner, 1991).

The personally meaningful experience. As a child's set of internalized
psychological tools expands and develops, his or her capacity for interpreting and attributing meaning to experience changes. For Vygotsky, it
is the personally meaningful experience emerging in the child–
environment relationship that guides the further process of development
(Van Der Veer & Valsiner, 1991): thus, "It is the child's experiencing of the
environment, organized by the use of meanings (the socially constructed
'stimulus-means') that constitutes the essence of the study of environment
for Vygotsky's paedology" (p. 316).

Development as revolutionary shifts in cognition. Because of the major
discontinuous changes in quality of cognition wrought by the processes
discussed earlier, Vygotsky saw development not as a steady stream of
quantitative increments, but in terms of fundamental revolutionary shifts.
Transition points in development are associated with either the introduction of some new form of mediation (e.g., the initial acquisition of language) or with the transition to a more advanced version of an existing
form of mediation (e.g., the onset of verbal–conceptual thought). At these
points of revolutionary dislocation, the essential nature of development
changes (Vygotsky, 1978; Wertsch, 1985). Vygotsky (1960/1981a) maintained that traditional child psychology had tended to overlook such points
of revolutionary dislocation in child development:

> Child psychology does not want to know about the sudden, violent, and
> revolutionary changes that appear throughout ontogenesis and that are
> so often encountered in the history of cultural development. To naive
> observers, revolution and evolution do not appear to coincide. Historical
> development seems to proceed along a straight path. When a revolu-
> tion, the rupture of the historical fabric, or a leap occurs, naive observ-
> ers see nothing but catastrophe, gaps, and precipices. For them, his-
> torical progression stops at this point until it alights anew on a straight
> and smooth path.
>   Scientific observers, on the other hand, consider revolution and evo-
> lution as two mutually connected forms of development that presuppose
> one another. They see sharp changes in the child's development that
> occur simultaneously with other, similar changes as the determining
> point in the whole line of development. (p. 151)

Vygotsky and the Child of Extraordinarily High IQ

Vygotsky's interest in the development of higher psychological processes
also led him to explore abnormal child development—especially the repercussions of disabling conditions precluding the normal route of development for mental functions. Thus, some of his research dealt with children who are blind, have mental retardation, and are deaf–mute who
required compensatory assistance to develop normal mental functioning
and adequate adaptation to their sociocultural environment (Blanck, 1990;
Kozulin, 1990; Van Der Veer & Valsiner, 1991). Interestingly, however, one
avenue of important research was left unexplored by Vygotsky—those
children who precociously develop the higher psychological process of abstract verbal–conceptual thought. Children of extraordinarily high IQ
would appear to be a valuable source of information about what happens
when verbal–conceptual thought becomes internalized and cerebralized
before the normally expected time in the course of development.
   The previously referenced case study of one extraordinarily high-IQ
child, Jennie Cartwright (Morelock, 1991), will be used to highlight how
Vygotskian developmental theory may provide insights into the nature of
gifted development. In the following section, qualitative data are presented describing my impressions of the Cartwright family as well as Jen-

nie's developmental history as recounted by her mother Mrs. Cartwright and Dr. London, the clinical psychologist who worked with Jennie. The case study data are organized along the lines of Vygotsky's recommendations for the optimally designed study of child development. Thus, I examine Jennie's development from a longitudinal perspective spanning the period before, during, and after the cognitive leap took place. From analyzing shifts in external symptomatology I then reconstruct, in Vygotskian theoretical terms, the causal system leading to Jennie's psychological development. Jennie's organizational state before the leap took place becomes the control condition for understanding her organizational state after the leap was revealed to have taken place. For each segment of the developmental trajectory, after the qualitative data comprising it are presented, I return to Vygotskian concepts for analysis in light of the newly presented data.

Jennie Cartwright

In April 1990, Mrs. Cartwright contacted Tufts University concerning her daughter Jennie, who was at the time almost 5 years old. Mrs. Cartwright described her daughter as profoundly gifted and extremely emotionally vulnerable because of her giftedness. Mrs. Cartwright was seeking sources of assistance for academic planning for her child as well as for guiding Jennie socially and emotionally. In talking with Mrs. Cartwright, I explored the possibility of conducting a case study of her daughter. Mrs. Cartwright was agreeable to the idea. The information presented here is drawn from in-depth interviews with Mrs. Cartwright and Dr. London, Jennie's psychologist, as well as from records of Jennie's two assessments on the Stanford–Binet L–M.

The Cartwrights lived in a rural area of New England. The family consisted of Mr. and Mrs. Cartwright and their three children, Jake, Jennie, and Mitchell. At the time of my first visit, Jake was 8 years old, Jennie was 5½ years old, and Mitchell was 2½ years old. The Cartwright home was spacious and spotless, reminding one of the dream houses shown in *Better Homes and Gardens*. Yet, it was cheerfully and liberally sprinkled with toys, books, and other indications that children lived there. This impression was completed by four resident pets—a German Shepherd and three kittens that lived in peaceful coexistence.

At the time of my home visit, Mr. Cartwright was a small business owner while Mrs. Cartwright was a stay-at-home wife and mother. Whereas Jennie's father appeared "laid back," her mother was intense. Indeed, my initial impression was that Mrs. Cartwright exuded an aura of compressed energy at the point of release. Her speech was rapid and filled with information. Watching her interact with Jennie—for example, during home schooling sessions—I got the sense that the child was being barraged with information. Mrs. Cartwright easily jumped from fact to fact, from association to association. Simply going to the back porch overlooking the swimming pool became an opportunity for discussing the pipes that were laid underneath the ground when the pool was installed. Curiously, this mode of interaction was not so obvious with the other children. Mrs. Cartwright reported that Jennie had, from infancy, demanded stimulation. It was as if this type of interaction was an unconscious manifestation of a type of "goodness of fit" (Thomas & Chess, 1984), where Mrs. Cartwright had adapted to Jennie's need for an unusual amount of stimulation and information provided at a rapid pace.

When I first met Jennie, I recorded that she was attractive and tall for her age, with light eyes and blonde hair. There was a certain appealing fragility about her—reminding one of a porcelain doll. Her speech did not appear unusual for a 5-year-old child. It belied the depth of comprehension of her thought processes. One of my first thoughts on meeting Jennie was how easily one could overlook this gifted child.

Dr. London's report (Morelock, 1991), completed in December 1989, when Jennie was 4 years, 7 months gives an idea of how Jennie performed in terms of standardized measures:

> On the Stanford–Binet, Jennie scored a mental age of 7 years 10 months, and an IQ of 176 which places her within the exceptionally gifted range of intellectual functioning. In fact, this score may still be somewhat of an underestimate due to her anxiety and slight lapses of attention as she fatigued. Her score places her in the top .001% of children of her age in the nation. . . . On the Wide Range Achievement Test, Jennie scored at the 99.98% in reading recognition (SS 155+); the 99.96% in spelling (SS 153) and the 99.7% in arithmetic (SS 145). These scores were obtained using the norms for 5-year-old children and, as she is 6 months below this age, her real standard scores and percentages are much higher.

The first case study segment, which is recounted below, presents highlights from Jennie's development before the cognitive leap period, as was recounted by her mother.

Case Study Segment 1: Before the Cognitive Leap

Mrs. Cartwright reported that, from infancy, Jennie demonstrated an inner drive for mastering academic material. Before the child was age 3 years, she had begun reading beginner books. And before that, Mrs. Cartwright had found it necessary to encourage Jennie to sound out the spellings of words for herself when her daughter's requests that Mrs. Cartwright orally spell various words began to be too much of an interference in daily life. When Jennie was 3, an incident took place that precipitated a significant improvement in the level of her reading abilities. Mrs. Cartwright reported that at the time of the incident, Jennie could read "little baby books," but she could not read more sophisticated, larger ones. Jake was in first grade at the time, and Mrs. Cartwright would read with him at night so that he could practice his reading skills.

One night, Jennie was sitting next to her mother and brother while they read. She kept interrupting them, insisting "Well, I can read those, too. I can read those, too." When Mrs. Cartwright let Jennie try, however, it became obvious that the child really could not read her brother's books, and Jennie became extremely frustrated. Ordinarily, she was a very self-controlled child, holding tears back even when she was physically hurt and wanted to cry. But on this occasion, Mrs. Cartwright said,

> she got very upset and she went into the other room and started *crying*, sobbing and sobbing and sobbing. And I came and I put my arms around her and I said "Jennie, what's the matter?" And she said "*I can read, too. I* can do it. *I* can do it." She was just so *beside* herself. Her body was shaking, she was *so* upset. And of course, I felt terrible, you know. And I said "OK, I'll help you, Jen. I'll help you."
>
> So the next three to four days, we wrote together and we read together. And she would be up until like 9:00 at night, 9:30 at night, wanting to read in bed. And I was trying to teach her. And within four days, she was reading fluently—really fluently. And she would go to bed and she'd fall asleep, and she'd be repeating the words in her mouth and spelling things in her sleep. And she'd wake up in the morning and she'd be all ready to go.

Mrs. Cartwright reported that Jennie's drive to indulge in academic projects was constantly present. When Jennie had easy access to materials for satisfying that drive, it receded a bit into the background of their lives. When she was deprived of adequate outlet for it, however, her need became more obvious, and her efforts to satisfy that need increased dramatically —sometimes to a frenetic level. Mrs. Cartwright described her at such times as being like a "whirlwind," rising early and going nonstop for hours reading and doing workbooks and art projects. At a certain point, she would become satisfied and then was able to slow down and relax into fantasy play or watching television. It was as if she had to get a certain amount of stimulation before she could go on to any other type of play.

When Jennie was 3 years, 9 months she was moved from a nonacademically oriented preschool to a Montessori preschool, which resulted in a period during which she was apparently energized by the increased academic stimulation offered by the new program. This period of comparative peace was not to last, however. By the time Jennie was 4 years, 6 months she began again to show signs of restlessness, frustration, and unsatisfied need. She became withdrawn and quiet on the way to school, refusing to talk with her mother. At first, Mrs. Cartwright thought that her daughter was not feeling well. Then she noticed that Jennie's activities at home began increasing the way they had in the past when her need for intellectual stimulation was not satisfied. Jennie started to wake up earlier and go to bed later in an apparent effort to include enough sufficiently stimulating activities in her day.

After about 3 weeks of Jennie's not talking about the problem, suddenly she began to ask daily whether her mother thought there would be anything new for her to do in school. Finally, after one of the extended days when the school still had not provided anything adequately stimulating, Jennie seemed to reach the breaking point. After a quiet ride home, she suddenly announced that school was boring and that she did not want to go back. In an extraordinarily apparent effort to stimulate herself, she then turned on both the record player and the television and began working in a third-grade math book while talking with her mother all at the same time. Mrs. Cartwright sensed that Jennie's actions expressed her extreme frustration at recognizing that while school was not providing her with the stimulation she needed, neither could she any longer satisfy that drive herself. At home she had begun to go through the workbooks so quickly that it had become obvious to Mrs. Cartwright that the work was no longer at a level complex enough to satisfy her.

The frustration escalated that night to a point where at bedtime, Jennie began having a tantrum, crying inconsolably and hitting her mother. It was the only tantrum that she had ever had, and Mrs. Cartwright reported that it ended with Jennie collapsing, exhausted, in her mother's arms.

A Vygotskian analysis before the cognitive leap. Analyzing this developmental period from a Vygotskian perspective, the workbook-based academic activities that Jennie pursued with such passion from an early age may be seen as external mediational instruments that were provided by a structured environment and that facilitated the development of higher psychological processes. In addition, the relationship between Jennie and Mrs. Cartwright served on an ongoing basis as an especially powerful mediational means for Jennie's development. It was Mrs. Cartwright to whom Jennie turned when she wanted to learn how to spell. It was Mrs. Cartwright who responded to Jennie's needs by providing books, workbooks, art supplies, and so forth and, when needed, assisting her daughter in their use. The role of this relationship was especially striking when Jennie, at age 3, enlisted Mrs. Cartwright's facilitation for her passionately conducted campaign to read more fluently.

Implications for future research. More qualitative research is needed exploring the family milieus of extraordinarily high-IQ children. The relationship between Jennie and her mother is particularly intriguing—the goodness-of-fit phenomenon in which Mrs. Cartwright's cognitive style and intensity appear to complement Jennie's need for stimulation, for example. The general psychological literature supports the concept of reciprocal influences between parent and child so that a particular dynamic interrelationship is established in which responses of each participant serve as stimuli for the other and also change as the result of the same stimulus exchanges (Bell, 1979; Bell & Harper, 1977). More recently, Gottfried, Gottfried, Bathurst, and Guerin (1994) conducted a study of the development of infants and toddlers who eventually attained IQs within the gifted range (IQ 130+) by age 8. The researchers found that whereas enriched environments were characteristic of their sample, there was also evidence that the children played an active role in eliciting environmental stimulation.

> Although it is impossible to determine from our data whether these children are more demanding from the early infancy period or whether they develop into more demanding children because parents provide more for them, one would hypothesize that process is one that is continuous, interactive, and effectual: that is, children affect their environment. (Gottfried et al., 1994, pp. 167–168)

With regard to extreme giftedness and talent, parent–child mutualities in terms of preferred talent areas and modes of interaction have been documented through in-depth case studies of families of prodigies (Feldman, 1991; Morelock & Feldman, 1997, in press) and in families with children above a 200 IQ (Morelock, 1995). And in a review of the literature on case studies of cognitive precocity, Fowler (1981) noted that "precocious children, with few exceptions, develop in professional–academic milieus enjoying a remarkable intellectual ambiance, in which the child (or children) is often personally included from earliest infancy" (p. 327). More research is needed on such dynamics.

Jennie's use of egocentric speech when she was working with her mother to increase her reading skills at age 3 is of particular interest. Mrs. Cartwright noted that during this intense period, Jennie would "go to bed at night and she'd fall asleep, and she'd be repeating the words in her mouth and spelling things in her sleep." Vygotsky saw egocentric speech as an important aid in organizing thought when a child is working hard at trying to comprehend a particularly challenging problem (Vygotsky, 1934/1986). Jennie's use of it under the circumstances in question supports Vygotsky's contention.

During this period of Jennie's development, perhaps most striking is her aggressive persistence in seeking out and using mediational psychological tools. Mrs. Cartwright's description gives a sense of a driving need for stimulation which, when left unsatisfied, causes Jennie to experience extreme frustration. It is as if Jennie is driven to extract the structural support from her environment that will facilitate the development of higher psychological processes. During this period of Jennie's development, the most salient aspect of her inner experience is this need and the resultant frustration when it is left unsatisfied.

The passionate attraction that Jennie showed for academic activities is common among children of extraordinarily high IQ (Morelock, 1995; Morelock & Feldman, 1997). In general, the literature reports that "gifted babies" tend to need less sleep than their agemates (Lewis & Michalson, 1985; Silverman & Kearney, 1989) and can be characterized as alert, expressive, and interactive with the environment. Recent research documents that gifted children from infancy are intrinsically motivated to seek out and engage in activities geared toward cognitive mastery and the acquisition of academic knowledge (Gottfried et al., 1994). The intensity of this phenomenon in extraordinarily high-IQ children like Jennie leads to speculation that it is undergirded by a structural or functional difference in brain development resulting in neuropsychological requirements for a specific quality and level of stimulation. Thus, the gifted child appears driven to extract from the environment the degree and quality of stimulation and the type of socioculturally evolved structural support required for the development of higher psychological processes.

In their study of gifted development, Gottfried et al. (1994) concluded that

> At the heart of superior intellect may be motivation for or pleasure inherent in acquiring knowledge, that is, intrinsic motivation. Our data indicate that cognitive mastery motivation and eventually academic intrinsic motivation are characteristics of the intellectually gifted from infancy and thereafter. (p. 171)

If this natural attraction to cognitive mastery and engagement with academic tasks is indeed the result of some neuropsychologically based requirement for environmental stimulation, this holds definite (and perhaps alarming) implications for educational environments failing to provide the required level of stimulation. Should schools failing to respond to the needs of these young brains be held accountable in some way (Benbow & Stanley, 1996; Henderson & Ebner, 1997; Morelock & Morrison, 1999)?

Case Study Segment 2: Behavioral Concomitants of the Cognitive Leap and Its Aftermath

The evening of the tantrum marked a turning point in the qualitative tone of Jennie's cognition. Mrs. Cartwright reported that as of the next morning, Jennie embarked on a 3-week period of intense questioning at a markedly different level from any before. She began by asking questions about the origin of common household items. That led to questions about the universe, how the oceans and life began, and how human knowledge had accumulated and been transmitted over the ages. All of this questioning was accompanied by emotional turmoil. It appeared as if question after question were arising in Jennie's mind, tormenting her and demanding to be answered. Her mother reported that Jennie could not fall asleep at night:

> She'd lay in bed and she'd be asking questions that would lead to another question that would lead to another question to another question, and she would just take it to the nth degree—anything, she would just take to the nth degree. So she had a hard time even getting to sleep. And we had this list of things that she wanted to know.

Jennie's attempt to grapple with the question of beginnings brought her naturally to the question of endings. She tried to comprehend death:

> She talked about death for a few nights in a row, and she'd have a really hard time about it. Her grandfather had died the year before. She was very upset because she *wanted* to believe in God and that everybody goes to Heaven, but in her mind, it wasn't rational enough

for her. She'd say "Well, does God love everybody?" And it'd be "Of course Jennie, He loves everybody." "Well, where do the *bad* people go? Don't *they* go to Heaven?" If God *loves* everybody, then *all* people would go to Heaven. And therefore the concept of being a God who is all-loving, there *can't* be, 'cause that doesn't make sense to her.

   And she'd lay at night with tears in her eyes and not wanting to cry, 'cause she was so self-controlled, knowing that *she* could die at any time. 'Cause she knew her own mortality. . . . You'd say to her "Oh, you're gonna be fine, of course." "You're gonna live, and I'm gonna be a Nana and. . . ." And she'd say "Well, nobody knows for sure what's gonna happen, Mom. Nobody knows for sure. You can get in an accident, and nobody knows really when they're gonna die. It's nice if everybody lives to be old, but that's not always what happens, 'cause children die sometimes."

Dr. London supported Mrs. Cartwright in helping Jennie through this period of upheaval. In addition, the psychologist taught Jennie some relaxation exercises—showing her how to focus on one image so that her mind would not race. The techniques succeeded in helping Jennie get to sleep at night. It was also during this period that Dr. London administered the second Stanford–Binet IQ test and the Wide Range Achievement Test (WRAT–R) (Jastak & Wilkinson, 1984).

At the end of this 3-week period, another period of striking change ensued. It began when Jennie was 4 years, 8 months and continued for a month. Mrs. Cartwright reported that instead of relying on workbooks and other externally provided materials, Jennie began to be absorbed in her own thought. No longer drawn to textbook-structured learning activities, Jennie became content to stay at home reading fiction or engaging in self-orchestrated fantasy play, such as playing "school" by herself in her room. When Jennie played school she would begin by looking at a picture that she had of the children in her class. She would then put it down and proceed to act out a fantasy play incorporating all 20 or so of the children —pretending to read to them or carry on various activities normally taking place during the school day.

It was also during this period that Mrs. Cartwright noticed a sudden change in Jennie's reading ability. She went from reading books written at the 2nd-grade level to reading 5th- and 6th-grade-level books, such as *Mathilda, Charlotte's Web*, and *Little House on the Prairie*. Whereas before she would become frustrated trying to read higher level books, suddenly Jennie's reading skills jumped to a new level, and her tolerance for more complex reading increased noticeably. She totally absorbed herself in reading—sometimes sitting and reading for as much as 3 hours at a time and devouring two books in a single day.

At about 4 years, 10 months Jennie began to return to her schoolwork activities, "but never like it was before," according to Mrs. Cartwright. Both Mrs. Cartwright and Dr. London saw Jennie as having made a shift to a different level of thought—one that sprang from a more internal source and that was self-directed. Her increased abilities also manifested themselves through rapidly improved reading skills. Jennie no longer gained the same satisfaction from workbook activities. In addition, although Jennie continued to wonder about things, she did so, according to Mrs. Cartwright, at a "more normal level. She can get caught up sometimes, but it isn't *anything* like it was in that three weeks."

An interview with Dr. London in December 1990 provided additional validation for Mrs. Cartwright's observations. Dr. London was the first one to use the phrase "cognitive leap" to describe what had taken place. She compared the Stanford–Binet L–M test results obtained when she administered the test to Jennie to those from the test conducted 10 months before. On the first test, Jennie had scored 148 and had missed a number of the more abstract questions, responding as if she had failed to understand them. The results of the second test, however, showed that Jennie could answer questions that she had not been able to answer before. Scoring 176 IQ, she demonstrated an ability to answer questions of a different kind. Rather than only being able to answer questions requiring her to form abstract categories (e.g., correctly identifying how two things are alike or different), she was now able to successfully handle questions requiring abstract problem solving—for example, to detect what is absurd in a verbally presented scenario.

Dr. London noted that generally children do not begin to be able to detect verbal absurdities until they reach a mental age of about 8 or 9 years. Before that mental age, children are not yet able to answer more complex "why" questions. Jennie's results on the second administration of the Stanford–Binet L–M corresponded with her sudden desire to understand abstract phenomena such as time, God, and the universe and how they fit together—at the age that most 4-year-olds are still thinking about "my house and my family and myself and my school."

Dr. London thought that the emotional turmoil that accompanied this experience for Jennie was due partly to the speed with which the cognitive leap had taken place. Because of the sudden onset and rapid development of the cognitive changes, Jennie had felt deluged with sudden new thoughts and information. Such a dramatic shift is not the normal developmental trajectory. Most children appear to go through these changes at a more moderate pace. For all children, when the shift does occur, it brings with it a need for more complex programming in school. Whereas other children can still be satisfied with more advanced work in a teacher-provided workbook format, children who have gone through this cognitive shift require more self-generated structure and direction.

A Vygotskian analysis of the cognitive leap. Vygotsky's general genetic law of cultural development is helpful in explaining what may have been happening in terms of cognitive development when Jennie, at approximately age 4 years, 6 months, began her incessant questioning during the post-tantrum 3-week period. It may be that, because the higher level deductive and inductive thought processes she was using were but newly developing, Jennie needed to verbalize the chains of reasoning in the context of interpsychological interaction with her mother to fully incorporate these psychological processes into her cognitive repertoire. This is in keeping with Vygotsky's notion that all higher mental functions are internalized social relationships (Vygotsky, 1960/1981a).

In addition, one can argue that Jennie's articulated chains of reasoning reflected the ongoing logicalization of her thought processes—a logicalization process that was beginning at an earlier point in the developmental trajectory and continuing at a more rapid pace than is typically the case in children's development.

Inextricably woven into the fabric of Jennie's cognitive experience is her affective response to that experience. In Vygotskian terms, as Jennie's cognitive capacities expanded, her emotions became dialectically interrelated with her cognition—forming an interfunctional unit. It appears that, as the result of the logicalization process, Jennie experienced a concomitant emotional need for logical consistency in her understanding of the world. This may have culminated in the emotional turmoil she experienced during the period of the cognitive leap.

As Jennie grappled with the sudden onslaught of increased abstract capacity, she was forced to deal with the emotional repercussions of her own thought. Thus, in Jennie's mind at age 4, God could not possibly be a loving God if He would refuse heaven to anyone. And the terrible realization of her own mortality could not be softened by her mother's reassurances because "Nobody knows for sure ... children die sometimes." In spite of her impressive capacity for abstract thought, Jennie was only 4. Her emotional needs, like those of other 4-year-olds, included a trust in the strength and reliability of her parents and in the predictability of a secure world. However, her advanced cognitive capacities—or, from the Vygotskian perspective, the precocious logicalization of her thought processes and her increased ability to interpret and attribute meaning to experience—left her emotionally defenseless in the face of her own reason.

Implications for future research. There is evidence that cognitive leaps such as the one that Jennie experienced are not unusual in the development of extraordinarily high-IQ children. Hollingworth (1942) reported that she had found significant increases in successive Stanford–Binet scores among the profoundly gifted children she studied. "Child G," for example, at the age of 6 years, 7 months measured an IQ of 163. At eight years, he achieved an IQ of 192, prompting Hollingworth to note in his record that "the increase over the IQ obtained at the age of 6 is not unusual for a very young, very bright child, although it would be unusual for an average child" (p. 178).

Certainly, the idea of a cognitive leap would come as no surprise to Vygotsky, who saw revolutionary shifts as a central aspect of cognitive development.[4] Unfortunately, we do not have on record detailed accounts

---

[4]Larisa V. Shavinina (1999) saw cognitive leaps such as Jennie experienced as manifestations of "sensitive periods" in development. The Russian researcher and scholar N. S. Leites was apparently the first to apply Vygotskian theory to questions of giftedness, drawing mainly on Vygotsky's notion of "sensitive periods" (L. V. Shavinina, personal communication, May 28, 1999). These are windows of time during which conditions are optimal for

of the emotional concomitants of Hollingworth's subjects' leaps in cognition. Nevertheless, the idea of revolution seems appropriate to Jennie's case, not only because of supporting psychometric and reading achievement documentation, but also because of the extraordinary emotional turmoil she experienced.

More qualitative research is needed exploring in detail—contextually and phenomenologically—the developmental patterns of extraordinarily high-IQ children. Is the cognitive leap pattern indeed common among these children? What triggers cognitive leaps? Do they result in emotional turmoil? Always? Sometimes? Rarely? Under what conditions? Longitudinal case studies paired with cross-case comparisons, as was recommended by Vygotsky, would be especially of value.

The issue of the cognitive leap brings up another area of concern and possible direction for research. The Stanford–Binet L–M provided valuable substantiating evidence of Jennie's cognitive leap. In spite of its outdated norms due to the Binet's revision as the *Fourth edition*, the L–M remains the most sensitive instrument for differentiating types and levels of verbal–conceptual reasoning in highly and profoundly gifted children (Lovecky, 1992; Morelock & Feldman, 1992, 1997; Silverman & Kearney, 1989). Had it not been available in Jennie's case, an important source of confirmational evidence would have been lost.

Research is needed toward developing assessment instruments to sensitively discern and differentiate higher levels of verbal–conceptual ability. This will enable researchers and clinicians to trace the developmental trajectories of children like Jennie.

A Vygotskian analysis after the cognitive leap. During the time when Jennie was between 4 years, 8 months and 4 years, 9 months—after the increase in the Stanford–Binet performance had been documented—Jennie appeared to go through a resolution phase. Her mother described her as going inward and getting satisfaction from thinking on a deeper level. She no longer used textbooks or workbooks and seemed content to rely on her own thinking processes to satisfy her cognitive needs. As previously noted, the workbook-based academic activities may be seen as external mediational instruments provided by a structured environment. It is especially intriguing that her involvement with these activities significantly decreased at the same time that she began to manifest a capacity for internal thought at a higher level. This is substantiated not only by Mrs. Cartwright's descriptive account of Jennie's behavior at home during the cognitive leap period, but also by the significant change in Jennie's performance on the Stanford–Binet L–M, as reported by Dr. London, and in the abrupt increase in difficulty level of Jennie's chosen reading material. When Jennie was able to satisfy her needs through self-directed thought (i.e., a more advanced form of internalized, centralized verbal–conceptual

cognitive development to proceed at a rapid pace and children are especially likely to actualize their potentially extraordinary abilities. Unfortunately, Leites's work (1960, 1996) is not available in English.

activity), she no longer required the external stimulation and structure provided by the workbooks serving earlier to mediate internalization of these processes. This speculated role played by the workbooks gains support from Dr. London's observation that she had seen this change take place in other children, as well—although not in such an abrupt way—and that children whose cognitive skills have not yet developed to the level of Jennie's still need the structure provided by workbook activities.

It was during this resolution phase as well that Jennie began to indulge in imaginative play at a more intense and complex level than her mother had observed her to do before—peopling her fantasy schoolroom with all of the children from her normal classroom and participating in elaborate fantasy scripts. From a Vygotskian perspective, the increased complexity of her imaginative play and her intense absorption in it would be seen as the direct result of her enhanced capacity for abstract verbal–conceptual thought. Vygotsky viewed not only the emergence of language, but also the onset of the major stages in its development as a critical factor in the evolution of children's imagination (Vygotsky, 1987). The revolutionary shift taking place in the quality of Jennie's cognition would, therefore, of necessity initiate major changes in her imaginative faculties as well.

Implications for future research. A number of studies appear to support Vygotsky's contention regarding the relationship between language development and the emergence of imaginative faculties. For example, research has demonstrated relationships between the acquisition of language and the appearance of symbolic play behaviors (Bates, 1976; McCune-Nicolich, 1981; McCune-Nicolich & Carroll, 1981; Morelock, Brown, & Morrissey, 1996; Spencer, Deyo, & Grindstaff, 1990). Furthermore, findings from in-depth case studies of profoundly gifted children (Morelock, 1995, 1997a, 1997b) have suggested that such children are more likely to develop extraordinarily keen imaginative powers. More research is needed exploring the relationship between enhanced verbal–conceptual abilities and the capacity for heightened imagination.

Implications for Concepts of Giftedness

It is only recently that efforts have been made to incorporate a phenomenological perspective into contemporary concepts of giftedness. One such concept, that of the Columbus Group (Morelock, 1992, 1996, 1997c, 1997d; Silverman, 1997a), draws on Vygotskian thought in its construction. The Columbus Group definition asserts that "asynchronous development" (i.e., when the rates of a child's cognitive, emotional, and physical development are out of sync)—and the emotional consequences and altered quality of life stemming from it—is at the very heart of giftedness:

> *Giftedness* is asynchronous development in which advanced cognitive abilities and heightened intensity combine to create inner experiences

and awareness that are qualitatively different from the norm. This asynchrony increases with higher intellectual capacity. The uniqueness of the gifted renders them particularly vulnerable and modifications in parenting, teaching and counseling in order for them to develop optimally. (Columbus Group, 1991, p. 7, emphasis added)

The Columbus Group definition is in line with Vygotsky's cautionary admonition that developmentalists must study both child–environmental interaction and the child's inner psychic reality if they are to completely understand development. Part of the strength of Vygotsky's theory lay in his insistence on considering a phenomenon in its entire complexity. Thus, when he considered the development of higher psychological processes such as logical memory and abstract thought, he pondered not only the socioculturally evolved psychological stimuli contributing to their development, but also the resultant changes in inner experience as development occurred and the subsequent impact that those changes in inner awareness then had on continued development. The asynchrony characterizing gifted development means that socioculturally derived psychological tools become interiorized and begin to structure thought and experience at an earlier point in development than is typically the case. The logicalization of thought processes takes place earlier and at an accelerated pace. Emotion becomes dialectically interrelated with complex, abstract thought more rapidly and perhaps even prematurely if one is comparing gifted with more typical development. Thus, as the Columbus Group definition states, inner experiences and awareness become qualitatively different from the norm. The results of this, from a Vygotskian perspective, is the emergence of certain difficulties in sociocultural adaptation—thus, the requirement for modifications in parenting, teaching, and counseling. From this stance, an IQ score representing verbal–conceptual capacity beyond that expected for a child's chronological age is, most importantly, an index of the degree of underlying asynchrony, although certainly a minimal and imperfect one (Morelock, 1996, 1997c; Silverman, 1997a, 1997b).

Another Vygotskian contention is captured in the Columbus Group definition. Vygotsky recognized the centrality of the personally meaningful experience in guiding the process of development (Van Der Veer & Valsiner, 1991). The importance of environmental stimuli in helping to structure further development lay in the child's organizing of experience through the use of meaning attributed to those stimuli. Thus, the child's inner experience is central for Vygotsky. Socioculturally evolved tools are vital in channeling and shaping the development of human thought. Products and external manifestations are of interest. But for Vygotsky the essence lies in meaningful, emotionally reverberating inner experience.

In the past two decades or so, contextual views of talent development have become more visible in the field (Bloom, 1985; Csikszentmihalyi, Rathunde, & Whalen, 1993; Csikszentmihalyi & Robinson, 1986; Feldhusen, 1998; Feldman, 1991; Gardner, 1993). The proponents of these perspectives equate giftedness with talented performance, calling for a view recognizing the major role played by familial, social, and cultural influences in shaping extraordinary achievement. Giftedness—according to this view —lies not within the child but in the specific match between child and culturally provided opportunities for expression. Traditional psychometric gauges of giftedness, such as an IQ score, are considered only as limited predictors of future achievement—and that only within a very restricted range of talent areas mostly associated with academic ability.

As the case study of Jennie exemplifies, however, to focus solely on talents or potential achievement can be diversionary from what may be most important in questions of giftedness—the inner processes and awareness that are its essence. It would appear that what is most needed is simultaneous and integrated research into both the inner psychic reality of giftedness and the individual–environmental mutuality allowing for the external expression of talented performance (Gagné, 1997a, 1997b; Morelock, 1993, 1996, 1997c, 1997d). For Vygotsky, this would pose no contradiction. Perhaps we should take a lesson from him.

Conclusion

One of the most valuable aspects of looking at Jennie through a Vygotskian lens is that we begin to see her as an intriguing example of a form of gifted development that has not yet been adequately explored. In today's all-too-prevalent atmosphere of nouveau sophistication discounting the significance of psychometric tests and pleading for broadened views of what constitutes giftedness, too often children of extraordinarily high IQ are dismissed as simply children who happen to score high on IQ tests. Looking at Jennie through a Vygotskian lens reveals that such a stance is premature and naive. It is instead important that we return to the question of gifted development and study it freshly—without the constraints of preconceptions and prejudices.

References

Bates, E. (1976). *Language and context: The acquisition of pragmatics*. New York: Academic Press.

Bell, R. Q. (1979). Parent, child, and reciprocal influences. *American Psychologist, 34*(10), 821–826.

Bell, R. Q., & Harper, L. V. (1977). *Child effects on adults*. Hillsdale, NJ: Erlbaum.

Benbow, C. P., & Stanley, J. C. (1996). Inequity in equity: How "equity" can lead to inequity for high-potential students. *Psychology, Public Policy, and Law, 2*(2), 249–292.

Blanck, G. (1990). Vygotsky: The man and his cause. In L. C. Moll (Ed.), *Vygotsky and education: Instructional implications and applications of sociohistorical psychology* (pp. 31–58). New York: Cambridge University Press.

Bloom, B. S. (Ed.). (1985). *Developing talent in young people*. New York: Ballantine Books.

Bruner, J. (1987). Prologue to the English edition. In R. W. Rieber & A. S. Carton (Eds.), *The collected works of L. S. Vygotsky: Vol. 1. Problems of general psychology* (pp. 1–16). New York: Plenum.

Columbus Group. (1991, July). [Transcript of meeting]. Columbus, OH: Author.

Csikszentmihalyi, M., Rathunde, K., & Whalen, S. (1993). *Talented teenagers*. New York: Cambridge University Press.

Csikszentmihalyi, M., Rathunde, K., & Whalen, S. (1993). *Talented teenagers*. New York: Cambridge University Press.

Csikszentmihalyi, M., & Robinson, R. E. (1986). Culture, time, and the development of talent. In R. Sternberg & J. Davidson (Eds.), *Conceptions of giftedness* (pp. 264–284). New York: Cambridge University Press.

Curtiss, S. (1977). *Genie: A psycholinguistic study of a modern-day "wild child."* New York: Academic Press.

Feldhusen, J. F. (1998). A conception of talent and talent development. In R. C. Friedman & K. B. Rogers (Eds.), *Talent in context: Historical and social perspectives on giftedness* (pp. 193–209). Washington, DC: American Psychological Association.

Feldman, D. H. (with Goldsmith, L. T.). (1991). *Nature's gambit: Child prodigies and the development of human potential*. New York: Teachers College Press. Original work published 1986.

Fowler, W. (1981). Case studies of cognitive precocity: The role of exogenous and endogenous stimulation in early mental development. *Journal of Applied Developmental Psychology, 2*, 319–367.

Gagné, F. (1997a). Critique of Morelock's (1996) definition of giftedness and talent. *Roeper Review, 20*(3), 76–85.

Gagné, F. (1997b). Much more than a semantic glitch: A rejoinder to Morelock's response. *Roeper Review, 20*(3), 87–88.

Gardner, H. (1993). *Frames of mind: The theory of multiple intelligences* (10th ed.). New York: Basic Books.

Gazzaniga, M. S., & Smylie, C. S. (1984). What does language do for a right hemisphere? In M. S. Gazzaniga (Ed.), *Handbook of cognitive neuroscience* (pp. 199–209). New York: Plenum Press.

Gottfried, A. W., Gottfried, A. E., Bathurst, K., & Guerin, D. W. (1994). *Gifted IQ: Early developmental aspects: The Fullerton Longitudinal Study*. New York: Plenum Press.

Henderson, L. M., & Ebner, F. F. (1997). The biological basis for early intervention with gifted children. *Peabody Journal of Education, 72*(3–4), 59–80.

Hollingworth, L. (1942). *Children above 180 IQ: Stanford–Binet origin and development*. Yonkers-on-Hudson, NY: World Book.

Jastak, S., & Wilkinson, G. S. (1984). *Wide Range Achievement Test—Revised*. Wilmington, DE: Jastak Associates.

Kozulin, A. (1990). *Vygotsky's psychology: A biography of ideas*. Cambridge, MA: Harvard University Press.

Leites, N. S. (1960). *Intellectual giftedness*. Moscow: APN Press.

Leites, N. S. (Ed.). (1996). *Psychology of giftedness of children and adolescents*. Moscow: Academia.

Lewis, M., & Michalson, L. (1985). The gifted infant. In J. Freeman (Ed.), *The psychology of gifted children* (pp. 35–57). New York: Wiley.

Lovecky, D. V. (1992). The exceptionally gifted child. *Understanding Our Gifted, 4*(4), 3–4.

Luria, A. R. (1976). *Cognitive development: Its cultural and social foundations* (M. Cole, Ed.). Cambridge, MA: Harvard University Press.

McCune-Nicolich, L. (1981). Toward symbolic functioning: Structure of early pretend games and potential parallels with language. *Child Development, 52*, 785–797.

McCune-Nicolich, L., & Carroll, S. (1981). Development of symbolic play: Implications for the language specialist. *Topics in Language Disorders, 1*, 1–15.

Morelock, M. J. (1991). *The case study of Jennie, a profoundly gifted child*. Unpublished manuscript, Tufts University, Eliot-Pearson Department of Child Development, Medford, MA.

Morelock, M. J. (1992). Giftedness: The view from within. *Understanding Our Gifted, 4*(3), 1, 11–14.

Morelock, M. J. (1993). Imposing order on chaos: A theoretical lexicon. *Understanding Our Gifted, 5*(6), 15–16.

Morelock, M. J. (1995). *The profoundly gifted child in family context*. (University Microfilms No. 0234 TUFTS-D 9531439)

Morelock, M. J. (1996). On the nature of giftedness and talent: Imposing order on chaos. *Roeper Review, 19*(1), 4–12.

Morelock, M. J. (1997a, July 29–August 2). Fantasy proneness and profound giftedness. Paper presented at the 12th World Conference of the World Council for Gifted and Talented Children, Seattle, WA.

Morelock, M. J. (1997b). Imagination, logic and the exceptionally gifted child. *Roeper Review, 19*(3), A1–A4.

Morelock, M. J. (1997c). In response to Gagné's critique. *Roeper Review, 20*(2), 85–86.

Morelock, M. J. (1997d). A semantic glitch with major implications. *Roeper Review, 20*(2), 88–89.

Morelock, M. J., Brown, M., & Morrissey, A. M. (1996). *Gifted development in infancy: A study of maternal–child interactions and the precocious emergence of symbolic play.* Paper presented at the Sixth Annual Esther Katz Rosen Symposium on the Psychological Development of Gifted Children, University of Kansas, Lawrence.

Morelock, M. J., & Feldman, D. H. (1992). The assessment of giftedness in preschool children. In E. Vazquez Nuttall, I. Romero, & J. Kalesnik (Eds.), *Assessing and screening preschoolers: Psychological, social, and educational dimensions* (pp. 301–309). Boston: Allyn & Bacon.

Morelock, M. J., & Feldman, D. H. (1997). High IQ children, extreme precocity, and Savant Syndrome. In N. Colangelo & G. Davis (Eds.), *Handbook of gifted education* (2nd ed., pp. 439–359). Boston: Allyn & Bacon.

Morelock, M. J., & Feldman, D. H. (in press). Prodigies and savants: What they reveal about the cognitive underpinnings of talent. In K. Heller, F. Mönks, R. Sternberg, & R. Subotnik (Eds.), *International handbook of research and development of giftedness and talent* Oxford, England: Pergamon Press.

Morelock, M. J., & Morrison, K. (1999). Differentiating "developmentally appropriate": The Multidimensional Curriculum Model for young gifted children. *Roeper Review, 21*(3), 195–200.

Ratner, C. (1991). *Vygotsky's sociohistorical psychology and its contemporary applications.* New York: Plenum Press.

Sacks, O. (1989). *Seeing voices: A journey into the world of the deaf.* Berkeley: University of California Press.

Shavinina, L. V. (1999). The psychological essence of the child prodigy phenomenon: Sensitive periods and cognitive experience. *Gifted Child Quarterly, 43*(1), 25–38.

Silverman, L. K. (1995, August). *On the universal experience of being out-of-sync.* Keynote address presented at the 11th World Conference on Gifted and Talented Children, Hong Kong.

Silverman, L. K. (1997a). The construct of asynchronous development. *Peabody Journal of Education, 72*(3–4), 36–58.

Silverman, L. K. (1997b, July 29–August 2). *The human being as the instrument of evaluation: Using test results to support clinical judgement.* Paper presented at the 12th World Council for Gifted and Talented Children, Seattle, WA.

Silverman, L. K., & Kearney, K. (1989). Parents of the extraordinarily gifted. *Advanced Development, 1,* 41–56.

Spencer, P. E., Deyo, D., & Grindstaff, N. (1990). Symbolic play behavior of deaf and hearing toddlers. In D. F. Moores & K. P. Meadow-Orlans (Eds.), *Educational and developmental aspects of deafness* (pp. 390–406). Washington, DC: Gallaudet University Press.

Thomas, A., & Chess, S. (1984). Genesis and evolution of behavioral disorders: From infancy to early adult life. *American Journal of Psychiatry, 141*(1), 1–9.

Van Der Veer, R., & Valsiner, J. (1991). *Understanding Vygotsky: A quest for synthesis.* Cambridge, MA: Blackwell.

Vygotsky, L. S. (1978). *Mind in society: The development of higher psychological processes* (M. Cole, V. John-Steiner, S. Scribner, & E. Souberman, Eds.). Cambridge, MA: Harvard University Press.

Vygotsky, L. S. (1981a). The genesis of higher mental functions. In J. V. Wertsch (Ed.), *The concept of activity in Soviet psychology* (pp. 144–188). Armonk, NY: M. E. Sharpe. (Original work published 1960 as *Razvitie vysshikh psikhicheskikh* [The development of higher mental functions], pp. 224–231)

Vygotsky, L. S. (1981b). The instrumental method in psychology. In J. V. Wertsch (Ed.), *The concept of activity in Soviet psychology* (pp. 134–143). Armonk, NY: M. E. Sharpe. (Original work published 1960 as *Razviti vysshikh psikhicheskikh* [The development of higher mental functions], pp. 224–231)

Vygotsky, L. S. (1986). *Thought and language* (A. Kozulin, Ed.). Cambridge, MA: MIT Press. (Original work published 1934 as *Myschlenie I rech'* [Thinking and Speech])

Vygotsky, L. S. (1987). Imagination and its development in childhood. In R. W. Rieber & A. S. Carton (Eds.), *The collected works of L. S. Vygotsky: Volume 1—Problems of general psychology* (pp. 339–349). New York: Plenum Press.

Wertsch, J. V. (1985). *Vygotsky and the social formation of mind.* Cambridge, MA: Harvard University Press.

Wertsch, J. V. (1991). *Voices of the mind: A sociocultural approach to mediated action.* Cambridge, MA: Harvard University Press.

4

The Giftedness Matrix:
A Developmental Perspective

Howard Gardner

The example of Wolfgang Amadeus Mozart has been put to many uses—not least by psychologists (H. Gardner, 1997, 1999a; Morris, 1994). Such exploitation is not surprising, because Mozart's work has spoken *to* so many individuals over so many years in so many powerful ways. Mozart also has been spoken *of* in many ways: as a genius, a prodigy, an expert; as an individual who was talented, creative, intelligent, and gifted. I hope it will be seen as a token of respect, rather than as a mark of further exploitation, if I draw on the case of Mozart for yet two further purposes: (a) to clarify the nature of the terminology we use in talking about exceptional individuals and (b) to introduce a particular perspective I have brought to bear in the study of human gifts.

Mozart evokes a plethora of positive characterizations. He is our prototype of a prodigy, as precocious as Pablo Picasso or John Stuart Mill, as preternaturally talented as his fellow musicians Felix Mendelssohn or Camille Saint-Saëns. He is seen as infinitely creative, as unmistakably individualistic as Igor Stravinsky or Richard Wagner, although exhibiting an ingenuity that was evolutionary rather than revolutionary in character. He was as productive as his prolific contemporaries, the historically hapless Antonio Salieri or the euphonically dubbed Karl Ditters von Dittersdorf. And he is granted a deep wisdom, an insight into the human condition as profound as that associated with Samuel Johnson or Johann Wolfgang von Goethe, with Diego Rodríguez de Silva y Velasquez or Rembrandt van Rijn.

Students of Mozart and, for that matter, students of psychology might well leave this as it is. Terminology tends to proliferate, and ordinarily, little harm is done by a cornucopia of terms. Yet it can be valuable to step back to consider how one might extend and apply terminology consistently. If such application is based on a coherent theoretical framework, it can sometimes aid discussion, research, and understanding. In what follows I introduce a general framework for the consideration of a giftedness matrix, in the process presenting a set of distinctions I hope will prove useful.

A Framework for Analysis

Every cognitive act involves an agent who carries out an action or a set of actions in some task or domain. Even when the agent operates alone, his or her acts can be evaluated by someone competent in that particular task or domain space (Csikszentmihalyi, 1988, 1996; Feldman, 1986/1991; Feldman, Csikszentmihalyi, & Gardner, 1994; H. Gardner, 1988a, 1993a). Whether one considers the most remarkable acts of genius or the most modest accomplishment of the average citizen, the analytic perspective is applicable.

In the social sciences, the analytic framework has been decomposed as follows:

> The *biopsychological* perspective examines the agent and his or her capacities, inclinations, values, and goals. Included are a consideration of the genetic and neurological substrates of behavior, as well as the analysis of an individual in terms of cognitive powers, traits, and temperamental disposition. (H. Gardner, 1988b)

A perspective from the point of view of *domains* or *tasks* examines a task or activity as it has been realized within a societal domain or discipline. Traditionally, tasks have been analyzed by philosophers or by experts in a domain; since the advent of computer science, experts in artificial intelligence have brought forth analyses of the structural and procedural properties of a task.

Finally, evaluations or judgments of actions (or works) performed in a domain are made by those who are knowledgeable in that domain—by members of the *field*, in Csikszentmihalyi's (1988, 1996) term. In the absence of a judgment by knowledgeable individuals or groups, it is impossible to tell whether a task has been executed satisfactorily or commendably. It is not the case that, in the absence of such judgment, a task or work is necessarily inadequate; rather it is simply impossible to render a judgment. The disciplines that can clarify the operation of the field are sociology and social psychology.

The Words

Using the analytic framework as a point of departure, one can return to the lexical members of the giftedness matrix to offer some provisional definitions.

Intelligence is a biopsychological potential (H. Gardner, 1999b). Whether and in what respects an individual might be deemed intelligent is a product in the first instance of genetic heritage and psychological properties, ranging from cognitive powers to personality dispositions. I return later to the issue of how best to conceptualize intelligence in light of recent advances in cognitive study.

Giftedness is a sign of early or precocious biopsychological potential in the domains of a culture (Winner, 1996). A person who advances quickly, who is "at promise" in an available task area or domain, earns the epithet "gifted." Individuals can be gifted in any area recognized as involving intelligence.

Prodigiousness is extreme giftedness, and it usually applies to a single domain (Feldman, 1986/1991). Mozart qualified as a prodigy because of his extraordinary musical gifts. The giftedness of the youthful mathematician Karl Friedrich Gauss was quite different from the precociousness of the English painter John Everett Millais or the prodigiousness of the chess player Samuel Reshevsky. Similarly, Mozart differed from other "merely" gifted youngsters, including his sister Nannerl. On occasion, however, there are universal or omnibus prodigies.

The terms *expertise* or *expert* are appropriately invoked only after an individual has worked for a decade or so within a domain (Ericsson, Krampe, & Tesch-Romer, 1993). By this time, a person has mastered the skills and lore requisite to performance at the highest levels of the domain. There is no implication of originality, dedication, or passion in expert performance, however; expertise is better understood as a kind of technical excellence. Colleagues of Mozart (long since forgotten) who could produce virtually on demand a set of concerti or symphonies might have attained expertise without evincing any particular originality.

Creativity is a characterization reserved for those who produce what initially is seen as novel within a domain but that ultimately is recognized as acceptable within an appropriate community (Csikszentmihalyi, 1996). Judgments of originality or creativity can properly be made only by knowledgeable members of a field, whether ancient or newly constituted. There is a tension between creativity and expertise: Certainly one can be expert without being creative, and, quite possibly, one's tell-tale symptoms of creativity can be manifest before one attains the rank of master.

It is with some trepidation that I introduce the final term into the discussion: *genius* (H. Gardner, 1997). I reserve this label for persons whose works are not only expertly executed and creative but that also assume universal, or quasiuniversal, meaning or application. Within science, the genius discovers a principle of universal significance. In the arts, the genius creates works that "speak to" audiences of diverse cultures and eras. We are comfortable in applying the epithet to Shakespeare, Goethe, Rembrandt, and Mozart, because their works transcend their times. Presumably, individuals from other cultures and eras also merit the term, but the determination can be made only when they have passed the test of various relevant fields.

Traditional Psychological Approaches to the Giftedness Matrix

In most traditional approaches, the focus has fallen sharply on the individual agent. As a result of this bias, there has been too little consideration of the specific tasks or domains in question. At least among psychologists, the assumption has obtained that abilities will emerge irrespective of the domains available in one's culture. Also as a result of this bias, there has been little consideration of the processes by which judgments of quality are made. At least among psychologists, the field has been as little visible as the domain.

The most influential approach to the giftedness matrix has been a direct descendant of work in the area of intelligence and intelligence testing. In the Binet–Spearman tradition, intelligence is the trait of the isolated individual, who can be assessed alone; there is typically the additional assumption that all people are born with a certain amount of intelligence, which can be measured early in life and which proves relatively insensitive to environmental factors, such as training. Even when there have been efforts to pluralize intelligence, as in the work of Thurstone, intelligence is still seen as a relatively fixed trait that is readily elicited through the administration of paper-and-pencil instruments (cf. H. Gardner, 1983, 1993b, 1999b).

Given this standard view of intelligence, an ensemble of moves can be made with respect to the giftedness matrix. The gifted are those with high IQs; prodigies are those with even higher IQs. "Genius" can be applied either to a youngster or to an adult, so long as his or her IQ is high enough —perhaps over the legendary 180. By some definitions, creativity and intelligence are related, other definitions stress their relative independence. Recently, an informal consensus has emerged that, above an IQ of 120, creativity is not connected to psychometric intelligence. Yet from my point of view, the measures of creativity that have grown out of the psychometric tradition are even more impoverished than are the measures of intelligence. They focus almost exclusively on the most mundane instances of creativity—the type associated with clever repartee at cocktail parties— rather than on human accomplishment of scope and depth. Finally, the word *expert* seems somewhat anomalous in the context of intelligence testing, because it typically makes contact with specific areas of competence, whereas intelligence is styled as the most general property of an individual. Certainly, many members of Mensa are expert at nothing much valued by society—except perhaps taking intelligence tests.

A Contemporary View of Intelligence and Related Matters

Countering the notion of a single intelligence has been the view, which has recurred from time to time, that intellect is better conceived of as pluralistic. Typically, this conclusion has been reached as the result of factor-analytic studies of test scores, and so it is limited by the nature of the instruments used to assess various competences.

In my own work, I have approached issues of intelligence from a different perspective. The problem I set myself some years ago was this: Given the wide range of competences, of "end states" that are valued around the world, what is the nature of the mind that can give rise to a plethora of possibilities? Posing the question in this way was heterodox: It made no use of standardized tests, it focused on meaningful roles as elaborated in a society rather than on abstract competences, and it harbored a culturally relative perspective. So long as a capacity is valued in a culture, it can count as an intelligence, but in the absence of such a cultural or "field" endorsement, a capacity would not be considered an intelligence.

Having adopted this definition, I developed a method for determining what might qualify as a candidate intelligence. Briefly, my colleagues and I surveyed a wide set of literatures on human competence. The areas included information about the development of human capacities; their dissolution under conditions of brain damage; the existence of special populations, such as prodigies, idiot savants, and persons with autism; cognition in different species; cognition in different eras and cultures; susceptibility to codification in a symbol system; and, finally, two forms of psychological evidence—the results of factor-analytic studies of human ability and findings about the attainment (or nonattainment) of transfer across tasks.

Collating the information, I identified eight human competences, talents, or "intelligences" (H. Gardner, 1999b): linguistic, logical–mathematical, musical, spatial, bodily–kinesthetic, natural, interpersonal, and intrapersonal. My conclusions are that, as a species, humans have evolved to respond to at least these eight kinds of content that can be apprehended in our world, that all humans possess all of these intelligences, but that humans differ from one another in the configuration of their intelligences at any historical moment. Each of these intelligences itself has subcomponents and distinctive processes, and if there are eight intelligences, there almost certainly must be more. But the goal has not been to establish an unassailable list of intelligences; rather, it has been to pluralize the concept of intelligence and to align it more closely with what individuals do productively around the world.

The decision to adopt the term *intelligences* is deliberate: One should call all of these capacities *talents*, or one should call them *intelligences*. I find no motivated reason to call linguistic facility *intelligence* but consign musical ability to *talent*, nor do I find the capacity to deal with numbers in any way different from the capacity to deal with spatial information or with knowledge of other individuals.

Should one build on this conception of intelligence (H. Gardner, 1983, 1993b, 1999b), it is possible to devise a new and consistent way to speak about the giftedness matrix. An individual is gifted if he or she is "at promise" in any domain where intelligences figure; and the term *prodigy* would be applied to an individual of extreme promise and ease in acquiring skill and knowledge. An *expert* is a person who achieves a high level of competence within a domain, irrespective of whether any of his or her approaches are novel or experimental. Conversely, an individual is *creative* if he or she regularly solves problems or fashions products in a domain in a way that is initially seen as novel but that ultimately is recognized as appropriate. No definition of genius flows directly from this work. But I would propose that someone merits the epithet "genius" to the extent that his or her creative work in a domain exerts a material effect on the definition and delineation of that domain—so that, in the future, others who work in that domain must wrestle with the contributions made by that individual. The more universal the contribution, the more it travels across cultures and eras, the greater the genius. That is why young writers shudder when confronted with the example of Shakespeare or Goethe; these titans cast a formidable shadow over the future dimensions of the domain.

In the preceding discussion, I introduced an innovative way of conceiving of intelligence; I then suggested how the remainder of the giftedness matrix can be conceptualized with reference to this view. The effectiveness of the analysis can be determined in part on the basis of its internal coherence but, for a behavioral scientist, a more important test is the extent to which the analysis is consistent with what is known about human behavior and the extent to which the analysis can lead to productive research and to increased understanding.

Accordingly, in what follows, I carry out a developmental analysis. I examine four points in the developmental trajectory of individuals, with special reference to the issues of intelligence, giftedness, and creativity (cf. H. Gardner, 1998). Then, I touch on a few educational implications of this perspective.

The Five-Year-Old: Indifferent to Domain and Field

In the first years of life, children develop powerful theories and conceptions of how the world works—the physical world and the world of other people. They also develop at least a first-draft competence with basic human symbol systems—language, numbers, music, and two-dimensional depiction. What is striking about these acquisitions is that they do not depend on explicit tutelage. Children develop symbolic skills and theoretical conceptions largely by dint of their own spontaneous interactions with their world. This is not to deny that specific cultures exert specific effects, but it is to assert that the kinds of capacities that evolve would be difficult to thwart, given any reasonably rich and supportive environment.

With respect to most youngsters, then, one can speak of early development as being "predomain" and "prefield." That is, youngsters develop with only a dim alertness to the domains that exist in their culture and with even less sensitivity to the existence of fields that judge. At young ages, children are sometimes attracted to specific domains by what I have elsewhere called *crystallizing experiences* (Walters & Gardner, 1986). For the most part, however, those who are attracted are more interested than they are proficient.

There are exceptions. Mozart was certainly one. There is the occasional prodigy who early on discovers an affinity to a culturally approved domain and who evinces an early mastery of that domain. In such instances, the child has a head start on the attainment of expertise and, perhaps, of creativity.

The issue of childhood creativity is vexed. In many ways, all young children partake of the elixir of creativity. They are willing to transcend boundaries of which they are at least peripherally aware, they throw themselves into their play and work with great passion, they create products that often strike "the field" as more impressive than do those of older children (H. Gardner, 1982, 1989). And yet it is fair to say that such creativity occurs outside of the field. Even though the field might be impressed by works of young children—legitimately so—the young child proceeds in sublime indifference to the operations of the field.

The Ten-Year-Old: Mastering the Rules of the Domain

Shortly after the age at which school ordinarily begins, youngsters begin to assume a different stance toward the opportunities in their culture. Whether or not this is abetted by school, it seems evident that youngsters want to know the principles of the domains—the conventions of the culture—and they seek to master these as rapidly, as expeditiously, as possible. In the arts, we encounter a period of literalness—students averting metaphor, striving to produce works of art that are as representationally accurate as possible. But the same trends occur in every domain—students want to know the rules of the game.

And so one might say that the existence of the domain arises with a vengeance. To the extent that students choose, or are chosen, to work in a specific domain, they attempt to gain expertise as quickly as possible. And even with reference to the wider society, the student attempts to become acculturated as fully as possible.

This period functions as an apprenticeship en route to expertise in specific domains, an apprenticeship en route to expertise in the ways of one's culture. Those who advance most rapidly could be called gifted or even prodigious (Bloom, 1985). But reference to creativity or genius still seems inappropriate. The free-ranging explorations of the young child cease, and the informed exploration of the boundaries of the domain cannot yet be undertaken.

If creative work is not yet forthcoming, the conditions for a creative (or noncreative) life already are falling into place. For creativity depends heavily on dispositional and personality traits and on the accidents of demography (H. Gardner, 1988a, 1988b, 1993a; Perkins, 1981; Sternberg, 1988). Youngsters who are marginal within their culture, those who are ambitious and stubborn, those who can ignore criticism and stick to their guns, are "at risk" for a creative life. Those who feel comfortably a part of a group, those who advance in their domains with little feeling of pressure or asynchrony, are probably consigned to the life of the expert.

The Adolescent: At the Crossroads

The period between the ages of 15 and 25 constitutes a critical phase in the development of the giftedness matrix. The possibility for prodigiousness is already at an end—and genius lurks in the future. The crucial issue surrounds expertise. Individuals who devote themselves for a decade to one domain are likely to attain the level of expert and have the option of continuing to make at least modest contributions. They also might become members in good standing of the dominant field. Their intelligences are deployed in the service of the normal, productive functioning of their current society. Here they work comfortably within the tastes of the current field.

But at least some persons do not remain simply at the level of expertise. At some point, typically in adolescence, but possibly earlier, they make a decisive turn toward greater risk taking, increased testing of limits, determined iconoclasm. No longer do they wish simply to follow in the steps of their mentors; they raise challenges and seek to go beyond what has come before. This heightened tension can result in a so-called midlife crisis and, indeed, some adolescents cease their creativity altogether, either temporarily or permanently (Bamberger, 1982; Csikszentmihalyi, Rathunde, & Whalen, 1993). Others directly challenge the field, with unpredictable and varying degrees of success. If this period of crisis can be navigated, the opportunities for sustained creative achievement remain alive.

The Mature Practitioner: Ensconced Somewhere on the Matrix of Giftedness

Speed forward another decade or two, up to the age of 30–35, and encounter the individual whose ultimate location on the giftedness matrix is likely to have been determined. On an actuarial basis, most who are committed to a domain will be contented experts, discontented experts, or those who sought but failed to transcend expertise.

Of special interest, however, are people who, for whatever reason, transcend mere intelligence, giftedness, or expertise to seek an existence swathed in creativity. We know some of their characteristics: ambition, self-confidence, mild neuroticism, adventurousness (Albert & Runco, 1986; Barron, 1969; MacKinnon, 1961). My own studies confirm that creative individuals, whatever their domain differences, have comparable personalities and that they are frequently irascible, self-centered, and disagreeable (H. Gardner, 1993a).

I have sought to understand what it is like to operate on the edge of current knowledge and expertise (H. Gardner, 1993a). It is a bracing but frightening prospect to consider ideas and practices that have never, to your knowledge, been envisioned before. Such individuals, no matter how solitary, seem to need both cognitive and affective support at such times. And in a way that approaches the uncanny, they are reminiscent of the caretaker who is teaching a first language and introducing an initial culture to the child. For to confirm that they are not mad, creators must be able to convince at least one other person that they have invented a language, a way of seeing things, that makes sense. Without an unusual set of intellectual, social, affective, and personality traits, such dedication to the enterprise of creativity is difficult to fathom.

My studies suggest a pattern to the enterprise of the highly creative individual. After the first decade of expertise, he or she goes on to make a radical statement, one that shakes up the domain and challenges the field. A more synthetic statement is likely to emerge a decade later. In some domains, such as mathematics, the physical sciences, or lyric poetry, the prospects of continuing breakthroughs are modest. In others, it is possible to continue to effect additional breakthroughs for decades more. This is why such artists as Pablo Picasso, Igor Stravinsky, or Martha Graham led creative lives to the end, and why some scientists, such as Sigmund Freud and Charles Darwin, locate a lode they can mine for the rest of their active lives.

Understanding creativity is difficult enough; shedding light on genius borders on the impossible. Let me simply propose that the genius is a creative individual who arrives at insights that are novel and yet that sooner or later strike a deeply responsive chord across the world's diverse cultures. It is difficult enough to make an advance within one's domain; to make an advance that can reverberate across human society borders on the miraculous. Perhaps it is not fanciful to consider Mozart or Shakespeare or Jesus Christ to be miraculous—the incredible coincidence of the mind and the projects of a single human with the secrets of the universe.

With the genius, the developmental path comes full circle. The young child creates without respect to domain or field. The expert accepts the domain and the field, whereas the would-be creator challenges the domain and field. Challenge is the special province of the genius, who arrives ultimately at a product or a solution that constitutes a new, more comprehensive domain—that perhaps even transcends domain and field—to reveal an insight of broad human significance.

In speaking of genius, one moves rather far from the province of behavioral science—invoking a term that seems more appropriate to literary or artistic pages than to the volumes of the scientific literature. Yet, even if we cannot explain genius, we cannot pretend it does not exist. Whether or not he can inspire social scientific progress, Mozart is a perennial reminder of the heights to which humans occasionally rise (H. Gardner, 1999a).

Educational Implications

A developmental scheme designed to describe giftedness and its corollaries leads naturally to a question, What can be done to foster or educate giftedness? It has sometimes been quipped, more in sorrow than in joy, that it is easier to thwart gifted and creative youngsters than it is to encourage their flowering. And, indeed, precisely because we know so little about these precious phenomena, it is most important that parents and teachers "first do no harm."

The foregoing discussion yields at least a few modest implications. To begin with, the very delineation of the varying forms that constitute gift-edness, expertise, creativity, and the like can aid educators in that it raises a question, What kind of extraordinary performances or achievements are wanted? To develop an individual who is creative is a far different challenge than to nurture one who is prodigious or to train one to be an expert. What is deemed a gift in China may seem a frill or even a burden in Chicago—or vice versa. The desirability of disaggregating these end states and deciding which are desired, which are not, seems a useful step for any educator.

A second implication is entailed in the adoption of a developmental approach. Once one recognizes that children of different ages or stages have different needs, attend to different forms of cultural information, and assimilate content to different motivational and cognitive structures, then the kinds of educational regimens we design ought to account for developmental factors. It is as inappropriate to subject a five-year-old to the critique of the field as it is to withhold such critique from the aspiring (or accomplished) master.

A third point concerns the kinds of educational models we provide to children. Quite different messages are gleaned by the child, depending on whether the adults, or masters, embody expertise, creativity, or even some form of genius and which sorts of early intimations of these end states they encourage or discourage. A simple decision about which teachers or mentors to include in a "giftedness" program carries powerful signals about the direction in which children should venture.

Overshadowing the decision about specific individuals is the broader question of the messages about giftedness conveyed in the wider society. As a study of arts education in China and the United States has revealed (H. Gardner, 1989), two societies can convey sharply contrasting messages about the uses to which talents can be put and the ways in which they can be developed within a culture. Within our own society, as well, there can be contrasting and even contradictory models of what counts as a gift —and about what should count in the future.

Perhaps inevitably, discussions of giftedness and education in our cultural contexts highlight the importance of the individual child. Yet, if the above discussion is valid, it reminds us that gifts of all sorts can never be properly conceptualized as existing solely within the head or the body of the individual. By calling attention to the "domain" and "field" characteristics that surround any activity—and, in particular, any extraordinary activity—I hope to remind educators that they too should remember the extrapersonal factors that are so important in the development (or thwarting) of talent.

Discussions of values may seem out of place in a contribution that purports to be scientific. Yet if there is any societal realm in which issues of value are prominent, it is terrain that must wrestle with the questions of what constitute gifts and how they should be identified, fostered, and mobilized within a community. Equity and excellence need not be in direct conflict (J. Gardner, 1961), but there is undeniable tension between them, particularly in times of limited resources. Those of us who devote our energies to the exploration of such fascinating topics have a special obligation to keep these issues of value in mind and, when possible, to help make the value considerations and choices clear to colleagues, educators, and the wider public.

References

Albert, R., & Runco, M. (1986). The achievement of eminence: A model of exceptional boys and their parents. In R. J. Sternberg & J. E. Davidson (Eds.), *Conceptions of giftedness* (pp. 332–357). New York: Cambridge University Press.

Bamberger, J. (1982). Growing up prodigies: The midlife crisis. In D. H. Feldman (Ed.), *Developmental approaches to giftedness* (pp. 61–78). San Francisco: Jossey-Bass.

Barron, F. (1969). *Creative person and creative process.* New York: Holt, Rinehart, & Winston.

Bloom, B. (Ed.). (1985). *Developing talent in young people.* New York: Ballantine.

Csikszentmihalyi, M. (1988). Society, culture and person: A systems view of creativity. In R. J. Sternberg (Ed.), *The nature of creativity* (pp. 325–339). New York: Cambridge University Press.

Csikszentmihalyi, M. (1996). *Creativity.* New York: HarperCollins.

Csikszentmihalyi, M., Rathunde, K., & Whalen, S. (1993). *Talented teenagers: The roots of success and failure.* New York: Cambridge University Press.

Ericsson, A., Krampe, R. T., & Tesch-Romer, C. (1993). The role of deliberate practice in the acquisition of expert performance. *Psychological Review, 100*(3), 363–406.

Feldman, D. H. (with Goldsmith, L.). (1991). *Nature's gambit.* New York: Basic Books. (Original work published 1986)

Feldman, D., Csikszentmihalyi, M., & Gardner, H. (1994). *Changing the world: A framework for the study of creativity.* Westport, CT: Greenwood.

Gardner, H. (1982). *Art, mind, and brain.* New York: Basic Books.

Gardner, H. (1983). *Frames of mind.* New York: Basic Books.

Gardner, H. (1988a). Creative lives, creative works. In R. Sternberg (Ed.), *The nature of creativity* (pp. 298–321). New York: Cambridge University Press.

Gardner, H. (1988b). Creativity: An interdisciplinary perspective. *Creativity Research Journal, 1,* 8–26.

Gardner, H. (1989). *To open minds: Chinese clues to the dilemma of contemporary education.* New York: Basic Books.

Gardner, H. (1993a). *Creating minds: An anatomy of creativity seen through the lives of Freud, Einstein, Picasso, Stravinsky, Eliot, Graham, and Gandhi.* New York: Basic Books.

Gardner, H. (1993b). Intelligence in seven phases. In H. Gardner (Ed.), *Multiple intelligences: The theory in practice* (pp. 213–230). New York: Basic Books.

Gardner, H. (1997). *Extraordinary minds: Portraits of exceptional individuals and an examination of our own extraordinariness.* New York: Basic Books.

Gardner, H. (1998). Extraordinary cognitive achievements: A symbol systems approach. In W. Damon (Ed.-in-Chief), *Handbook of child psychology: Theoretical models of human development* (5th ed., Vol. 1, pp. 415–466). New York: Wiley.

Gardner, H. (1999a). *The disciplined mind: What all students should understand.* New York: Simon & Schuster.

Gardner, H. (1999b). *Intelligence reframed: Multiple intelligences for the 21st century.* New York: Basic Books.

Gardner, J. (1961). *Excellence.* New York: Harper & Row.

MacKinnon, D. W. (1961). Creativity in architects. In D. W. MacKinnon (Ed.), *The creative person* (pp. 291–320). Berkeley, CA: Institute of Personality Assessment Research.

Morris, J. (1994). *On Mozart.* Washington, DC: Woodrow Wilson Center Press.

Perkins, D. N. (1981). *The mind's best work.* Cambridge, MA: Harvard University Press.

Sternberg, R. (1988). A three-facet model of creativity. In R. J. Sternberg (Ed.), *The nature of creativity* (pp. 125–147). New York: Cambridge University Press.

Walters, J., & Gardner, H. (1986). Crystallizing experience. In R. J. Sternberg & J. E. Davidson (Eds.), *Conceptions of giftedness* (pp. 306–331). New York: Cambridge University Press.

Winner, E. (1996). *Gifted children*. New York: Basic Books.

5

Tracking Trajectories of Talent: Child Prodigies Growing Up

Lynn T. Goldsmith

Although rare, child prodigies are a nonetheless common part of our culture, and most of us have images or expectations of them. Yet when people encounter examples of prodigious achievement, few feel adequately prepared for the experience. The works of child prodigies not only engender appreciation and pleasure, but also wonder, disbelief, and even discomfort or distress. Consider, for example, excerpts from a child's short play (Feldman, 1986/1991) written in 1978, which was based on Bram Stoker's novel *Dracula*. In this version, Jonathan Harker, a real estate agent, is sent to Transylvania by his boss, Mr. Hawkins, to sell some real estate to the mysterious count.

Scene 1
Mr. Hawkins's office in London.
Hawkins: Come in, Harker. I've got a very important assignment for you.
Harker: (taking a seat) Will I be traveling, sir?
Hawkins: To Transylvania, Harker, to see a certain Count Dracula. He is in urgent need of a large estate in England. I'd like you to go and see the man and take care of the particulars. You might find him an odd sort of chap. Lives in a castle on the side of a mountain, sounded very curious on the phone . . . ah well, there's big money involved, Harker, do your best lad.

Scene 2
A hotel in Bucharest. Harker is shaving when he hears a knock on the door.
Harker: (hears door knock) Come in (door opens).
Gypsy: I have come to warn you that Count Dracula is a very strange man.

I would like to thank Trudy Goodman, Jim Guttmann, Ilene Kantrov, Erica Wilsen, and Ellen Winner for a variety of interesting conversations about this work. Keffie Feldman, Betsy Goldman, and Danny Feldman graciously forbore silent car rides while I worked out ideas and occasionally took vehicular dictation. Reva C. Friedman, Frances Degen Horowitz, Meredith Porter, and Bruce M. Shore have my thanks for being supportive editors and facilitators of this chapter. Most of all, I extend my thanks to the six young men and their families who so generously opened their homes and their lives to this study.

Harker: Oh nonsense. Who are you, and what do you want?
Gypsy: I am an old gypsy, and I know many things. Count Dracula is a vampire. And there are only a few things that can stop them. Take this garlic, my son, and this cross. Either one will stop that hideous fiend. . . . You will know the truth of what I am saying when you see that Dracula casts no reflection in the mirror. Take this small mirror and see for yourself. . . .
Harker: Thank you. When he takes one look he'll go wild.

Scene 3
At the gate of Castle Dracula. Driver takes Harker's bags into the castle and disappears. Harker waits at the gate, which finally opens with a loud creak.
Harker: Hello, is anyone there?
Dracula: Velcome to Castle Dracula, my frant. You must be able to recognize me. I am Count Dracula.
Harker: Very good meeting you, Count.
Dracula: You must be hungry after your long journey, my frant.
Harker: I am very well, Count.
Dracula: Then come in (bows), come in.
Harker: I will, Count. . . . [Feldman, 1986/1991, pp. 67–68]

This play was authored, and typed, by Mac Randall, a boy age 4½ years. Reflect for a moment on your reaction to this information. Did you exhale, raise your eyebrows, laugh, read the sentence a second time to be sure that you had understood it correctly? Despite our abstract understanding that child prodigies demonstrate unusually sophisticated abilities, actually confronting a very young child's accomplishments can be unsettling. Reading about the talented childhoods of historical greats such as Wolfgang Amadeus Mozart or Pablo Picasso is altogether different than directly experiencing examples of prodigious abilities in children who are growing up today.

When we do encounter evidence of prodigious talent, we tend to construe the child's life in terms of this talent: Because their achievements are so striking it is difficult to imagine prodigies' futures as anything but unbounded potential waiting to be crafted and polished. If such children are this accomplished as youngsters, just imagine how extraordinary they will be as practitioners in 10 or 20 more years. There is a precedent for such expectations, for many of the historical cases of prodigies are of children who continued to enjoy premier adult careers, for example, Mozart, Picasso, Norbert Weiner, Yehudi Menuhin, Bobby Fischer. Yet the historical record is skewed in the direction of such successes, for there are fewer efforts to preserve the life stories of individuals who fall out of the public eye. Those stories we do have, for example, that of mathematics *wunderkind* turned marginalized eccentric William James Sidis (Montour, 1977; Wallace, 1986), tend to be preserved as sad and sobering tales of lives somehow gone disappointingly, if not terribly, wrong. It is as if we believed that such gifted children have an obligation to the rest of us to make continued, productive use of their unusual talent. We may view their failure to do so not only as a seriously wasted opportunity, but also somehow as a breach of faith.

But in fact, "failed prodigies" are quite common. The best prediction about the adult outcome for child prodigies is that, like Sidis, California artist Janel Lessing (Seidenbaum, 1961), writer Winifred Stoner (Goldsmith, 1987), and countless children whose names we do not know, prodigies will *not* continue to perform at the forefront of their fields. A vivid illustration of this is provided by the "San Francisco cohort" of musical prodigies (Goldsmith, 1990).

During the 1920s and 1930s, the San Francisco area proved to be a particularly fertile area for the identification and development of young musicians. The reasons for this flowering of talent remain unexplored and would make an interesting investigation in its own right. But whatever the causes, more than 70 musical prodigies were actively performing in the area in the '20s and '30s: this amounts to better than one musical prodigy for every square mile of the San Francisco city limits.

Of these 70 unusually talented young musicians, only six had notable musical careers as adults: pianists Leon Fleisher, Ruth Slenczynski, and Hephzibah Menuhin and violinists Issac Stern, Ruggiero Ricci, and Yehudi Menuhin. We know nothing of the musical fates of the remaining 64 children, nothing of the events and decisions that shaped their life courses. In all likelihood, some continued in less visible musical careers, perhaps teaching music or playing professionally in orchestras, chamber groups, or bands. Others may have chosen to integrate music into their lives avocationally rather than professionally.

This example illustrates clearly that early prodigious achievement does not necessarily guarantee adult acclaim. Prodigies' accomplishments represent a confluence of a number of factors at a particular time: individual talent and commitment to study, a domain of endeavor that is highly structured and organized, parents' and teachers' commitment to promote the development of perceived talent, family resources to do so, and a cultural milieu that values performance in the prodigy's domain of expertise (Bloom, 1982; Csikszentmihalyi, Rathunde, & Whalen, 1993; Feldman, 1986/1991; Goldsmith, 1990; Goldsmith & Feldman, 1989; Howe, 1990; Sosniak, 1997). All of these factors must continue to intercoordinate if the prodigy's talent is to continue to grow.

At present, we know little about how these factors interact over the course of a prodigy's middle life or about the kinds of issues or circumstances that lead prodigies to reevaluate their commitment to pursue their original talents. This chapter offers some first glimpses at the extended course of development of several child prodigies who were first studied in the middle 1970s and raises questions about the development of talent.

The Middle Years in the Lives of Six Child Prodigies

A number of years ago David Feldman and I wrote a book about the early lives of six child prodigies (Feldman, 1986/1991). All six were boys. Two were gifted chess players (alias Ricky Velazquez and Franklin Montana), one was a musician (Nils Kirkendal), one was mathematically precocious

(Billy Devlin), and one was a prolific writer (Randy McDaniel). (As Randy and his parents are no longer concerned with protecting his anonymity, I will refer to them in this chapter by their given names: Mac Randall and his parents Janice and Dean.) The sixth child, Adam Konantovich, seemed to be a polymath even at the age of 3 years, expressing a large range of interests including musical composition, mathematics, and foreign languages.

Most of the regular contact with these children was between 1975 and 1980). It began with some formal assessments of Piagetian reasoning (Feldman, 1979) but was soon transformed to a more ethnographic inquiry including observations at home, in lessons, and in performance, as well as interviews with teachers, parents, and mentors. The intention of this approach was to take a broad perspective to examine the range of factors influencing the development of extraordinary talent.

The case studies as reported to date have focused on the boys' early to middle childhoods. The boys ranged in age from 5 (Adam) to 15 years (Nils) at the end of the study in 1980. As Albert (1994) has noted, however, longitudinal studies are rarely ever really over, even if the investigator intends to get on to other projects and to stop collecting more information. So it seems to be with this project. The symposium that occasioned this chapter provided the opportunity for me to take another look into the lives of the six boys I have known and to ask about what has happened to them over the ensuing 12 years. How have they fared with respect to developing their original area of talent over this time? What else has become important to them as they have journeyed from childhood to young adulthood?

The detail of the updates I can provide vary, for my contact with the boys and their families over the intervening years has been irregular. By the time the formal research agenda ended more than a decade ago our relationships had eased into friendships, some of which have included fairly regular contact, and some of which have not. Billy's and Franklin's families have moved, and I have not been in touch with them recently; my information about their activities and interests will therefore be sparse. I was able to have at least one extended conversation with each of the other four in the fall and winter of 1992.

These conversations were guided by a general framework of questions designed to catch up on the chronology of their lives, discuss important life events, learn about their current intellectual interests and work, and provide them with an opportunity to reflect on their childhood talents. In each of these four cases I was also able to have at least brief telephone conversations with their parents. Nils's, Ricky's, and Adam's conversations took place over the telephone, and I spoke with Mac in person. Mac's and Nils's conversations were audiotaped and later transcribed; conversations with Ricky, Adam, and assorted parents were documented through written notes. As I was unable to reach either Billy's or Franklin's families, the only additional information about them comes from occasional notes and records of telephone conversations from several years back.

In all six of these cases the original trajectories of the boys' talents have experienced some perturbations. Only in the case of violinist Nils

Kirkendahl would his development be perceived as steady, continuous, and without significant deviation. Mac, Adam, and Billy have each turned to new areas of interest that represent some transformation or translation of their earliest expressions of ability, and Ricky and Franklin have taken off in directions that seem rather far afield from the game that provided the vehicle for expressing a remarkable early ability.

Nils Kirkendahl: A Relatively Unperturbed Trajectory

Nils began playing the violin when he was age 3 and has not stopped since. Of the six children I have studied, his is the story that most closely resembles the historical cases of prodigies who have continued on to significant adult careers. At the time of our conversation he was age 27 and well on his way to developing a world-class reputation as a solo violinist. He had made two compact disc recordings with a major label and maintained a busy national and international performance schedule. These accomplishments reflect not only Nils's talent, but also his focus and commitment to keeping his artistic path a clear and straight one.

This path began as a toddler. His mother Helen noticed that Nils was very taken with a recording of the Tchaikovsky violin concerto[1] and invited him to take violin lessons when he turned age 3. He expressed interest in the prospect, and she enrolled him in a local Suzuki class shortly after his birthday. He loved to play and seemed to catch on quickly and easily. By the time he was age 5, it was clear that he needed a different level of instruction; he seemed quite talented and was obviously committed to more intensive study than the Suzuki teacher could offer. Helen found a teacher to begin formal studies with a child who was already making lovely music on a quarter-sized violin.

Nils's interests and talent both continued to develop rapidly. He began to compose around age 6, and within a year or two was straining his second teacher's instructional expertise. Thus, before Nils had entered the third grade, he (and his mother) began the first of several appraisals of his talent and commitment to the serious study of music. The overall pattern of decision making about his musical education is consistent with that observed by Bloom and colleagues in their studies of mathematicians, pianists, swimmers, and research scientists (Bloom, 1985). The first of these decisions involved determining that he was ready for the next level of teacher (Bloom, 1982). This decision made, it fell to Helen to figure out to whom they should entrust Nils's continuing musical education. She researched the music scene in and around their hometown and concluded that the teachers he needed could not be found within 100 miles. Despite the distance, they decided that the strength of Nils's talent and dedication warranted the 200-mile round trip for lessons. Eight-year-old Nils intensified his studies, and the three other members of the Kirkendahl family made adjustments in their lives to accommodate his schedule. Nils and

---

[1]I think it is interesting that one of Nils's first professional recordings is of this same concerto.

Helen, and sometimes Nils's younger brother Loki drove 2 hours each Saturday morning so he could take 4 or 5 hours' worth of lessons. Nils studied solfege, piano, and composition; played in ensembles; and took master classes. After the lessons they would turn around and make the 2-hour trip home. During the week, Nils would practice 4 or 5 hours each day.

A second assessment was precipitated several years later by his composition teacher and concerned the focus of his musical studies. As both a promising young composer and a gifted violinist, Nils was a teacher's dream—"too good to be true" in the words of his composition teacher. This teacher was not often blessed with composition students of any age as thoughtful and talented as Nils. He was eager to share his art with his brilliant young student and found it difficult to accept that Nils's heart seemed to lie in performing. He began to press Nils to forgo serious study of the violin and declare himself first and foremost a composer—at age 10. Nils resisted this push for further specialization for a time but eventually agreed that he did have to declare his allegiance to one or the other. Before he was age 11, then, he had cast his lot with performing and organized his musical training toward that end.

A third appraisal came at about age 12 when Nils, his mother, and his teachers decided that it was time to place his future education in the hands of a mentor and master teacher. He was accepted for precollege studies at Juilliard and began to work with Dorothy DeLay, one of the country's most respected violin teachers. Nils's weekend commuting took on a southerly, rather than an easterly, direction, and this time he often traveled on his own. He would take the train into New York by himself on Saturday, stay overnight with family friends, and return home on Sunday in time to get ready for school the next day.

By the time he was 15 Nils moved around New York City like a pro, was responsible about looking after himself for the weekend, and was developing into a strong young violinist. In addition to making an increasing number of performances with local orchestras, before his 15th birthday Nils had performed Paganini as a guest soloist at Carnegie Hall and had debuted with the Boston Pops.

All this time Nils was fitting his regular education around the interstices of his music. He had begun high school at a private day school and was considered a very strong student academically, despite frequent absences caused by his demanding performance schedule. Although the school recognized Nils's talent and accepted his musical commitments, many teachers wished that he could be as interested in their subjects as he was in his music, for he was exceptionally bright, thoughtful, and articulate. Nils tended to think about his schoolwork as interesting, but of secondary importance. By the end of his freshman year he knew that he wanted to begin full-time studies in New York as soon as possible. He had already auditioned and been accepted into Juilliard's degree-granting program, but admission was contingent on his graduation from high school. Eager to get on with his "real" education, Nils decided he would finish high school the following year. Curriculum requirements at the day school made this impossible, so Nils enrolled in a public high school that would allow him to collapse his sophomore, junior, and senior years into one. Although the logistics were fearsome, he completed three years of coursework in one (noting that the courses, themselves were really very easy, and that it was the scheduling that was really the challenge). Nils entered Juilliard at age 15 on a scholarship, continuing his private studies with Dorothy DeLay. He moved into an apartment with other Juilliard students and began another phase in his life as a musician.

In his second or third year of studies at Juilliard Nils experienced the largest perturbation to his musical career, suffering a crisis of confidence. Although he can no longer recall the precipitating factors (or even exactly when this period of time occurred), he does remember that he "didn't want to play anymore. . . . I didn't know *what* I wanted to do." This period of time was relatively brief, but intense. He stopped playing entirely for about a month and mused about his musical career. He found the lack of overall intellectual rigor at Juilliard disappointing and debated enrolling at Columbia University, where he would be able to explore academic interests in an atmosphere of serious inquiry. He wondered how to rekindle his inspiration.

After a month or so he decided that the answer to his dilemma did not lie in broadening his intellectual interests, but in focusing even more sharply on his music. He took a semester's leave from school and devoted himself entirely to practice and private instruction. His teacher

> knew I was going through some problem, so she was very encouraging. And then I really started working again, and she lent me her violin to play on for a while. Part of it was I wasn't happy with my instrument, and she kind of could sense what was going on, so she lent me this fantastic instrument to use for a while. And that reinspired me to really start working. (N. Kirkendahl, personal communication, December 8, 1992)

Nils devoted 6 months to intensive study of and on the instrument. At the end of this time he entered and "won a competition or something," which seemed to renew his confidence that he could make the kind of music he envisioned for himself.

Nils received his degree from Juilliard at age 19, signed with New York management, and spent the next 8 years developing an international career. He aims for passionate and energetic performances, ones that are spontaneous and interpretively exciting as well as technically "clean." Appraisals of his performances would indicate that he is succeeding at achieving this goal. Pianist Vladimir Ashkenazy heard Nils play shortly after graduating from Juilliard and opined "I have not enjoyed such good violin playing for a long time. His presence is compelling, his technique is fabulous, he is unpretentious, direct and magnetic" (N. Kirkendahl, personal communication, December 8, 1992).

Nils is also aware that his success as an artist involves understanding the business end of his profession. He is careful to observe other musicians' careers, to attend carefully to his mentor's advice, and to generate and pursue potential contacts and engagements. It is particularly important to him to conduct the business side of his career with integrity, without feeling like he has "sold out" artistically just to have work. In this regard, he is also thoughtful about selecting works for his repertoire. He wants to balance the classic pieces that audiences expect to hear with the opportunity to introduce new works to the public. He is happy to perform works he described as "old chestnuts" as long as he can bring a freshness of interpretation and emotional depth to his performances. He also feels a responsibility to offer richer and more varied musical experiences to his audiences in the form of new compositions. He understands, however, that he must develop a standing with audiences so that they will trust his taste and artistry.

Looking at Nils's life thus far, I am struck by the focus and sense of direction with which he has undertaken his journey. He has long been committed to becoming the finest musician he possibly can and has deliberately, but not relentlessly, organized his life in service of this goal. With help from wise teachers he has nurtured and paced his own growth, taking the time to develop a deep and rich artistry. As he looks at his life, he is accepting and optimistic.

> Now I feel like I'm starting to come into some beginnings of maturity musically—how I approach things. But, you know, it takes a really long time, and you should relax and enjoy the ride and not make yourself crazy about by what age you accomplish such and such because life just doesn't work that way. . . . Sometimes I feel like I wish it were faster, because I get impatient but, in general, I don't worry about it. I think as long as you have your goal, and you have a means to work toward that goal and opportunities to try your stuff out, that's all you can ask for. And there are some people who want to get famous right away and start doing outrageous things to get famous. But if you really want playing that you're absolutely happy with, and proud of, I don't think you can rush that.
>
> I'm glad I wasn't pushed really hard a few years ago and made to do a lot of things I wasn't ready to do yet. . . . I probably wouldn't be playing any more. I would have been good enough in one sense, but not really—I would have known. . . . When I hear playing [of those performers] who were pushed very early, and achieved fame very early, a lot of the time I feel like it sounds half-baked. And I'm not fooling myself. I would have sounded half-baked too at that age. I don't want to sound that way. I want to sound fully formed. (N. Kirkendahl, personal communication, December 8, 1992)

Nils is well on his way to a rewarding career. He has worked long and hard, striving with passion and discipline, humor and focus to become an intelligent and exciting artist. His efforts seem to have been well placed, for all the indications are that we will be hearing from him in the future.

Mac Randall: Revisions in a Writer's Life

"You never want to back into a story," Mac related to me over lunch at a bustling restaurant at the edge of Harvard Square. "If you have the lead in the fourth paragraph, that's a mistake. You have to get people interested right away." This advice came to me through two generations of journalists: Mac's dad Dean, veteran newspaperman, had offered it to Mac, and he, the 20-year-old assistant editor of *Musician* magazine, was passing the tip on to me.

Mac is something of a veteran himself. He has been writing since the day that Dean discovered him, at age 3, sitting at the electric typewriter and pounding out a short description of himself and his parents. In the intervening years Mac has explored writing in a variety of genres and in both literary and musical modalities.

Long before he decided to explore his father's typewriter Mac had reveled in the spoken and the written word, moving to the rhythms of nursery rhymes as an infant, delighting in his father's broadcast-style commentaries on family life and popular subjects, and spending large parts of each day reading and discussing stories with his parents. When I met Mac at age 8 he was already the author of dozens of carefully researched essays and stories, many of which were lovingly bound and illustrated. The story of Mac's development has been one with more twists and turns than Nils's, but in large measure it, too, is a tale about how a writer has continued to explore his craft.

Like Nils and his music, Mac's development as a writer proceeded almost entirely outside of school until his teenage years. By the time he was age 6 he was accustomed to discussing with Dean how authors conveyed ideas to their readers. In his own writing, Mac experimented with different styles and forms, producing original versions of stories that he had read (such as *Dracula* excerpted earlier), as well as poems, plays, and reports of library research on a variety of historical and scientific topics. (For other examples of Mac's early writing, see Feldman, 1986/1991.) In this enterprise Dean served as Mac's literary guide and mentor.

As there is no formal pedagogy for the instruction of child writers, Mac's education as a writer has been idiosyncratic. There are no curricula, or even general plans of attack, for helping a very young writer develop the craft. Nor is there a system for identifying and training young writers —no nationally known group of teachers, summer camps, or institutes that serve to develop youngsters with literary talent. Becoming a serious writer is generally considered an adult's aspiration, not a child's.

Thus, Dean's work with Mac has been based primarily on his own knowledge—about being a writer himself, about the workings of his son's mind, about mentoring aspiring adult journalists over the years. From the first, Mac's education has been an apprenticeship. He read and wrote. Dean read and wrote. Together, they read and thought about ideas and talked. Dean was always ready to listen to what was on Mac's mind. Sometimes this meant reading and discussing something that Mac wrote, other times he served as a sounding board for Mac's thoughts about things that had happened in school or in the news. Rarely did Dean's role as mentor involve critiquing Mac's writing directly. Most of his teaching revolved around stimulating an awareness of literary expressiveness and encouraging Mac to explore ways to say what he wanted to say.

Much of Mac's early writing (until age 10 or 11) can be seen as technical explorations of the tone and structure of different literary forms. He wrote his own abridged versions of famous stories, as well as original short stories, poems, and reports of the research that he and Dean conducted together. Around age 8 he embarked on an ambitious program of book writing, creating his own version of the *Dr. Who* series (see Feldman, 1986/1991, for an example). These books, each with its own cover art, illustrations, and copyright page, contained original fantasies based on the *Dr. Who* characters. They were written in a style corresponding closely in both tone and texture to the prose in the actual science fiction series. As the stories themselves go, however, the tales were somewhat lackluster, being short on significant plot or character development. Mac worked on these books for four or five years, having promised himself that he would produce an entire series of some 30 books. In the end, he notes,

> I stayed with that [series] just out of habit, more than anything else. . . . But you make a certain commitment. I had set out a whole plan of stories—all these stories that all involved this character, and so the idea, of course, was to actually write all these stories, which I didn't do. I had them all generally plotted out, but I never actually wrote them all down in detail. . . . Part of it is to actually live up to the commitment that you made to yourself. . . . But I just moved on to other things after a while, and I started writing more journalistic sorts of things. (M. Randall, personal communication, October 22, 1992)

During the time that Mac was working on *Dr. Who* he was also developing a strong interest in music. He had loved classical music since infancy, with a particular and abiding fondness for Beethoven, Tchaikovsky, and Grieg. When Mac was about age 8 or 9, Dean suggested that he try branching out to popular music. Mac found the contemporary rock offerings of the late '70s uninspiring but developed a serious attachment to the Beatles after listening to the album *Sgt. Pepper's Lonely Hearts Club Band*. In short order he owned every Beatles album, memorized all their songs, and sang them constantly. Soon singing *a capella* was not good enough: Mac wanted to be able to play popular tunes on the guitar. As always, Mac was certain about what he wanted to do. He did not want a general introduction to music; he wanted to be able to play the rock music he knew and loved. Dean and Janice set out to find a teacher who would start right in with Mac's agenda rather than at the beginning of some lesson book.

They found a bluegrass musician who taught by ear, and within 2 or 3 months Mac was playing the guitar for hours on end, eagerly picking out every Beatles tune ever written. He started a rock band with some friends at school. The band was notable for its personnel, for there was not a single musician among them. No one but Mac had even held an instrument before. As the band's manager and lead guitarist, Mac busily wrote songs (to be performed at some later time) and even designed a series of album covers complete with liner notes. These musical projects shared much in common with the *Dr. Who* series in that he was interested in creating both the substance and the form of the genre.

The band disbanded in relatively short order, given that Mac was the only member with enough of an Eastern philosophical learning to imagine the sound of a nonmusical band playing. However, he continued to hone his own instrumental and song writing skills by taking lessons, playing constantly, listening to records and live music, reading music reviews, and hanging out with musicians.

Whereas his interest in music may feel like a departure from his writing (Feldman, 1986/1991), for Mac, himself, writing and music are simply two ways to explore and communicate his ideas. He has also managed to integrate music and writing by writing about music. When he first became interested in music, Mac would write short reviews of albums he was listening to just for fun. He didn't care that no one else read them, for they were a way for him to practice listening to music and to experiment with writing intended to inform and critique. In more recent years, he has begun to write similar kinds of pieces for publication in *Musician* magazine and several local newspapers.

Mac's life is currently a full one. After graduating as valedictorian of his high school class, he and his parents moved to southern Massachusetts so Janice could attend graduate school. Mac used this time to focus on developing both his literary and musical crafts. He was very productive, writing the better part of every day, and felt as if the time was critical to developing his style and voice. It was also during this time that he began to work for *Musician*. The Randalls returned to Boston about two years later, which gave Mac the opportunity to reconnect with the Boston rock scene.

In 1992 he decided to enroll in Harvard Extension's degree-granting program and was a full-time student there when I spoke to him (as well as a half-time staffer on *Musician* and a freelance writer). He was thoroughly enjoying his academic work, much of which is bringing him back to the exploration of themes that had first preoccupied him 15 years ago: commonalities among myths in different cultures, studies of the ancient world, the history of scientific ideas. He was continuing to develop his writing, both in school and out. At *Musician* he was taking advantage of the opportunity to learn the business of music journalism from several perspectives—as a freelancer, an editor, and a production assistant. And he was continuing to compose music when he could make the time in a crowded schedule.

Like Nils, Mac has pursued his interests with extraordinary focus and determination. But unlike the violinist, Mac has done so in the face of less external approval and assistance. Outside of the encouragement provided by his parents, Mac has been on his own. Nils's development has progressed in the context of formal and informal systems designed to promote the development of musical talent; Mac has learned his craft in greater isolation. His focus and determination to develop his writing have carried him along a path that others might have found too lonely and dangerous to travel alone. He has always drawn strength from the knowledge that he had a special way of thinking about the world and interesting things to say. As he has grown older he has found better matches between his interests and culturally supported opportunities for expression. Whereas it is odd and disconcerting for a 4-year-old to write a short essay on *Being*, it is a perfectly reasonable theme for a college student to tackle. And whereas it seems a little precious for a 10-year-old to be constructing faux music reviews, it is fairly easy to believe that a 19-year-old musician might have an opinion worth listening to about an album or a performance. As he has grown up, Mac seems to have grown into his work in a way that is more understandable, and therefore more acceptable, to the world at large.

How the different facets of Mac's life will come together over the next decade or two remains an open question, but it seems highly likely that he will make things happen for himself. And perhaps waiting to see how things fit together is part of the fun for the Randall family. When I suggested to Mac that his life seemed like an adventure, he replied cheerfully, "It is. Always is. Never stops. I'll be as interested to see what happens as anybody."

Adam Konantovich: Tending to His Talent, Tending to His Life

As we were driving to meet the Konantovich family for the first time I remember wondering whether 3½-year-old Adam would be wearing diapers. It was the kind of question one asks when uncertain of what to expect next. Previsit conversations with Adam's parents had prepared me to meet a child who, by their accounts, had carried on extended conversations at age 6 months, asked for an explanation of logarithms' mantissas at age 1 year (noting that he thought he understood the characteristic), had been reading children's classics since he was age 18 months, was composing music at age 3 years, and had a passing knowledge of several languages. I wondered whether all of this was really possible for a child.

I did, in fact, meet a child, who was not only toilet trained but also astoundingly verbal, cheerful, knowledgeable, witty, and comfortable around adults. His language and manner was somewhat formal for one so young, but he was neither intimidating nor obnoxious. He was playful and affectionate with his parents, self-possessed, and politely friendly with visitors.

I also met unusual parents. Fiona and Nathaniel Konantovich were extremely dedicated to providing a rich and responsive environment for their son from the first days of his life. They had given a good deal of thought to their philosophies and strategies of childrearing before Adam's birth and brought their newborn son home to a house where music and song, dance, visual arts, and conversation were an integral part of daily living. They thought carefully about how they would provide for the emotional, social, and intellectual nourishment of their child. However, Adam challenged their ability to enact their philosophy from the beginning by being far more responsive and rapid in his development than they had expected. In their pre-Adam days Fiona and Nathaniel had imagined providing an enriching and stimulating environment for their child at their own pace and discretion. In reality, sometimes they felt they were at the mercy of Adam's insatiable quest to know more.

To a significant extent, it became Nathaniel and Fiona's dedication to their son, in concert with Adam's own wide-ranging interests, that drove the dynamic of their family. And often this driving was literal, as the family trekked to New York, Philadelphia, Boston, and Washington (both DC and state) to provide Adam with opportunities to visit museums, attend concerts and special events, meet with tutors and to attend school. Adam's mother had described her son as having an omnivorous intellect and often spoke of the enormous amounts of energy that she and Nathaniel spent simply keeping up with his interests. Within a year of Adam's birth they had begun to consult with academic experts; scour the country for educational programs; take out memberships in museums across the Eastern seaboard; buy thousands of books; and search for teachers, mentors, and other resources. They did all this with a strong sense of mission, but also with good humor, high spirits, and a sense of adventure. Only occasionally did they admit to the exhaustion and loneliness that also came with the territory. Protecting Adam's specialness and providing him with the means to develop his extraordinary intellectual gifts was a serious responsibility. They recognized and accepted it and served it as best they knew how.

Over the years the Konantoviches developed a tight family system. They relied on each other for stimulation, security, and emotional sustenance. They knew many people through their professional contacts, interests in folk dancing and music, and educational quests on Adam's behalf, but they seemed to look toward each other for support and companionship. Adam's contacts with other children were often disappointing. He found little in the way of common interests and seemed ill-equipped to deal with the kinds of slights, disagreements, and conflicts that are common to interactions among youngsters. His social world became filled almost exclusively with adults. The Konantoviches built friendships for the family, just as they worked together to build Adam's education.

Before Adam turned to intensive study of music (which occurred at around age 8 years, just as the formal research was ending), his studies were fairly informal and unstructured. If possible, one parent served as guide through the domains he wanted to learn about; otherwise, they hired an outside tutor. Adam and his parents identified an extensive collection of areas to study (Feldman, 1986/1991). It seemed to me that he moved fairly frequently from topic to topic, weaving back and forth as interest and availability of instructors dictated. Fiona observed that he needed only to visit a domain briefly to understand it deeply. I, myself, observed relatively little of Adam's course of study firsthand, hearing about his current interests and accomplishments from his parents. From time to time, I wondered about some of the more subtle textures to Adam's learning. Were there, for example, some aspects of Adam's studies that were more resistant to mastery than others? How did he deal with concepts and skills that did not come easily? Did he feel some obligation to be brilliant, or was he relatively unconscious about the scope and depth of his intellect?

Adam's parents did not promote their son, but neither were they shy about his gifts, and the expectations for Adam's abilities and for his future were substantial. From early on Fiona and Nathaniel spoke of the major contributions he would be able to make to the world if he were afforded the education and stimulation his intellect required. Adam's success in matching these expectations was considerable, particularly in the domain of music. He had requested violin lessons when he was age 2 and began with Suzuki lessons about a year later. He also experimented with writing music. At age 4, he composed a solo violin piece he called *Hail to Gaul*. Fiona reported that his violin teacher, a violinist with the New York Philharmonic, described it as "exceedingly very difficult to play, but well worth the effort" (F. Konantovich, personal communication, March 8, 1983). Ten years later, he won an Aaron Copland Young Composers Award for a piece he had written on his 13th birthday, a bar mitzvah composition about coming of age as a Jew in the diaspora. Yet there was a certain grandiosity to the vision of Adam's future that may have become increasingly burdensome to him. For example, by Fiona's account, his mastery of the violin was exceptional from the very first. Adam's own recent assessment of his ability is that he is a good violinist but hardly a brilliant one, being particularly limited technically with respect to his intonation.

It was against a background of high expectations that Adam continued his studies into his teenage years. These studies increasingly focused on music. He worked first with private teachers near home and then flew weekly to the Cleveland Institute of Music for a day's worth of composition and instrumental lessons. These arrangements were not entirely satisfactory, however. Adam's access to the music faculty in Cleveland was limited, and the commute made his life feel more disjointed than it already was. His progress slowed somewhat, and he seemed to be less interested in continuing to work at a breakneck pace. He and Fiona would sometimes become impatient and short with each other when she tried to supervise his practicing or studying. Fiona began to feel that Adam was becoming undisciplined, and Adam began to feel that Fiona was trying to manage too much of his studies.

When Adam was 16, Nathaniel decided that Adam would benefit from more structure in his life. Other than his weekly commute to Cleveland, Adam had few lessons or regular obligations to help organize his time. Nathaniel felt that it was time for Adam to experience more typical rhythms and responsibilities in his life. He felt that Adam needed to learn to live more on his own, to be allowed to experience some failures and frustrations, to make friends, and to learn firsthand that "despite his enormous talents, he's more like other people than he is different" (N. Konantovich, personal communication, December 20, 1992). He enrolled Adam at a nearby state college that enjoys a good reputation for its music department. Although the music curriculum was not as challenging as it could have been, the school had the advantage of being close enough that Adam, who had never spent a night away from his parents, could commute. Fiona objected to Adam's matriculation on the grounds that it was a second-rank school—one where Adam might more reasonably be teaching rather than studying music—but the men prevailed, and Adam began his life as a college student.

Nearly coincidental with this change in Adam's life came a significant change in the Konantovich family itself. After nearly 30 years together, Nathaniel and Fiona separated in 1991. In some important ways, the mission to educate Adam may have been the glue that held the family together. With Adam's increasing ability to advocate for his own needs and to set the course of his own education, some of the bonds that held them together seem to have weakened and dissolved.

Perhaps paradoxically, Adam himself described the previous two years as the best ones of his life. Although watching his family's harmony become discordant has produced its share of pain, this time was also full of eager exploration and fun. His agenda in school was largely a personal one. He had a lot of catching up to do socially and described himself as "drinking up life like a dry sponge." He worked hard at his music, but it comprised only part of his life. In addition to being the music director of an all-college musical and setting William Blake's *Songs of Innocence* to music, he was busy making friends for the first time in his life, experimenting with being an adequate (rather than a brilliant) student some of the time, earning some money on his own, and just generally learning to take care of himself. As Adam reflected in 1992 on his experiences over the previous two years, he noted that the only thing that wasn't perfect was the absence of a girlfriend.

For years the Konantoviches focused their lives on the development of Adam's extraordinary gifts. As Adam finished his teenage years, he chose to focus more on his ordinary development as a young man. Seemingly confident and secure about his gifts, he felt the need to turn for a time to other, less developed parts of his life. In 1992 he was reluctantly planning on graduating from college this year at age 18, noting that he was having such a wonderful time that he would like to stay longer. His plan was to enter graduate school as a composition student, preferably at a university in another state.

The circumstances that have helped Adam learn how to nurture his talent according to his own agenda have in some ways been difficult. When he was a young child, Fiona and Nathaniel gave their son their own gifts of commitment, support, and energetic advocacy for his unusual needs. More recently, Adam has been able to take from them his independence and autonomy. As he takes charge of his life and talents it will be interesting to see how he chooses to focus his efforts.

Ricky Velazquez: A Passion for Playing

Unlike Nils, Mac, and Adam, Ricky's tenure as a child prodigy was relatively short. He began playing chess at about the age of 5 years, had gained a B-level tournament rating by age 8, and had given it all up by the time he was 10. Chess was simply a game to Ricky, not a way of being and thinking.

He liked many games, particularly team sports. These were, in fact, his first loves. He was an avid baseball player and later a talented soccer player. Even during the two or three years he played competitive chess the conflict between playing sports and tournaments was a keen one for him. Eventually, the sports won out.

Ricky, in fact, began his serious chess career when a broken collarbone sidelined him from his usual sports regime during the summer he was age 5. Bored with his enforced inactivity, Ricky began "fooling around with" the chess set his father had shown him some months earlier. When his family went to the local swimming pool, Ricky found that he could keep himself amused with a game or two with one of the parents there. By the end of the summer he could take on most of the adults he knew. He was hooked. He began to take lessons with Life Master John Collins, one of the doyens of the New York chess scene, and soon was making a good showing at local tournaments.

What Ricky seemed to like best about chess was the winning. He liked the competition and took some considerable pleasure in besting opponents four and five times his age. While clearly engaged by the intellectual challenges intrinsic to the game itself, Collins noted that Ricky did not appear to think "chessically"—to feel the logic and aesthetics of the game in his very bones. Despite his delight in cutthroat competition, Ricky was also a very sociable player. In fact, in earlier writings I had described him as the Pearle Mesta of the tournament scene (Feldman, 1986/1991). He would make his moves quickly and confidently and then be off to look at other boards and kibbitz with other players. This was in sharp contrast to general tournament ambiance of deep and quiet concentration. After a year or two, though, chess seemed to offer neither the kind of excitement nor the sociability that baseball did. In the end, it seemed that chess was too isolating. Not only was it a relatively solitary form of competition—just one-on-one—but it was a game that was beginning to set him apart from his friends, and this was a serious problem.

Ricky did not want to be different. Playing chess distinguished him too much from his classmates. In our 1992 conversation he noted that one of the reasons he quit the game was that the publicity he was receiving made him increasingly uncomfortable. And so, after several years of serious involvement, Ricky gave up chess and turned his attention full-time to physical sports. He still enjoyed the game, but he loved baseball more. His father encouraged this decision, for he felt that athletics was a more mainstream interest that would serve Ricky better in the long run.

By the time that Ricky was in middle school it was important enough for him to fit in with the other kids that he did not advertise his chess experience. He was similarly unassuming about his other abilities. Although academically gifted, Ricky downplayed his abilities at school, taking a casual attitude toward his studies (yet doing extremely well nonetheless). He was correspondingly modest about his athletic talent, emphasizing the importance of overall teamwork rather than his individual contributions. He did not seem to be interested in being outstanding if it meant standing out.

Although Ricky's accomplishments over the past 10 years are impressive, he is still low key about the extent of his achievements. He sailed through high school, playing chess briefly, first as a ringer on the high school team and then in regular tournament play for several months. He was surprised by the quality of his play, noting that he was much stronger in high school, even after 6 or 7 years' absence, than he had been when he was younger; he was now more disciplined and less focused on going straight for the win. Although Ricky (who now prefers Richard) enjoyed his return to chess, it soon slipped out of his stack of priority activities.

He had his pick of colleges and decided on one noted for its soccer team. There he played varsity with teammates who were among the best young players in the country. He enjoyed college, deciding that he would go to law school. He told me that he did not know exactly why or how he made the decision, just observing that it seemed like a good career. Richard decided that he did not want to settle down into another three years of school, however, so he and a friend went to Zimbabwe for a year to teach mathematics at a local high school and to play on the national soccer team. Richard's description of the year in Africa was also understated: it was "excellent, fun, the people were great" (Velazquez, personal communication, October 17, 1992).

Richard returned from Africa in 1989 and entered Columbia Law School. When I spoke to him in 1992 he was 26 and finishing his last year there. Throughout this period of his life he had also maintained his commitment to teaching and community service. Although the opportunity to play soccer in Africa was an exciting one, Richard had been equally drawn by the chance to teach math there. Back home, he had been a Big Brother in Harlem during his first two years in law school and had continued the teaching and tutoring he had done since high school. After working as a Stanley Kaplan tutor, Richard developed his own College Board review course. When we spoke, he was offering LSAT preparation classes that were taking up more of his time than his own studies.

At the time of our conversation Richard had been offered a position at one of the most prestigious New York City law firms and was planning to begin his professional life by practicing general law. I expect that the sharp analytic skills that allowed him to develop so rapidly as a young chess player will find a comfortable home with the law. In fact, the most energetic part of our conversation involved his cross-examination of my research methodology for this follow up. He questioned whether my information would stand up to serious scrutiny, how I might go about collecting compelling evidence, and what strategies I might take to shore up the limitations of a longitudinal research design.

Although he was positive about the prospect of being a lawyer, he neither seemed fascinated by the study of law nor wholly dedicated to its practice. It felt more like Richard had decided that being a lawyer will offer a reasonable way to make a living, but not necessarily a source of deep personal or intellectual satisfaction. I am sure that he will make an excellent attorney, but I wonder how much pleasure he will derive from it. In fact, he said that he does not expect his work to provide a deep-seated satisfaction. For the moment, he expected this part of his life to come from his involvement with friends and sports.

Richard wondered whether his life might not be too boring to merit further study, noting that he had stopped playing chess long ago and had not done anything really remarkable since then. He saw his life as progressing smoothly and steadily, without watershed events. Both work and play come easily for him; in fact, he observed that he regretted he had not learned how to work harder. Something always seems to have worked out for him, and Richard seems to have moved gracefully from opportunity to opportunity. He seems to lack the strong drive, focus, and connection to chosen work that Nils, Mac, and Adam display. His interests are more diversified, and his investment in any given part of his life seems correspondingly less intense. It will be interesting to see where Richard chooses to invest his energies in the future.

Billy Devlin and Franklin Montana: Two Cases (at Least Temporarily) Out of Service

My information about Billy and Franklin is less current, as I have lost touch with both of their families within the past few years (another hazard of longitudinal research). When I last heard of Billy in his family's annual holiday note around 1989, he had decided on a scientific career rather than a strictly mathematical one. After graduating from college at age 18 with joint majors in physics, astronomy, and English, he went to work at the Goddard Space Center—a place he had often visited as a youngster. His parents reported in their letter that Billy spent much of his free time playing music and had also taken up marathon running just for fun.

Billy's decision to study and work in a scientific field squares with the Billy that I had known 10 or 15 years ago, for he was always fascinated by a variety of scientific disciplines. His decision to major in English is one that I would not have expected. He was an extremely avid reader as a youngster, but it had seemed to me that his reading was more focused on mathematics, science, and science fiction than on literature. Perhaps the original research interest in Billy's quantitative skills had led to a focus on only a limited subset of Billy's interests at the time, or perhaps he became intrigued with more humanistic pursuits in high school and college. I am curious about how he is currently weaving these different intellectual threads.

I tried to contact Billy at Goddard in 1992 and found that he no longer worked there. His parents have also moved, and it seems as if the Devlin family is, at least temporarily, lost to me. I wonder whether Billy has gone to graduate school. Maybe I'll see him next spring at the Boston Marathon.

Franklin Montana had stopped playing chess by the time he was in junior high school, like his peer and sometime opponent Ricky Velazquez.

He wrestled for a time, competing at the state level in middle school, but wrestling, too, held his attention for only a year or two. In his early adolescence, Franklin was most interested in cultivating a variety of entrepreneurial concerns. He started a neighborhood house-sitting and snow-shoveling business at about age 10, which he parlayed into part ownership of a gas station and landscaping business by the end of high school. He then sold these and began dabbling, quite successfully, in the stock market.

Franklin's focus on financial concerns was not matched by his attention to his schoolwork. He completed high school with an undistinguished record and a somewhat limited set of college options. In this regard, Franklin had changed little since I had first met him. He was capable of directing unusually intense and focused attention toward those activities that captivated his interest and imagination. He was equally capable of ignoring much of what was happening around him if it was not intriguing. If the discussion in English class raised an interesting point, he might continue musing over it long after everyone else had moved on to another discussion (and he might bring up some point that was therefore unrelated to the current conversation). If he was not interested in his physics homework, he was very likely not to bother doing it, regardless of whether he annoyed or alienated people in the process.

When last I heard about Franklin, he was trying to transfer from a local community college to a more challenging school. Unfortunately, my version of his story ends rather abruptly there. Given that Franklin had consistently marched to his own drummer during the time that I knew him, I would not be surprised to find that he has continued to make his way according to his own rules since then.

Some Reflections of Prodigies' Development During Their Middle Years

The earlier work with these six boys sought to identify factors contributing to the expression of early prodigious achievement. As these children have grown into young men, some new issues have arisen with respect to these factors that would benefit from continued examination.

Talent, Motivation, and the Whole Child

As child prodigies approach the adolescent years they must necessarily shed their status as remarkable children. It is no longer enough for them to demonstrate unusual proficiency and insight for a child. If they are to continue to show extraordinary connection to the field, they must begin to develop the depth, expressivity, and subtlety that distinguishes world-class work from merely mature performance. For those prodigies who have pursued their talents through their early and middle childhoods, adolescence can represent the first time they seriously question their own abilities or experience significant, prolonged confusion or frustration with their studies.

Jeanne Bamberger (1982, 1986) has explored some of the dimensions of this period of doubt among gifted young musicians, dubbing it the "mid-life crisis." She suggested that this crisis is precipitated by changing demands for further mastery within the domain. To continue to grow, young musicians must transform their original understanding of music, which has been grounded in concrete, figural, and kinesthetic understanding of performance on an instrument, into an abstract, formal, conceptually driven system of knowing. This transformation is driven both by their own developing intellectual capacities and by the changing criteria for continued development within the music community itself. Technical prowess becomes less valued in and of itself and more as a vehicle for interpretation and communication with the audience. This transformation requires the prodigy to recognize the music at a different level, both conceptually and experientially. Although Bamberger has described this crisis of confidence specifically in terms of the lives of gifted musicians, it may be a more commonly occurring phenomenon that marks the transition out of the prodigy phase of mastery.

Whether prodigies continue to develop their talent is not only a question of whether they can make the intellectual transition to more abstract and interpretive ways of knowing, but whether their talents, themselves, can ripen and mature into individual, expressive forces. As these children approach the middle years of their training it becomes less impressive that they have passed certain milestones at particularly early ages and more important that they have something to say in their chosen medium or domain of expertise. It increasingly becomes the depth and richness of understanding, the power and grace of communication, that signals the presence of a serious talent, not the rate of mastery. The elements that contribute to the crafting of a mature talent may or may not necessarily be part of the collection of talents that characterize the child prodigy.

Even if a prodigy is blessed with a talent for substantial interpretive and expressive contributions, there is no guarantee that the child will be motivated to continue to develop that talent. One of the hallmarks of prodigies in their first years is that they are clear and insistent about creating opportunities for themselves to learn the subjects they love, often sweeping bemused and incredulous parents into action in response to the intensity of their interests. If prodigies do not continue to feel this commitment and dedication, the development of their special gifts may slow or stop regardless of the virtuosity of their talent. Those prodigies who do continue to pursue their original area of talent do so in large measure by maintaining their strong identification and commitment to the field. They retain their sense of direction and purpose, self-confidence, and focus on the practice of their craft. The importance of these factors are also emphasized in other researchers' formulations of talent development (cf. Csikszentmihalyi et al., 1993; Gruber, 1989; Horowitz & O'Brien, 1985; Howe, 1990, 1993; Renzulli, 1986; Sosniak, 1997).

Other motivational issues involve more general aspects of the children's development. Most parents of prodigies understand that they are raising children who are more than a violinist or a writer or a mathematician. Their children have additional needs and agendas that are also important to healthy development. When these needs are ignored or unrecognized, children are at risk, as a case like William James Sidis illustrates (Montour, 1977). When these issues are attended to, the focus may shift from the single-minded pursuit of talent, at least for a while. This may be clearest in my own sample in the case of Adam, whose efforts to achieve some separation and autonomy from his family have currently taken precedence over attention to more intellectual pursuits, but it is true of all the young men I have studied.

Domains and Fields

Prodigies are commonly found only in a relatively small number of domains: music (particularly instrumental performance), chess, visual and theater arts, and occasionally writing or mathematics (Feldman, 1986/ 1991). I am not aware of child prodigies in domains like medicine or law (although there are traditions of prodigious learning of religious texts, as in the case of Talmudic scholars).

Those domains that support early prodigious achievement seem to have certain characteristics in common. They are emotionally and experientially accessible to children. They involve the mastery of symbolic or notational systems and are well structured—they have clear rules for the production and manipulation of the elements of the domain. In mathematics, for example, the rules for arithmetic operations are well defined and explicit, and the behavior of mathematical objects under these rules is lawful. In the visual arts, children can develop techniques for rendering likenesses, depth, and texture. Such characteristics allow the young child an initial foothold into the domain and then support the acquisition of its fundamental conceptual and technical aspects: for example, developing the "felt paths" for musical expression (Bamberger, 1986); learning the patterns and possibilities of the chessboard; manipulating mathematical objects and learning canons for mathematical reasoning and argument; and exploring the expressive potential of language, paint, or clay.

Yet these characteristics may become less important the further one progresses in the domain, and this may be reflected in shifting criteria for outstanding performance. Evaluation of talent begins to focus on the development of increasingly abstract and complex conceptualization of domains, individual interpretation and reconceptualization of ideas, and personal expression of understanding. The characteristics of the domain that are most important for future work, for example, sensitivity to the subtleties of ideas and nuances of expression or the ability to recognize and develop interesting new problems, may be different than the ones that facilitated the prodigy's early achievements. Prodigies' gifts may or may not include strengths in these areas.

As prodigies grow older, they also begin to meet domains that were previously inaccessible to them, for example, philosophy, art criticism, engineering, business, even psychology. These may call on abilities and sensibilities that are similar to the ones prodigies had applied to their original domains of accomplishment and yet be engaging in their own way. They may also offer intellectual work that is more relevant to the adolescent's developing interests and goals, and prodigies may find themselves intrigued by the possibility of studying something new. It seems more than serendipity to me, for example, that Richard has selected a career that involves logical analysis, anticipation of opponents' moves, and the development of strategies for winning.

Because the achievements of prodigies appear so stunning, we may feel that these children have some kind of obligation to continue their commitment to their earliest expression of ability. But, just as the changing demands of the domain may result in a mismatch with the prodigy's particular talents and strengths, it is possible that in the end the developing interests and abilities of the prodigy are better matched to some other area of intellectual work. Thus, it is important that child prodigies retain the opportunity to be captivated by the exercise of their talent, but not captured by it. Albert (1994) has made this point as well.

Prodigies must also begin to participate in the culture of the field if they are to continue to develop (Csikszentmihalyi & Robinson, 1986; see also Gardner, this volume, chapter 4). There is no guarantee that the prodigy's earliest appearing talent includes the abilities and accommodations required to negotiate successfully the more socioculturally based elements of practice. Those prodigies who are willing and able to enter into the culture of the field will have created conditions that are most supportive and favorable to their continued development within the domain. Those who are either unwilling or unable to do so are less likely to continue to develop at the forefront of the field's mainstream.

This is not to suggest that very talented individuals (prodigies and others) unwilling to play by all of the rules of their fields are necessarily prohibited from making important contributions, only that it is harder. There are cases of individuals who have made principled decisions to pursue work that is out of favor with the existing *zeitgeist* in their fields (see, for example, Keller, 1983). However, without an understanding of the canons of performance and communication established by the field and without some level of support from colleagues or powerful players in the field, it is difficult to make a living practicing one's craft.

Finally, with reference to domains I think that it is noteworthy that three of the children I have studied—half of the original group—are now actively involved in music and that a fourth plays a variety of instruments for fun. I am not sure what this means, but I feel it is important. There is something very immediate, compelling, and perhaps uniquely accessible about music within the human experience. Although its forms vary across cultures, no society is without music as a powerful source of communication and expression. Because it is accessible at an emotional as well as a conceptual level, there is a way in which virtually everyone can welcome music into their lives. Not all of us can become expert performers, but nearly everyone forges some kind of connection to music, even if it is only to sing in the shower or dance in the car at the stoplight with the radio turned up high. Perhaps someday we will know more about why music seems to enjoy a privileged status within the realm of experience and accomplishment.

Teachers

Without new observations of the study participants and their teachers, it is possible only to speculate about the nature of the teacher–prodigy relationship during prodigies' middle years. From the boys' conversations and from other researchers' observations, it is possible to sketch some of the dimensions of this relationship, which could serve to direct future investigation.

The teaching of prodigies during the first phases of their development involves introducing them to the fundamentals of the domain (as it would any aspiring novice), but teachers of prodigies have the additional challenge of creating an educational environment for a child who is learning at an extrordinarily rapid rate. Prodigies present strong developmental asynchronies. They learn a specific domain very quickly (or at least, they learn aspects of a specific domain with unusual speed), but in many other psychosocial and cognitive respects they still function as young children. Yet simply accelerating a standard curriculum may not be the best way to promote prodigies' development, because such acceleration may presume more general maturity or cognitive sophistication than such children possess. The disparity between the maturity of the person and that of the talent presents a particular challenge to the teachers of prodigies. The kinds of pedagogical decisions that teachers make for prodigies are not necessarily the ones that they would make for students learning at a more typical pattern and pace. Eventually, many first teachers pass their prodigious students on to others who are more experienced in developing talent of significant proportions (Bloom, 1982). And because prodigies make this shift when they are still quite young, the new teacher must also keep in mind that, overall, the children displaying these talents are not as mature as their gifts would suggest. By exploring the similarities and differences in pedagogical approaches that teachers take to the education of prodigies and to their less precocious students, we may learn more about the intellectual structure of the discipline.

As prodigies master the technical and conceptual fundamentals of their domains, their teachers can begin to concentrate on exploring possibilities for multiple ways of representation, conceptualization, and expression. Teachers begin to guide their students toward internalizing the field's particular methods, values, and ways of thinking and performing. They encourage their students to become thoughtful and reflective critics of their own work and to develop their own voices.

Some master teachers approach the task of acculturating their most talented students by establishing a certain distance from them, demanding complete commitment to the discipline and loyalty to the teacher's regimen for advanced training (Bloom, 1982). Yet adolescence is a time of possibility and choice, of introspection and reflection, and teachers of adolescent prodigies may find that their requiring blind allegiance to a regimen or particular perspective feels too constraining or controlling for a youth beginning to imagine a world of options and opportunity. Adolescence is also a time for recognizing others' thoughts and accomplishments and for exploring one's own place in the world relative to these. Such an approach may alienate students who feel that there is no room for them to acknowledge their own individuality. Teachers may also find that some prodigies begin to experience challenges in their studies, which lead to a need for a kind of support and encouragement that was previously unnecessary. Some teachers, like Nils's, are able to sustain their students through slumps and moments of uncertainty; others are not. Those who are unable or unwilling to do so may increase the likelihood that their students will turn their attention to other pursuits.

Families

During prodigies' early development the support and assistance of their families are of central importance. Although the children provide most of the energy and determination necessary for pursuing their interests, they cannot secure the opportunities they need to develop their talent all alone. Usually the responsibility for mobilizing and monitoring the required resources falls to one (or both) of the parents; this can easily develop into a demanding and involving task. The nature and extent of parental involvement may vary. In some families it is limited to putting in the extra time and resources needed to create opportunities for their child—for example, arranging for lessons; making visits to libraries, museums, and lectures; providing the transportation to all of these various events; assuming the financial responsibilities for these activities; and making allowances in the daily flow of family life to accommodate the prodigy's special needs. In other families the involvement extends deeper as parents and prodigies forge unusually strong alliances to support and foster the development of extraordinary talent. In some cases, parents give up their own careers to promote the continued progress of their children; relocate to be near teachers, schools, or cultural centers; or divide the family so that the prodigy's education can continue. In all cases, the families of prodigies make adjustments, reorganizations, and sacrifices to accommodate the pursuit of prodigious talent.

Although prodigies need a high degree of family commitment, availability, and support in their early years, this changes with time. If they are to continue to grow, adolescent prodigies must begin to develop separate and autonomous lives, both with respect to their areas of talent and with respect to their own psychosocial development. If this requires the reworking of well-established patterns of interdependence that had earlier served an important function in the family, this period of family life could be one of upheaval and conflict.

In fact, the adolescences of the boys I have studied have been relatively calm—more so than I had expected 9 or 10 years ago. They developed independence and self-confidence, autonomy and self-reliance. Several had made educational choices at very young ages that required large amounts of personal responsibility. Billy left home to attend a nearby college at age 13, Adam was jetting off once a week to Cleveland for the day when he was 14, and Nils was living on his own in New York City before he was old enough to drive. The boys' parents seem to have facilitated the process of individuation by respecting their sons' judgment and giving them the space to grow up without trying to challenge or control them in a way that required the boys to grow away. As young men, they generally seem to enjoy close, caring, and warm relationships with their parents.

Other researchers have explored the development of gifted adolescents with relation to particular family variables and dimensions such as independence, cognitive style, and family complexity (Albert & Runco, 1989; Rathunde, 1991). These studies point to the importance of the family environment for acculturating children into a set of values, expectations, and strategies for engaging in productive work. Although this process is an ongoing one that begins at birth, it may become particularly salient as children begin to take charge of the management of their own talent.

Questions and Directions for Future Research

Tracking the Specifics of Talent as It Develops

There remains much to be known about what, exactly, child prodigies know and understand about their domains and about how prodigious talent develops over time. If we are to extend our understanding we must make more detailed, domain-based studies of how such talent develops. Despite abilities that are remarkably advanced for children, prodigies are neither mature nor faultless practitioners. It is important to learn more about how their understanding develops. It is particularly important to take a critical stance toward exploring the outer edges of their understanding and ability, for it is at the places where understanding is stretched or still shaky that the intellectual action is likely to proceed.

By gathering a number of detailed case studies within a particular domain—for example, musical performance, visual arts, mathematics, or writing—we could begin to develop a more general picture of the course of prodigious development within specific fields. We may also want to compare patterns of development for children who make early entries into domains with those of students who begin serious study at a later age. Comparisons of this sort will provide information about whether it is the rate of mastery alone that characterizes early prodigious achievement or whether the structure and nature of prodigies' understanding is different.

Although in-depth explorations are crucial for extending the understanding of the phenomenon of early prodigious achievement, they are difficult to accomplish. Work of this kind demands a wide range of expertise: a sophisticated understanding of the particular domain or domains under investigation, a psychological perspective on issues of development and transformation, and the ability to collaborate with both prodigy and teachers. Because of this requisite mix of abilities, significant work of this kind may require a collaborative venture.

Early Prodigious Achievement in Girls

The study of child prodigies has essentially been the study of boys (Goldsmith, 1987). Before we can be confident that we understand the factors contributing to the development of prodigious talent in all of its forms, we will need to know much more about the abilities and experiences of talented girls. Because we have primarily anecdotal information about the lives and work of a few female prodigies who have gained media attention (Goldsmith, 1987, 1992; Goldsmith & Feldman, 1989; Winner, 1996), systematic research on this issue will have to begin with some fundamental questions: How are gifted young girls identified, what are their areas of talent, what are their educational experiences, what are the supports or impediments to the development of their talent, how does the process of developing their talent compare with that of boys, and how do they fare as adults? When we can answer questions like these, we will have a more complete picture of the phenomenon of early prodigious achievement and a more articulated understanding of the factors contributing to its occurrence.

Exploring the Nature of the Teacher–Student Relationship

We currently know little about the dynamics of the educational partnership between teacher and student. Exploring this relationship would illuminate both our understanding of the developmental course of early-appearing talent and also our knowledge of effective ways of facilitating that development. For example, how does the unusual mixture of childlike and adult sensibilities we find in the prodigy (Baumgarten, 1930) affect teachers' decisions about the structure, organization, and content of lessons? Some teachers of prodigies are deliberate about organizing lessons in spirited and playful ways that are designed to capture a child's interest; others take a more disciplined and adult approach to the work (Feldman, 1986/1991).

Are talented teachers of prodigies talented teachers in general? We do not know much about the important dimensions for gifted teaching of gifted students. Today's national climate of general educational reform has created an interest in understanding what makes master teachers of any kind (Goldsmith & Schifter, 1997; Lampert, 1990; Schifter & Fosnot, 1993; Shulman, 1987). Further study of teachers entrusted with fostering the development of unusual talent may help in general to articulate the dimensions of gifted teaching in general.

Attending to the Affective Aspects of Talent and Its Development

What does it feel like to be unusually talented, and how do these feelings influence the course of the prodigy's development, both as a child and as a prodigy? At present, we also know little about the affective side of talent development, yet it may be emotions that are the prime drivers of the process (Csikszentmihalyi & Csikszentmihalyi, 1993; Csikszentmihalyi et al., 1993). Interest, passion, competitiveness, and the joy of mastery all move these children toward achievement. Confusion, frustration, and loss of confidence makes the mid-life crisis an important turning point in the lives of many.

Similarly, prodigies' feelings about themselves may also mediate their interpersonal relationships. In what ways do they feel different from other children, and how does this influence their peer relations and self-image? We can learn much about the experiences of child prodigies, and perhaps also about the intersection between thought and feeling in general, by paying attention to the affective side of their development.

Conclusion: Development of Mature Talent

What does it mean to have been a child prodigy? This question raises issues about the phenomenology of the experience for the prodigy and about societal decisions regarding national investment in talent development. With respect to this latter issue, we must ask whether prodigies are gifted in ways that will allow them to mature into creative, or even expert, practitioners of their domains (Goldsmith, 1987, 1990; Wallace & Gruber, 1989). Does the study of child prodigies further the goal of improving the identification and education of individuals at promise for significant contributions to socially valued domains?

The answer to these questions may be no. By and large, the children I have studied have not gained national attention for their work, although they are still young enough that they may yet do so in the future. Some have long since given up their original areas of achievement, so if they are to develop national visibility, it will be in some other domain of accomplishment. If we are interested in understanding how to nurture talent that will lead to adult expertise and creativity, perhaps we should focus on the development of promise in older individuals—adolescents or young adults. This would offer a focus population that is more likely to continue to pursue their identified talent. It would also allow us to choose individuals working in domains that are viewed as important for the well-being and advancement of the nation.

With respect to the individual development of talent, the study of prodigies may be quite informative. Research on child prodigies has pointed to the importance of understanding the contributions of a number of different factors to the development of individual gifts. It has emphasized that the process of talent development is dependent on the match between individual interests and proclivities, the structure and organization of particular domains, and the support of a variety of environmental enablers. By studying child prodigies as striking examples of the successful interaction among these factors, we may learn much about how to support and educate the gifts of many individuals.

But because the prodigy presents such striking complementarity between individual and domain at such an early age, understanding the phenomenon of the child prodigy will probably not provide the key that unlocks the secret of how to best develop talent in general. (Surely there is no single key, nor a single secret, in any event.) At the very least, though, it helps us to understand the importance of responding to the expression of strong interest and commitment to learning. Perhaps the most striking characteristic of child prodigies is their intense involvement with their studies, their desire to master, and their eagerness to know. These are the qualities that mobilize their parents to action, more than the maturity and sophistication of their accomplishments. If we are committed to creating optimal conditions for fostering the development of talent in our society, then we must be responsive to the expressions of interest and the desire to learn. If we are, then regardless of whether particular individuals go on to make remarkable progress or significant contributions, we will have provided them with the opportunity to do satisfying work.

References

Albert, R. (1994). The achievement of eminence: A longitudinal study of exceptionally gifted boys and their families. In R. F. Subotnik & K. D. Arnold (Eds.), *Beyond Terman: Contemporary longitudinal studies of giftedness and talent* (pp. 282–315). Norwood, NJ: Ablex.

Albert, R. S., & Runco, M. (1989). Independence and the creative potential of gifted and exceptionally gifted boys. *Journal of Youth and Adolescence, 18*(3), 211–230.

Bamberger, J. (1982). Growing up prodigies: The mid-life crisis. In D. H. Feldman (Ed.), *Developmental approaches to giftedness and creativity* (pp. 61–77). San Francisco: Jossey-Bass.

Bamberger, J. (1986). Cognitive issues in the development of musically gifted children. In R. J. Sternberg & J. E. Davidson (Eds.), *Conceptions of giftedness* (pp. 388–413). Cambridge, England: Cambridge University Press.

Baumgarten, F. (1930). *Wunderkinder psychologische untersuchungen*. Leipzig, Germany: Johann Ambrosius Barth.

Bloom, B. S. (1982). The master teachers. *Phi Delta Kappan, 63*, 664–667.

Bloom, B. S. (Ed.). (1985). *Developing talent in young people*. New York: Ballantine Books.

Csikszentmihalyi, M., & Csikszentmihalyi, I. S. (1993). Family influences on the development of giftedness. In G. R. Bock & K. Ackrill (Eds.), *The origins and development of high ability* (Ciba Foundation Symposium Series, Vol. 178, pp. 187–206). Chichester, England: Wiley.

Csikszentmihalyi, M., Rathunde, K., & Whalen, S. (1993). *Talented teenagers: The roots of success and failure*. Cambridge, MA: Cambridge University Press.

Csikszentmihalyi, M., & Robinson, R. (1986). Culture, time, and the development of talent. In R. J. Sternberg & J. E. Davidson (Eds.), *Conceptions of giftedness* (pp. 264–284). Cambridge, England: Cambridge University Press.

Feldman, D. H. (1979). The mysterious case of extreme giftedness. In A. H. Passow (Ed.), *The gifted and talented: Their education and development* (pp. 335–351). Chicago: National Society for the Study of Education.

Feldman, D. H. (with Goldsmith, L. T.). (1991). *Nature's gambit: Child prodigies and the development of human potential.* New York: Teachers College Press. (Original work published 1986)

Feldman, D. H., & Goldsmith, L. T. (1989). Child prodigies: Children straddling two worlds. In *Health and medical update* (pp. 32–51). Chicago: Encyclopedia Britannica.

Goldsmith, L. T. (1987). Girl prodigies: Some evidence and some speculations. *Roeper Review, 10*(2), 74–82.

Goldsmith, L. T. (1990). The timing of talent: The facilitation of early prodigious achievement. In M. J. A. Howe (Ed.), *Encouraging the development of exceptional skills and talents* (pp. 17–31). Leicester, England: British Psychological Society.

Goldsmith, L. T. (1992). Stylistic development in a Chinese painting prodigy. *Creativity Research Journal, 5*(3), 1–13.

Goldsmith, L. T., & Feldman, D. H. (1989). Wang Yani: Gifts well given. In W.-C. Ho (Ed.), *The brush of innocence* (pp. 51–62). New York: Hudson Hills.

Goldsmith, L. T., & Schifter, D. (1997). Understanding teachers in transition: Characteristics of a model for the development of mathematics teaching. In E. Fennema & B. S. Nelson (Eds.), *Mathematics teachers in transition* (pp. 19–54). Mahwah, NJ: Erlbaum.

Gruber, H. E. (1989). The evolving systems approach to creative work. In D. B. Wallace & H. E. Gruber (Eds.), *Creative people at work* (pp. 3–15). New York: Oxford University Press.

Horowitz, F. D., & O'Brien, M. (1985). Epilogue. Perspectives on research and development. In F. D. Horowitz & M. O'Brien (Eds.), *The gifted and talented: Developmental perspectives* (pp. 437–454). Washington, DC: American Psychological Association.

Howe, M. J. A. (1990). *The origins of exceptional abilities.* Cambridge, England: Basil Blackwell.

Howe, M. J. A. (1993). The early lives of child prodigies. In G. R. Bock & K. Ackrill (Eds.), *Ciba Foundation Symposium 178: The origins and development of high ability* (pp. 85–105). Chichester, England: Wiley.

Keller, E. F. (1983). *A feeling for the organism: The life and work of Barbara McClintock.* New York: Freeman.

Lampert, M. (1990). When the problem is not the question and the solution is not the answer: Mathematical knowing and teaching. *American Educational Research Journal, 27*(1), 29–63.

Montour, K. (1977). William James Sidis, the broken twig. *American Psychologist, 32,* 265–279.

Rathunde, K. (1991, April). *Family influences on interest and talent development.* Paper presented at the annual meeting of the American Educational Research Association, Chicago, IL.

Renzulli, J. S. (1986). The three ring conception of giftedness: A developmental model for creative productivity. In R. J. Sternberg & J. Davidson (Eds.), *Conceptions of giftedness* (pp. 53–92). Cambridge, England: Cambridge University Press.

Schifter, D., & Fosnot, C. T. (1993). *Reinventing mathematics education: Stories of teachers meeting the challenge of reform.* New York: Teachers College Press.

Seidenbaum, A. (1961, June 9). Paintings by a prodigy. *Saturday Evening Post,* pp. 36–37.

Shulman, L. S. (1987). Knowledge and teaching: Foundations of the new reform. *Harvard Educational Review, 57,* 1–22.

Sosniak, L. A. (1997). The tortise, the hare, and the development of talent. In N. Colangelo & G. A. Davis (Eds.), *Handbook of gifted education* (2nd ed., pp. 207–217). Boston: Allyn & Bacon.

Wallace, A. (1986). *The prodigy.* New York: Dutton.

Wallace, D. B., & Gruber, H. E. (Eds.). (1989). *Creative people at work: Twelve cognitive studies.* New York: Oxford University Press.

Winner, E. (1996). *Gifted children: Myths and realities.* New York: Basic Books.

Part II

Giftedness and Cognition

Is it appropriate that development typically is seen as discontinuous? How good are the chances that high potential will, in fact, be realized, and what are the essential conditions for its emergence? In chapter 6, "Cognition, Development, and Exceptional Talent in Infancy, " John Colombo, D. Jill Shaddy, and W. Allen Richman provocatively review and challenge the arguments for discontinuity of intellectual development and summarize evidence for the continuity of intellectual development from infancy. They propose that the discontinuity conclusion is an artifact of inappropriate assessment. This proposal is consistent with Howard Gardner's (chapter 4) framework, and their conclusion that there are indeed links between infant preverbal cognition and later giftedness is couched in language similar to David Henry Feldman's (chapter 12)—that is, new measures provide evidence for the risk of exceptionality, not a guarantee—and includes the caveat that intervention is required to ensure that later giftedness is realized. Intervention in many forms is well illustrated in the case studies that inspire this and several other chapters.

In "Life-Span Cognitive Giftedness: The Development of Relativistic Thinking," chapter 7, MaryLou Fair Worthen unravels some of the complexity of relativistic thinking in 100 research participants from ages 12 through 82 and other groups. Her observations that early differences in relativistic thinking (e.g., perspective taking, compromising, negotiating, and managing uncertainty) may level off in time raise questions repeated elsewhere in this book: Is the apparent leveling off an artifact of insufficiently sensitive instruments or unsupportive life experiences? Are early signs of such thinking (e.g., awareness of interconnectedness of rules in different settings such as home and school) indicative of the webbed knowledge base that distinguishes experts? Do the skills of more able adults decline more because they reached a higher peak? Worthen cautions that the passage of time alone offers little to intellectual development. She hypothesizes that relativistic thinking may be one of the vehicles that allows cognitive giftedness to continue to grow well past adolescence, and she aptly demonstrates its growth, and sometimes decline, as a component of exceptional thinking.

Bruce M. Shore concludes part II with an overview of several years of research that partially maps the existence and nature of several domain-general characteristics of expertise (cf. Keating, 1990), although these are expressed in specific contexts, most often mathematics and science. Chapter 8, "Metacognition and Flexibility: Qualitative Differences in How Gifted Children Think" concentrates on two of these domain-general abilities that are discernible across ages from early childhood onward. These studies collectively address metacognition and flexibility from three perspectives: qualitative differences in thinking, the nature of the development of children's skills toward adult competence, and the smoothness or continuity of this development. The review reveals several conclusions. First, the nature of high ability becomes more complex with age and gifted children are distinguished largely by their enhanced ability to call on a repertoire of intellectual skills that are, nevertheless, typically available to others. Similar types of differences were observed across ages, but gifted children's performance did not match that of experts in all respects, and the concept of *novice* warrants study. Second, cognitive components are necessary but not sufficient parts of a definition of giftedness. The roles of motivation, formally learned knowledge, and domain-general habits of mind are large. Third, some of the development is continuous or smoothly progressive toward adult levels, and some is discontinuous. For example, there appears to be a relatively smooth development of monitoring and self-evaluation, key parts of metacognition, but large leaps are evident in preference for complexity and working with a plan. Adult models of exceptional intellectual performance are useful as frameworks, but children's performance is not adult-like in every way.

Reference

Keating, D. P. (1990). Charting pathways to the development of expertise. *Educational Psychologist, 25,* 243–267.

6

Cognition, Development, and Exceptional Talent in Infancy

John Colombo, D. Jill Shaddy,
and W. Allen Richman

The purpose of this chapter is to address some of the issues surrounding giftedness and exceptional talent (G/ET) in the cognitive or intellectual domain during infancy. We write this chapter as developmental psychologists with a research focus on early cognition. As such, we are outsiders to the field of giftedness and gifted education. However, our perusal of the extant literature on G/ET suggests that considerations of early development, and of infancy in particular, have long been salient in the field. Indeed, this literature suggests that G/ET researchers have long understood the potential importance of studying infancy for understanding the development of G/ET (Bock & Ackrill, 1993; Dalzell, 1998; Gardner, 1993; Gottfried, Gottfried, Bathurst, & Guerin, 1994; Horowitz & O'Brien, 1985, 1986; Klein & Tannenbaum, 1992; Obler & Fein, 1988; Storfer, 1990; Subotnik & Arnold, 1994a; Zigler & Farber, 1985) and for the possible early identification of individuals who may attain the status of G/ET (Gottfried et al., 1994; Gross, 1999; Horowitz, 1992; Shaklee, 1992; Sternberg, 1993; Tannenbaum, 1992). As such, we assume that a developmental approach to the study of G/ET would presumably represent a viable, desirable, and ultimately useful research program.

In the course of addressing this fundamental purpose, we hope to attain several goals. First, we will review the extant literature on the prediction of cognitive and intellectual status from infancy in the hope that this will draw interest to the study of cognitive processes in infancy and early childhood as a possible component of research on the development of G/ET. Second, by reviewing some of the traditional approaches for studying early manifestations of G/ET, we hope to turn the reader's attention to current approaches to developmental causation. These approaches

Preparation of this chapter was supported in part by NIH grants MH14326, HD29660, and HD35903. Jeff Coldren, Janet Frick, Reva C. Friedman, Frances Horowitz, Aletha Huston, Wayne Mitchell, Dale Walker, and John Wright have all offered comments and discussion on the issues presented here. Thanks are also due to Meredith Porter and Sheila Gorman for their assistance at various times in the production of the many final versions of this chapter.

provide what is perhaps a more accurate account of developmental processes and determinants than the traditional nature–nurture dichotomy. In addition, however, we believe that these approaches call for a careful consideration of developmental course in the empirical investigation of emergent phenomena, and we hope to build an argument that the future of research on the development of G/ET will require an intensive longitudinal approach.

Having laid out what we hope to do, we think it may be useful for the reader to consider some limitations that we acknowledge in addressing this literature. First, we are cognizant that the concept of G/ET is not a simple one. Previous authors in the field have noted that the definition of G/ET is complexly determined (Renzulli, 1998; Sternberg, 1993; Sternberg & Davidson, 1986). Although G/ET may begin with some precocious or advantageous characteristic, the presence of such a characteristic per se is not a sufficient condition for ultimately classifying an individual as having G/ET status. The classification also depends on, for example, the value placed on the traits by the individual (e.g., whether the individual attains or retains motivation to achieve within the domain of precocity). It also depends on the degree to which the individual's precocity/advantage is valued by his or her immediate social environment. We find this conceptualization of G/ET to be compelling. We also find these latter sets of determinants to be beyond the reach of prediction from early in life. As such, we find it unreasonable to make a claim for the possibility of predicting G/ET status from infancy. What we think we may be able to do, however, is build a reasonable argument for the possibility of detecting precocity in some domains of cognitive function during infancy. That is, although it may not be feasible to expect the ultimate bestowal of the G/ET classification, it may be possible to detect the precursors that indicate some promise (or risk) for that classification.

Can Cognitive Precocity Be Detected in Infancy?

We attempt this task by first reviewing the more general literature on the prediction of cognitive–intellectual status from infancy and then reviewing the data that exist on the identification of G/ET itself from infancy.

General Prediction of Cognitive Status From Infancy

The current status of the literature on the prediction of later intelligence from early cognitive measures in infancy is clearly relevant to the consideration of early detection of G/ET. In the past decade, there has been a considerable amount of work in this area. Our own research program at the University of Kansas has been concerned for more than a decade with the prediction of cognitive and intellectual status from infancy, although research on this topic obviously precedes our involvement. In our view (see also Bornstein, Slater, Brown, Roberts, & Barrett, 1997), this literature has progressed through three distinct periods, which are reviewed in chronological order below.

Belief in the discontinuity of intelligence from infancy. From the 1950s through the early 1980s, it was known that intellectual function stabilized within individuals at some point during childhood (e.g., Stott & Ball, 1965). However, it was also routinely taught that such stability of intellectual function did not extend from any point earlier than perhaps the third or fourth year of life. The basis for advocating the "discontinuity" of intellectual function from infancy and toddlerhood was strongly empirical in nature. Indeed, the position was based on the pattern of correlation between performance on standardized infant assessments (such as Cattell, 1940; Gesell & Amatruda, 1947; & Bayley, 1970) with later IQ test performance. Comprehensive reviews (see, e.g., McCall, 1979, 1983) have shown that such standardized assessments of infant development administered during the first year of life correlated very poorly (only about +.10) with intelligence or cognitive achievement later in childhood. However, the predictive power of these tests begins to rise somewhat during the second and third years, such that correlations attain magnitudes of over +.50 by the end of the third year (McCall, 1979).

The most widely accepted explanation for this increase in prediction was that intellectual function was *discontinuous* from this early period of life, that is, those behaviors or domains that could be considered as intellectual or cognitive competence during early infancy were qualitatively different from those behaviors or domains that constituted intellectual function at maturity. A plausible alternative position, however, was that intellectual function might indeed be continuous from infancy but that the traditional infant tests tapped skills that were largely irrelevant to later intellectual or cognitive function (Colombo, 1993). That is, the domains largely assessed on infant tests during the first year of life (gross and fine motor skills, simple sensory-motor coordination, and immediate and non-generalized imitation) might be irrelevant to individual differences in later cognitive development. This alternative position predicted that if one assessed skills or domains in infancy that overlapped more with those assessed at later ages, continuity for such skills might emerge.

Initial findings of continuity. In the early 1980s, a few reports emerged showing that a number of laboratory tasks that were designed to assess various cognitive and neurocognitive functions in human infants were significant predictors of language and intelligence test performance in childhood and adolescence. The reader may be referred to numerous other reviews of this area that have been published in the past decade (Bornstein, 1990; Bornstein & Sigman, 1986; Bornstein et al., 1997; Colombo, 1993, 1997; Colombo & Fagen, 1990; Colombo & Frick, 1999; Colombo & Janowsky, 1998; Colombo & Mitchell, 1990; J. F. Fagan, 1990; J. F. Fagan & McGrath, 1981; J. W. Fagen & Ohr, 1990; McCall & Carriger, 1993; McCall & Mash, 1995; Mitchell & Colombo, 1997; S. A. Rose & Feldman, 1990; Sigman & Mundy, 1993). However, it will suffice to note that measures designed to tap visual attention, recognition memory, long-term retention, reaction time, and anticipation of stimulus events during infancy have been consistently found to be moderately correlated with meaningful measures of language and cognitive status later in childhood and adolescence.

Relative to previous attempts at prediction, the general magnitude of the initial correlations reported for these measures was fairly striking. Although performance on standardized infant scales accounted for only about 1% of the variance in later intelligence (McCall, 1983), initial reports suggested that these measures accounted for up to 40% or 50% of the variance in the later measures (e.g., Rose, Slater, & Perry, 1986). Although such magnitudes represented extremes in the prediction literature, even the typical (median) level of prediction attained with these measures (about 20%; see Colombo, 1997) represented a substantial improvement over the traditional standardized infant scales. Of particular note was the fact that such prediction was realized with measures whose reliability rarely exceeded +.50 (Colombo, 1993). Given that the reliability of any instrument places mathematical constraints on its power to correlate with other instruments, it seemed that the arrival of reliable tools in early screening and identification awaited only refinement and further testing (Colombo, 1993). In spite of such promise, it has been duly and accurately noted that, although the ability to predict 20% of the variance may be theoretically important or relevant, it does not provide a level of prediction that is practically useful (McCall & Carriger, 1993).

Challenges to a simple model of prediction. The thoughtful reader will have probably noted by now that the literature reviewed so far is predicated on a relatively simple approach to developmental prediction. The research in this area has generally involved the assessment of infant cognitive performance at a few points (most often, only one). This belies an expectation that the processes that underlie such performance will remain stable across time and remain accessible later during the life span. This approach has yielded a level of prediction that is statistically relevant and thus has provided a valuable clue as to the general feasibility of the predictive endeavor. However, it is also true that the amount of variance accounted for by such early measures in later outcome measures has been limited. What factors may be responsible for such limited levels of prediction?

One possibility has to do with the reliability of the measures. Perhaps modest prediction is a function of modest reliability. If so, then if reliability is increased, the magnitude of prediction will be improved correspondingly. One problem for the field of early prediction that became evident during the 1990s was that improving the reliability of the infant measures was more easily said than done. Despite the use of tried-and-true psychometric techniques, attempts at increasing the reliability of the various predictive measures have been largely unsuccessful. For example, despite extensive standardization and item selection (Fagan & Shepard, 1986–1987), the internal consistency of infant recognition memory scores remains abysmal (Andersson, 1996; Benasich & Bejar, 1992). For example, aggregate measures of infant look duration (a measure of infant visual attention that has been reported to be negatively correlated with later IQ) generally show inconsistent and puzzling patterns of variability and reliability across ages (see Colombo & Frick, 1999). Thus, these measures do not appear to conform readily to the assumptions of the standard measurement or psychometric model. This may be due to the predominance of state variables in test performance during early infancy, to the influence of fundamental stimulus properties on cognitive measures, or perhaps to the fact that some variables exhibit distinct nonlinear developmental courses. In any event, such conditions would be to the strong disadvantage of prediction research that assumes a simple psychometric model.

A second problem is that the data also suggest that infant cognition may be more "modular" in nature than was previously believed (see, e.g., Rose & Feldman, 1995a, 1995b). Initial reviews of the literature (Colombo, 1993; McCall & Carriger, 1993) have suggested that the various measures of infant cognition correlated with one another and might thus be reducible to a single general underlying mechanism (or perhaps two mechanisms that were intercorrelated). If this were in fact true, it should be feasible to conduct limited assessments of this mechanism early in life and then expect that such assessments would predict to later manifestations of the same mechanism. However, in the case of multiple independent (i.e., "modular") cognitive mechanisms, such an approach would be problematic.

Evidence for this latter case was first provided by Jacobson et al.'s (1992) factor analyses of look duration, novelty preference, and reaction time. The notion has since been further supported by the observation that, although infant cognitive measures are sensitive to prenatal or perinatal exposure to environmental toxins, different measures appear to be sensitive to the effects of different toxins (Jacobson, Fein, Jacobson, Schwartz, & Dowler, 1985; Jacobson et al., 1993). For example, infant recognition memory is affected by prenatal exposure to polychlorinated biphenyls (PCBs, a toxic environmental pollutant) but not by prenatal exposure to alcohol (see also Singer et al., 1999); infant look duration is affected by prenatal exposure to alcohol but not by exposure to PCBs (see also Mayes, Bornstein, Chawarska, & Granger, 1995). In addition, infant look duration (but not recognition memory) is sensitive to some dietary enhancements in early life (Carlson & Werkman, 1995, 1996; Reisbick, Neuringer, & Gohl, 1997; Werkman & Carlson, 1996). Indeed, recent theoretical models of the processes that mediate individual differences in infant cognitive task performance (Colombo & Janowsky, 1998) suggest that the two most commonly used measures may well reflect the function of two independent neural substrates. The implication of such modularity is of particular importance for longitudinal work, in that if myriad independent cognitive functions may be assessed during infancy, not all measures will be equally sensitive or predictive at all times. Again, this is at odds with a simple psychometric approach to the problem of prediction.

Finally, the expectation that a measure taken early in life will predict to a measure taken later is based on the assumption that there will be no Ability × Environment interactions after the early measures of ability are taken. For example, in the absence of such an interaction, we might expect that memory at age 7 years would be strongly correlated with memory at 10 years. However, what if some 7-year-olds with poor memories received instruction in mnemonic strategies (i.e., what if the environment changed or adapted, depending on the particular strengths or deficiencies of individuals)? Of course, under those conditions, we would expect that correlation between memory abilities at ages 7 and 10 would be attenuated. The analogous situation with respect to the prediction literature would be that the infant's caregiving environment might interact with, for example, early attentional skills that are predictive over the long term. There is some evidence for simple additive effects of infant cognition and the quality of early interaction in determining cognitive outcome (Bornstein, 1985; Bornstein & Tamis-LeMonda, 1994; Mitchell, McCollam, Horowitz, Embretson, & O'Brien, 1991; Tamis-LeMonda & Bornstein, 1989). However, recent results from our laboratory suggest the possibility that a more complex set of interactions are probably at work. For example, at 6 months of age, infants' attentional profiles are correlated with some aspects of their mothers' interaction styles (e.g., Saxon, Frick, & Colombo, 1997). We cannot definitively say whether mothers are actively adjusting their styles or whether particular interactive styles are merely elicited by their infants' attentional characteristics. In any event, however, such covariance in and of itself raises the possibility that a simple causal model may not be appropriate. Furthermore, longitudinal data from a small sample of mother–infant dyads suggests that cognitive outcome is related to particular types of "matches" between the infant's attentional characteristics and caregiving styles in the immediate environment (Colombo & Saxon, in press). Again, this situation is at odds with a simple psychometric approach to prediction and, as such, has important implications for what must be measured, and how one must measure it, if a satisfactory level of prediction is to be attained.

Summary. This area of inquiry has evolved from the belief that prediction from infancy was not possible, followed by a reconsideration based on research guided by a simple model based on straightforward psychometric assumptions. Although this research showed prediction to be possible, the levels of prediction realized were not practically useful. Finally, the plot has thickened considerably in the past 5 years, and the extant data suggest that successful prediction may necessitate a careful consideration of many variables and the measurement of the developmental course of those variables across time. Indeed, we have shifted the emphasis of our own research program to such an intensive, prospective longitudinal approach, with some promising results (see Colombo, Harlan, & Mitchell, 1999).

Research on the Early Development and Identification of G/ET

The preceding sections clearly suggest that some modest prediction of cognitive ability is possible from infancy. As useful as this suggestion might be, this general literature has not directly addressed the question of whether the precursors of G/ET might themselves be detected in infancy. To do this, we now turn our attention to work that has specifically sought to predict or identify G/ET early in life.

Can the cognitive precursors of G/ET be identified during infancy? It appears to be a basic assumption within the literatures on G/ET and gifted education that the factors contributing to G/ET are operative very early in life. For example, there is a considerable amount of material on "gifted preschoolers" (Creel & Karnes, 1988; Gross, 1999; Isaacs, 1987; Klein, 1992; Koopmans-Dayton & Feldhusen, 1987; Lehweld & Friedrich, 1987; Moss, 1992; Sankar-DeLeeuw, 1999; Shaklee, 1992; Smutny, 1998; Williams & Gonzalez, 1998). The apparent acceptance of G/ET in pre-schoolers implies that the developmental course of G/ET begins before pre-school and may thus be in some way identifiable during infancy or toddlerhood.

Methodological considerations. Subotnik and Arnold (1994b) have provided a summary of several longitudinal studies on G/ET. The review and introduction to their edited volume (Subotnik & Arnold, 1994a) shows that, except for a very small ($n = 9$) study of the development of children's singing ability from ages 1 to 6 years (Davidson & Scripp, 1994), little or no longitudinal research on G/ET has included measurement during infancy or toddlerhood. Similarly, edited volumes on psychometric approaches to G/ET (Benbow & Lubinski, 1996) and the developmental determinants of G/ET (Bock & Ackrill, 1993) include virtually no data relevant to infants or toddlers. Interestingly, of an entire volume devoted to early manifestations of G/ET (Klein & Tannenbaum, 1992), only three chapters make any mention of infancy, and only one (Robinson & Robinson, 1992) presents data on children younger than age 4. Thus, perhaps one of the first conclusions that we can draw about research into the origins or early identification of G/ET is that, although many think the topic area is important, there is very little empirical work on the issue.

Some of what is available with respect to this topic exists as unsystematic retrospective reports of precocious talent in infants and toddlers. Indeed, there are many retrospective case studies of children who were eventually identified as G/ET in some domain or other that include anecdotal descriptions of precocious abilities as early as during the first year (Gross, 1992; Smith, 1996; Tannenbaum, 1992; see also Section III of Obler & Fein, 1988). One may take issue with many aspects regarding these kinds of data, but perhaps the most serious deficiency in such reports is that they represent only a portion of the universe of events that are relevant to the prediction or understanding of the early development of G/ET. Table 6.1 makes this point schematically.

Essentially, such reports provide a good example of what cognitive psychologists have called *hindsight bias* (Fischoff, 1975, 1982a, 1982b), in which knowing an outcome of an event will change one's perception of the

Table 6.1. Confirmatory Bias in Retrospective Reports

	Individuals Identified As	
Events/Talents Reported As	Exceptional	Nonexceptional
Exceptional	A	B
Nonexceptional	C	

Note. *A* denotes the type of data provided by retrospective case reports of G/ET individuals. *B* and *C* denote the type of important convergent data that are relevant and critical to the evaluation of prediction but that are often missing or not emphasized in such reports, although *B* does represent data that bear somewhat on reports of "failed prodigies."

inevitability or predictability of the event.[1] The report of exceptional events or talents in the life of someone who is eventually identified as G/ET unduly biases belief in the idea of the unequivocal (and perhaps inevitable) prediction of exceptionality. However, such reports do not provide information that is critical to the scientific evaluation of predictive validity. That is, they do not provide detailed reports of early unexceptional events or talents in individuals who are eventually classified as exceptional. In addition, such reports usually do not provide any sense of the base rate of exceptional events or talents in individuals who are not precocious. The literature on "failed" child prodigies (see, e.g., Radford, 1990; Tannenbaum, 1992) might well be a rich source of such data, but such cases have not been interpreted in this way and, as a result, have generally not been subjected to such statistical analysis.

The case study has an obvious place in the behavioral sciences (Cook & Campbell, 1979), but it does not substitute for large-scale nomothetic work with appropriate controls. What is necessary to draw proper conclusions about early signs of G/ET are prospective and longitudinal studies that seek to identify the precursors of G/ET from a sample that includes both gifted and nongifted individuals. This point has been made before (Horowitz, 1987; Horowitz & O'Brien, 1985, 1986; Robinson, 1987). However, to our knowledge, there has not been a review of the few studies that have G/ET in infancy from a longitudinal framework. We provide a brief summary of those reports that have followed participants from infancy in an effort to identify the precursors of G/ET.

Longitudinal studies of G/ET from infancy. The prospective studies of G/ET involving infants and toddlers generally fall into two categories. In one category, infants and young children are identified as G/ET by some criterion and are enrolled for further study. In some cases, the criterion is precocious performance on some standardized measure (e.g., Jackson, 1992; Robinson, Dale, & Landesman, 1990), whereas in others it may simply be nomination by a parent (Klein, 1992; Robinson & Robinson, 1992).

---

[1]The influence of hindsight bias is by no means limited to the social–behavioral sciences and education. Indeed, Gould (e.g., 1989) has written extensively about how hindsight bias has affected both scholarly and popular views of human evolution across the course of two centuries.

Robinson and Robinson cited data from several unpublished studies involving over 550 young children (ages 3–4 years) referred by their own parents as candidates for G/ET. Within this data set, over 250 of these children (i.e., 47%) actually tested in the gifted range on standardized assessments. Given a base rate of giftedness of between 2.0% and 2.5%, Robinson and Robinson suggested that parents are fairly accurate assessors of precocity in their own children. In addition, follow-up of those children who tested in the gifted range at these young ages indicated that they generally maintained their gifted status or increased their advantage over time.

Although such studies may be informative, however, they have not generally included infants or toddlers. Furthermore, they do not directly address the issue of whether G/ET can be accurately "picked out of the crowd" using measures taken in infancy. Our review of the literature shows only four published studies (involving three different samples) that do address this issue. These are reviewed below, with special emphasis on one truly prospective longitudinal project, the Fullerton Longitudinal Study (FLS).

Willerman and Fiedler (1974) retrospectively identified a sample of 100 children who at age 4 years were found to have IQs of 140 or above and who had been administered the Bayley Scales of Infant Development at age 8 months. Although the high-IQ group did have significantly higher mean Bayley scores on both the Mental ($p < .05$) and Motor ($p < .01$) subscales than control children drawn from the same population, the magnitude of the differences was less than 2 points on each of the subscales. Furthermore, the mean Bayley scores for the high-IQ sample were far from the exceptional range. The same sample was retested at age 7 years (Willerman & Fiedler, 1977), and the results were much the same. These findings are generally cited as evidence for the lack of continuity in high intelligence from infancy (e.g., Robinson & Robinson, 1992). It appears clear that these data do suggest that superior standardized test scores do not foreshadow precocious preschool performance in infancy. However, several cautions are warranted with regard to overinterpreting Willerman and Fiedler's (1974, 1977) data. First, it has been argued that first-year Bayley scores do not predict well to intellectual outcome in any population (McCall, 1983), such that the range of domains tested on the 8-month assessment would probably not include any domains relevant to the standardized IQ instruments administered at ages 4 and 7 (Colombo, 1993). Furthermore, Willerman and Fiedler's (1977) follow-up report indicates that, in fact, the mean IQ for the sample of 100 children at age 7 had dropped from "near-genius" level (i.e., 140+) at age 4 to slightly above 120. Thus, on average, by age 7, this sample would probably no longer be considered to be gifted.

Shapiro et al. (1989) subsequently reported the results of a similar study with a larger sample ($N = 200$) of infants who were tested on the Bayley Scales between ages 11 and 25 months and whose motor and language milestones were observed at various points between 2 and 24 months. Of this sample, 36 (18%) were identified as gifted based on a

WISC–R full- or subscale performance of 135 or above at age 7.5 years. Shapiro et al.'s data address some of the cautions raised with regard to Willerman and Fiedler's (1974, 1977) sample in that individuals actually meet standard criteria for G/ET at the final age point of the study. Essentially, Shapiro et al.'s findings replicate and bolster the Willerman and Fiedler (1974) results, in that the gifted group showed a number of statistically significant advantages over the nongifted group. However, Shapiro et al. noted that the early differences between the gifted and nongifted groups were not clinically significant: On average, the gifted group scored higher on the Bayley Scales by about 5 points, walked about 3 weeks earlier, and showed slightly steeper slopes of receptive and expressive language acquisition. A discriminant analysis of the various infant measures showed relatively weak sensitivity and specificity for the identification of the gifted and nongifted groups; of the 36 children age 7.5 years classified as G/ET, only 2 had Bayley scores of 135 or above. Of particular interest here was that even a Stanford–Binet administered at age 3 years did not predict gifted-group membership at a level of precision that was accurate for individual classification.

Perhaps the best-designed prospective longitudinal study for the early identification of G/ET is the FLS. In a clearly written, detailed, and systematic exposition (Gottfried et al., 1994), the authors described the recruitment of 107 infants at age 1 year and the longitudinal tracking of that sample through age 8 on measures within a number of psychological domains. The sample was selected from a population in the upper/middle socioeconomic status in anticipation of attaining higher proportions of G/ET than the national norm (i.e., about 2.0–2.5%). Indeed, by age 8, 20 of the 107 participants (18.7%) had been identified as G/ET, based on full-scale Wechsler IQ scores of 130 or above. At that point, the authors could inspect cognitive, achievement, personality, and home–environment data collected before the classification. In essence, this study provides the kind of design advocated by previous developmentalists who have attended to the G/ET literature (e.g., Horowitz, 1987, 1992). In return for this investment, the FLS has yielded particularly striking findings with regard to the development of cognitive intellectual giftedness. Gottfried et al. (1994) reported that gifted and nongifted groups are statistically indistinguishable at 1 year on the Bayley Scales, thus supporting the previous Willerman and Fiedler (1974, 1977) and Shapiro et al. (1989) studies. However, the group of infants who will eventually be classified as G/ET at 8 years separates sharply from the larger, nongifted group on the Bayley Scales shortly thereafter, showing mean differences of about 1 standard deviation (SD) at 1.5 years and nearly 1.5 SD at 2 years. Although the two groups remain statistically discrete at each of the measurement points reported through age 8, there are interesting age-related fluctuations. For example, the difference between the groups is reduced to 1 SD or less during years 2.5 through 5. It is not entirely clear whether this is caused by the introduction of different instruments (McCarthy and Kaufman Scales) for these age ranges, although the convergence of the two groups to within 1 SD is observed across both of these measures and persists with the introduction of the Wechsler tests at age 6 years. However, after age 6 the groups begin to diverge again, and by age 8 they are separated by more than 1.5 SD. Thus, the possibility that the different instruments may be differentially sensitive to G/ET during the preschool period cannot be ruled out definitively. However, these data provoke the hypothesis that there may be two developmental "spurts" that separate gifted from nongifted groups within the cognitive–intellectual domain. Furthermore, one of these is squarely set during the period of infancy and toddlerhood.

In addition to reporting means for the two groups, Gottfried et al. (1994) have provided individual graphs of the developmental profiles on standardized intellectual–cognitive test performance for all 20 of the children eventually identified as gifted. The authors declined to draw any sweeping generalizations from the individual graphs, although they did point out that each of the individuals showed at least one testing session during infancy with a standardized score at or above 130 on the Bayley Scales. In examining the graphs ourselves, we note a particular commonality among them, which is that in each of the 20 cases, the standardized score rises considerably between ages 1.0 to 2.0 years. In a few cases the rise is distinctly linear, whereas in some a rise occurs between 1 and 1.5 years and is maintained through 2.0 years, and in others the rise occurs between 1.5 and 2.0 years. In each case, however, the 2.0-year score is higher than the 1.0-year score.

It is of interest that this rise seems to occur irrespective of the fact that many of the infants showed standardized scores well above average at 1.0 year; that is, even infants testing at 120 at 1.0 or 1.5 years show such an increase. Furthermore, the fact that these are rises in standardized scores suggests that these infants are outstripping the norms at an extremely rapid rate. Gottfried et al. (1994) did not provide the individual graphs for all of the children eventually classified as nongifted and so it is not possible to determine the degree to which this exceeds the normal course of development across 1.0 to 2.0 years. However, it is the case that the average change for the nongifted group from 1.0 to 2.0 years is an increase of less than one-half a scale point.

Summary. Overall, the evidence on the prediction of G/ET from infancy and toddlerhood within the cognitive–intellectual domain shows a surprising concordance with the literature on prediction of general intellectual function from infancy. The large-scale retrospective studies indicate that group differences do exist between infants who are eventually identified as G/ET versus those who are not. However, although the differences are statistically reliable, they are not practically relevant in that they are not powerful enough for the classification of individuals (e.g., Shapiro et al., 1989). Like those studies of infant cognition that have been guided by a simple psychometric approach, the studies reviewed in this section may be taken to indicate the feasibility (but not the practical reality) of early identification of cognitive precocity leading to a G/ET classification. The one prospective study that has included a truly longitudinal approach (Gottfried et al., 1994) provides a strong suggestion that, if developmental course is carefully observed, G/ET may be evident in infancy, even with standardized scales that generally have not shown very good prediction to later IQ. It remains to be seen whether such findings are sample specific. However, it is worth noting that the study actually corroborates the more negative trends culled from "reconstructed" longitudinal designs featuring measures during the first year (Shapiro et al., 1989; Willerman & Fiedler, 1974, 1977) while at the same time showing the powerful nature of a careful and prospective longitudinal investigation. Indeed, Gottfried et al. (1994) have identified that G/ET within the cognitive or intellectual domains may emerge before the end of the second year; future work might be focused on this time period for more intensive study.

The extant data from both literatures suggests that the early detection of precocious cognitive ability during infancy is a feasible (if perhaps not a fail-safe) endeavor. Thus, we now turn to the issue of what the developmental origins of the early manifestations of G/ET might be. In so doing, we examine both traditional and current positions with respect to developmental causation.

From Where Do the Precursors of G/ET Come?
A Developmental Analysis

Nature–Nurture and G/ET

Questions about the origins of any behavior or personal trait usually leads to a discussion of the two obvious sources of behavioral variation (i.e., genes and environment).[2] It is thus possible to place speculations about the origins of the precursors of G/ET within the context of the nature–nurture debate (Atkinson, 1993). Traditionally, the nature–nurture model has been conceptualized in terms of two continuous, independent, parallel, and additive "streams" or "tracks" of developmental causation (see Figure 6.1).

Behavior–genetic studies. There has been some discussion of the possible genetic basis of G/ET, but the substance of this argument is usually based on a general discussion of the evidence for the heritability of IQ (e.g., Tannenbaum, 1992) rather than on the inheritance patterns of G/ET per se. However, Plomin and Thompson (1993) have conducted an analysis of the heritability of high ability. This was done by selecting MZ (monozygotic) (n = 29) and DZ (dizygotic) (n = 24) twins with IQ scores 1.25 standard deviations above the mean (this translates to an IQ of slightly

---

[2]It is worth noting that the best known early volumes in the area of G/ET are labeled *Genetic Studies of Genius* (Cox, 1926; Terman, 1925, 1930; Terman & Oden, 1947, 1959). However, it would seem that the word *genetic* in those publications might also reflect the archaic use of the term as a synonym for development (as in G. Stanley Hall's *Journal of Genetic Psychology*) rather than as an attribution of G/ET to biological inheritance.

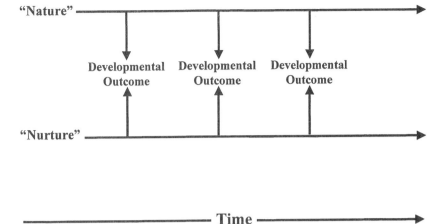

Figure 6.1. Paths of influence of genetic ("nature") and environmental ("nurture") determinants on individual development, according to the traditional nature–nurture model. Here, both genetic and environmental factors contribute to developmental outcome in an additive or independent fashion.

less than 120, which meets the more widely accepted criteria for G/ET). Plomin and Thompson reported a fairly high heritability of IQ for this selected subsample: 0.67 ± 0.24. Concordance for the high-ability classification was more than twice as high for the MZ twins than for the DZ twins. It is perhaps worth noting, however, that the value reported for the concordance for the MZ twins (i.e., 62%) was itself far from perfect; indeed, 11 of the 29 MZ pairs were discordant for high IQ (DZ concordance was 25%). Thus, although these data indicate some involvement of genetic factors in the distribution of high cognitive ability, it is obvious that genes are not its sole determinant.

This conclusion is echoed by other studies that have examined the relationship between giftedness in children and their parents. This approach, of course, does not conclusively support either side of the nature–nurture-inspired approach to G/ET, but the data are nonetheless valuable in informing various hypotheses about the G/ET's etiology. For example, Benbow, Stanley, Kirk, and Zonderman (1983) studied 35 families (children and both parents) of participants selected from the national Study of Mathematically Precocious Youth (SMPY) on the basis of scoring in the top 0.03% of the large ($N = 10,000$) longitudinal sample that comprises that project. In this study, these highly capable children were found to have highly capable parents, although it was also found that parents did not score as highly as their children on the various instruments administered to the sample. In a subsequent report, Benbow, Zonderman, and Stanley (1983) found that parents of such children were much more alike than is typically found in the general population. This suggests that the patterns of assortative mating may be somehow different for families with children who show exceptionality within this domain. Of further interest is the finding from that same article that children in this extremely capable group were less like their parents within their domain of excellence than is typically found in the general population. These results led the authors to two interesting conclusions. One was that "extreme giftedness cannot be predicted reliably solely as a result of the mating of bright parents" (Benbow, Zonderman, & Stanley, 1983, p. 153). Another was that "the etiology of individual differences at the high end of the distribution of intellectual abilities may *not* be similar to that in the rest of the distribution" (Benbow, Stanley, Kirk, & Zonderman, 1983, p. 151). Both points suggest that the determination of G/ET is complex.

Environmental studies. Other investigators have examined the early environment for clues to the determinants of G/ET, under the assumption that high-quality early environments can lead to exceptional cognitive outcome. Such work is always vulnerable to the criticism that environmental differences between gifted and nongifted groups might only be correlates of a G/ET genotype; however, in light of the literature reviewed in the preceding section, the strength of this contention is not particularly overwhelming.

In any case, the environmental evidence is suggestive but somewhat equivocal. Some of the musings on this point are based on retrospective analyses of case studies (e.g., Gardner, 1993). As noted previously, such evidence has its limitations, and negative findings often are more informative than are positive confirmations. For example, as Csikszentmihalyi and Csikszentmihalyi (1993) noted, "Highly creative individuals are likely to have had either very disrupted childhoods . . . or very good early environments" (p. 197). However, some good prospective and objective data on this issue are available. For example, Gottfried et al. (1994) reported that the parents of gifted children have a higher socioeconomic status and are better educated than those of nongifted children; gifted children also have fewer siblings and older parents (see also Barbe, 1956; Freeman, 1979) than nongifted children. Overall, Gottfried et al. found that the quality of the home environment of gifted children was remarkably more enriched than that observed for nongifted children. Moreover, the differences between the groups on this variable were not pronounced during infancy but were fairly marked at age 3 years and beyond. Interestingly, Gottfried et al. did not find that parents of gifted children had higher IQs than those of nongifted children.

Gottfried et al. (1994) examined global familial variables, but other investigators have provided a more fine-grained analysis of the interactions between gifted and nongifted children and their parents. Moss (1992; Moss & Strayer, 1990) studied dyads composed of 20 gifted and 20 nongifted children ages 3 to 4 and their mothers in problem-solving situations. Relative to mothers of nongifted children, the mothers of gifted children were more likely to engage in activities that solicited metacognitive activity on the part of their children during the problem-solving sessions (e.g., asking "what if" questions, encouraging the child to empirically test his or her assumptions within the session). They were also less likely to engage in activities that did not directly facilitate the child's understanding or solving of the problems at hand (e.g., directly providing the child with the solution to the problem, redirecting the child's attention to the task). In turn, the gifted children were observed to engage in more activities that reflected the use of metacognitive strategies. This finding would normally elicit chicken-and-egg questions about the nature of the interaction (i.e., were mothers encouraging metacognitive activity in their gifted children, or were they just responding to it when it occurred?). However, analyses of the sequential dependencies of maternal and child behaviors suggested that metacognitive behavior on the part of the child was a consequence of the metacognitive content of the preceding maternal utterance. Of course, even this analysis does not relieve all forms of causal ambiguity; it is always possible that mothers of gifted preschoolers more often encourage metacognitive strategies because they know their children are capable of using them.

The ideal situation, of course, would be to use random assignment of infants or toddlers to different environments and then document the relative frequency of exceptional outcomes. In fact, something very much like such an experiment has been conducted within the realm of providing enriched language experiences beginning at ages 3 to 7 months and following children through to formal schooling (Fowler, Ogston, Roberts-Fiati, & Swenson, 1992; Fowler & Swenson, 1979; Ogston, 1983; Swenson, 1983). Unfortunately, definitive inferences from these studies are hampered by very small sample sizes, and there are some indications that the intervention may have "bled" or "spilled over" to the control families enrolled in the project. However, the data suggest that enriched language stimulation during infancy may be associated with later assignment to G/ET educational curricula: 72% of language-stimulated infants were placed in gifted classes or advanced grades, whereas only 33% of the control infants achieved such status.

Summary. The extant literature suggests that both genetic and environmental factors contribute to the origins of G/ET, with two caveats. First, a clear case for direct influence of either source has not been definitively or convincingly made. Second, it is clear that neither genes nor environment in and of themselves are sufficient to guarantee G/ET status. Certainly this summary is not surprising; it seems that nearly every empirical test of the nature–nurture debate is resolved in this manner, and as such it is not particularly helpful or enlightening in truly understanding the origins of such characteristics. Perhaps what is surprising, however, is that no more sophisticated models of the developmental origins of G/ET have been substantively considered. In the next section, we provide a brief sketch of an emergent developmental approach that may be applied to the investigation of G/ET.

A Developmental-Systems Approach

During the 1980s and 1990s, a number of authors have proposed alternative ways of conceptualizing developmental causation. The positions espoused by these authors vary in scope. Some represent general approaches, such as developmental or developmental–psychobiological systems theory (Gottleib, 1992, 1997; Gottleib, Wahlstein, & Lickliter, 1998; Oyama, 1985) or dynamical systems theory (Thelen, 1990; Thelen & Smith, 1994, 1998), whereas others represent more specific hypotheses about the development of neural substrates (Edelman, 1987) or simulations of cognitive processes that are based on biologically feasible principles (Elman et al., 1996). All of the positions, however (which we refer to generically as *developmental-systems approaches* from here on), share the fundamental assumption that development may be characterized in terms of self-organizing processes that involve continuous interactions between genetic and environmental factors across time (see Figure 6.2). Furthermore, the concept of self-organizing processes renders the classification of behavioral or cognitive phenomena as innate (traditionally attributed to "nature") or acquired (traditionally attributed to "nurture") as somewhat moot.

As is perhaps evident from the different paths shown in Figure 6.2, the central feature of the developmental-systems approach is the rejection of the independent and parallel paths of causation inherent in traditional formulations of the nature–nurture debate. That is, traditional nature–nurture models hold that developmental outcome is a function of a simple additive formula (i.e., some proportion of variance attributable to genetic endowment plus some proportion of variance attributable to environmental quality). On the other hand, the developmental-systems model proposes that outcome will vary at different times, owing to continuous dynamic transactions between the environment and the individual. Furthermore, the standard clusters of developmental determinants,

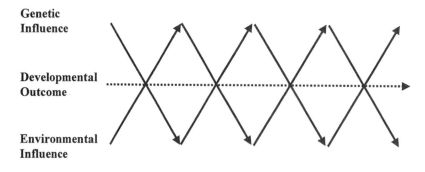

Figure 6.2. Interactive nature of developmental-systems type models in the determining of individual development. Genetic and environmental factors interact with one another on a continuous basis across time, and developmental outcome at any point is a product of the interactions that have occurred before. This figure is similar to a more complex representation of developmental causation appearing in Gottleib (1992).

innate–genetic–biological versus acquired–environmental–behavioral, readily break down under such analysis. For example, biological measures (including those related to gene expression) may reflect the influence of environmental input, and the individual's choice of environmental conditions may be influenced by the genotype.

To a few, this approach is frustrating, in spite of the fact that it may accurately represent the reality of development, because it is not readily subject to disproof. To others, the approach is simply disappointing, because it clearly implies that a static variable (or set of variables) measured once or twice early in life will not predict later developmental outcome very well. As Thelen (1990) wrote, a systems approach imposes "real limits on our ability to predict long-range developmental outcome from any set of precursor variables" that will not simply be attributable to "imperfect measurement instruments or incomplete statistical models" (p. 37). On the other hand, the systems approach clearly implies that if any satisfactory level of developmental prediction can be attained, it must come through the tracking of the dynamic gene–environment–behavior transactions that are proposed to occur. Practically speaking, the key to prediction from early portions of the life span will be longitudinal research featuring multiple measures at different levels of the organism. In such research, the developmental profile of the putative precursors may be more useful as a predictor unit rather than a single assessment or an aggregate mean of assessments.

Implications and Suggestions for the Study of G/ET in Infancy

As we close this chapter, we hope that we have made clear the prospects for the early detection of the precursors that may lead to G/ET. Furthermore, we hope that we have also made a case for the fact that this endeavor may most likely be realized using methodologies derived from a complex, interactive, and transactional perspective on the determinants of developmental outcome. We are not the first developmentalists to advocate for a developmental systems approach to the study of G/ET or its early precursors. The importance of the role of longitudinal research in the study of G/ET was advocated more than a decade ago by Horowitz and O'Brien (1985, 1986), and the application of complex developmental models to the emergence of G/ET was proposed by Horowitz (1992). At this point, we make some concrete suggestions for what this approach implies for future work toward the identification and understanding of G/ET from infancy and toddlerhood.

First, a developmental-systems-based approach necessitates an intensive longitudinal strategy. We think it likely that a cognitive precursor of G/ET may not be conspicuously precocious at all points during the individual's early life span. Rather, based on the extant literature (e.g., Gottfried et al., 1994) and on the developmental-systems approach (Horowitz, 1992), it seems probable that such precocity may develop as a function of continuous interactions among the various influences that contribute to developmental outcome. As such, plotting the development of cognitive precocity will be the *sine qua non* of future work in the area. Such a strategy is not entirely new to research on G/ET. Indeed, longitudinal work in the area is common (Klein & Tannenbaum, 1992), and Terman's (e.g., 1925) early work in the field followed this general blueprint. Furthermore, it is worth noting that Benbow's (e.g., 1988) speculations concerning the possible effects of prenatal hormonal exposure on precocious mathematical ability in the SMPY sample approximates a developmental-systems type of hypothesis. One problem with these research programs, however, is that they typically commence with the classification of the individual as G/ET. As a result, these studies are ill equipped to provide definitive insights into what processes in early life may have led to the manifestation of G/ET characteristics in the first place. However, future work can be designed to remedy this situation by taking an intensive and prospective approach. Given Gottfried et al.'s (1994) data, such longitudinal studies should begin before the end of the second year.

Second, we have reviewed evidence indicating that measures of infant cognition reflect abilities that may well be modular in nature. This raises the possibility that the precursors that may lead to G/ET in a particular domain may be strongly domain specific. If this is the case, investigators studying the precursors of G/ET during infancy will need to devise specific cognitive tasks that are relevant to the domain of G/ET that they wish to predict. This departs somewhat from Horowitz's (1992) proposal that generic cognitive tasks such as habituation (a measure of visual learning) and paired comparison (which yields a short-term recognition memory measure) might be successfully applied to the early identification of precocious cognition in infancy. The technology and methodology for testing infant cognitive abilities has grown remarkably in the past 5 years, and thus many other tasks are now available or are waiting to be devised. We contend that if one is interested in, for example, G/ET in the visual–spatial domain, then one should seek precocity in the developmental course of that domain across infancy. The same formula holds for other abilities; in some cases, perhaps a generic procedure could be used, but it might be implemented with stimuli (or stimulus discriminations) that are relevant to the domain under study.

Furthermore, we recommend that the domain be studied with dependent variables that span both behavioral and biobehavioral levels. This provides an important convergent validation of the phenomena and provides for the possibility that exceptionality that may not be evident behaviorally early in life may be evident in the measurement of the underlying substrates that will eventually mediate such behavior later. It is possible that the precursors of G/ET can be validated by examination of that neural substrate or by observation of other behavioral functions to which that substrate contributes (see Fein & Obler, 1988). For example, both recent and not-so-recent work has hinted that exceptional talent in the domain of theoretical physics may be indicated by particular structural configurations of the parietal lobe (Dehaene, Spelke, Pinel, Stanescu, & Tsivkin, 1999; Donaldson & Canavan, 1928; Witelson, Kigar, & Harvey,

1999). It seems probable that precocity in highly modular abilities might be most evident from an analysis of this type.

Conclusion

In our opinion, the outright prediction of G/ET from infancy is not a reasonable expectation. However, the detection of cognitive precocity in infancy which, in turn, holds some promise for the understanding and early identification of individuals at promise or risk for G/ET, is certainly within the realm of possibility. Perhaps it is worth noting even the impact of null results in such an endeavor; consider the value of knowing those domains in which the attainment of G/ET is predated by an early precocity and those in which it is not.

In any case, such an endeavor will necessitate the use of reliable infant tasks whose designs are based on a solid understanding of the components underlying the mature form of the domain of G/ET under investigation. Furthermore, the dependent measures from those tasks will ideally be validated on multiple levels of response. Finally, given the assumption that such precocity will always be a developmental "work in progress" rather than a psychometric *fait accompli*, all of this will need to be incorporated into intensive longitudinal designs. Thus, although early detection may be possible, it will most certainly not be easy. At the same time, we are in agreement with those who have studied or are currently studying G/ET (e.g., Bock & Ackrill, 1993; Gottfried et al., 1994; Horowitz & O'Brien, 1985; Klein & Tannenbaum, 1992; Obler & Fein, 1988; Subotnik & Arnold, 1994a; see also chapters in this volume by Jackson and Feldman) and who suggest that such an endeavor will be useful and worthwhile. We hope that the reader agrees.

References

Andersson, H. W. (1996). The Fagan Test of Infant Intelligence: Predictive validity in a random sample. *Psychological Reports, 78*, 1015–1026.

Atkinson, R. C. (1993). Introduction. In G. R. Bock & K. Ackrill (Eds.), *The origins and development of high ability* (Ciba Foundation Symposium 178, pp. 1–4). Chichester, England: Wiley.

Barbe, W. B. (1956). A study of the family background of the gifted. *Journal of Educational Psychology, 47*, 302–309.

Bayley, N. (1970). *The Bayley scales of infant development.* New York: The Psychological Corporation.

Benasich, A. A., & Bejar, I. I. (1992). The Fagan Test of Infant Intelligence: A critical review. *Journal of Applied Developmental Psychology, 13*, 153–171.

Benbow, C. P. (1988). Sex differences in mathematical reasoning ability in intellectually talented preadolescents: Their nature, effects, and possible causes. *Behavioral and Brain Sciences, 11*, 169–183.

Benbow, C. P., & Lubinski, D. (1996). *Intellectual talent: Psychometric and social issues.* Baltimore: Johns Hopkins University Press.

Benbow, C. P., Stanley, J. C., Kirk, M. K., & Zonderman, A. B. (1983). Structure of intelligence in intellectually precocious children and in their parents. *Intelligence, 7*, 129–152.

Benbow, C. P., Zonderman, A. B., & Stanley, J. C. (1983). Assortative marriage and the familiality of cognitive abilities in families of extremely gifted students. *Intelligence, 7*, 153–161.

Bock, G. R., & Ackrill, K. (Eds.). (1993). *The origins and development of high ability* (Ciba Foundation Symposium 178). Chichester, England: Wiley.

Bornstein, M. H. (1985). How infant and mother jointly contribute to developing cognitive competence in the child. *Proceedings of the National Academy of Science, 82*, 7470–7473.

Bornstein, M. H. (1990). Attention in infancy and the prediction of cognitive capacities in childhood. In J. T. Enns (Ed.), *The development of attention: Research and theory* (Advances in Psychology Vol. 69, pp. 3–19). Amsterdam, Netherlands: North Holland.

Bornstein, M. H., & Sigman, M. D. (1986). Continuity in mental development from infancy. *Child Development, 57*, 251–274.

Bornstein, M. H., Slater, A., Brown, E., Roberts, E., & Barrett, J. (1997). Stability of mental development from infancy to later childhood: Three "waves" of research. In G. Bremner, A. Slater, & G. Butterworth (Eds.), *Infant development: Recent advances* (pp. 191–215). Hove, England: Psychology Press/Taylor & Francis.

Bornstein, M. H., & Tamis-LeMonda, C. S. (1994). Antecedents of information-processing skills in infants: Habituation, novelty responsiveness, and cross-modal transfer. *Infant Behavior and Development, 17*, 371–380.

Carlson, S. A., & Werkman, S. H. (1995). Preterm infants fed formula with compared to without docosahexaeonic acid (DNA) have shorter look duration ten months after DNA is discontinued. *Pediatric Research, 37*, 14A.

Carlson, S. A. & Werkman, S. H. (1996). A randomized trial of visual attention of preterm infants fed docosahexaeonic acid until two months. *Lipids, 31*, 85–90.

Cattell, P. (1940). *The measurement of intelligence of infants and young children*. New York: The Psychological Corporation.

Colombo, J. (1993). *Infant cognition: Predicting later intellectual functioning*. Newbury Park, CA: Sage.

Colombo, J. (1997). Individual differences in infant cognition: Methods, measures and models. In J. Dobbing (Ed.), *Developing brain and behavior: The role of lipids in infant formulas* (pp. 339–385). London: Academic Press.

Colombo, J., & Fagen, J. W. (Eds.). (1990). *Individual differences in infancy: Reliability, stability, and prediction*. Hillsdale, NJ: Erlbaum.

Colombo, J., & Frick, J. E. (1999). Recent advances and issues in the study of preverbal intelligence. In M. Anderson (Ed.), *The development of intelligence* (pp. 46–71). East Sussex, England: Psychology Press.

Colombo, J., Harlan, J. E., & Mitchell, D. W. (1999, March). *Look duration in infancy: Evidence for a triphasic developmental course*. Poster presented at the annual meeting of the Society for Research in Child Development, Albuquerque, NM.

Colombo, J., & Janowsky, J. S. (1998). A cognitive neuroscience approach to individual differences in infant cognition. In J. E. Richards (Ed.), *The cognitive neuroscience of attention: A developmental perspective* (pp. 363–392). Hillsdale, NJ: Erlbaum.

Colombo, J., & Mitchell, D. W. (1990). Individual and developmental differences in infant visual attention: Fixation time and information processing. In J. Colombo & J.W. Fagen (Eds.), *Individual differences in infancy: Reliability, stability, and prediction* (pp. 193–227). Hillsdale, NJ: Erlbaum.

Colombo, J., & Saxon, T. F. (in press). Infant attention and the development of cognition: Does the environment mediate continuity? In H. Fitzgerald, K. Karraker, & T. Luster (Eds.), *Infant development: Ecological perspectives*. Washington, DC: Garland Press.

Cook, T. D., & Campbell, D. T. (1979). *Quasi-experimentation: Design and analysis issues for field settings*. Boston: Houghton-Mifflin.

Cox, C. M. (1926). *Genetic studies of genius. II. The early mental traits of three hundred geniuses*. Palo Alto, CA: Stanford University Press.

Creel, C. S., & Karnes, F. A. (1988). Parental expectancies and young gifted children. *Roeper Review, 11(1)*, 48–50.

Csikszentmihalyi, M., & Csikszentmihalyi, I. S. (1993). Family influences on the development of giftedness. In G. R. Bock & K. Ackrill (Eds.), *The origins and development of high ability* (Ciba Foundation Symposium Series, Vol. 178, pp. 187–206). Chichester, England: Wiley.

Dalzell, H. (1998). Giftedness: Infancy to adolescence—A developmental perspective. *Roeper Review, 20(4)*, 259–264.

Davidson, L., & Scripp, L. (1994). Conditions of giftedness: Musical development in the preschool and elementary years. In R. F. Subotnik & K. D. Arnold (Eds.), *Beyond Terman: Contemporary longitudinal studies of giftedness and talent* (pp. 155–185). Norwood, NJ: Ablex.

Dehaene, S., Spelke, E., Pinel, P., Stanescu, R., & Tsivkin, S. (1999). Sources of mathematical thinking: Behavioral and brain-imaging evidence. *Science, 284*, 970–974.

Donaldson, H. H., & Canavan, M. M. (1928). A study of the brains of three scholars. *Journal of Comparative Neurology, 46*, 1–95.

Edelman, G. (1987). *Neural Darwinism*. New York: Basic Books.

Elman, J. L., Bates, E. A., Johnson, M. H., Karmiloff-Smith, A., Parisi, D., & Plunkett, K. (1996). *Rethinking innateness: A connectionist perspective on development*. Cambridge, MA: MIT Press.

Fagan, J. F. (1990). The paired-comparison paradigm and infant intelligence. *Annals of the New York Academy of Sciences, 608*, 337–364.

Fagan, J. F., & McGrath, S. K. (1981). Infant recognition memory and later intelligence. *Intelligence, 5*, 121–130.

Fagan, J. F., & Shepard, P. A. (1986–1987). *The Fagan Test of Infant Intelligence*. Cleveland: Infantest.

Fagan, J. F., & Singer, L. T. (1983). Infant recognition memory as a measure of intelligence. In L. P. Lipsitt & C. K. Rovee-Collier (Eds.), *Advances in infancy research* (Vol. 2, pp. 31–79). Norwood, NJ: Ablex.

Fagen, J. W., & Ohr, P. S. (1990). Individual differences in infant conditioning and memory. In J. Colombo & J. W. Fagen (Eds.), *Individual differences in infancy* (pp. 155–192). Hillsdale, NJ: Erlbaum.

Fein, D., & Obler, L. K. (1988). Neuropsychology study of talent: A developing field. In L. K. Obler & D. Fein (Eds.), *The exceptional brain: Neuropsychology of talent and special abilities* (pp. 3–15). New York: Guilford Press.

Fischoff, B. (1975). Hindsight ≠ foresight: The effect of outcome knowledge on judgment under uncertainty. *Journal of Experimental Psychology: Human Perception and Performance, 1*, 288–299.

Fischoff, B. (1982a). Debiasing. In D. Kahneman, P. Slovic, & A. Tversky (Eds.), *Judgment under uncertainty: Heuristics and biases* (pp. 422–444). Cambridge, England: Cambridge University Press.

Fischoff, B. (1982b). For those condemned to study the past: Heuristics and biases in hindsight. In D. Kahneman, P. Slovic, & A. Tversky (Eds.), *Judgment under uncertainty: Heuristics and biases* (pp. 335–351). Cambridge, England: Cambridge University Press.

Fowler, W., Ogston, K., Roberts-Fiati, G., & Swenson, A. (1992). Accelerating language acquisition. In G. R. Bock & K. Ackrill (Eds.), *The origins and development of high ability* (Ciba Foundation Symposium 178, pp. 207–217). Chichester, England: Wiley.

Fowler, W., & Swenson, A. (1979). The influence of early language stimulation on development. *Genetic Psychology Monographs, 100*, 73–109.

Freeman, J. (1979). *Gifted children: Their identification and development in a social context*. Baltimore: University Park Press.

Gardner, H. (1993). The relationship between early giftedness and later achievement. In G. R. Bock & K. Ackrill (Eds.), *The origins and development of high ability* (Ciba Foundation Symposium 178, pp. 175–182). Chichester, England: Wiley.

Gesell, A., & Amatruda, C. S. (1947). *Developmental diagnosis: Normal and abnormal child development. Clinical methods and pediatric applications* (2nd ed.). New York: Hoeber.

Gottfried, A. W., Gottfried, A. E., Bathurst, K., & Guerin, D. W. (1994). *Gifted IQ: Early developmental aspects*. New York: Plenum.

Gottlieb, G. (1992). *Individual development and evolution*. Oxford, England: Oxford University Press.

Gottlieb, G. (1997). *Synthesizing nature–nurture*. Mahwah, NJ: Erlbaum.

Gottlieb, G., Wahlstein, D., & Lickliter, R. (1998). The significance of biology for human development: A developmental psychobiological systems view. In R. M. Lerner (Ed.), *Handbook of child psychology* (Vol. 1, pp. 233–274). New York: Wiley.

Gould, S. J. (1989). *Wonderful life*. New York: Norton.

Gross, M. U. M. (1992). The early development of three profoundly gifted children of IQ 200. In P. S. Klein & A. J. Tannenbaum (Eds.), *To be young and gifted* (pp. 94–138). Norwood, NJ: Ablex.

Gross, M. U. M. (1999). Small poppies: Highly gifted children in the early years. *Roeper Review, 21*(3), 207–214.

Horowitz, F. D. (1987). A developmental view of giftedness. *Gifted Child Quarterly, 31*, 165–168.

Horowitz, F. D. (1992). A developmental view on the early identification of the gifted. In P. S. Klein & A. J. Tannenbaum (Eds.), *To be young and gifted* (pp. 73–92). Norwood, NJ: Ablex.

Horowitz, F. D., & O'Brien, M. (Eds.). (1985). *The gifted and talented: Developmental perspectives*. Washington, DC: American Psychological Association.

Horowitz, F. D., & O'Brien, M. (1986). Gifted and talented children: State of knowledge and directions for research. *American Psychologist, 41*, 1147–1152.

Isaacs, A. F. (1987). Identifying and parenting the gifted-talented-creative child beginning with preschool. *Creative Child and Adult Quarterly, 12*, 21–30.

Jackson, N. E. (1992). Precocious reading of English: Origins, structure, and predictive significance. In P. S. Klein & A. J. Tannenbaum (Eds.), *To be young and gifted* (pp. 171–203). Norwood, NJ: Ablex.

Jacobson, S. W. (1995, April). *Evidence for speed of processing and recognition memory components of infant information processing*. Paper presented at the Society for Research in Child Development, Indianapolis.

Jacobson, S. W., Fein, G. G., Jacobson, J. L., Schwartz, P. M., & Dowler, J. K. (1985). The effects of intrauterine PCB exposure on visual recognition memory. *Child Development, 56*, 853–860.

Jacobson, S. W., Jacobson, J. L., O'Neill, J. M., Padgett, R. J., Frankowski, J. J., & Bihun, J. T. (1992). Visual expectation and dimensions of infant information processing. *Child Development, 63*, 711–724.

Jacobson, S. W., Jacobson, J. L., Sokol, R. J., Martier, S. S., & Ager, J. W. (1993). Prenatal alcohol exposure and infant information processing. *Child Development, 64*, 1706–1721.

Klein, P. (1992). Mediating the cognitive, social, and aesthetic development of precocious young children. In P. S. Klein & A. J. Tannenbaum (Eds.), *To be young and gifted* (pp. 245–277). Norwood, NJ: Ablex.

Klein, P. S., & Tannenbaum, A. J. (Eds.). (1992). *To be young and gifted*. Norwood, NJ: Ablex.

Koopmans-Dayton, J. D., & Feldhusen, J. F. (1987). A resource guide for parents of gifted preschoolers. *Gifted Child Today, 10*(6), 2–7.

Lehweld, G., & Friedrich, G. (1987). Developmental–psychological problems of the early recognition of gifted children. *Psychologie fuer die Praxis* (Supplement), 5–12.

Mayes, L. C., Bornstein, M. H., Chawarska, K., & Granger, R. H. (1995). Information processing and developmental assessments in 3 month old infants exposed prenatally to cocaine. *Pediatrics, 95*, 539–545.

McCall, R. B. (1979). The development of intellectual functioning in infancy and the prediction on later IQ. In J. D. Osofsky (Ed.), *Handbook of infant development* (pp. 707–741). New York: Wiley.

McCall, R. B. (1983). A conceptual approach to early mental development. In M. Lewis (Ed.), *Origins of intelligence* (2nd ed., pp. 67–106). New York: Plenum.

McCall, R. B., & Carriger, M. (1993). A meta-analysis of infant habituation and recognition memory performance as predictors of later IQ. *Child Development, 64*, 57–79.

McCall, R. B., & Mash, C. (1995). Infant cognition and its relation to mature intelligence. In G. Whitehurst (Ed.), *Annals of child development* (Vol. 11, pp. 27–56). Greenwich, CT: JAI Press.

Mitchell, D. W., & Colombo, J. (1997). Infant cognition and general intelligence. In W. Tomic & J. Kingma (Eds.), *Advances in cognition and educational practice: Reflections on the concept of intelligence* (pp. 101–119). Greenwich, CT: JAI Press.

Mitchell, D. W., McCollam, K., Horowitz, F. D., Embretson, S. E., & O'Brien, M. (1991, April). *The interacting contribution of constitutional, environmental, and information processing factors to early developmental outcome.* Society for Research in Child Development (poster session), Seattle.

Moss, E. (1992). Early interactions and metacognitive development of gifted preschoolers. In P. S. Klein & A. J. Tannenbaum (Eds.), *To be young and gifted* (pp. 278–318). Norwood, NJ: Ablex.

Moss, E., & Strayer, F. F. (1990). Interactive problem-solving of mothers and gifted and nongifted preschoolers. *International Journal of Behavioral Development, 13,* 177–197.

Obler, L. K., & Fein, D. (Eds.). (1988). *The exceptional brain: Neuropsychology of talent and special abilities.* New York: Guilford Press.

Ogston, K. (1983). The effects of gross motor and language stimulation on infant development. In W. Fowler (Ed.), *Potentials of childhood* (Vol. 2, pp. 177–208). Lexington, MA: Lexington Books.

Oyama, S. (1985). *The ontogeny of information.* Cambridge, England: Cambridge University Press.

Plomin, R., & Thompson, L. A. (1993). Genetics and high ability. In G. R. Bock & K. Ackrill (Eds.), *The origins and development of high ability* (Ciba Foundation Symposium 178, pp. 67–79). Chichester, England: Wiley.

Radford, J. (1990). *Child prodigies and exceptional early achievers.* New York: Free Press.

Reisbick, S., Neuringer, M., & Gohl, E. (1997). Visual attention in infant monkeys: Effects of dietary fatty acids and age. *Developmental Psychology, 33,* 387–395.

Renzulli, J. S. (1998). The three-ring conception of giftedness. In S. M. Baum, S. M. Reis, & L. R. Maxfield (Eds.), *Nurturing the gifts and talents of primary grade students.* Mansfield Center, CT: Creative Learning Press.

Robinson, N. M. (1987). The early development of precocity. *Gifted Child Quarterly, 31,* 161–164.

Robinson, N. M., Dale, P. S., & Landesman, S. (1990). Validity of Stanford–Binet IV with linguistically precocious toddlers. *Intelligence, 14,* 173–186.

Robinson, N. M., & Robinson, H. (1992). The use of standardized tests with young gifted children. In P. S. Klein & A. J. Tannenbaum (Eds.), *To be young and gifted* (pp. 141–170). Norwood, NJ: Ablex.

Rose, D., Slater, A., & Perry, H. (1986). Prediction of childhood intelligence from habituation in early infancy. *Intelligence, 10,* 251–263.

Rose, S. A., & Feldman, J. F. (1990). Infant cognition: Individual differences and developmental continuities. In J. Colombo & J. W. Fagen (Eds.), *Individual differences in infancy* (pp. 229–246). Hillsdale, NJ: Erlbaum.

Rose, S. A., & Feldman, J. F. (1995a, March). *Cognitive continuity from infancy: A single thread or a twisted skein?* Presented at the meeting of the Society for Research in Child Development, Indianapolis.

Rose, S. A., & Feldman, J. F. (1995b). Prediction of IQ and specific cognitive abilities at 11 years from infancy measures. *Developmental Psychology, 31,* 685–696.

Sankar-DeLeeuw, N. (1999). Gifted preschoolers: Parent and teacher views on identification, early admission, and programming. *Roeper Review, 21*(3), 174–179.

Saxon, T. F., Frick, J. E., & Colombo, J. (1997). Individual differences in infant visual fixation and maternal interactional styles. *Merrill–Palmer Quarterly of Behavioral Development, 43,* 48–66.

Shaklee, B. D. (1992). Identification of young gifted students. *Journal for Education of the Gifted, 15,* 134–143.

Shapiro, B. K., Palmer, F. B., Antell, S. E., Bilker, S., Ross, A., & Capute, A. J. (1989). Can it be predicted in infancy? *Clinical Pediatrics, 28,* 205–209.

Sigman, M. D., & Mundy, P. (1993). Infant precursors of childhood intellectual and verbal abilities. In D. F. Hay & A. Angold (Eds.), *Precursors and causes in development and psychopathology* (pp. 123–144). Chichester, England: Wiley.

Singer, L. T., Arendt, R., Fagan, J. F., Minnes, S., Salvator, A., Bolek, T., & Becker, M. (1999). Neonatal visual information processing in cocaine-exposed and non-exposed infants. *Infant Behavior and Development, 22*, 1–16.

Smith, S. B. (1996). Calculating prodigies. In L. K. Obler & D. Fein (Eds.), *The exceptional brain: Neuropsychology of talent and special abilities* (pp. 19–47). New York: Guilford Press.

Smutny, J. F. (Ed.). (1998). *The young gifted child: Potential and promise.* Cresskill, NJ: Hampton Press.

Sternberg, R. J. (1993). The concept of "giftedness": A pentagonal implicit theory. In G. R. Bock & K. Ackrill (Eds.), *The origins and development of high ability* (Ciba Foundation Symposium 178, pp. 5–16). Chichester, England: Wiley.

Sternberg, R. J., & Davidson, J. E. (1986). Cognitive development in the gifted and talented. In F. D. Horowitz & M. O'Brien (Eds.), *The gifted and talented: Developmental perspectives* (pp. 37–74). Washington, DC: American Psychological Association.

Storfer, M. D. (1990). *Intelligence and giftedness: The contributions of heredity and early environment.* San Francisco: Jossey-Bass.

Stott, L. H., & Ball, R. S. (1965). Infant and preschool mental tests: Review and evaluation. *Monographs of the Society for Research in Child Development, 30*(3: Whole 101).

Subotnik, R. F., & Arnold, K. D. (Eds.). (1994a). *Beyond Terman: Contemporary longitudinal studies of giftedness and talent.* Norwood, NJ: Ablex.

Subotnik, R. F., & Arnold, K. D. (1994b). Longitudinal study of giftedness and talent. In R. F. Subotnik & K. D. Arnold (Eds.), *Beyond Terman: Contemporary longitudinal studies of giftedness and talent* (pp. 1–23) Norwood, NJ: Ablex.

Swenson, A. (1983). Toward an ecological approach to theory and research in child language acquisition. In W. Fowler (Ed.), *Potentials of childhood* (Vol. 2, pp. 121–175). Lexington, MA: Lexington Books.

Tamis-LeMonda, C. S., & Bornstein, M. H. (1989). Habituation and maternal encouragement of attention in infancy as predictors of toddler language, play, and representational competence. *Child Development, 60*, 738–751.

Tannenbaum, A. J. (1992). Early signs of giftedness: Research and commentary. In P. S. Klein & A. J. Tannenbaum (Eds.), *To be young and gifted* (pp. 3–32). Norwood, NJ: Ablex.

Terman, L. M. (1925). *Genetic studies of genius: Vol. 1. Mental and physical traits of a thousand gifted children.* Palo Alto, CA: Stanford University Press.

Terman, L. M. (1930). *Genetic studies of genius: Vol. 3. The promise of youth.* Palo Alto, CA: Stanford University Press.

Terman, L. M., & Oden, M. H. (1947). *Genetic studies of genius: Vol. 4. The gifted child grows up.* Palo Alto, CA: Stanford University Press.

Terman, L. M., & Oden, M. H. (1959). *Genetic studies of genius: Vol. 5. The gifted group at mid-life.* Palo Alto, CA: Stanford University Press.

Thelen, E. (1990). Dynamical systems and the generation of individual differences. In J. Colombo & J. W. Fagen (Eds.), *Individual differences in infancy* (pp. 19–43). Hillsdale, NJ: Erlbaum.

Thelen, E., & Smith, L. B. (1994). *A dynamic systems approach to the development of cognition and action.* Cambridge, MA: MIT Press.

Thelen, E., & Smith, L. B. (1998). Dynamic systems theories. In R. M. Lerner (Ed.), *Handbook of child psychology* (Vol. 1, pp. 563–634). New York: Wiley.

Werkman, S. H., & Carlson, S. A. (1996). A randomized trial of visual attention of preterm infants fed docosahexaeonic acid until nine months. *Lipids, 31*, 91–97.

Willerman, L., & Fiedler, M. F. (1974). Infant performance and intellectual precocity. *Child Development, 45*, 438–486.

Willerman, L., & Fiedler, M. F. (1977). Intellectually precocious preschool children: Early development and later intellectual accomplishments. *Journal of Genetic Psychology, 131*, 13–20.

Williams, N., & Gonzalez, V. (1998, April). *Identification of giftedness in preschoolers: Are parents' perceptions related to home environment factors and cognitive assessments?* Paper presented at the annual meeting of the American Educational Research Association, San Diego.

Witelson, S. F., Kigar, D. L., & Harvey, T. (1999). The exceptional brain of Albert Einstein. *Lancet, 353,* 2149–2153.

Zigler, E., & Farber, E. A. (1985). Commonalities between the intellectual extremes: Giftedness and mental retardation. In F. D. Horowitz & M. O'Brien (Eds.), *The gifted and talented: Developmental perspectives* (pp. 387–408). Washington, DC: American Psychological Association.

7

Life-Span Cognitive Giftedness: The Development of Relativistic Thinking

MaryLou Fair Worthen

Many cognitive psychologists consider relativistic thinking to be a hallmark of advanced thought. Jean Piaget, possibly an undeclared relativist, wrote that it is nearly impossible to understand and justify the validity of our knowledge without presupposing the existence of relations (Piaget, 1977). Intellectual descendants of Piaget's work in cognitive development have studied relativistic thinking specifically (e.g., Benack, 1984, 1988; Powell, 1984; Sinnott, 1984, 1989a, 1989b, 1998). In addition, other psychological researchers not coming directly from the Piagetian tradition have empirically supported the inclusion of relativism as a cognitive advance (Belenky, Clinchy, Goldberger, & Tarule, 1986; Blanchard-Fields & Norris, 1996; Collins, Luszcz, Lawson, & Keeves, 1997; Kitchener & King, 1981; Kramer, 1986; Lee, 1989; Perry, 1970, 1981).

Describing Relativistic Thinking

Generally, *relativistic thinking* can be described as an advanced epistemological orientation (Perry, 1970), as a developed way of knowing (Belenky et al., 1986), or as postformal operations (Sinnott, 1984, 1998). More specifically, relativistic thinking involves the following:

- An awareness and tolerance of uncertainty, change, flux, ambiguity, contradiction, and paradox (Blanchard-Fields & Norris, 1996; Kitchener & King, 1981; Kramer, 1983; Perry, 1970; Sinnott, 1984). This form of relativistic thinking is considered to be advanced be-

These studies were conducted as partial fulfillment of the Doctor of Philosophy degree in Human Development and Communication Sciences at the University of Texas at Dallas. I acknowledge Professor T. G. R. Bower, doctoral candidate Sara J. Henry (deceased), and my husband Deuard Worthen for their special assistance in conducting this research. I also thank the participants who contributed their thinking for these studies.

cause the thinker maintains a cognitive balance or dialectic between or among apparently opposite options.

- Contextualism, or interactive judgments based on circumstances, motives, and intentions (Bar-Tal & Nissim, 1984; Kitchener & King, 1981). This kind of relativistic thinking is thought to be advanced because the thinker considers specifics of the situation and modifies thinking as his or her awareness of current reality changes.
- Subjective, self-referential, reflective thought (Kitchener & King, 1981; Labouvie-Vief, 1992; Sinnott, 1989a). This aspect of relativistic thinking incorporates the concept of the observer as part of the system. It is relativistic because the thinker keeps in mind not only his or her limited perception or awareness of the system, but also that he or she as an observer affects the system itself.
- The individual's active participation in knowledge (Belenky et al., 1986; Kitchener & King, 1981; Lee, 1989). This feature refers to the advanced awareness that knowledge is formed, created, and discovered by people and that the thinker himself or herself can create and add to such knowledge for humankind.
- Multidimensional, metasystematic, or cross-paradigmatic thinking (Benack, 1988; Benack & Basseches, 1989; Richards & Commons, 1984; Sinnott, 1989a; Sinnott & Cavanaugh, 1991). A meta-thinker bridges systems of thought by integrating them along dimensions of similarity while also mentally maintaining their distinctions as in tolerance of contradiction described earlier.

Sinnott (1989a) determined two especially salient features that make up relativistic thinking: self-reference and metasystematic thinking. A relativist knows that she or he functions within a mental framework or logic system (i.e., she or he self-references), and also a relativist can understand or bridge frameworks or logic systems (i.e., she or he thinks beyond the self-system).

Relativistic Thinking as Cognitive Giftedness

For more than 100 years, intelligence has been measured using a psychometric approach (see Anastasi, 1988, as well as Gardner & Clark, 1992, for histories of intelligence testing). In this century-old tradition, intelligence has been found to involve two major abilities (Horn & Hofer, 1992; Sternberg & Powell, 1983; Wechsler, 1972): (a) crystallized intelligence and (b) fluid abilities. Although crystallized intelligence (i.e., general information, vocabulary) has been found to increase with age (Arbuckle, Maag, Pushkar, & Chaikelson, 1998; Sternberg & Powell, 1983), fluid intelligence (performance abilities such as abstract thinking) has been found repeatedly to peak during the third decade of life and to decline thereafter (Arbuckle et al., 1998; Horn & Hofer, 1992). Because fluid intelligence is found to begin to decline in young adulthood, the concept of cognitive giftedness has been applied within the psychometric tradition to youthful people who are pre-cocious in informational knowledge or reasoning abilities.

As in the psychometric tradition, the Piagetian perspective has viewed cognitive development as peaking in youth as a fluid ability to reason abstractly or as formal operations (Bower, 1979; Inhelder & Piaget, 1958; Piaget & Inhelder, 1969). The work of Perry (1970, 1981), however, expanded the study of the development of formal operations into the college years. Moreover, neo-Piagetians have begun to consider the existence of a postformal stage of intellectual development and to study adult thinking (Cavanaugh, Kramer, Sinnott, Camp, & Markley, 1985; Commons, Richards, & Armon, 1984; Commons, Trudeau, Stein, Richards, & Krause, 1998; Kramer, 1983; Sinnott, 1994b, 1998). Thus, the possibility of lifelong intellectual growth has begun to receive research attention.

The topic of intellectual development in adulthood involves the areas of precociousness, giftedness, and wisdom. In the current context, *precociousness* refers to highly advanced development that is premature for chronological age. If the endpoint of cognitive growth does not occur during young adulthood, then the possibility of being cognitively precocious can extend later into adulthood. On the other hand, *giftedness* may not be inherently developmental because it refers to superior skill, aptitude, or ability. An adolescent or an adult may be endowed with superior thinking skills and, thus, will be gifted. Superior, however, is a relative term. If an adolescent's thinking is superior to normative adolescent thinking or even adult thinking, then superior and gifted are developmental terms. In addition, an adolescent or an adult may be "wise beyond her or his years." Because most people do not achieve wisdom even by older age (Smith & Baltes, 1990; Smith, Staudinger, & Baltes, 1994), being wise at any age could be considered to mean intellectual giftedness, even in oldest adulthood.

Within the present perspective, cognitive development that is measurably advanced beyond peers, agemates, or cohort group suggests exceptional cognitive ability or intellectual giftedness. Yet both the possibility for intellectual growth beyond a "modal point" in young adulthood and a way to measure advanced cognitive development are required to determine cognitive abilities in middle and older adulthood. The current conceptualization of relativistic thinking could fulfill these two requirements and, in so doing, also could address the issue of cognitive giftedness across the life-span. Two studies were undertaken to address life-span development of relativistic thinking.

Study 1

Scant evidence has been found that the development of relativistic thinking occurs during the teenage years. In one study, Bar-Tal and Nissim (1984) found a shift toward relativism from age 12 to age 17 years. In another study, Wilkinson and Schwartz (1987) found that young gifted adolescents ages 12 to 15 years held relativistic beliefs. A review of the literature of studies with older adolescents shows that only some late adolescents consistently produce evidence of the ability to think relativistically (Erwin, 1983; Kitchener & King, 1981; Perry, 1981; Ruck, Keating, Abramovitch, & Koegl, 1998; Ryan, 1984a, 1984b; Schwartz & Wilkinson, 1988; Singh & Forsythe, 1989; Stonewater, Stonewater, & Hadley, 1986; Wainryb, 1993; Worthen, 1992b). Thus, evidence for relativistic thinking was produced only by older or gifted adolescents. In Study 1 of the current research, the presence of relativistic thinking was examined as a possible indicator of developmentally advanced intellectual growth or cognitive giftedness in adolescents. Because all people do not achieve relativistic thinking even in adulthood (Sinnott, 1984), adolescents who can think relativistically are said here to be gifted with exceptional ability and are considered to be cognitively precocious.

Predictions

Two main predictions were made in this pilot study. First, more responses from adolescents who have been identified as gifted will be rated as more advanced than will the responses of nongifted adolescents. Second, more responses of the gifted adolescents will be rated as relativistic thinking than will be the responses of the adolescents of normative intellect.

Method

Participants. Sixty-four adolescents (mean age = 14.6 years) were matched for socioeconomic status, gender, ethnic background, age, educational level, and intellectual giftedness. Participants were determined to be gifted or nongifted based on having been so identified by a public school system in the Dallas area (see Worthen, 1992b). The criteria for giftedness in the school system from which most of the participants were drawn included (a) scoring in the 99th percentile for verbal or quantitative ability on any of several nationally standardized and administered tests of aptitude or achievement, (b) recommendations from teachers and parents, and (c) approval of a portfolio of the student's school work as outstanding.

Measures. Relativistic thinking was assessed quantitatively using the Preformal, Formal, or Postformal–Relativistic Thinking (PFPR) Test, a multiple-choice questionnaire concerning neo-Piagetian developmental ways of thinking (Worthen, 1992a). In addition, relativistic thinking was assessed qualitatively with participants' responses to reasoning situations (Worthen, 1992a).

Data scoring. Scores on the PFPR were used to place participants in a neo-Piagetian category of preformal, formal, or postformal–relativistic. Responses to problem situations were judged by two blind raters using a manual (see Worthen, 1992a). Responses were also categorized as one of three neo-Piagetian categories listed earlier. A Cohen's κ on 40% of the rated responses was .90, which can be interpreted as 90% of the joint judgments being in agreement after chance agreement was excluded.

Results

Chi-squared analyses confirmed both predictions of this study. Younger gifted adolescents (mean age = 13.0 years) were more relativistic than younger nongifted adolescents (mean age = 13.3 years) [χ^2 (2, n = 32) = 6.24, p < .05], as represented in Figure 7.1. Although younger gifted adolescents were not more relativistic than were older nongifted adolescents [χ^2 (2, n = 32) = 5.86, NS], this nevertheless suggests that younger gifted adolescents are at least as advanced in their thinking as are older nongifted adolescents. In addition, a chi-square analysis comparing all gifted adolescents to all nongifted adolescents showed significant differences. The gifted adolescents scored as more relativistic than the nongifted adolescents [χ^2 (2, N = 64) = 6.62, p < .05], as presented in Figure 7.2.

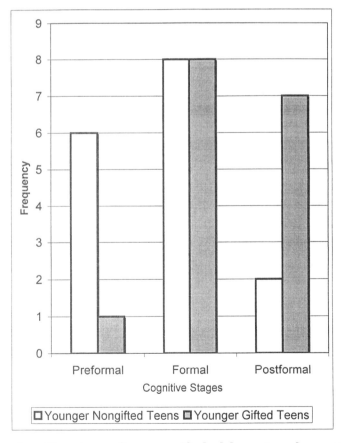

Figure 7.1.   Cognitive stages of younger gifted adolescents and younger nongifted adolescents.

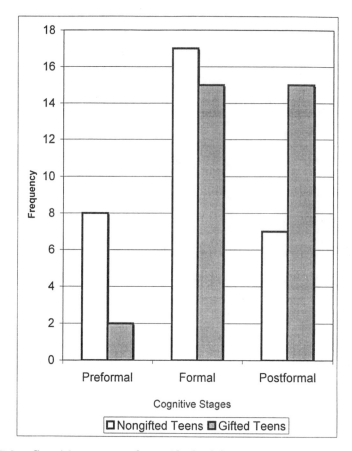

Figure 7.2.   Cognitive stages of nongifted adolescents and gifted adolescents.

Discussion

Results of this pilot study suggest not only that adolescents sometimes think relativistically, but also that gifted adolescents are more relativistic in their thinking than are nongifted adolescents. These findings have several implications for the future of gifted adolescents.

Adult relativistic thinkers have been shown to be empathetic (Benack, 1984, 1988; Powell, 1984; see also Worthen, 1995); affectively committed to participation in life (Perry, 1970, 1981; Sinnott, 1989a); advanced in moral and ethical thinking (Perry, 1970, 1981; Worthen, 1996; see also Folsom, 1998; Sinnott, 1997); and pragmatic, subjective, able to handle paradoxes cognitively, and advanced in everyday problem solving (Collins et al., 1997; Sinnott, 1984, 1989a, 1989b, 1993). Adult relativistic reasoners, suggests Kramer (1986), are able to accept contradictory perspectives. Adolescents who are postformal–relativistic thinkers, therefore, not only may be of exceptional intellectual ability, but also may be at promise for cognitively maintaining several human perspectives simultaneously while not forcing closure on any issues. This mental openness, tolerance, or intellectual balancing mechanism may be both an identifying feature of cognitive relativity as well as a process, which defines exceptional promise in gifted adolescents. The social promise of relativism, especially among precocious adolescent relativists, may be the abilities to empathize, to negotiate, to balance tensions, and to solve ill-structured societal problems. It may be that our hope for future diplomacy, détente, and solution finding, whether on the individual or international level, lies in encouraging, promoting, and developing fledgling relativistic thinking among our current intellectually advanced adolescents.

Study 2

In the second study of relativistic thinking, the use of the Perry Scheme was added to the psychometric tradition and the Piagetian perspective. Also, adults were included with adolescent participants.

The Perry Scheme

William Perry (1968, 1970, 1981, 1990) formulated a scheme in which intellectual development is viewed as proceeding along 9 hierarchical epistemological positions. The first 3 encompass cognitive duality (i.e., either–or thinking) that in Positions 2 and 3 are modified by a recognition of diversity of opinion (Perry, 1981). The next 3 are levels of relativism in which judgments are made in context. The final 3 include awareness of relativism and allow commitment amid uncertainty. Perry's own longitudinal data from the late 1950s through the early 1980s, as well as other research on his scheme (in Perry, 1981), indicated to Perry that the course of cognitive development outlined in his scheme is a constant phenomenon of a pluralistic culture (Perry, 1981).

The Perry Scheme of intellectual development and the Piagetian perspective of cognitive development are similar in major ways. Perry (1970) wrote that his theory depended on Piagetian concepts of schema and constructivism and that his methodology is similar to Piaget's clinical interview method. Several differences exist between these approaches, however. One conceptual difference is that whereas Perry (1970) places relativistic thinking within Piagetian formal operations, some neo-Piagetians say it is postformal (e.g., Sinnott, 1984). In addition, Perry includes ethical development in his scheme, but the Piagetian perspective is viewed as more exclusively cognitive. Methodologically, Perry has emphasized epistemological probes, whereas Piaget used a physics, cause-and-effect framework and neo-Piagetians often stress everyday problem solving. Nevertheless, both theories of cognitive development include relativistic thinking as intellectually advanced beyond typical adolescent cognitive development.

Research involving Perry's intellectual positions has found that high schoolers were aware of relativism (Chandler, Boyes, & Ball, 1990) and that gifted teenagers in junior high school were relativistic (Wilkinson & Schwartz, 1987). Research with late-adolescent college students and very young adults showed relativistic thinking in the Perry Scheme to be more cognitively advanced than formal operations (B. Perry et al., 1986). Also, compared to dualistic thinking, relativism was associated with better performance among college students on a variety of cognitive tasks (Schwartz & Wilkinson, 1988). In adults, Perry relativism was associated with increased educational level compared to dualistic thinking (Benack & Basseches, 1989). Together, these studies indicate that in early adolescence through adulthood, relativistic thinking in the Perry Scheme will be associated with developmentally advanced cognitive performance.

Predictions

Based on the reasoning that relativistic thinking would be associated with giftedness, the first prediction of the second study includes participants across the life span. The responses of gifted participants will be more relativistic than the responses of nongifted participants.

The second prediction concerns only adolescents. In past research, adolescents normatively have not been rated in the highest cognitive positions in the Perry Scheme (Perry, 1970, 1981; Worthen, 1992a, 1992b, 1993b). The second prediction of the second study is that adolescents will be less cognitively advanced than adults.

The third prediction concerns only adults. As discussed earlier, the psychometric tradition indicates that reasoning and other fluid abilities decline with age. Another approach to cognitive aging involves a contextualist perspective of psychological longevity and growth in the intellect (Baltes, 1987; Schaie & Willis, 1986; Sinnott, 1994a; Worthen, 1993a). Longitudinal studies indicate maintenance of some intellectual functions, especially verbal abilities, until almost 80 years of age (Arbuckle et al., 1998; see also Schaie & Willis, 1986; Sinnott, 1994a). It is predicted here that the oldest adults will not be different in relativistic reasoning from other, younger adults.

Method

Participants. A pool of participants ranging in age from 12 through 82 years was divided into four age groups: pre-college adolescents, young adults, middle-aged adults, and older adults. Groups were matched for gender, ethnic background, socioeconomic status, recent physical health, and daily functional competence (e.g., passing in school for youth; noninstitutionalized living for older adults).

Measures. A multiple-choice vocabulary test using words from the Wechsler Adult Intelligence Scale (Wechsler, 1955) was used to assess intellectual ability. Verbal ability was chosen to assess giftedness for its involvement with cognitive development (see Slobin, 1992). Gerrig and Banaji (1994) reported that evidence supports cognitive attainments as preceding linguistic attainments and also offered that it is likely that cognitive development has a more profound impact on language development than language development has on cognitive development. People with high language ability, therefore, are likely to have high cognitive ability as well (see Blanchard-Fields & Norris, 1996, on verbal ability and relativistic thinking across the life span).

Relativistic thinking was assessed in the Piagetian perspective with both the PFPR and responses to the two problem situations used in Study 1. Perry's positions were assessed with the Measure of Intellectual Development (see Moore, 1989; Perry, 1981; Worthen, 1993a, 1993b) that presents seven sentence stems for completion and two essays for prose responses.

Data scoring. Vocabulary was scored after Wechsler (1955) and was used to categorize participants as gifted or not by tables in the Wechsler manual. The PFPR Test, along with blind raters' coded scores of responses to problem situations (judge's manual in Worthen, 1992a), were used to assess level of thinking as preformal, formal, or postformal–relativistic. Interrater agreement was Cohen's (1960) κ = .94. Relativistic thinking in the Perry Scheme was also rated by blind coders who, using a judge's manual (in Worthen, 1993a), placed each subject into one of Perry's nine epistemological positions. Cohen's κ for the Perry positions = .91.

Results

Chi-square analyses were conducted. The prediction of differences in relativistic thinking between gifted and nongifted participants was not supported in either cognitive–developmental approach: not in Piagetian reasoning [χ^2 (2, N = 64) = .33, NS], nor in the Perry Scheme (χ^2 (2, N = 64) = 5.3, NS]. Nevertheless, the other two predictions were supported by results of this study.

Development of relativistic thinking beyond adolescence was found when comparing adolescents to young adults in both the Piagetian data [χ^2 (2, n = 32) = 16.57, p < .001] and in the Perry Scheme [χ^2 (2, n = 32) = 16.67, p < .001]. These results are presented in Figures 7.3 and 7.4.

Also as predicted, the oldest participants were not different in relativistic thinking from other adults as seen in comparisons to middle-aged adults both in the Piagetian perspective [χ^2 (2, n = 32) = .51, NS] and in the Perry Scheme [χ^2 (2, n = 32) = 4.32, NS]. In addition, an overall chi-square analysis comparing Piagetian cognitive stages to Perry's intellectual positions showed no significant differences [χ^2 (4, N = 64) = 2.89, NS].

Discussion

Results of the life-span study do not support the idea that throughout life verbal giftedness is associated with improved reasoning ability. This cross-

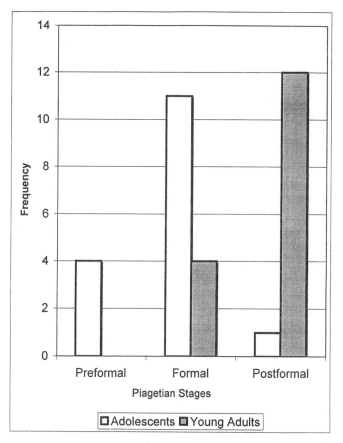

Figure 7.3. Piagetian stages of adolescents and young adults.

sectional result that across the whole of the life span from adolescence
through older adulthood those higher in verbal performance were not significantly higher in relativistic thinking suggests that in this study, it was
not just the development of verbal ability (i.e., normative word fluency as
opposed to giftedness in verbal functioning) that was being tested in the
reasoning measures. Thus, the cognitive development instruments of this
study probably measured something separate from verbal development or
something in addition to verbal development. That much is good news.
Remaining, however, is interpretation of what might be going on concerning cognitive development in relationship to these cross-sectional results.

Within the psychometric tradition of cognitive deterioration in older
adulthood, the above results can be interpreted as follows. With age, people of normative ability decline steadily in reasoning, whereas people of
high intellectual ability have a comparatively greater decline and also decline more rapidly due to the higher starting point of cognitively gifted
adolescents. Differences in reasoning ability that are visible at adolescence
decrease to nonsignificance some time in adulthood so that life-span com-

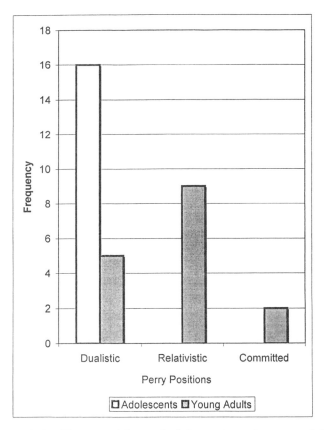

Figure 7.4.   Perry positions of adolescents and young adults.

parisons of intellectual ability do not show differences between gifted and nongifted adults.

Another look at the data, however, does not show decline with age. An alternative interpretation is possible. Within a contextualist perspective of cognitive longevity, high verbal ability may provide an advantage for adolescent relativists, but this advantage may diminish across the life span if gifted reasoning is not supported by other advantages in education, vocation, or life experiences. Thus, adults who are and who are not verbally gifted increase in reasoning across the life span—but those who are gifted increase less. There may be some ceiling effect for high-level thinking that gifted people approach much more quickly in development than do nongifted reasoners. It remains to be seen if increasing the saliency, face validity, or ecological validity of problems presented to older people would increase performance for gifted adults, for nongifted adults, or for both groups. Although differences in reasoning between verbally gifted and verbally normative adults were not found in this second study, these results can be interpreted as indicating growth in reasoning ability for both categories of adults.

This study provides more evidence for intellectual growth beyond adolescence toward relativistic thought in the adult years. In addition, more support was found for a lack of necessary cognitive decline in the older adult years. Instead, cognitive longevity is supported.

Implications for Future Research

Together these two studies provide input for speculations on implications for future research on relativistic thinking across the life span. These speculations concern conceptualizing, understanding, and assessing life-span advanced cognitive development and considering what may be beyond relativistic thinking.

Conceptualizing Life-Span Cognitive Giftedness

On a basic level, relativistic thinking is a cognitive balancing of more than one concept, idea, or system. Pre-adolescents might exhibit understanding of different sets of interpersonal rules, such as Mom's rules being different from Dad's rules, and the teacher's rules being different still. At the same time, young pre-relativists might also understand an underlying universality among the systems of rules, such as "All adults want me to be respectful and polite." Such children might recognize interconnectedness and apply what was learned in one setting, such as with siblings, to another setting, such as with peers. These could be early examples of future cross-paradigmatic or cross-systematic thinking. In adolescence, the concept of cognitive giftedness almost certainly must involve the self-referential or subjective aspect of relativistic thinking due to adolescents' normative increases in recursive thinking ability. Cognitively gifted older adolescents can be conceptualized as being beyond simple subjectivity and as being able to grasp the idea of intersubjectivity as mutual interactivity. Cognitive giftedness in adulthood could mean fully developed relativistic thinking (i.e., integration of logic systems; continual awareness of the influence of self in context). In oldest age, cognitive giftedness would involve not only the contextualism of relativistic thinking, but also the other features of wisdom, including value relativism and cognitive management of uncertainty (Smith & Baltes, 1990).

Understanding Life-Span Intellectual Giftedness

Early differences in relativistic thinking as intellectual giftedness may be quantitative and level in time due to ceiling effects or influences of unsupportive life experience. Alternatively, early differences in relativistic thinking may predict qualitative differences that are maintained in adulthood. Although longitudinal research could more definitively speak to the issue of quality versus quantity in relativistic thinking across the life span, cross-sectional research can provide some clues into the nature of cognitive giftedness in adults.

Study 1 of the current cross-sectional research on life-span development of relativistic thinking suggests that differences between gifted relativistic adolescents and adolescents of normative intellect are qualitative in nature. Given the same general life conditions and experiences, cognitively gifted relativistic people might continue to advance and not level out in later years with people of normative intellectual development. As the second study indicates, with different life conditions, across the years of adulthood, leveling appears to occur. Early cognitive advantages probably cannot overcome all of life's limiting experiences. The study of advanced intellectual development on the form of relativistic thinking would do well to take a cue from epistemology on the relativity of time itself. For some—gifted or not—the simple passage of time offers little in the way of progress in the intellect. Developmentally appropriate intellectual challenges sometimes go lacking. For others—gifted or not—life has supplied many opportunities to stimulate the mind, propelling cognitive development forward. It may be that the richness of phenomenological experience made available through relativistic thinking allows cognitively gifted people to continue to grow intellectually. Research on the developing intellect of gifted adults could reveal treasures of relativistic abilities that go beyond barely coping, beyond mere compensation, and beyond dualistic problem solving toward purposefulness, mastery, and life enhancement. In old age, giftedness as relativistic thinking might be understood as a quality of generativity in which interpersonal (i.e., metasystematic) knowledge leads the oldest gifted adults to pass their well-lit intellectual torches from their generation (that is, their system) to the next.

Assessing Life-Span Advanced Thinking

Along with Schaie (1993), I advocate a movement in lifespan research away from groupings based strictly or solely on chronological age. Research on advanced thinking across adulthood needs to move toward comparison among salient aspects of cognitive and psychological experiences such as occupation, education, and current mental activities, as well as participants' health and physical condition. Moreover, in the practice of assessing advanced cognitive ability across the life span, possibly inaccurate findings, such as necessary decline in reasoning, have almost certainly resulted from a failure to present developmentally appropriate (i.e., interesting, challenging, applicable to life) tasks for older adults. Motivation to perform to highest ability on difficult intellectual tasks appears to be increasingly critical with higher cognitive development and giftedness and with more-experienced participants. In engaging a gifted person, an older person, or most especially a cognitively gifted older person, tasks probably need to be viewed by the person as being important, as personally salient, or as in some way applicable to improving the human condition. Assessors, who apply relativistic thinking in their practice of determining levels of intellectual capability or degree of cognitive giftedness of members within varying populations, could probably achieve more accurate measurements of cognitive potential when they contextualize or "person-alize" some of their assessment procedures to the interests of the person being assessed.

Beyond Relativistic Thinking

In the beginning, there was only chaos. Out of chaos developed cognitive order that consisted mainly of superstition and belief in magic—until Aristotle. Next, making sense of the world meant embracing dualistic logic —until Copernicus, Galileo, and Newton. Understanding then centered on a Newtonian, deterministic, clockwork universe—until Einstein. Initiated by theories of relativity, the cognitive development paradigm is shifting again. Relativistic thinking is spreading from physics to other sciences, ranging from cultural relativism in Margaret Mead's anthropology to social relativism (e.g., Raven, Tijssen, & deWolf, 1991) to cognitive psychology's direct examinations of the intellectual mechanisms in relativistic thinking and finally, to social cognition. These examinations have opened scientific inquiry to the study of highly advanced thought and to the world, or universe (or "multi-verse"?), of cognitive giftedness in adults.

Where might cognitive development in gifted adults lead us from here? Directions toward even more advanced intellect already exist in math (e.g., nonlinearity, multidimensionality, fractals), in physics (e.g., the dual nature of particles/waves in quantum theory, second-order organization in chaos theory, the uncertainty principle, string theory), in computer science (e.g., interactivity, the Net, alternative logic systems), and in the social sciences (dialectical thinking, integrative complexity, wisdom). These advanced forms of thought may originate with the ability to think relativistically. In all probability, relativistic thinking is an advanced form of cognition. Yet further advancement in cognitive development—in making sense of one's universe—probably exists and may extend from relativism. For gifted adults, continued cognitive development may involve increasing understanding of complex dynamics in human motivations and affect. Very advanced intellect may also involve self-aware participation in consensus building and in the construction or the weaving together of intercultural networks. In addition, mature cognitive advancement may involve wise acceptance of differences, of paradox, and of dialectical interaction. Ultimately, adult cognitive giftedness that allows recognition of diversity may go beyond intellectual acceptance of differences into promoting visible celebrations of diversity (see Worthen, 1994). Raven et al. (1991) offered that relativism is no longer a threat; it is a resource. People can learn from each other, these authors have explained, precisely because their cognitive adaptations are different. The current author adds, Long live the difference!

References

Anastasi, A. (1988). *Psychological testing* (6th ed.). New York: Macmillan.
Arbuckle, T. Y., Maag, U., Pushkar, D., & Chaikelson, J. S. (1998). Individual differences in

trajectory of intellectual development over 45 years of adulthood. *Psychology and Aging, 13*, 663–675.

Baltes, P. B. (1987). Theoretical propositions of life-span developmental psychology: On the dynamics between growth and decline. *Developmental Psychology, 23*, 611–626.

Bar-Tal, D., & Nissim, R. (1984). Helping behaviour and moral judgement among adolescents. *British Journal of Developmental Psychology, 2*, 329–336.

Belenky, M. F., Clinchy, B. M., Goldberger, N. R., & Tarule, T. M. (1986). *Women's ways of knowing: The development of self, voice, and mind.* New York: Basic Books.

Benack, S. (1984). Postformal epistemologies and the growth of empathy. In M. L. Commons, F. A. Richards, & C. Armon (Eds.), *Beyond formal operations: Late adolescent and adult cognitive development* (pp. 340–356). New York: Praeger.

Benack, S. (1988). Relativistic thought: A cognitive basis for empathy in counseling. *Counselor Education and Supervision, 3*, 216–232.

Benack, S., & Basseches, M. A. (1989). Dialectical thinking and relativistic epistemology: Their relation in adult development. In M. L. Commons, J. D. Sinnott, F. A. Richards, & C. Armon (Eds.), *Adult development: Vol. 1. Comparisons and applications of developmental models* (pp. 95–109). New York: Praeger.

Blanchard-Fields, F., & Norris, L. (1996). Causal attributions from adolescence through adulthood: Age differences, ego level, and generalized response style. *Aging Neuropsychology and Cognition, 1*, 67–86.

Bower, T. G. R. (1979). *Human development.* San Francisco: Freeman.

Cavanaugh, J. C., Kramer, D. A., Sinnott, J. D., Camp, C. J., & Markley, R. P. (1985). On missing links and such: Interfaces between cognitive research and everyday problem-solving. *Human Development, 28*, 146–168.

Chandler, M. J., Boyes, M., & Ball, L. (1990). Relativism and stations of epistemic doubt. *Journal of Experimental Child Psychology, 50*, 370–395.

Cohen, J. (1960). A coefficient of agreement for nominal scales. *Educational and Psychological Measurement, 20*, 37–46.

Collins, K., Luszcz, M., Lawson, M., & Keeves, J. (1997). Everyday problem solving in elderly women: Contributions of residence, perceived control, and age. *Gerontologist, 37*, 293–302.

Commons, M. L., Richards, F. A., & Armon, C. (1984). *Beyond formal operations: Late adolescent and adult cognitive development.* New York: Praeger.

Commons, M. L., Trudeau, E. J., Stein, S. A., Richards, F. A., & Krause, S. R. (1998). Hierarchical complexity of tasks shows the existence of developmental stages. *Developmental Review, 18*, 237–278.

Erwin, T. D. (1983). The scale of intellectual development: Measuring Perry's scheme. *Journal of College Student Personnel, 24*, 6–12.

Folsom, C. (1998). From a distance: Joining the mind and moral character. *Roeper Review, 20*, 265–270.

Gardner, M. K., & Clark, E. (1992). The psychometric perspective on intellectual development of childhood and adolescence. In R. J. Sternberg & C. A. Berg (Eds.), *Intellectual development* (pp. 16–43). Cambridge, England: Cambridge University Press.

Gerrig, R. J., & Banaji, M. R. (1994). Language and thought. In R. J. Sternberg (Ed.), *Thinking and problem solving: Handbook of perception and cognition* (2nd ed., pp. 233–261). San Diego: Academic Press.

Horn, J. L., & Hofer, S. M. (1992). Major abilities and development in the adult period. In R. J. Sternberg & C. A. Berg (Eds.), *Intellectual development* (pp. 44–99). Cambridge, MA: Cambridge University Press.

Inhelder, B., & Piaget, J. (1958). *The growth of logical thinking: From childhood to adolescence.* New York: Basic Books.

Kitchener, K. S., & King, P. M. (1981). Reflective judgment: Concepts of justification and their relationships to age and education. *Journal of Applied Developmental Psychology, 2*, 89–116.

Kramer, D. A. (1983). Post-formal operations? A need for further conceptualization. *Human Development, 26*, 91–105.

Kramer, D. A. (1986). A life-span view of social cognition. *Educational Gerontology, 12*, 277–289.

Labouvie-Vief, G. (1992). A neo-Piagetian perspective on adult cognitive development. In R. J. Sternberg & C. A. Berg (Eds.), *Intellectual development* (pp. 197–228). Cambridge, England: Cambridge University Press.

Lee, D. (1989). Everyday problem solving: Implications for education. In J. D. Sinnott (Ed.), *Everyday problem solving: Theory and applications* (pp. 251–265). New York: Praeger.

Moore, W. S. (1989). The "Learning Environment Preferences": Exploring the construct validity of an objective measure of the Perry Scheme of intellectual development. *Journal of College Student Development, 30,* 504–514.

Perry, B., Donovan, M. P., Kelsey, L. J., Paterson, J., Statkiewicz, W., & Allen, R. D. (1986). Two schemes of intellectual development: A comparison of development as defined by William Perry and Jean Piaget. *Journal of Research in Science Teaching, 23,* 73–83.

Perry, W. G. (1968). *Patterns of development in thought and values of students in a liberal arts college: A validation of a scheme.* Cambridge, MA: Harvard University, Bureau of Student Counsel. (ERIC Document Reproduction Service No. ED 024 315)

Perry, W. G. (1970). *Forms of intellectual and ethical development in the college years: A scheme.* New York: Holt, Rinehart & Winston.

Perry, W. G. (1981). Cognitive and ethical growth: The making of meaning. In A. Chickering (Ed.), *The modern American college* (pp. 76–116). San Francisco: Jossey-Bass.

Perry, W. G. (1990). Foreword. In W. L. Bateman (Ed.), *Open to question: The art of teaching and learning by inquiry* (pp. xi–xiii). San Francisco: Jossey-Bass.

Piaget, J. (1977). *Psychology and epistemology* (A. Rosen., Trans.). Harmondsworth, England: Penguin.

Piaget, J., & Inhelder, B. (1969). *The psychology of the child.* New York: Basic Books.

Powell, P. M. (1984). Stage 4a: Category operations and interactive empathy. In M. L. Commons, F. A. Richards, & C. Armon (Eds.), *Beyond formal operations: Late adolescent and adult cognitive development* (pp. 326–339). New York: Praeger.

Raven, D., Tijssen, L. V., & deWolf, J. (1991). *Cognitive relativism and social science.* New Brunswick, NJ: Transaction.

Richards, F. A., & Commons, M. L. (1984). Systemic, metasystemic, and cross-paradigmatic reasoning: A case for stages of reasoning beyond formal operations. In M. L. Commons, F. A. Richards, & C. Armon (Eds.), *Beyond formal operations: Late adolescent and adult cognitive development* (pp. 92–119). New York: Praeger.

Ruck, M. D., Keating, D. P., Abramovitch, R., & Koegl, C. J. (1998). Adolescents' and children's knowledge about rights: Some evidence for how young people view rights in their own lives. *Journal of Adolescence, 21,* 275–289.

Ryan, M. P. (1984a). Conceptions of prose coherence: Individual differences in epistemological standards. *Journal of Educational Psychology, 76,* 1226–1238.

Ryan, M. P. (1984b). Monitoring test comprehension: Individual differences in epistemological standards. *Journal of Educational Psychology, 76,* 248–258.

Schaie, K. W. (1993). Ageist language in psychological research. *American Psychologist, 48,* 49–51.

Schaie, K. W., & Willis, S. L. (1986). Chapter Nine: Intellectual development. In *Adult aging and development* (2nd ed., pp. 278–323). Boston: Little, Brown.

Schwartz, N. H., & Wilkinson, W. K. (1988). The relationship between epistemological orientation and cognitive abilities. *Educational and Psychological Research, 8,* 129–139.

Singh, B., & Forsythe, D. R. (1989). Sexual attitudes and moral values: The importance of idealism and relativism. *Bulletin of the Psychonomic Society, 27,* 160–162.

Sinnott, J. D. (1984). Postformal reasoning: The relativistic stage. In M. L. Commons, F. A. Richards, & C. Armon (Eds.), *Beyond formal operations: Late adolescent and adult cognitive development* (pp. 298–325). New York: Praeger.

Sinnott, J. D. (1989a). Life-span relativistic postformal thought: Methodology and data from everyday problem solving studies. In M. L. Commons, F. A. Richards, J. D. Sinnott, & C. Armon (Eds.), *Adult development: Vol. 1. Comparisons and applications of developmental models* (pp. 239–278). New York: Praeger.

Sinnott, J. D. (1989b). A model for solution of ill-structured problems: Implications for everyday and abstract problem solving. In J. D. Sinnott (Ed.), *Everyday problem solving: Theory and applications* (pp. 84–99). New York: Praeger.

Sinnott, J. D. (1993). Yes, it's worth the trouble! Unique contributions from everyday cognitive studies. In J. M. Puckett & H. W. Reese (Eds.), *Mechanisms of everyday cognition* (pp. 73–94). Hillsdale, NJ: Erlbaum.

Sinnott, J. D. (Ed.). (1994a). *Interdisciplinary handbook of adult lifespan learning.* Westport, CT: Greenwood Press.

Sinnott, J. D. (1994b). The relationship of postformal thought, adult learning, and lifespan development. In *Interdisciplinary handbook of adult lifespan learning* (pp. 105–119). Westport, CT: Greenwood Press.

Sinnott, J. D. (1997). Developmental models of midlife and aging in women: Metaphors for transcendence and for individuality in community. In J. M Coyle (Ed.), *Handbook on women and aging* (pp. 149–163). Westport, CT: Greenwood Press.

Sinnott, J. D. (1998). *The development of logic in adulthood: Postformal thought and its applications.* New York: Plenum Press.

Sinnott, J. D., & Cavanaugh, J. C. (1991). *Bridging paradigms: Positive development in adulthood and cognitive aging.* New York: Praeger.

Slobin, D. I. (1992). *The crosslinguistic study of language acquisition* (Vol. 3). Hillsdale, NJ: Erlbaum.

Smith, J., & Baltes, P. B. (1990). Wisdom-related knowledge: Age-cohort differences in response to life-planning problems. *Developmental Psychology, 26,* 494–505.

Smith, J., Staudinger, U. M., & Baltes, P. B. (1994). Occupational settings facilitating wisdom-related knowledge: The sample case of clinical psychologists. *Journal of Consulting and Clinical Psychology, 62,* 989–999.

Sternberg, R. J., & Powell, J. S. (1983). The development of intelligence. In J. H. Flavell & E. M. Markman (Eds.), *Handbook of child psychology: Vol. 3. Cognitive development* (4th ed., pp. 341–419). New York: Wiley.

Stonewater, B. B., Stonewater, J. K., & Hadley, T. D. (1986). Intellectual development using the Perry scheme: An exploratory comparison of two assessment instruments. *Journal of College Student Personnel, 27,* 542–547.

Wainryb, C. (1993). The applications of moral judgments to other cultures: Relativism and universality. *Child Development, 64,* 924–933.

Wechsler, D. (1955). *Manual for the Wechsler Adult Intelligence Scale.* New York: Psychological Corporation.

Wechsler, D. (1972). "Hold" and "don't hold" tests. In S. M. Chown (Ed.), *Human aging.* New York: Penguin.

Wilkinson, W. K., & Schwartz, N. H. (1987). The epistemological orientation of gifted adolescents: An empirical test of Perry's model. *Psychological Reports, 61,* 967–978.

Worthen, M. F. (1992a, April). *The development of relativistic thinking: Evidence for a postformal cognitive stage.* Paper presented at the annual meeting of the Southwestern Psychological Association, Austin, TX.

Worthen, M. F. (1992b, February). *The role of the development of relativistic thinking in identifying adolescents of intellectual promise.* Paper presented at the Second Annual Esther Katz Rosen Symposium on the Psychological Development of Gifted Children, Lawrence, KS.

Worthen, M. F. (1993a, February). *Development of relativistic thinking across the lifespan: The Piagetian perspective and the Perry scheme.* Paper presented at the Third Annual Esther Katz Rosen Symposium on the Psychological Development of Gifted Children, Lawrence, KS.

Worthen, M. F. (1993b, March). *Cognitive development and empathy in adolescents: Intellectual and affective decentering.* Paper presented at the annual meeting of the Society for Research in Child Development, New Orleans, LA.

Worthen, M. F. (1994, September–October). *Development of acceptance of diversity: Is it related to intellectual giftedness or to age-associated experience?* Paper presented at the Fourth Annual Esther Katz Rosen Symposium on the Psychological Development of Gifted Children, Lawrence, KS.

Worthen, M. F. (1995, September). *Is the loss of empathy an emotional price of cognitive excellence?* Paper presented at the Fifth Annual Esther Katz Rosen Symposium on the Psychological Development of Gifted Children, Lawrence, KS.
Worthen, M. F. (1996, September). *Cognitive giftedness and ethical development: Taking the moral high ground or sharing the caring common ground?* Poster presented at the Sixth Annual Esther Katz Rosen Symposium on the Psychological Development of Gifted Children, Lawrence, KS.

8

Metacognition and Flexibility: Qualitative Differences in How Gifted Children Think

Bruce M. Shore

Since the late 1970s, my colleagues, students, and I have conducted a number of studies of how gifted students might think differently from other learners.[1] We have focused especially on differences in metacognitive processes—that is, the monitoring, evaluation, and control of thinking strategies—and on the flexibility of use of those strategies. We have also been interested in the juxtaposition of the gifted and cognitive literatures with regard to thinking processes. After briefly describing some overarching issues, this chapter describes some of our studies bearing on these topics and concludes with implications for quality education of all students, the impetus of all of our research efforts.

Qualitative or Quantitative Questions

Halbert Robinson (1977) was one of the first psychologists to examine giftedness in very young children. He posed an important challenge to the conceptualization of gifted education by noting that, on the basis of the evidence available at the time, one could not conclude that the thinking of gifted children was qualitatively different from that of others not so identified. In other words, the evidence then supported the notion that giftedness was precocity, although Robinson did suggest that some qualitative differences might one day be demonstrated.

His challenge is critical to one of the most central issues in the identification and education of gifted students: If giftedness is merely precocity, then acceleration appears to be the most appropriate form of educational enrichment, and extremely high psychometric test scores (IQ and achievement data in particular) would be confirmed as the most suitable means

---

[1]The principal researchers over the years (Bruce M. Shore, F. Gillian Rejskind, Glenn F. Cartwright, Lannie S. Kanevsky, Marcia A. B. Delcourt, and Mark W. Aulls) are all teachers who have added qualifications in general or educational psychology rather than psychologists who have taken an interest in education. One of our collaborators (Andrew Carson) was a counseling psychologist.

of identification. On the other hand, if giftedness involves different ways of thinking, then a differentiated curriculum (a concept promoted by Ward, 1961) would have to include more than just increasing the level of difficulty and the pace at which teaching and learning are encountered.

Of those whose work supported the latter perspective, Flavell (1976), who is known to educators as an interpreter of Piaget, proposed that one must look not only at quantitative differences in performance, but also at how children solve problems and how they monitor, evaluate, and adjust their performance while doing so. "Try to find out what is running through the child's mind as he or she wends his or her way through the task" (p. 234). Flavell (1980) later inquired about the target of development in terms of adult-like knowledge and behavior toward which gradual progress occurs. Would gifted children follow such a gradual path? The question has yet to be answered as to whether such processes, which I call *metacognitive strategies*, may contribute beyond precocity to our understanding of giftedness.

Creating the link to flexibility was prompted by research on academic learning by Kirby and Das (1977). They compared simultaneous and successive processing in college students and found that the highest performance was achieved by students who used both kinds of processes, depending on the demands of the task. Jaušovec (1994, especially see chapter 3; reviewed by Shore, 1996) summarized the literature on strategy flexibility and metacognition in relation to giftedness and, aided by additional studies of his own, supported our conclusions about their importance in understanding giftedness. His studies focused on the effects of two years of training flexible thinking skills on school children's solutions of well- and ill-defined problems. Such training closed the gap between average-ability and gifted students on the well-defined problems, but the gap persisted on open-ended problems requiring greater creativity. Jaušovec only briefly addressed developmental issues, primarily in reference to Vygotsky.

Cognitive–Developmental Questions

First, if giftedness is precocity, then how can one account for giftedness in adults? This topic has been addressed theoretically (e.g., Rabinowitz & Glaser, 1985), but the weight of published evidence remained in favor of Robinson's assessment—namely, that there were not qualitative differences in the thinking of gifted children (Rogers, 1986).

A second unanswered (and relatively unexplored) question concerns the relatedness of giftedness and the cognitive processes that experts (in contrast to novices) use in solving problems. Examples of the expert behavior that we have explored in highly able children include (cf. Coleman & Shore, 1991, for additional cross-references to original sources) the following:

- Experts develop and use more self-regulatory processes—such monitoring, evaluating, and correcting are encompassed by the term *metacognition* (Glaser, 1985).

- Experts develop automaticity, particularly with regard to simpler tasks or parts of tasks, presumably freeing working memory for more complex or novel task demands and for self-regulation (Perfetti & Lesgold, 1979).

- Experts take longer pauses during early stages of problem solving, such as data gathering, and execute the overall problem with fewer errors (Ericsson & Simon, 1980; Larkin, 1979).

- Experts are goal driven, and their problem-solving behavior reflects a mental representation of the problem and its categorization in relation to more extensive and interconnected (or webbed) prior knowledge (Chi, Glaser, & Rees, 1982; Glaser, 1985; Sternberg, 1981).

- Experts solve problems with a "forward" strategy, one in which they evaluate steps or groups of steps (corresponding to subroutines to computer programmers) in terms of their expected effect on their progress toward the goal (Simon & Simon, 1978).

In the course of exploring these and other qualities of expert adult thinking in relation to giftedness, it was necessary to select tasks that were appropriate to children who, at the very least, may have had less knowledge and less practice using this knowledge while addressing novel or complex tasks. Smaller components of expertise must therefore be studied, at least initially or especially with younger children.

Metacognition and flexibility, as addressed in this chapter, refer to two related parts of expert performance: (a) self-regulation and (b) the combination of a more extensive repertoire of knowledge (whether procedural or declarative) and the selective use of this knowledge as circumstances warrant. The parts are related at least at the level of adjusting strategies in response to monitoring and evaluating that one's course of action will not lead to the desired outcome (or that another kind of error, such as grammar or miscalculation, has been made along the way). A person must also have a store of suitably interconnected knowledge to be flexible.

There is also an underlying issue to keep in mind as context. The relation of thinking processes of gifted children and of adult experts has important implications for the development of both children who are gifted and those of average ability. In the cognitive literature, the key comparison is between experts and novices. In the gifted education literature, it is between identified gifted children and others not so identified. The literature on giftedness is burdened with the hereditary argument that dominates the literature on IQ. That may be a consequence of working in an area of study that traces its modern empirical origins to Galton's (1869/ 1979) *Hereditary Genius* and having a label ("gifted") invented by Terman in the course of the standardization of the Stanford–Binet IQ test (cf. Harry Passow's "Foreword" to Shore, Cornell, Robinson, & Ward, 1991). In contrast, novices learn—indeed, are taught—to become experts. If it can be shown that gifted children exhibit thinking processes similar to those of adults deemed experts, would this mean that a certain degree or some portion of giftedness can be learned? A serious gap in the expert–novice cognitive literature is that there is no agreement on the definition of a novice and no clear idea about how one becomes a novice within a domain of expertise—a cognitive and affective question. Novices (persons at some early point in the acquisition of adult expertise) are, in most instances, already motivated and highly selected (for example, on the basis of interest, prior performance, or knowledge). The relative importance of selection and training in the development of expertise is largely uncharted, but the focus in the literature has been on elements that can be taught and learned at least in substantial part.

Flavell (1980) had not specified the extent to which or the manner in which the progression toward adult-like performance had to be mediated, that is, as educators might use this term, guided in some systematic way by adults or children functioning at a more advanced level. Others who have influenced our work, such as Vygotsky (1978; also see Wertsch, 1979), argued that mediation was essential, as would Feuerstein (Feuerstein, Rand, & Rynders, 1988). That still does not tell us if we are dealing with intellectual skills that await optimal conditions to evolve from within, skills that need to be transmitted pedagogically, or in some combination of the two. In terms of providing capable or other students with intellectual skills needed to thrive in the 21st century, this is an important educational question. This chapter stops considerably short of an answer, but the question is part of the context for examining the relatedness of giftedness and expertise.

The third cognitive–developmental question concerns the smoothness or unevenness of the development of intellectual skills in expertise that might also be associated with giftedness.

The general cognitive hypothesis underlying our studies is that performance should be enhanced by the flexible use of metacognitive strategies. That is, learners who have a repertoire of problem-solving strategies and are able to monitor, evaluate, and correct their thinking processes flexibly in the course of problem solving should do better than those who do not exhibit such strategies (Shore, 1981, 1982, 1991). A second hypothesis is that those who are labeled as gifted will exhibit such metacognitive strategies to a greater extent than those not so identified. Finally, we have hypothesized that the performance of those labeled as gifted will resemble expert performance.

The three sections that follow provide an overview of our research in developmental context, our interim conclusions, and some plans for and speculations about this work, which is still in progress. In the following research summaries I attempt to shed some light on both the qualitative dimension of giftedness and the relation between thinking processes of gifted students and adult experts.

An Overview of the Research

Preschool

Three of our studies involved preschool children, the youngest of whom were age 3 years. Ellen Moss (1983, 1990) observed children ages 3 and 4 years with high and average IQs doing a series of puzzles in interaction with their mothers. While explaining the tasks to the children and being with them while they did the puzzles, the mothers of the higher-IQ children typically uttered instructions that gave the children principles by which they could do the tasks or that modeled self-monitoring. Mothers of the average-IQ children more often gave specific solutions. For example, in a jigsaw puzzle, mothers in the high-IQ group would evoke rules from their children, such as looking for matching colors or straight edges around the outside; in a block-building game, they asked their children what they would like to build and to think about how they should go about it. The other mothers more often showed where specific pieces fit or suggested—sometimes very directly—what to build (examples from both sets of protocols are available in Shore, Coleman, & Moss, 1992). The children's performance varied correspondingly. The high-IQ children created more elaborate block structures and voiced judgments about the quality of match between their block constructions and the goal (e.g., a fire engine). In the puzzle, the high-IQ children more often used rules (procedural knowledge) to search for pieces to fit.

We cannot conclude from this study that the mothers' teaching caused the enhanced performance, because the teaching could also have been a response to perceived ability in the child, and a possible methodological limitation of the study is that observations of the mothers' and children's performance was not conducted independently. The recurring nature-versus-nurture issue is not hereby resolved. Moss is continuing to study these interactions as a faculty member at the Université du Québec à Montréal. This research supports continued attention to the possible learning of behavior that might be described as gifted. Equally interesting is the possibility that the relationship between the child as learner and the parent as teacher might be informed by studies of the cultural transmission of talent or giftedness. The skills needed by parents to teach thinking strategies should be explored, as well as conditions that enhance or hinder parents' and children's performance. Up to this point, we have observed in preschool children performance that in adults would be described as metacognitive, and we observed more of it in a group that by one common definition (high IQ) could be described as gifted.

A second study with the same children examined their perspective taking (Tarshis & Shore, 1991). Being able to take the view of another, or perhaps coordinating alternative perspectives, would seem to be an important step in learning alternative approaches to a problem and to the development of flexibility.

Classic Piagetian tasks were easily adapted to our research. We replaced the rather abstract conical mountains with a colorful toy barnyard scene, because we did not want the perspective-taking task to be confounded by the need to make sense of abstract objects. After walking around the table with the toy barnyard, each child was seated at a chair facing the toys and was then shown eight photographs taken at 45-degree intervals where the children just walked. A familiar puppet was placed at each of the eight positions, and each child was asked to select the photograph depicting what the puppet would see from each position. The higher IQ group more often correctly recognized that the view of someone 45 degrees to either side was indeed another person's view. The difficulty with these adjacent views is that the two viewers do have many common elements in their sight; distinguishing them (in effect, not being egocentric) is a considerable accomplishment in terms of taking a subtly different perspective. Even at ages 3 or 4 years there are ability-related differences in this performance; however, we cannot tell if it is learned. We suggest, nonetheless, that some young children demonstrate rather early progress toward adult-like performance on a task where the elements to be manipulated are within their experience. The idea that performance on some Piagetian tasks may be "learning confounded" has also been suggested by Porath (1992), who concluded also that young high-IQ children performed like their mental-age peers when such confounding occurred. In the light of the next study, the effects of learning in such performance may require further consideration.

The third study was conducted by Lannie Kanevsky (now at Simon Fraser University) at Columbia University just before she joined our research team for three years. Kanevsky (1990, 1992) compared four groups of preschool children matched variously on mental and chronological age and assessed their transfer between physical and computerized adaptations of the classic Missionaries and Cannibals problem. Performance by the younger, higher-mental-age group was not matched in all respects by older children of similar mental age and exceeded that observed in other children of the same chronological age. The differences between equal-mental-age groups were found especially in such performance as being able to explain illegal moves (e.g., a larger ring may not be placed over a smaller) and in superior attitudes toward challenging learning situations. The explanations of illegal views reflect the monitoring and evaluating components of metacognition. The attitudinal differences are indirectly related: They allude to the heightened motivation of novices and attraction to complexity among gifted children (Bowen, Shore, & Cartwright, 1992; Maniatis, Cartwright, & Shore, 1998).

Elementary School

We have conducted three groups of studies at this level. The first arose in part from one of the commonly studied learning-styles taxonomies, that of reflectivity versus impulsivity (Kagan, Moss, & Siegel, 1963). Slow, accurate performance (labeled *reflective*) on the Matching Familiar Figures test was supposed to be superior to fast, inaccurate performance (labeled *impulsive*). Nothing was said about the fast, accurate performers? Who are they, and whom are they most like? Why are they not considered in discussions of this construct, even if most subjects fall into the two labeled categories? From a series of regression analyses we concluded that both speed and accuracy significantly predicted IQ scores. Speed did not significantly add to the prediction made by accuracy alone, but accuracy significantly improved the prediction from speed alone (Lajoie & Shore, 1986, 1987). Accuracy was the salient characteristic of high ability, at whatever speed the student was most comfortable operating. The admonition to slow down to improve accuracy may be ill directed; the better instruction might be to directly attend to accuracy. Bright students who work quickly and make errors should presumably attend to the problem, which is the errors rather than the speed. Improving accuracy demands self-monitoring of performance and, on occasion, corrective action. Whether or not the advice to attend to accuracy applies to all students is a different question, and it was partly addressed in another study noted later in this section. Respect for what may be differences in personal style or the effects of extended repetition or practice (in this case speed) is reasonable when dealing with adults and may also be warranted when examining the components of behavior that are associated with high IQ.

Our second set of studies also drew on a classic research paradigm, the water-jar mixture or "Einstellung" problems most extensively explored by Luchins (cf. Dover & Shore, 1991). The task involves breaking an induced set that is presumed to predispose the problem solver to use a particular solution strategy. After two demonstration examples, the set is established in the 3rd to 6th of a series of 11 problems. The 9th problem can be solved only with an alternative strategy; it serves as a test of flexibility. The 7th and 8th can be solved by the method required in problem 9, or the "set" method; more flexible solvers might elect an alternative (and simpler, two-step) solution when it is available rather than only when required. The participants were school-identified gifted and control-group 11-year-old students; most previous research with the water-jar task had been done with college students.

We examined flexibility, speed, and metacognitive knowledge on the water-jar problems. The key result was a three-way interaction among giftedness, speed, and flexibility, with metacognitive knowledge as the criterion. Metacognitive knowledge was assessed by an interview after the task that probed awareness of different kinds of solutions and of the unique characteristics of problems 7 and 9. At all speeds, the inflexible gifted children demonstrated less metacognitive knowledge than the flexible gifted children. Flexible gifted children who took less time revealed more metacognitive knowledge (in an interview) than those who took more time. At all speeds, inflexible average children had less metacognitive knowledge, but slower, flexible nongifted children indicated greater metacognitive knowledge. The gifted students were also more aware of the potential influence on their performance of the availability of an alternative solution at problem 7.

Flexibility and metacognition appear to be linked to each other and to high ability. They are invoked relatively quickly by more able students, and there is a suggestion here that metacognition is not merely part of a specific solution strategy, but an active state of mind. To return to the issue of speed versus accuracy, taking one's time may be to the advantage of less able students and might encourage their use of metacognition. The advice to attend to accuracy rather than speed might be most appropriate for more capable students, who also demonstrate that they have available a repertoire of suitable solution strategies that they can invoke as required by the demands of a task.

This classic design also left one group of students on the sidelines, as in the research on reflectivity and impulsivity. This time it was the students who are assumed not to have fully formed the response set on the 3rd to 6th trials; more precisely, they do not give the "Einstellung" response to all of these four problems. They have traditionally been dropped from the analyses. Why do they not form the set? Do they share a strength of resistance to forming sets, or are they less able to do so? Quite simply, who are they? This question was pursued (Shore, Koller, & Dover, 1994), including a re-examination of the data on hand. In general, including the children who did not meet the criterion for the trial items would not have changed the overall results as they are usually reported. However, one special insight was gained. Our first study pointed to the metacognitive superiority of gifted children who work quickly and demonstrate flexibility in their strategies. Average children who worked more slowly demonstrated greater metacognition. The second study limited the conclusion about gifted children to those who work with higher accuracy; less accurate gifted children were deficient in metacognitive knowledge and made other kinds of errors. Accuracy and metacognition seem to be the critical variables. This might imply that able, accurate students with good metacognitive skills are better suited to working more quickly than any student, gifted or not, who may be deficient in either metacognition or accuracy. The latter may need extra time to work on both of the latter. This is consistent with the work by Lajoie and Shore (1986), who also suggested that there was more to be gained by focusing on accuracy than speed.

The third group of elementary-age studies examined differences between gifted and other children's performance in computer environments. Computers are appropriate to this type of research because they provide some control for teacher variance, and they especially favor students exploring alternative views: "What makes the computer stand out (among information technologies) is its ability to represent information in many different ways, and to switch instantly between alternative representations" (Shavelson & Salomon, 1986, p. 24). In the first of these studies, Maniatis (1983), supervised by Cartwright, compared 9- to 11-year-old school-identified gifted children who also had above-average IQs with a group of average-IQ children on LOGO turtle graphics problems, which they devised and worked out (problem finding and solving). The gifted pairs generated and completed a greater number of complex projects. The tree structures of these projects contained more levels (indicating nested routines or subroutines). They made similar numbers of corrections, but the average group made more corrections during the design of the tasks, and the gifted group made more after the program was drafted and while it was being tried. The corrections made by the average-ability teams typically involved specific, small inputs. The gifted students made more global revisions related to the general operation of the program and that often affected more steps. In other words, they "chunked" larger numbers of elements and steps. The gifted dyads also used strategies more consistently. The groups did not differ on overall numbers of errors or the kinds of errors. They used the same strategies to detect what errors they sought. A simple psychometric account of the performance would not have revealed most of the differences that were found. This was taken to support the argument for qualitative differences in favor of gifted students and that their performance more closely resembled that which would have been expected of expert adults (Maniatis et al., 1998).

Complementary results were obtained in an examination of high-achieving and average children's responses to an instructional computer game, The Factory (from Sunburst Software), which had received an award as outstanding software by the Association for the Gifted of the Council for Exceptional Children (Bowen et al., 1992). The program simulates an imaginary machine shop that can be used to drill, groove, and rotate a block of material so as to make a displayed object. Expert strategies such as working with a plan and metacognition are advantageous to efficient and successful performance. The more able group more often worked with a plan and offered a greater number of suggestions for improving the software. Many of their suggestions would have increased its complexity and challenge.[2]

Our studies with elementary-age pupils suggest that children who obtain higher IQ scores or who do better at school more often create for themselves and solve relatively sophisticated problems using strategies that are commonly found in adult experts, such as working with a plan, metacognition, favoring complexity, and organizing their knowledge hierarchically.

Elementary and High School

A third set of studies, still being analyzed, used a different software environment with slightly older children (grades 7 and 8) who could be in elementary, middle, or secondary school, depending on the jurisdiction. The task was to identify a pattern of lily pads on a partial view of an imaginary pond (the software is The Pond, also from Sunburst Software). Only a portion of the pattern is visible through the window provided by the computer screen. The cursor keys can be used to move a frog across the pads to explore the pattern (the number of steps is selected in advance by the user). For example, a three-step problem could be two jumps up, three right, and one left. Repetition of this pattern will lead safely across the pond without falling in. Once the user has a hypothesis about the pattern, pushing one key changes the mode to allow the answer to be

---

[2]The program offers an option for pairs of students to construct items and then challenge each other to build it. This offers the possibility of comparing interactions in variously composed dyads, as was done in the LOGO study. This process of interaction may be useful in studying the possible acquisition of the intellectual skills useful for success on this task. It is also compatible with Piagetian theory regarding the importance of peer interaction in intellectual development.

given. In other words, there are explicit planning and execution stages. We were therefore able to compare the planning and execution times of our participants on this task, as well as various other measures of error, success, and time. The most important result so far is that the expert–novice contrast in planning and execution times is clearly visible between the high-IQ and average groups (Shore & Lazar, 1996). The planning times are relatively greater for the high group, although not absolutely, perhaps because the task is comparatively simple. The effects of the difficulty or novelty of the task remain to be assessed. Also, is it possible to talk about an "expert" on a novel task? Is this dilemma merely semantic? Taking relatively more time to plan possibly contradicts the idea of automaticity. We are awaiting conclusion of a replication (with Kathryn Macdonald) in which talk-aloud protocols were collected to verify if the observed differences are corroborated by evidence that different thinking processes were used.[3]

We have confirmed that more able students are relatively slower on the exploratory parts of problem solving but not absolutely slower if, it appears, the problem is easy for them. As Sternberg (1986) and others (see Bowen et al., 1992) have pointed out, the degree of novelty in the situation is important. What is going on in the children's heads at the exploratory stage has not yet been examined with this age group, but it has at the high school level. We shall return to this matter; for now it is sufficient to offer the conjecture that taking more time in the exploratory stage of problem solving (or problem finding) might allow scope for the consideration of alternatives and may be especially compatible with the notion of strategy flexibility.

Our most ambitious mixed-age study of cognitive processes in gifted students involved pupils at both the elementary and high school levels. If metacognition and flexibility especially distinguish the thinking of gifted children, then both types of processes should be especially discernible in a situation wherein learning would not occur without their use (in contrast to the potential for their use when they may not be essential—as in the contrast between problems 9 and 7 in the water-jar studies). Lynne Hannah (now on the faculty of Shepherd College) combined her interest in gifted children with learning disabilities with the issues we were studying (cf. Hannah, 1989; Hannah & Shore, 1995). Because students with reading impairments must use alternative strategies to manage in a literate world (and the reading literature has pioneered many of the best studies of metacognition, including numerous studies by Ann Brown and Campione, 1986, among others), we asked if these strategies are especially present in gifted students with learning disabilities. Are the thinking strategies of the latter group on a comprehension-monitoring task more similar to "ordinary" gifted students, average students, or reading-impaired students

---

[3]The sensitivity of such simple software as The Pond and The Factory to cognitive processing differences between gifted and other children is interesting. It remains to be shown if such software can be used to train such "gifted" or "expert" thinking skills in children, which both programs (and others) are intended to do.

not in any other category? The learning-disabled gifted children made sense of unfamiliar and unreasonable terms in a text within their reading ability by using strategies (including evidence of monitoring and metacognitive statements) in ways most similar to those of the gifted group at both age levels. There was, however, a grade-by-giftedness interaction. At the secondary level, the gifted and learning-disabled gifted students did not perform better than the average group specifically on metacognitive knowledge and comprehension of the material. Did this finding support the precocity argument at the same time? We think not. A better explanation is a ceiling effect, because these skills have been shown in numerous studies to improve with age. We also noted that the oldest children in previous studies reporting improvement of these skills with age were the same age as our elementary-age sample (grades 4 and 5). The high school situation requires further study.

The general conclusion to be carried forward from this study is that the metacognitive characteristics associated with giftedness are found in gifted children both with and without a specific learning disability, notably at the elementary level. The learning disability is not critical to this study; it enabled another perspective of the nature of high ability and how it is manifested in cognitive terms.

High School and College

Our studies exclusively at the secondary level especially addressed strategy flexibility, beginning with an examination of gender differences in how students use spatial or verbal strategies to solve a spatial task, specifically, an embedded-figures discrimination task. Girls' and boys' factor loadings for measures of field-independence–dependence loaded on different factors drawn from a large battery of different tests (Shore, Hymovitch, & Lajoie, 1982). The field-independence–dependence tests appear on the surface to be very spatial, and for boys they loaded on the same factor as a group of spatial tests, but for girls they loaded with verbal measures.[4]

Girls may have been reinterpreting or restating the task in ways that linked successful performance with their relatively superior verbal performance that is common in early teenage years. S. W. Brown and Yakimowski (1987) observed different Wechsler Intelligence Scale for Children–Revised (WISC–R) factor structures for gifted students and also inferred that different solution strategies may have been used.

This hypothesis of selectively responding to tasks from the perspective of procedural strengths was consistent with Getzels and Csikszentmihalyi's (1976) observation that art students who later became successful artists reframed still-life assignments in terms that better suited them-

---

[4]When Witkin and colleagues (Witkin, Dyk, Faterson, Goodenough, & Karp, 1963) conducted their original studies, they reported that females were highly field dependent and thus carried out most of the research with males only. This created a bias in the concept; we took care to avoid assuming that there were gender differences. We were interested only in explaining accurate performance on the measures.

selves. It also allowed us to restate the problem as one of intellectual strength rather than gender. In a follow-up study (Shore & Carey, 1984) we worked with 69 boys and 53 girls in our summer demonstration program for gifted pupils, all of whom would be entering grades 6 to 10 the following September. The numbers of boys and girls were about equal across grades. Each child was tested on the Block Design and Vocabulary subtests of the WISC–R IQ test and categorized according to which was the higher. We had not yet come across protocol analysis, so we kept detailed notes from tapes of comments made by each student as they worked with the portable rod-and-frame apparatus as a test of field-independence–dependence. The higher vocabulary scorers, male and female, were more verbal during their efforts on the task; they guided their solutions with verbal instructions and were better able to verbalize how they solved the problem. This led to further exploration of the hypothesis that more able students might adopt problem-solving strategies more closely linked to their intellectual strengths.

We explored this in a still ongoing series of studies involving mathematical tasks, some of them based directly on school curriculum. Some partial results are available. First, we selected two groups of students from an advanced mathematics class in the final year of high school. All had done exceptionally well in the regular course the year before. The first group was doing very well in the advanced course, and the second was demonstrating mediocre performance (roughly the top and bottom thirds of the advanced class). We asked them all to solve a selection of Krutetskii's (1976) mathematical word problems, which differed in the ease with which they could be solved by verbal–logical and visual strategies. Verbal strategies were used pervasively, perhaps an artifact of the tasks being word problems. Less competent students more often used trial-and-error. We particularly observed what happened when students encountered difficulties. Both groups changed strategies, so it appears that the part of flexibility that triggers a change in approach did not differ at these levels of performance. The difference was that the higher performing group changed to another suitable solution strategy (e.g., between verbal and visual), but the lower performing students more often reverted from either verbal or visual strategies to unsystematic trial and error (Kaizer & Shore, 1995). High performance in regular high school mathematics may better reflect the ability to execute the sequence of a solution than to select an appropriate strategy. Extremely high competence was associated with being able to select an appropriate alternative when one approach failed. This is consistent with experts' more extensive and more extensively webbed previous knowledge of content and strategies (procedures) in a domain.

We then asked at what point in the solution of a problem alternatives might be considered. Is it only at the point when one strategy fails? Perhaps an active metacognitive thinker is open to alternatives at all stages of working on a problem. We decided to look at problem categorization, a feature of expert performance also central to Krutetskii's research and one of the first steps in considering a problem and selecting a solution strategy.

A selection of problems from Canadian provincial high school graduation examinations was presented in three different forms: words, equa-
tions, and graphics (Pelletier & Shore, 1989; Shore, Kaizer, & Pelletier,
1990). The problems also differed in underlying mathematical content and
could be categorized in a completely crossed fashion. The subjects included
three groups: (a) the top 8 students in an advanced high school mathematics class, (b) 4 students from the lower end of performance in the same
class with 4 volunteers from a regular class taught by the same teacher
who taught in the same manner in both classes, and (c) 8 mathematics
graduate students. We asked the students not to solve the problems,
merely to categorize them into groups of problems according to the mathematical structure.

Higher-achieving students and graduate students were, however,
more similar to each other and different from the lower achieving students
in the advanced course in the following way. The former used fewer categories in their initial sort and spontaneously had subgrouped (hierar-
chized) some problems. The groupings were typically on the basis of substantive similarity of the problems. The lower achieving students offered
many more categories with fewer problems in each category, often only
one problem on its own. For this to happen, surface variables (in this case
presentation format) might have been invoked more often as a basis for
categorization (of course, the response may also have been much less systematic). When prompted to subcategorize, all groups did so, but the two
superior groups once again took further spontaneous steps and further
grouped some of the problems. However, some graph problems were so
categorized because the word "graph" appeared, others because there was
a graph. Word problems were so categorized by some average-ability students as a result of their being "wordy" or their resemblance to examples
the teachers used, but some experts focused on their multistep character
or on their resembling "public school" mathematics examples. Further
analysis is needed of the role of surface variables in problem categorization, because there were also unexpected confounding results in what was
interpreted to be a word problem.

From this as yet unpublished study (done with Pelletier), we have
evidence of flexibility associated with high ability and corroboration of the
hierarchization differences observed in the LOGO study. The parallels between gifted students and experts appear to be sustained even in an early
stage of problem solving, namely problem categorization.

In the earlier discussion of the differential use of time in exploratory
and execution stages of problem solving, it was noted that we had not (up
to that point) studied what was happening in students' thinking during
the exploratory stage. Another piece of software, The King's Rule (also
from Sunburst), was built around number-series tasks. It allows an examination of hypothesis making in the course of problem solving, because
the rule behind a number series is tested with probes (e.g., does this sequence fit the rule?). Michèle Godrie and I generated data now being analyzed from high- and average-achieving high school mathematics students and graduate mathematics students on this software. Impressions

gained during the collection of the data suggest that we shall confirm the use of hypothesis generation (a form of question asking) as one distinguishing element in the thinking by highly able high school students and graduate students during the exploratory stage of problem solving. This study used 8th-grade students, students who were 3 years younger and less differentiated in their mathematical accomplishments than the high school students in the two other studies reported earlier. The software can be used with much younger students to explore how early such performance may be observed.

Our final two studies to date in this sequence of research addressed performance in physics rather than mathematics. The first paralleled the enriched mathematics course studies with high and low performers in an advanced high school physics course (Coleman & Shore, 1991). Two physics graduate students and a high school physics teacher were the "experts." The students thought aloud while doing five physics problems. From the protocols it was determined that the high performers and the adult subjects made more correct metastatements (statements indicating monitoring, evaluation, or adjustment of strategy) in the course of their solutions, as well as more references to prior knowledge and fewer references to information given in the problems.

Finally, we have conducted one study at the junior college level. This project explored the importance of prior knowledge and the webbing of that knowledge with new learning. Students in a physics course were given brief training in concept mapping. A second group taught by the same instructor received practice reviewing the same list of concepts but did not learn to map until the end. There were three main results. The students who learned to map their concepts did better on conventional tests of physics performance, especially on multistep problems that required the interpolation of information or a transformation not given in the problem as stated, and on a mapping exercise (Austin & Shore, 1994, 1995). The maps were an excellent diagnostic guide to misunderstandings of concepts. In addition, students with outstanding performance on the conventional tests organized their concepts into maps, which more completely encompassed all the concepts, and their maps were more complex and hierarchical (Austin & Shore, 1993).

Contributions of the Research

Cognitive Implications

There are two main issues. First, are there qualitative differences between the thinking of gifted and other learners? No and yes. Gifted learners do not seem to use strategies that others never use. There is something broadly human about thinking across ability levels that affirms the thrust in cognitive psychology to search for universals. On the other hand, there are clearly differences in the extent to which different strategies are invoked and the fluency and speed with which they are used. Some of these differences are very persistent within and among individuals; they are recognizable between learners deemed "gifted" by a number of definitions and other learners, and they are observable in very young children. It may be fair to conclude from our and others' research that "qualitative" differences exist, but that just as learners can improve their scores on tests, so might they be able to improve their thinking processes.

Second, does gifted performance resemble expert performance? The answer seems to be yes, and in several ways. These include metacognition, strategy flexibility, strategy planning, the use of hypotheses (which may be related to forward chaining), preference for complexity, and the hierarchical and extensive webbing of knowledge about both facts and procedures.

Our research raises a series of questions about the nature of expertise. It is important to set this point in context. There is little agreement about the universal nature of expertise (cf. Ericsson & Smith, 1991). This is partly a consequence of the insistence by many cognitive psychologists that expertise is "situated," specific to tasks within domains. This implies that one cannot be an expert on a novel task, although one can legitimately ask how an expert on task A might perform on novel task B. Some of our research uses this paradigm. Before one masters task B, is it fair to be described as a novice on task B? The breadth of both terms, expert and novice, and the relation between them, are also not uniformly defined. The quality of automaticity, frequently stated as a characteristic of expertise, is a useful example. Automaticity was apparent in some of our data, such as the portable rod-and-frame task by students with high spatial ability, but more often we observed relatively greater planning time on novel tasks by our "gifted" students and by our "experts." Until cognitive psychology can agree on definitions of expert and novice, we can merely observe that thinking processes often associated with expertise are visible in persons not yet experts and who, in many cases, have not yet had the advanced formal training or experience that normally defines experts.

The research also implies some reconsideration of the idea of a novice. In retrospect, it is not always clear that our "experts" were not, in fact, novices, such as when physics graduate students and a physics teacher were treated together as an expert group. It would be useful to examine the formal and informal educational histories of persons regarded as novices in previous research. Might they have been gifted students a few years earlier? Is it appropriate to consider the state of being a beginner in a domain that requires specific skills as one in which all the skills are newly acquired? Is it possible that the novitiate is but a way station in the gifted learner's not-so-gradual progress to expertise? Can "novice" be used to describe someone who knows nothing about a topic, or does it refer to someone with a degree of knowledge and commitment? Examining the use of the term so far will be a helpful beginning to this discussion. If novices are found to be exceptionally able, motivated students embarking on specialized, advanced training, then the study of children deemed gifted might deserve a mainstream rather than the present fringe place in developmental studies of cognition. Novices may be highly selected candidates from a pool of very capable children.

Although problem-solving tasks have been central to decades of research on cognition, it has never been clearly established that this context is necessarily the trigger for expert thinking processes. Some of the intellectual skills that underlie expertise may not be invoked only as part of problem-solving strategy, but they may be on some kind of "active alert." Keating (1990) suggested the distinction between domain-general habits of mind and domain-specific expertise. This may be a useful conceptualization. It is an interesting coincidence that Keating's insight also follows many years of involvement with highly able young people who do not necessarily have a great amount of domain-specific experience; domain specificity may become a characteristic of expertise because such specialization is an important part of the culture for able adults, so it comes to dominate thinking. Flexibility may be a component or a consequence of domain-general skills and knowledge that could be operating even before categorization takes place in the course of solving a problem. Keating's conceptualization is consistent with our results on the water-jar experiments and provides a possible link between the study of personality (especially regarding learning style or cognitive style, cf. Keefe, 1982) and contemporary cognitive theory. It is also consistent with Kanevsky's (1992) report of related motivational differences in preschoolers. It is a small challenge to cognitive theory regarding the degree to which intellectual skills must be situated, that is, defined in terms of specific tasks in specific domains.

Developmental Implications

The first developmental issue we faced was Hal Robinson's (1977) precocity challenge. The state of the art seems to be that gifted children differ from others in the extent to which they draw on a repertoire of intellectual skills that are nonetheless available to others. There is a great fuzziness between quantitative and qualitative differences. The differences we have observed do require that thinking processes be discussed. If that is an adequate operational definition of qualitative differences, then they exist. The most striking result that we observed—even given that few of our studies specifically compared different age groups on comparable tasks, and none has yet been a longitudinal study—is that similar types of differences persisted across age ranges on a variety of tasks. If the link between giftedness and expertise is at all serious, then there is nothing precocious in this performance. Perhaps the gap in performance might even widen, let alone narrow, as learners build on their expanding knowledge and skills.

Even if the precocity argument could be laid to rest, we still need to account for the fact that something develops, as Siegler (cf. 1978 and later work) and many others have clearly shown. It is necessary to consider further what develops, from what bases (individual, familial, social, congenital, genetic, gender, etc.) and optimally under what conditions. Something called "intelligence" develops. Not only should the study of gifted children be more mainstream, but also should the study of giftedness. Understanding giftedness should inform our understanding of intelligence, at least as much as the other way around. We have proposed once before (Shore & Dover, 1987) that there may be a need to make a theoretical flip from giftedness as a subtheory of a theory of intelligence, to intelligence explained by a theory of giftedness. Furthermore, the theory would have to be developmental. This is by way of invitation to rather than criticism of Robert Sternberg (1981), who had the insight to bring the two concepts into a conceptual framework that went well beyond the idea of IQ. With regard to the learning underlying expertise and perhaps giftedness, there is almost certainly an experiential element in a human being's ability and propensity to cope with novelty and with automatization of performance.

The notion of gradual progression toward adultlike performance is challenged by the studies reported above but is not directly contradicted, because only longitudinal research could fully address this. The young ages at which some children demonstrate adultlike intellectual skills suggests rapid early unfolding of these skills. These children might lack only specific educational, interpersonal, or more general cultural experiences and the opportunity to interconnect these in their memory, in order to more fully close the gap with adult expertise. It is possible that domain-general and domain-specific thinking may leapfrog each other at different times during development, especially in highly able children. This does not readily lend itself to description as a gradual progression. Cohen (1988) observed that discontinuity is one of the hallmarks of creative giftedness, and some researchers are exploring quantum (Goswami, 1988) and chaos theory (Sterling, 1990) in relation to giftedness and creativity. These views may be helpful in explaining the big-bang-like explosion of intellectual skills that is observed in some children and the early appearance of metacognitive and other noteworthy performance. The research on gifted children with learning disabilities also suggests irregular and discontinuous development toward adultlike performance, because their giftedness rather than disability was prominent in their problem-solving skills, although the disability had a real impact on their general school performance.

Educational Implications

The central issue is the rationale for differential education, for curriculum and pedagogy specially adapted to the student's needs. Acceleration is merely one of the adaptations, not a solution in and of itself.

We have a mixed message. It appears that the greater and more efficient use of expertlike thinking skills opens learning opportunities for bright children that might be inappropriate for others, to the extent that the uniquely held or used skills are necessary to be able to perform well. It also appears that the stimulation of intellectual peers and the contemplation of personal futures may arguably call for at least some time in a differentiated curriculum with these peers.

On the other hand, a critical educational agenda for gifted education must also include the question of how and to what extent learning situations that are appropriate and advantageous for bright students are useful, advantageous, or necessary for others. To date, the more commonly posed question has addressed the suitability of general or average mainstream education for very bright students. The answers have fueled efforts by advocates of differentiated education for bright students for ability-segregated programs. Are these enhanced programs in all respects uniquely appropriate for gifted children? Perhaps not always (Shore et al., 1991—especially see chapter 4 in which 7 of 17 practices recommended to educators of gifted children were judged to be effective but suitable for all children). This might throw a much more positive light on programs for able students as pilot and model programs for improvements in general education, at least in part. A portion of the responsibility for bringing this about lies with those of us interested in giftedness; we are currently experiencing political marginalization of gifted education on many fronts, but for many years research on giftedness and gifted education has addressed issues that are poorly connected with priority concerns in general education (Delisle, 1992; Feldhusen, 1992) despite many opportunities for complementary links (see Clark & Shore, 1998).

Also, how important is the company of bright students to other students and vice versa? The small amount of empirical evidence available to date indicates a greater negative effect for the less able children than a positive effect for the more able children (Dar & Resh, 1986); all students seem to relatively thrive in high-ability classes, with less able students responding more to class norms (Veldman & Sanford, 1984). There is no less need for ethical consideration in educational practice than in any other profession. Is a win–win solution possible? Our study of concept mapping in physics and the work of others such as Novak (1984) and Okebukola (1990) indicate that some intellectual skills associated with expertise can be taught with facility. Equally elegant explorations of other skills require similar treatment. Of course the impact of such training may be to raise everyone's level of functioning, and the most proficient students might gain the most. That is another largely ethical or policy issue: Is the goal of intervention to close the gap between low and high performance, or to raise the level of performance by all students for whom this is a reasonable goal even if the gap widens? It is reminiscent of early studies of the impact of *Sesame Street* in which educationally disadvantaged children indeed learned, but middle-class children with substantial educational head starts in their own homes and nursery schools learned even more. It has been shown in second-language learning through immersion —programs that began and are still often thought of by some as especially suitable for more able students—that although the most able students achieve remarkable levels of bilingualism, even the least able students learn more than they would in a standard course of 40 minutes or so a day (Genesee, 1987). Answers will not be forthcoming from laboratory studies. Large-scale implementations are needed.

References

Austin, L. B., & Shore, B. M. (1993). Concept mapping of high and average achieving students, and experts. *European Journal for High Ability, 4,* 180–195.

Austin, L. B., & Shore, B. M. (1994). The use of concept mapping as an instructional strategy in college-level physics. *Scientia Paedagogica Experimentalis, 31,* 249–264.

Austin, L. B., & Shore, B. M. (1995). Using concept mapping for assessment in physics. *Physics Education, 30*(1), 41–45.

Bowen, S., Shore, B. M., & Cartwright, G. F. (1992). Do gifted children use computers differently? A view from "The Factory." *Gifted Education International, 8,* 151–154.

Brown, A. L., & Campione, J. (1986). Psychological theory and the study of learning disabilities. *American Psychologist, 14,* 1059–1068.

Brown, S. W., & Yakimowski, M. E. (1987). Intelligence scores of gifted students on the WISC–R. *Gifted Child Quarterly, 31,* 130–134.

Chi, M., Glaser, R., & Rees, E. (1982). Expertise in problem solving. In R. J. Sternberg (Ed.), *Advances in the psychology of human intelligence* (Vol. 1, pp. 7–75). Hillsdale, NJ: Erlbaum.

Clark, C., & Shore, B. M. (1998). *Educating students with high ability.* Paris: UNESCO.

Cohen, L. M. (1988). To get ahead, get a theory. *Roeper Review, 11,* 95–100.

Coleman, E., & Shore, B. M. (1991). Problem-solving processes of high and average performers in physics. *Journal for the Education of the Gifted, 14,* 366–379.

Dar, Y., & Resh, N. (1986). Classroom intellectual composition and academic achievement. *American Educational Research Journal, 23,* 357–374.

Delisle, J. R. (1992). Preaching to the converted. *TAG Update, 15*(1), 1.

Dover, A. C., & Shore, B. M. (1991). Giftedness and flexibility on a mathematical set-breaking task. *Gifted Child Quarterly, 35,* 99–105.

Ericsson, K. A., & Simon, H. (1980). Verbal reports as data. *Psychological Review, 87,* 215–251.

Ericsson, K. A., & Smith, J. (Eds.). (1991). *Toward a general theory of expertise: Prospects and limits.* Cambridge, England: Cambridge University Press.

Feldhusen, J. F. (1992). The response of gifted education to school reform: Physician, heal thyself. *Gifted Child Quarterly, 36,* 3.

Feuerstein, R., Rand, Y., & Rynders, J. E. (1988). *Don't accept me as I am: Helping "retarded" people to excel.* New York: Plenum Press.

Flavell, J. H. (1976). Metacognitive aspects of problem solving. In L. B. Resnick (Ed.), *The nature of intelligence* (pp. 231–235). Hillsdale, NJ: Erlbaum.

Flavell, J. H. (1980, August). *Metacognition.* Paper presented at the 88th Annual Convention of the American Psychological Association, Montreal, Quebec, Canada.

Galton, F. (1979). *Hereditary genius.* London: Julian Friedmann. (Original work published 1869)

Genesee, F. (1987). *Learning through two languages: Studies of immersion and bilingual education.* Cambridge, MA: Newbury House.

Getzels, J. W., & Csikszentmihalyi, M. (1976). *The creative vision: A longitudinal study of problem finding in art.* New York: Wiley.

Glaser, R. (1985). *The nature of expertise (Occasional paper No. 107).* Columbus, OH: National Center for Research in Vocational Education (ERIC Document Reproduction Service No. ED261190).

Goswami, A. (1988). Creativity and the quantum theory. *Journal of Creative Behavior, 23,* 9–31.

Hannah, C. L. (1989). The use of cognitive methodology to identify, investigate, and instruct learning-disabled gifted children. *Roeper Review, 12,* 58–62.

Hannah, C. L., & Shore, B. M. (1995). Metacognition and high intellectual ability: Insights from the study of learning-disabled gifted students. *Gifted Child Quarterly, 39,* 95–109.

Kagan, J., Moss, H. A., & Siegel, I. E. (1963). Psychological significance of style of concep-
    tualization. In J. C. Wright & J. Kagan (Eds.), *Basic cognitive processes in children
    Monographs of the Society of Research in Child Development, 28* (Whole No. 2).
Kaizer, C., & Shore, B. M. (1995). Strategy flexibility in more and less competent students
    on mathematical word problems. *Creativity Research Journal, 8*, 113–118.
Kanevsky, L. S. (1990). Pursuing qualitative differences in the flexible use of problem-
    solving strategy by young children. *Journal for the Education of the Gifted, 13*, 115–
    140.
Kanevsky, L. S. (1992). The learning game. In P. Klein & A. J. Tannenbaum (Eds.), *To be
    young and gifted* (pp. 204–241). Norwood, NJ: Ablex.
Keating, D. P. (1990). Charting pathways to the development of expertise. *Educational Psy-
    chologist, 25*, 243–267.
Keefe, J. (Ed.). (1982). *Student learning styles and brain behavior: Programs, instrumen-
    tation, research*. Reston, VA: National Association of Secondary School Principals.
Kirby, J. R., & Das, J. P. (1977). Reading achievement, IQ, and simultaneous-successive
    processing. *Journal of Educational Psychology, 69*, 564–570.
Krutetskii, V. A. (1976). *The psychology of mathematical abilities in schoolchildren*. Chicago:
    University of Chicago Press.
Lajoie, S. P., & Shore, B. M. (1986). Intelligence: The speed and accuracy tradeoff in high
    aptitude individuals. *Journal for the Education of the Gifted, 9*, 85–104.
Lajoie, S. P., & Shore, B. M. (1987). Impulsivity, reflectivity, and high IQ. *Gifted Education
    International, 4*(3), 139–141.
Larkin, J. (1979). Enriching formal knowledge: A model for learning to solve textbook phys-
    ics problems. In J. R. Anderson (Ed.), *Cognitive skills and their acquisition* (pp. 311–
    334). Hillsdale, NJ: Erlbaum.
Maniatis, E. (1983). *An analysis of the differences in problem-solving of gifted and non-gifted
    children using the LOGO programming language*. Unpublished MA thesis in educational
    psychology, McGill University, Montreal, Quebec, Canada.
Maniatis, E., Cartwright, G. F., & Shore, B. M. (1998). Giftedness and complexity in a self-
    directed computer-based task. *Gifted and Talented International, 13*, 83–89.
Moss, E. (1983). *Maternal teaching styles and giftedness*. Unpublished PhD dissertation in
    educational psychology, McGill University, Montreal, Quebec, Canada.
Moss, E. (1990). Social interaction and metacognitive development in gifted preschoolers.
    Gifted Child Quarterly, 34, 16–20.
Novak, J. D. (1984). Application of advances in learning theory and philosophy of science to
    the improvement of chemistry teaching. *Journal of Chemical Education, 61*, 607–613.
Okebukola, P. A. (1990). Attaining meaningful learning of concepts in genetics and ecology.
    Journal of Research in Science Teaching, 27, 493–504.
Pelletier, S., & Shore, B. M. (1989, April). *Ability, expertise, and the categorization of math-
    ematical problems*. Paper presented at the annual meeting of the American Educational
    Research Association, San Francisco.
Perfetti, C. A., & Lesgold, A. M. (1979). Coding and comprehension in skilled reading. In
    L. B. Resnick & P. Weaver (Eds.), *Theory and practice of early reading* (pp. 57–84).
    Hillsdale, NJ: Erlbaum.
Porath, M. (1992). Stage and structure in the development of children with various types
    of giftedness. In R. Case (Ed.), *The mind's staircase: Exploring the conceptual underpin-
    nings of children's thought and knowledge* (pp. 303–318). Hillsdale, NJ: Erlbaum.
Rabinowitz, M., & Glaser, R. (1985). Cognitive structure and process in highly competent
    performance. In F. D. Horowitz & M. O'Brien (Eds.), *The gifted and talented: Develop-
    mental perspectives* (pp. 75–98). Washington, DC: American Psychological Association.
Robinson, H. B. (1977). Current myths concerning gifted children. In W. Abraham, I. H.
    Berkovitz, M. R. Howard, R. C. W. Jenkins, & H. B. Robinson (Eds.), *Early childhood
    education for gifted/talented* (pp. 1–11). Ventura, CA: National/State Leadership Train-
    ing Institute on the Gifted and the Talented.
Rogers, K. B. (1986). Do the gifted learn and think differently? A review of recent research
    and its implications for instruction. *Journal for the Education of the Gifted, 10*, 17–39.
Shavelson, R. J., & Salomon, G. (1986). Reply to comment on "Information technology: Tool
    and teacher of the mind." *Educational Researcher, 15*(2), 24–25.

Shore, B. M. (1981, November). *Developing a framework for the study of learning style in high-level learning*. Paper presented at the Major Conference on Learning Styles and Brain Behavior, National Association of Secondary School Principals, New Orleans, LA.

Shore, B. M. (1982). Developing a framework for the study of learning style in high-level learning. In J. Keefe (Ed.), *Student learning styles and brain behavior: Programs, instrumentation, research* (pp. 152–156). Reston, VA: National Association of Secondary School Principals.

Shore, B. M. (1991). How do gifted children think differently? *AGATE (Journal of the Gifted and Talented Education Council of the Alberta Teachers Association), 5*(2), 19–23.

Shore, B. M. (1996). Strategy flexibility: On Jaušovec's *Flexible thinking: An explanation for differences in ability. Creativity Research Journal, 9*, 287–288.

Shore, B. M., & Carey, S. M. (1984). Verbal ability and spatial task. *Perceptual and Motor Skills, 59*, 255–259.

Shore, B. M., Coleman, E. B., & Moss, E. (1992). Cognitive psychology and the use of protocols in the understanding of giftedness and high level thinking. In F. J. Mönks & W. Peters (Eds.), *Talent for the future: Social and personality development of gifted children* (Selected proceedings of the Ninth World Conference on Gifted and Talented Children, The Hague, 1991; pp. 259–263). Assen, Netherlands: Van Gorcum.

Shore, B. M., Cornell, D. C., Robinson, A., & Ward, V. S. (1991). *Recommended practices in gifted education: A critical analysis*. New York: Teachers College Press.

Shore, B. M., & Dover, A. C. (1987). Metacognition, intelligence and giftedness. *Gifted Child Quarterly, 31*, 37–39.

Shore, B. M., Hymovitch, J., & Lajoie, S. P. (1982). Processing differences in the relation between ability and field-independence. *Psychological Reports, 50*, 391–395.

Shore, B. M., Kaizer, C., & Pelletier, S. (1990, October). *Metacognition, giftedness, and mathematical thinking*. Paper presented at the annual meeting of the European Council for High Ability, Budapest, Hungary.

Shore, B. M., Koller, M., & Dover, A. (1994). More from the water jars: Revisiting a cognitive task on which some gifted children's performance is exceeded. *Gifted Child Quarterly, 38*, 179–183.

Shore, B. M., & Lazar, L. (1996). IQ-related differences in time allocation during problem solving. *Psychological Reports, 78*, 848–849.

Siegler, R. S. (Ed.). (1978). *Children's thinking: What develops?* Hillsdale, NJ: Erlbaum.

Simon, D., & Simon, H. A. (1978). Individual differences in solving physics problems. In R. Siegler (Ed.), *Children's thinking: What develops?* (pp. 325–348). Hillsdale, NJ: Erlbaum.

Sterling, A. (1990). *Where chaos theory and creativity meet: A review of the research*. Unpublished manuscript, University of Oregon, Eugene, Department of Teacher School of Education.

Sternberg, R. J. (1981). A componential approach to intellectual giftedness. In R. J. Sternberg (Ed.), *Advances in the psychology of human intelligence* (Vol. 1, pp. 413–463). Hillsdale, NJ: Erlbaum.

Sternberg, R. J. (1986). A triarchic theory of intellectual giftedness. In R. J. Sternberg & J. E. Davidson (Eds.), *Conceptions of giftedness* (pp. 223–243). Cambridge, England: Cambridge University Press.

Tarshis, E., & Shore, B. M. (1991). Differences in perspective taking between high and above average IQ preschool children. *European Journal for High Ability, 2*, 201–211.

Veldman, D. J., & Sanford, J. P. (1984). The influence of class ability level on student achievement and classroom behavior. *American Educational Research Journal, 21*, 629–644.

Vygotsky, L. S. (1978). *Mind in society: The development of higher psychological processes*. Cambridge, MA: Harvard University Press.

Ward, V. S. (1961). *Educating the gifted: An axiomatic approach*. Columbus, OH: Merrill.

Wertsch, J. V. (1979). From social interaction to higher psychological processes: A clarification and application of Vygotsky's theory. *Human Development, 22*, 1–22.

Witkin, H. A., Dyk, R. B., Faterson, H. F., Goodenough, D. R., & Karp, S. A. (1963). *Psychological differentiation: Studies of development*. New York: Wiley.

Part III

Domain-Related Talent

Chapter 9, "Social Giftedness in Childhood: A Developmental Perspective," by Marion Porath presents two observational studies, one with children aged 2 to 5 years and one with 6- to 12-year-olds, their parents, and their teachers. Theoretically driven by Case's (1992) stage theory of cognitive development, Porath's conclusion regarding the argument of domain specificity or generality is that it is not an either–or situation but rather one of deciding under what circumstances each of these views applies. Particular or "encapsulated" abilities may develop very quickly, presumably in response to internal or external influences, whereas other, more general abilities may be age related. This is compatible with the observation by others that manifest giftedness may vary at different ages, but it does not contradict John Colombo, D. Jill Shaddy, and W. Allen Richman's (chapter 6) view either. Some intellectual development may be continuous, and some discontinuous. We simply have to ask the right questions and appropriately measure performance on relevant tasks, for instance, those that are set within the zone of proximal development.

Sandra I. Kay reports her research with 60 adult professional artists, semiprofessionals, and nonartists on a closely related topic in chapter 10, "On the Nature of Expertise in Visual Art." She also asks how problem finders find problems. Her chapter is linked to early work on problem finding through its focus on art as the domain of activity and to cognitive science through its choice of cognitive psychology rather than creativity as the theoretical foundation, including the analysis of verbal protocols generated while constructing problems. The research task was to build anything with an open-ended construction toy. Among Kay's results are confirmation that practice or preparatory time increased with level of expertise, as found in other domains (cf. chapter 8 by Bruce Shore), but that problem-finding time was highest for the semiprofessional artists and lowest for the professionals. This dilemma may be explained by Kay's proposal for the operation of a personal aesthetic bias that caused the most expert group to regard the task as trivial. This personal aesthetic influences the perception and therefore the nature of the task, sometimes by constraining it. Kay's work demonstrates well how additional layers or templates may be added to the competencies of highly able people as they grow and add expertise in various domains. She relates this to mathematicians' and others' high regard for elegance, for an aesthetic component to what might otherwise seem to be a very straightforward intellectual enterprise.

The question of problem finding is further explored in chapter 11, "Finding the Problem Finders: Problem Finding and the Identification and Development of Talent." Alane J. Starko examines creative giftedness and specifically how individuals so recognized decide which problems to solve or ideas to express. Similar work with young adult artists and the popularization of the phrase *problem finding* lies with Getzels and Csikszentmihalyi (1976). It is noteworthy that this work also found that not all promising young artists became successful career artists, and Getzels and

Csikszentmihalyi linked the future of young artists to the extent to which they could define or redefine original problems to solve. Starko reviews the extensive literature, including her own parallel work with very young children. She discovered that problem finding is not only a preliminary stage to artistic performance but that elements of it are found at many points throughout development. In some ways or in some domains, then, as Colombo and his colleagues hinted in chapter 6, giftedness does not entirely or necessarily change with age. Rather, it evolves, adds new elements, drops some old, and changes. As strongly emphasized in *Talent in Context: Historical and Social Perspectives* (Friedman & Rogers, 1998), giftedness is not a unitary construct. It is a constellation of qualities; as educators of teachers sometimes tell their classes, being gifted is like being learning disabled—to make sense of either it is necessary to ask in what ways it is manifested and how severely. Starko shows that a fairly reliable characteristic of young children considered to be highly creative is their problem-finding skill. This has been found through adulthood in many domains and forms the basis of inquiry-driven curricula in nearly all fields. Starko concludes with suggestions for assessing problem finding and encouraging it in school.

"Was Mozart at Risk? A Developmentalist Looks at Extreme Talent" by David Henry Feldman (chapter 12) asks what are the critical issues in bringing out extremely high potential. In a rather surprising conclusion, Feldman proposes that when the case is examined in detail, it is perhaps a fluke that Wolfgang Amadeus Mozart succeeded. Few of the usually expected favorable circumstances were present, with the exception of Mozart's father's devotion to the realization of his son's potential. Neither of Mozart's parents, we learn, came from a family in which there was any previous history of exceptional musical accomplishment. Leopold Mozart acquired his musical education as an adult. We do not know if he actually recognized his son's potential or set out to live vicariously through his achievements. In answer to his main question, Feldman concludes that early exposure to the domain is critical, as well as timing (both individually and culturally or societally). For example, a few years later the wave of revolution in Europe would have threatened the patronage Mozart received. What a developmentalist has seen is that conventional wisdom is inadequate and considerably more study is needed of the lives of exceptionally able people. Historical examples have their limitations, and Feldman's contribution to the study of contemporary prodigies was represented in the follow-up study by his partner in the original data collection, Lynn Goldsmith, in chapter 5.

References

Case, R. (1992). *The mind's staircase: Exploring the conceptual underpinnings of children's thought and knowledge.* Hillsdale, NJ: Erlbaum.

Friedman, R. C., & Rogers, K. B. (Eds.). (1998). *Talent in context: Historical and social perspectives.* Washington, DC: American Psychological Association.

Getzels, J. W., & Csikszentmihalyi, M. (1976). *The creative vision: A longitudinal study of problem finding in art.* New York: Wiley.

9

Social Giftedness in Childhood: A Developmental Perspective

Marion Porath

This chapter presents a developmental perspective on social giftedness. The idea that some people demonstrate a high degree of social intelligence is recognized by the general public, educators, and researchers. However, efforts to validate the construct have met with mixed success. Here it is argued that by using a theoretical approach that acknowledges both the various specific forms of human intelligence and the general influences on the development of children's thought and knowledge, a view of social giftedness emerges that can increase our knowledge of the *what* and the *how* of social expertise. After a short history of social intelligence and an examination of the state of knowledge of giftedness in the social domain, the contributions of developmental and modular theories of mind to understanding social giftedness are presented. Based on preliminary research findings, the conclusion is that the articulation of the nature of stages of development in the social domain could increase our ability to assess social intelligence and to plan appropriate instructional experiences for those children who demonstrate giftedness in the social domain.

Social Intelligence: A Short History

Research on social intelligence began with Thorndike's (1920) acknowledgment of social ability as a distinct intelligence involving the ability to understand and manage others in a wise fashion. There was interest in measuring social intelligence after Thorndike's recognition (e.g., Hunt, 1928; Strang, 1930), but the success of these and subsequent attempts was limited (see Walker & Foley, 1973). The construct was difficult to validate largely because measurement techniques involved measures that tapped

This research was supported by a University of British Columbia Humanities and Social Sciences Research Grant. I acknowledge the support and enthusiasm of the staff, parents, and children at the Child Study Centre and the Psychoeducational Research and Training Centre at the University of British Columbia. The contributions of Joellen Housego and Natasha Lozovsky-Burns to data collection and analysis and William McKee to the conception and organization of the Clinic on Ability and Development are acknowledged with thanks.

academic competence rather than social ability (Ford & Tisak, 1983; Janos & Robinson, 1985; Keating, 1978).

Despite these difficulties, interest in the definition and measurement of social intelligence endured. Guilford's (1959) lecture on the three faces of intellect acknowledged different facets of intelligence and referred to the interesting possibilities inherent in the identification of abilities relevant to understanding our own and others' behavior using the Structure of Intellect model. The publication of Howard Gardner's book *Frames of Mind* (Gardner, 1983) presented "personal intelligence," which consists of interpersonal and intrapersonal understanding and skills, as a human ability of validity and value equal to the logical–mathematical and verbal abilities so emphasized and prized in our culture. Gardner described various "end states" in personal intelligence—the gifted leaders, teachers, or therapists who, because of their exceptional ability to ascertain and respond to others' thoughts, feelings, and intentions, contribute greatly to social well-being.

The idea that some people demonstrate social intelligence in an exceptionally well-developed form ("social giftedness") has received research attention. Jarecky (1959) identified socially gifted adolescents by using a combination of sociometric ratings, peer and teacher evaluations of social behavior, and observational data. These adolescents were well-accepted, made positive contributions in social interactions, coped well with varied social situations, and treated others with respect. Jarecky found that above-average intelligence was necessary but not sufficient for social giftedness, supporting the idea of a separate domain for social understanding. Jarecky's study was, however, limited by its small sample size and its urban, middle-class study group.

Abroms and Gollin (1980) investigated psychosocial giftedness in intellectually gifted preschoolers and found the construct to be somewhat independent of IQ. They also found only a marginal relationship between measures of social cognition and prosocial behavior, and they posited that an important distinction must be made between "knowing *that*" one should behave in a moral, sensitive fashion and "knowing *how*" to do so in real-life situations (Janos & Robinson, 1985; Walker & Foley, 1973). Roedell, Jackson, and Robinson (1980) also found that high performers on measures of social problem-solving ability did not necessarily use this ability in peer interactions. The inclusion of a behavioral component in defining social intelligence dates to Thorndike (1920), who emphasized intelligent social behavior in real-world contexts, an idea revisited in current thinking on social intelligence.

State of Knowledge

Contemporary research supports the inclusion of behavioral effectiveness in the definition of social intelligence. Thorndike's (1920) suggestion was that understanding and wise management of others pertains to actual people in real situations, and more attention has been paid to intelligent social behavior in ecologically valid contexts. This has resulted in evidence supporting the existence of a separate domain of social understanding (Barnes & Sternberg, 1989; Ford, 1982, 1986; Ford & Tisak, 1983; Gardner, 1983; Matthews, 1990, 1997; Taylor & Cadet, 1989) and uniquely social "structures of knowing" (Case, 1992a; Chandler, 1982). However, despite interest in social intelligence, its inclusion in the form of leadership in a widely recognized definition of giftedness (Marland, 1972), and the recognition that the domains we consider in research and education must encompass more than logical–mathematical and verbal intelligence (Bruner, 1996; Feldman, 1986; Frederiksen, 1990; Gardner, 1983; Globerson, 1989), little research has focused on social giftedness, and there has been no demonstrable influence on educational practice (Globerson, 1989; U.S. Department of Education Office of Educational Research and Improvement, 1993).

Effective interpersonal relationships are crucial in a world of rapidly changing educational, political, cultural, and professional structures (Keating, 1995; Matthews, 1995). To encourage these relationships in our increasingly complex world, increased study of prosocial behavior is necessary (Eisenberg, 1992). Bruner (1996) argued that the study of intersubjectivity, or of "how people come to know what others have in mind and how they adjust accordingly" (p. 161), must be a central objective for contemporary research. A focus on prosocial expertise, or social giftedness, is especially important in ensuring effective communities (Csikszentmihalyi & Larson, 1984; Horowitz & O'Brien, 1986; Keating, 1995).

Social intelligence is an important factor in theories of giftedness (Okagaki & Sternberg, 1988). Horowitz and O'Brien (1986) review the state of the research on gifted children and emphasize that it is crucial to begin to study social intelligence to explain its roots and the conditions that foster it. Other researchers agree (Csikszentmihalyi & Larson, 1984; Eisenberg & Mussen, 1989; Gallagher & Courtright, 1986). This call for research speaks to a need to take a "front-end" approach to social giftedness by focusing on the formative years of early and middle childhood. It seems timely, therefore, to study this form of giftedness, to articulate its characteristics, and to better elucidate its developmental course.

Social Giftedness

Based on Gardner and Hatch's (1989) definition of interpersonal intelligence and Abroms and Gollin's (1980) work on psychosocial giftedness, *social giftedness* is the unusual ability to make inferences about others' thoughts, emotions, intentions, and points of view, evidenced in nurturance of and empathic responses to other children. In addition, following Fischer and Pipp's (1984) description of children with high ability, children with interpersonal expertise demonstrate frequent and flexible use of social roles in play situations and elaboration in social role-playing that captures the subtleties and details of different roles. Both components of the definition involve the ability to understand and act in ways that demonstrate social insight.

The focus in this chapter is on social giftedness in childhood. This focus, coupled with a developmental perspective, is appropriate for its potential to describe emergent abilities.

Developmental Perspective

The research on social giftedness extends a theoretical model of giftedness (Porath, 1992) to the social domain. The model has been applied previously to the logical–mathematical, artistic, and verbal domains (Porath, 1992, 1993, 1996a, 1997). Within the model, general characteristics of development are defined and unique specific abilities associated with outstanding performance in a domain are identified. General characteristics are discussed here.

Case's (1985, 1992a) description of children's thought and understanding is the theoretical framework for detailing age-related changes in conceptual knowledge. Case's neo-Piagetian theory of intellectual development is used to articulate general characteristics of development, but research in the neo-Piagetian tradition supports the view that development in the social domain is independent from that in other domains. It is because general systemic influences are believed to account for parallels in the form of children's conceptual thought across domains (Case, 1992a; Case, Marini, McKeough, Dennis, & Goldberg, 1986) that the theory is used to articulate general developmental characteristics.

Case (1992a) described children's "central conceptual structures" in several domains. These structures are "blueprints" of children's understanding. *Structure* is an internal mental entity consisting of the relations among a number of concepts. *Conceptual* refers to the semantic nature of the relations—the meanings, representations, or concepts that children assign to external entities in their world. Because a structure is believed to form the basis of a range of more specific concepts and to operate in enabling children to make the transition to new stages of thought, it is defined as central (Case, 1992a; Case & Griffin, 1989). There is evidence for several central conceptual structures, including one that is uniquely social (Case, 1992a; Case, Okamoto, Henderson, McKeough, & Bleiker, 1996). The central social structure develops with age (as do other structures), allowing children to think in increasingly complex and abstract terms about their social world.

The age-related nature of children's central conceptual structures is universal. That is, even children of exceptional ability demonstrate age-typical or only moderately advanced thinking on conceptual tasks (Fischer & Canfield, 1986; Globerson, 1985; Porath, 1992). This finding is important in explaining exceptionally able children's thinking, because it provides an age-appropriate description of how knowledge across domains is constructed and integrated (Fischer & Pipp, 1984), and it offers some instructional guidelines (Porath, 1991; Strauss, Globerson, & Mintz, 1983).

The idea of a central conceptual descriptor of gifted children's thinking is also relevant to the argument that it is not stage advancement that is characteristic of giftedness but what is done with the available level of thought, namely, unusually rich responses to developmental tasks (Fischer & Pipp, 1984; Lovell & Shields, 1967; Porath, 1991; Roeper, 1978; Webb, 1974). Following this argument, it is the speed with which gifted children learn and the resultant elaboration and complexity within a stage of development that accounts for individual differences (Case, 1992b; Fischer & Canfield, 1986; Fischer & Pipp, 1984; Porath, 1992). Fischer and Pipp (1984) suggested that very intelligent children acquire different levels of thought at the same time as do children of average intelligence but that they construct a wider range of skills at each level. There also might be variations in developmental pathways (Fischer, Knight, & Van Parys, 1993) such that a gifted child's "way in" to a concept is both efficient and elaborate because of ability, experience, and motivation.

In addition to age-related conceptual understandings, gifted children obviously do possess developmentally advanced abilities (Keating, 1990, 1991; Porath, 1992). These abilities are discussed in their specific forms by theorists who view the mind as modular and not subject to the general organismic constraints hypothesized by Case (1992a).

Modular Perspective

Modular theorists (e.g., Feldman, 1986; Gardner, 1983) have argued that each domain of knowledge is discrete and that development in an area of giftedness can proceed far in advance of other intellectual capacities. Any overall mechanism for coordinating specific skills is "self-contained" and unique to that domain. Internal structure within modules is present at birth, with the result that children are "pretuned" to attend to and interrelate given environmental features in particular ways (Spelke, 1988, cited in Case, Okamoto, Henderson, & McKeough, 1993). Thus, the gifts of the chess or music prodigy develop rapidly and are far ahead of their other abilities (Feldman, 1986). Following the modular argument, social giftedness involves particular attention to social situations and rapid learning of social concepts and skills, with the result that social ability far exceeds other abilities. It also could coexist with advanced development in other domains, following Gardner's (1983) recognition that an individual can be gifted in one or more intelligences and Feldman's (1986) description of an "omnibus prodigy."

How, then, can the developmental and modular perspectives on giftedness, with seemingly disparate views of knowledge, be reconciled? Significantly advanced development might involve abilities that are, at most, minimally influenced by the kind of understanding evident in central conceptual structures (Case, 1992a; Fischer & Canfield, 1986; Fischer & Pipp, 1984; Porath, 1992). For example, in narrative, gifted young storytellers' plot structures—a conceptual understanding (McKeough, 1992)—are somewhat developmentally advanced but still similar to the plot structures of their peers, whereas other language abilities, such as vocabulary, grammar, syntax, and creative expression, are considerably more advanced (Porath, 1996a). The latter abilities are believed to be "encapsulated" or modular (Porath, 1992), the result of rapid learning in a domain.

Integrated Theoretical Perspective

By integrating developmental and modular theories of mind in a model of giftedness, it is possible to address the need to define the roles of general cognitive strategies and domain-specific knowledge in the gifted child's thinking (Horowitz & O'Brien, 1986; Rabinowitz & Glaser, 1985). Certainly, conceptual knowledge and skills alike are important in elucidating social giftedness (Hatch, 1997). A developmental perspective on expertise is the most appropriate framework for research, both for theoretical and applied reasons (Keating, 1991). That is, current research in cognitive development focuses on the role of cognitive activity in emerging expertise rather than on the essentialist, or general, notion of ability (Keating, 1990), and the educational implications of such a focus result in more appropriate matches between students' abilities and curricula (Globerson, 1989; Keating, 1991; Malkus, Feldman, & Gardner, 1988).

How children behave and understand others is thought to be influenced by the nature of their central social structure (Case, 1992a; Schneider, 1993). A study of empathy in children aged 4–10 (Bruchkowsky, 1992) found that children's explanations for others' feelings change from references to external events to increasingly complex references to others' internal, or intentional, states (Griffin, 1992), that is, to others' feelings, desires, or judgments. Four-year-old children, in general, focus on external events in explaining why another might feel happy, sad, or angry. For example (see Bruchkowsky, 1992), when asked what made a story character sad after her dog died, a typical response was "Because he died." Six-year-olds tend to refer to the external event plus an internal dimension: "Mary is sad because her dog died, and she misses him." By about age 8, children can incorporate a second internal dimension: "Mary is sad because her dog died, and she really loved him, and still really misses him." In another two years, by about age 10, many children can elaborate on these responses: "Mary is sad because her dog died, and she really loved him, and still really misses him because he was her best friend." By this stage, children's responses are integrated and cohesive.

Similarly, in a study of 4- to 10-year-old girls' conceptions of their mothers' roles, the understanding of another's intentions progressed from action-oriented behavioral descriptions to increasingly complex understandings of intentionality (Goldberg-Reitman, 1992). For example, in responding to a cartoon scenario in which a little girl has trouble putting a piece into a puzzle, a typical 4-year-old response is that the girl's mother would put the piece in the puzzle "because the girl cannot." By 6 years, the mother's intention is recognized—"Because she doesn't want the little girl to be stuck with the puzzle"—and by age 10 a much more integrated response is evident—"Mother puts the piece close by but not actually in. Because she wants the little girl to learn about things, and she doesn't want her frustrated."

Parallel findings come from Fischer, Hand, Watson, Van Parys, and Tucker's (1984) study of children's understanding of parental and occupational roles in which roles were acted out by the children. Four-year-olds displayed a "behavioral role"; 6-year-olds displayed a "true role," in which internal motivation was considered; and 10-year-olds displayed multiple interacting roles, paralleling the more integrated nature of the responses found by Bruchowsky (1992) and Goldberg-Reitman (1992).

Socially gifted children's central social structures are hypothesized to be age-typical but elaborate, with rich descriptions of feelings, desires, and judgments. Similarly, in social role-playing, gifted children make frequent and flexible use of social roles and elaborate on the roles in a way that captures subtleties and details. From a modular perspective, social giftedness involves specific social skills, such as facilitation, leadership, nurturance (Krechevsky, 1994), positive interactions, and effective coping strategies (Jarecky, 1959). It also could be that just as gifted young artists demonstrate their gifts in different ways—some with elaborations on age-typical structures and others with advanced artistic technique, graphic ability, or expressiveness (Golomb, 1992; Pariser, 1987; Porath, 1993)—so too will socially gifted children.

Preliminary Research

Research focused on the above hypotheses involves two separate but related investigations. The first is exploratory and inductive, focusing on interpersonal expertise in early childhood (Porath, 1995). The second is longitudinal: It examines cognitive, social, and motivational aspects of giftedness (Porath, 1996b). Age of entry to the second study ranges from 6 to 12. Three basic methodologies are incorporated.

1. Analysis of videotapes of young children considered socially mature by the staff of the child development laboratory preschool at the University of British Columbia. This includes tallying and describing instances of interpersonal sensitivity and adeptness at social role-playing.
2. Naturalistic observation in a kindergarten classroom that is part of the preschool described above. The observations focus on the classes of behaviors hypothesized as characteristic of interpersonal expertise. This provides baseline information about how social understanding is coordinated with responses to classroom situations and about the nature of individual differences. Naturalistic observation is believed to provide a dependable and stable measure of prosocial behavior (Eisenberg & Mussen, 1989). The Peer Interaction Checklist (Krechevsky, 1994), completed by the researcher and teacher, is used as a source of validating infor-

mation. The checklist presents descriptors of behaviors believed to differentiate among preschool children. Raters check behaviors that distinguish a child; the behaviors then are summarized under different categories—leader, facilitator, independent player, and team player (Krechevsky, 1994). Most relevant to the topic of social giftedness are the categories of team player, facilitator, and leader. Team players are willing to cooperate with others and participate in social activities; facilitators share ideas, information, and skills; and leaders attempt often to organize other children (Krechevsky, 1994).

3. Analysis of social developmental and social skills data collected from the Clinic on Ability and Development, a gifted assessment clinic at the University of British Columbia, focused on the longitudinal study of gifted children and adolescents. The data include children's teachers' and parents' ratings of social skills using the Social Skills Rating System (Gresham & Elliott, 1990). That rating system provides a measure of social behaviors that can influence the development of social competence and adaptive functioning at school and at home. The instrument asks the rater to judge the frequency of specific behaviors that are representative of cooperation, assertion, self-control, responsibility, and empathy. Ratings of social acceptance and behavioral conduct from the Self-Perception Profile for Children (Harter, 1985) are part of the data set, as is a task believed to tap children's central social structure (Griffin, 1992), administered in a semistructured interview. Children are asked to define "happy," "sad," "proud," and "embarrassed" using the following set of questions: "What does it mean to be happy (sad, proud, embarrassed)? What else can it mean? What is happening when you are happy (sad, proud, embarrassed)?" (Griffin, 1992, p. 197). The task focuses on intrapersonal understanding—the child's "inner world" (Griffin, 1992)—but it has been found to resemble the levels of social knowledge elicited by tests of interpersonal understanding because of the event-intention relationships elicited by the task (Griffin, 1992; McKeough, 1992), and it has been found to load on a "social factor" (Case et al., 1993).

The next section suggests preliminary support for the hypothesized forms of social giftedness. Descriptions of children's thoughts and actions illustrate these forms.[1] Some children appear in more than one category.

Childhood Manifestations

Fischer and Pipp (1984) and Case (1992a) suggested models of development in the neo-Piagetian tradition. They posited stagelike se-

---

[1]Pseudonyms are used in descriptions of specific children.

quences in which development proceeds hierarchically. Fischer and Pipp's work is drawn on the examination of elaborate role-playing, Case's in an analogous examination of elaborated central social structure.

Elaborate Use of Social Roles

Sam was noted by the preschool staff as exceptionally advanced socially. Videotaped sequences of Sam at 2 years old show him on the telephone. It is hard to make out the words between "Hello! I fine!" and "Goodbye!" but it is clear from the exaggerated adultlike inflections that this is a dynamic and involved "conversation." He is aware of his playmate nearby and attempts to engage her by offering her the receiver: "Talk to you?"

He is very theatrical, a self-conscious performer at an early age, able to pick up on things that are funny when exaggerated—the things that characterize specific activities (he speaks in a characteristic "phone call" tone of voice; J. Housego, personal communication, August 1992). All the while, Sam plays with the telephone cord, twirling it around as an adult would, and he engages the teacher in having her turn on the telephone. He hangs up emphatically. Sam's behavior is clearly different from the other children, whose role-playing, when demonstrated, is much less complex.

Sam's behavior is typical of the level of development described by Fischer and Pipp (1984) as "single representations." This level emerges at about 2 years and, in social role-playing, is typified by behavioral actions related to a single role. Sam's behavior supports Fischer and Pipp's hypothesis that ability in a domain is demonstrated by complex skills at a particular level. Thus, Sam's use of many behavioral nuances while acting out "talking on the telephone" could be described as "within-stage" elaboration.

Sara, age 5, also uses the telephone in her role-playing. She sits in the kindergarten "office" calling "her real estate agent." Two boys sit nearby. They "receive calls" and, while clearly enjoying the activity, respond quickly and hang up. Sara's conversation is animated; her body language mimics exactly that of an adult who is attending to several other things while on the telephone. Sara asks questions about the house, consults her calendar, makes an appointment. Here, too, actions match prototypical behavior: At about 5 years, children can combine behavioral actions to form a social role—"representational mapping" (Fischer & Pipp, 1984). Sara attends to the business of buying a house while keeping "other business" on her desk in order. Her play suggests a recognition that one can have personal and professional roles. Sara's play is sustained and elaborate; it is a richer representational mapping than is seen elsewhere in the classroom. It stands out even in a group where attention spans are long and general knowledge is sophisticated.

Elaborated Central Social Structure

Mark, aged 6½, was assessed for giftedness at the request of his parents, who expressed a desire to know more about his academic and social abilities. Mark's reported strengths include attention to people's motivations, awareness of the social implications of language, and empathy for others. Mark's responses to two of the questions designed to elicit level of intrapersonal understanding showed the ability to integrate an event or action with one intentional state (a feeling, desire, or judgment), which is typical of children his age (Griffin, 1992). For example, in response to the question "What does it mean to be happy?" Mark replied, "You want to do lots of fun stuff (desire); climb trees (action)." However, Mark's responses when questioned about the meaning of "proud" and "embarrassed" were typical of children about 2 years older. He integrated an event or action with two intentional states; moreover, he did so in an elaborate way, incorporating a variety of examples and perspectives. To define "proud," Mark answered,

> Be *happy* about *something that someone has done* and they've done it *well*. Your mom and dad may be *proud* that *you can horseback ride*. You're really *doing something good*; you're *giving your best*. You *think* you're *just as good as* an expert. (actions and intentions in italics)

Mark's central social structure can be considered a "blueprint," showing the coordination of two intentional states with an event or action, but his structure contains multiple interpretations of this coordination. These interpretations can be considered elaborations on the "basic" structure (Porath, 1996a)—a difference suggested as one manifestation of socially intelligent behavior. Not all of Mark's responses fit this description. A similar phenomenon is apparent in gifted young artists. As Pariser (1987) found in his study of the childhood works of Pablo Picasso, Paul Klee, and Henri-Marie-Raymond de Toulouse-Lautrec, giftedness is not apparent in all of their childhood drawings, a finding replicated by Gardner (1980) and Porath (1993, 1997). It appears that use of multiple criteria and multiple observations is as important for the identification of social giftedness as it is for other instances of exceptional ability.

Andrew, age 10, was referred to the gifted assessment clinic by his mother, who reported social strength in the form of sensitivity to others' feelings and perceptions. Andrew was reported to be "a good judge of people." Andrew himself reported the ability to read others' intentions and to use this knowledge effectively. Andrew expressed a desire to be a psychologist when he grows up. Andrew's responses to questions designed to elicit level of intrapersonal understanding showed the ability to integrate events, feelings, and judgments typical of children his age (Griffin, 1992). As do Mark's, Andrew's responses differ from the prototypical. In Andrew's case, this difference is less that of elaboration on the basic form, but rather a depth of emotional insight. There was a qualitative difference in his responses that distinguishes him from other 10-year-olds. For example, a fairly typical reply to the question "What is happening when you are embarrassed?" is "You feel dumb because you've done something that you're not supposed to do." Andrew replied, "Inside of you seems to get very very small and you want to hide. . . ."

As is sometimes the case with intellectually gifted children, Andrew's social insight appears to make him different from others at school. Andrew's teacher rated his social acceptance as low, using the teacher rating form of the Self-Perception Profile for Children (Harter, 1985). Andrew's self-rating of acceptance was average, although he subsequently changed schools in an effort to find a better fit. Self-, parent, and teacher ratings of social skills were average, with a significant number of behaviors demonstrated "sometimes" rather than "often." This suggests that Andrew's depth of conceptual understanding in the social domain might not transfer to actual behaviors in a consistent way.

This hypothesis is partially supported by consideration of ratings of behavioral conduct. Andrew rated himself high on this dimension, as did his mother and teacher. The behavioral conduct items on the profile are framed more broadly and appear to take a more conceptual approach to behavior than do the items on the Social Skills Rating System (Gresham & Elliott, 1990). Raters are asked to indicate the degree to which descriptors, such as doing the right thing, acting the way one should, doing things one should not do, and behaving well (Harter, 1985) apply to the child being rated. At a 1-year follow up, both Andrew and his mother maintained very positive views of his behavioral conduct. His teacher was less positive. The rater's frame of reference and expectations could be moderating variables in the judgment of social competence.

Mark's and Andrew's responses highlight the understanding of emotions (both of self and others) evident in social intelligence. This raises the question of the degree to which emotional intelligence (Goleman, 1995; Salovey & Sluyter, 1997) operates in social giftedness. Does exceptional interpersonal understanding imply insightful understanding of emotions? Intrapersonal and interpersonal intelligence are intertwined (Gardner, 1983), and emotional intelligence is central to effective relationships and life success (Goleman, 1995). When children possess the language of thought and feeling, they are better able to conceptualize the mental world (Astington, 1993; Astington & Jenkins, 1995; Porath, 1998). Tasks that tap both abilities load on the same factor (Case et al., 1996). This suggests a fruitful direction for subsequent research and educational intervention (Salovey & Sluyter, 1997).

Advanced Social Abilities

In this section, abilities that are considered "encapsulated" are presented. Drawing on modular theory, these abilities are hypothesized to develop independently of children's conceptual understanding of the social world.

Positive Interaction

Sam and Annie are completing a puzzle together. Sam has welcomed Annie into his play, and they take turns adding pieces. "This goes here! That goes there!" Sam is congenial and remarkable in his capacity to engage others in activity and conversation. Upon completion of the puzzle, Sam exclaims, "We did it! We did it!" Both children jump up and down triumphantly. Not only is Sam's cooperative behavior advanced (cf. Lupkowski, 1989; Parten, 1932), but his recognition of what has been accomplished through cooperation demonstrates a reflective ability far in advance of his chronological age.

Facilitation, Nurturance, Leadership

A kindergarten class has three children who appear to have exceptional social abilities that are manifested in different ways. Elena is very focused on activities and, at the same time, appears completely aware of the children around her. She is helpful and considerate. Her academic abilities are advanced, and she offers assistance with writing and spelling. She demonstrates ("When it has that little black edge it goes around the frame somewhere") and supports ("That was a good try"). She seems to be able to offer a balance that allows peers to find their own way with a task yet know she is there to support them. After responding to a request asking how "dinosaur" is spelled, Elena showed the word's location on a poster and made sure the child had started copying it correctly ("Make a little dot at the top. That looks pretty good, Nancy"). She then said, "I'll go back there, then you can come and get me."

Elena has a strong sense of fair play; she ensures that materials are distributed equitably and that compromises are reached in group play. She appears to want everyone to feel happy and included. She admonishes two boys that whispering makes people feel "they're not part of the group" and reassures others "Don't be upset if we don't go to Dinosaur Park today because we can always go another day."

Both teacher and researcher ratings of Elena's behaviors on the Peer Interaction Checklist (Krechevsky, 1994) indicate strong abilities as a team player, a facilitator, and a leader. No other child in the kindergarten has such a strong profile. Her teacher observed that Elena has very adult social skills, and that some children are very accepting of this although others experience dissonance. Elena's teacher posed the question, "Does she understand why the difference in reactions?" Elena's social understanding shows up somewhat differently than Andrew's, but the same issue can be raised for both children: How do their abilities affect their classroom lives?

Sara is enthusiastic and influential. She is constantly part of a group, contributing in a lively and often creative fashion to conversations. Sara is always engaged. Children follow her lead, but she never seems to take advantage of this fact. She is quick to help other children and demonstrates genuine concern that they understand and enjoy activities. The researcher and teacher rated her on the Peer Interaction Checklist (Krechevsky, 1994). Both ratings indicate strong abilities as a team player and a leader. In a preschool class, emergence of clear social roles has been found to be limited to a small number of children (approximately 10%) and to single roles (Krechevsky, 1994). However, this finding is limited to one classroom; more data clearly are needed to confirm whether Elena's and Sara's abilities fall into the upper end of such a distribution.

Molly is very much engaged in classroom activities but much less "center stage" than Elena or Sara. Molly is clearly as concerned about other children's well-being as the other two girls are, but her approach is different. She is a quiet observer who appears to be able to understand others' feelings and motivations. Her approach to assistance or mediation is mature in its consideration of all class members. After a class vote in which the majority decided to remain inside rather than have an outdoor play period, one child cried loudly in disappointment. Others looked on in concern, but insisted the vote was fair. Molly said calmly, "I have an idea. Why doesn't one teacher take the children who want to go outside to the playground, and the other teacher can stay here with the rest." This suggestion met with enthusiasm (and some relief) from teachers and students alike. Molly is advanced in her ability to decenter from her own point of view and take the point of view of others whose situation is different (Bruchowsky, 1992). Ratings on the Peer Interaction Checklist (Krechevsky, 1994) showed that Molly has a strong ability as a facilitator.

Molly is a sensitive observer, but she is far less articulate than Elena and Sara. Her abilities raise the issue of the relationship between social competence and mature language. This issue is analogous to confounding between social intelligence and academic ability, which has plagued measurement of social cognition (e.g., Keating, 1978). Language ability must be controlled for, and the behavioral effectiveness criterion (Ford & Tisak, 1983; Thorndike, 1920) remembered, in investigations of social competence.

Different Manifestations of Social Ability

The examples that follow are of children whose performance on the task believed to tap central social structure is age typical and not elaborated in any way. The children's social skills are well developed.

Lucy, age 9, was assessed at the Clinic on Ability and Development. She was reported to be socially mature. Lucy responded in an age-typical fashion to the central social structure measure. Her social skills were, however, rated as high by her father—in the 98th percentile. Lucy's teacher rated her in the 70th percentile; Lucy rated her own skills in the 86th percentile. A more consistent pattern emerged in Lucy's second year at the clinic. Parent, teacher, and self-ratings were at the 93rd, 87th, and less than 98th percentiles, respectively. Lucy presents as a very well-mannered, self-assured, and cooperative child. This impression is validated by the high ratings of social skills and by high teacher, parent, and self-ratings of social acceptance and behavioral conduct over a 2-year period.

Kevin, age 8, also was assessed at the clinic. He was reported to have highly developed social skills and the ability to get along with children his own age, older children, and adults. Parental reports indicated that he listened well and was very understanding of others. Kevin, too, responded in an age-typical fashion to the task that tapped central social structure, but he was rated as demonstrating highly competent social behavior. The parental rating of his social skills was in the 98th percentile. (Self-ratings begin at the third-grade level; Kevin was in second grade. Teacher data were unavailable.) On follow up the next year, consistently high results were obtained, with parent, teacher, and self-ratings in the less than 98th, 87th, and 98th percentiles, respectively. Kevin, too, presents as a child who is socially adept. His own and others' ratings of his social acceptance and behavioral conduct are high.

The pattern of development evident in Lucy and Kevin does not necessarily mean that their conceptual understanding is unremarkable; rather, it means that they might not have demonstrated such understanding on these occasions and under these circumstances. Multiple measures of conceptual knowledge should provide more reliable indicators of "optimal level" of understanding, particularly when opportunities are present for practice and support (Fischer at al., 1993). What is evident is the children's well-developed ability to get along with others and to "do the right thing."

Given that measurement error is addressed, however, a question arises about the extent to which both elaborate conceptual understanding and specific social skills are necessary in defining social giftedness. Are these simply "good" behaviors, which, without depth of understanding, might contribute nothing to outstanding performance in the social domain? Or, with a repertoire of such "good" behaviors and prolonged experience in the social domain, will outstanding performance result? Analogous questions have been raised in the study of other forms of giftedness (e.g., Gardner, 1983) as has the question of the degree to which general intelligence influences performance in specific domains. Lucy's IQ is average; Kevin's is superior. How will this difference affect their contributions in the social domain? The results of Jarecky's (1959) and Abroms and Gollin's (1980) studies suggest that an above-average IQ is necessary but not sufficient for social giftedness.

Summary and Implications

Because the research reported in this chapter is exploratory, findings must be considered tentative. A research strand that combines observational research focused on different manifestations of social ability with more comprehensive formal measures of central social structure and specific skills is necessary to fully address the integrated nature of the theoretical framework. The model of social giftedness does, however, appear to have potential. The model is strongest in describing the *what* of social gifted-ness—elaborate conceptual understanding and social role-playing, specific social skills, and the different ways social giftedness is demonstrated. *How* social giftedness develops is described with reference to stage theories, which posit a dialectical cycle in development (with qualitative shifts in conceptual understanding at points in development related to general systemic factors) and to modular theory (which posits periodic conceptual reworkings within domains) (Case, 1992a; Case et al., 1993). Such a theory base can provide considerable explanatory strength, but there is a need to include in-depth analysis of contextual factors as well as theory-based analyses in subsequent research. The following sections present implications of the research for the identification and assessment of social giftedness and for educational planning. Both sections raise questions with the intent of provoking thinking about potential influences on the development of this important intelligence.

Identification and Assessment

There are prosocial behaviors that are identifiable and valued in our culture (Bruner, 1996; Eisenberg & Mussen, 1989; Gardner, 1983; Zahn-Waxler, Radke-Yarrow, Wagner, & Chapman, 1992). We recognize the exceptional leaders; facilitators and nurturers tend to be behind the scenes but are recognized nonetheless. These individuals' interpersonal expertise—their ability to understand others' intentions and feelings—is essential for a healthy society. How we identify and nurture such expertise must be informed by consideration of the following questions.

Are there social behaviors that are perceived differentially by children, their peers, parents, and teachers? For Andrew and Elena, the answer appears to be yes. Andrew's teacher was less positive about his social behavior than he or his mother were. Some of Elena's classmates perceived her behavior as too directive or as unusual. Andrew's insight also might have been perceived as unusual. "Unusual" can too easily become "weird." Assessment tools that allow for multiple perceptions of social competence are as important as are observations in different contexts and background information to frame interpretation of the perceptions.

In our search for the focus of ratings, it is important to consider the match between the construct of social intelligence and its operational definition. The Social Skills Rating System (Gresham & Elliott, 1990) is a good match to Ford and Tisak's (1983) behavioral effectiveness criterion of "one's ability to accomplish relevant objectives in specific social settings" (p. 197). In clinical work, parental feedback on the measure has validated this match. Parents, though, have expressed their desire for a measure that goes further, one that captures the degree to which integrity and concern for justice are displayed.

Education

To be optimal, education for gifted children should have domain-specific foci compatible with the abilities of the children being served, rather than the general problem-solving or general "enrichment" approaches so commonly used (Jackson & Butterfield, 1986; Keating, 1980; Matthews, 1988). Thus, children who demonstrate social expertise should be offered curricula that appropriately match their level of social development.

There are programs and teaching strategies that aim to increase social understanding (e.g., Battistich, Watson, Solomon, Schaps, & Solomon, 1991; Lickona, 1991). However, we have relatively little knowledge of the effect of programs and teaching on prosocial development (Battistich et al., 1991; Eisenberg, 1992; Zins, Travis, & Freppon, 1997). Where programs have been successful, the effects are not well understood because many procedures have been used and it is not clear which lead to success (Eisenberg, 1992). Efforts to enhance prosocial development in classrooms have shown weak positive effects on behaviors at school, but these effects have not generalized to out-of-school interactions (Battistich et al., 1991). Research is necessary to refine instructional approaches in the social domain and to consider the degree of depth and flexibility of pacing necessary for gifted learners in this domain. One approach that holds promise is that of "conceptual bridging" based on Case's (1992a) theory of development.

It is recognized that children's conceptual understandings are a necessary starting point in instructional planning (e.g., Case, 1991; Donaldson, 1989) and that instruction that aims to create a "conceptual bridge" from one developmental level to another is effective, generalizable, and stable (e.g., Griffin, Case, & Siegler, 1994; McKeough, 1992). This approach uses what is known about central conceptual structures at different stages of development, and it plans instruction to help children grow conceptually. Thus, one might envision conceptually based instruction in the social domain with opportunities to apply and extend social understanding.

In addition, the degree of contextual support (practice, modeling) offered to children has been shown to influence demonstrated developmental level (Fischer et al., 1993). The nature and degree of support for socially gifted youngsters must be considered. They might, for example, need little practice but plenty of opportunities to observe social experts at work.

Gender could be a relevant variable when considering contextual support. Differences between boys and girls have been found in social behaviors and interpretations, and those differences increase during childhood (Fischer et al., 1993). Matthews (1995) pointed out the importance of including human development courses in the curriculum to address issues of equity (girls are more interested in this domain than boys, particularly in early adolescence) and to facilitate boys' learning. Articulating the nature of the differences in early childhood could influence such courses.

Conclusion

Studying expertise is important in its own right, but it also is a valuable strategy for elucidating mainstream development (Gardner, 1995; Janos & Robinson, 1985). The study of the conceptual nature of expert social understanding, the developmental pathways to such understanding, and specific advanced social behaviors under varying degrees of contextual support, could provide a starting point for the ultimate enhancement of interpersonal expertise in the general population. Research on competence and the conditions that foster it can direct the way we build programs that have as their focus the optimization of successful development (Horowitz & O'Brien, 1986; Masten & Coatsworth, 1998; Meichenbaum & Biemiller, 1998).

What is necessary to keep social intelligence alive and well? This question has been addressed extensively in the literature on intellectually gifted children, and it is from this literature that we can take guidelines for optimizing the development of socially gifted youngsters. Taking a life-span perspective, it is speculated that the form social giftedness takes in childhood and the influences that direct it (teachers, parents, peers, mentors) have profound implications for its ultimate realization and contribution to society.

References

Abroms, K. I., & Gollin, J. B. (1980). Developmental study of gifted preschool children and measures of psychosocial giftedness. *Exceptional Children, 46,* 334–341.

Astington, J. W. (1993). *The child's discovery of the mind.* Cambridge, MA: Harvard University Press.

Astington, J. W., & Jenkins, J. M. (1995). Theory of mind development and social understanding. *Cognition and Emotion, 9,* 151–165.

Barnes, M. L., & Sternberg, R. J. (1989). Social intelligence and decoding of nonverbal cues. *Intelligence, 13,* 263–287.

Battistich, V., Watson, M., Solomon, D., Schaps, E., & Solomon, J. (1991). The Child Development Project: A comprehensive program for the development of prosocial character. In W. M. Kurtines & J. L. Gewirtz (Eds.), *Handbook of moral behavior and development: Volume 3. Application* (pp. 1–34). Hillsdale, NJ: Erlbaum.

Bruchkowsky, M. (1992). The development of empathic cognition in middle and early childhood. In R. Case (Ed.), *The mind's staircase: Exploring the conceptual underpinnings of children's thought and knowledge* (pp. 153–170). Hillsdale, NJ: Erlbaum.

Bruner, J. (1996). *The culture of education.* Cambridge, MA: Harvard University Press.

Case, R. (1985). *Intellectual development: Birth to adulthood.* New York: Academic Press.

Case, R. (1991). A developmental approach to the design of remedial instruction. In A. McKeough & J. Lupart (Eds.), *Toward the practice of theory-based instruction: Current cognitive theories and their educational promise* (pp. 117–147). Hillsdale, NJ: Erlbaum.

Case, R. (1992a). *The mind's staircase: Exploring the conceptual underpinnings of children's thought and knowledge.* Hillsdale, NJ: Erlbaum.

Case, R. (1992b). Neo-Piagetian theories of intellectual development. In H. Beilin & P. Pufall (Eds.), *Piaget's theory: Prospects and possibilities* (pp. 61–104). Hillsdale, NJ: Erlbaum.

Case, R., & Griffin, S. (1989). Child cognitive development: The role of central conceptual structures in the development of scientific and social thought. In C. A. Hauert (Ed.), *Developmental psychology: Cognitive, perceptuo-motor and neurological perspectives.* Amsterdam, Netherlands: Elsevier/North Holland.

Case, R., Marini, Z., McKeough, A., Dennis, S., & Goldberg, J. (1986). Horizontal structure in middle childhood: Cross-domain parallels in the course of cognitive growth. In I. Levin (Ed.), *Stage and structure: Reopening the debate* (pp. 1–39). Norwood, NJ: Ablex.

Case, R., Okamoto, Y., Henderson, B., & McKeough, A. (1993). Individual variability and consistency in cognitive development: New evidence for the existence of central conceptual structures. In R. Case & W. Edelstein (Eds.), *The new structuralism in cognitive development: Theory and research on individual pathways* (pp. 71–100). Basel, Switzerland: Karger.

Case, R., Okamoto, Y., Henderson, B., McKeough, A., & Bleiker, C. (1996). Exploring the macrostructure of children's central conceptual structures in the domains of number and narrative. In R. Case & Y. Okamoto (Eds.), *The role of central conceptual structures in the development of children's thought* (Monographs of the Society for Research in Child Development, *61*, pp. 59–82). Chicago: University of Chicago Press.

Chandler, M. J. (1982). Social cognition and social structure. In F. C. Serafica (Ed.), *Social-cognitive development in context* (pp. 222–239). New York: Guilford Press.

Csikszentmihalyi, M., & Larson, R. (1984). *Being adolescent*. New York: Basic Books.

Donaldson, M. (1989, March). The mismatch between school and children's minds. *Human Nature,* pp. 155–159.

Eisenberg, N. (1992). *The caring child*. Cambridge, MA: Harvard University Press.

Eisenberg, N., & Mussen, P. H. (1989). *The roots of prosocial behavior in children*. New York: Cambridge University Press.

Feldman, D. H. (1986). *Nature's gambit. Child prodigies and the development of human potential*. New York: Basic Books.

Fischer, K. W., & Canfield, R. L. (1986). The ambiguity of stage and structure of behavior: Person and environment in the development of psychological structure. In I. Levin (Ed.), *Stage and structure: Reopening the debate* (pp. 246–267). Norwood, NJ: Ablex.

Fischer, K. W., Hand, H. H., Watson, M. W., Van Parys, M. M., & Tucker, J. L. (1984). Putting the child into socialization: The development of social categories in preschool children. In L. Katz (Ed.), *Current topics in early childhood education* (Vol. 5, pp. 27–72). Norwood, NJ: Ablex.

Fischer, K. W., Knight, C. C., & Van Parys, M. (1993). Analyzing diversity in developmental pathways: Methods and concepts. In R. Case & W. Edelstein (Eds.), *The new structuralism in cognitive development: Theory and research on individual pathways* (pp. 33–56). Basel, Switzerland: Karger.

Fischer, K. W., & Pipp, S. L. (1984). Processes of cognitive development: Optimal level and skill acquisition. In R. J. Sternberg (Ed.), *Mechanisms of cognitive development* (pp. 45–80). New York: Freeman.

Ford, M. E. (1982). Social cognition and social competence in adolescence. *Developmental Psychology, 18,* 323–340.

Ford, M. E. (1986). A living systems conceptualization of social intelligence: Outcomes, processes, and developmental change. In R. J. Sternberg (Ed.), *Advances in the psychology of human intelligence* (Vol. 3, pp. 119–171). Hillsdale, NJ: Erlbaum.

Ford, M. E., & Tisak, M. S. (1983). A further search for social intelligence. *Journal of Educational Psychology, 75,* 196–206.

Frederiksen, N. (1990). Toward a broader conception of human intelligence. *Mensa Research Journal, 29,* 6–19.

Gallagher, J. J., & Courtright, R. D. (1986). The educational definition of giftedness and its policy implications. In R. J. Sternberg & J. E. Davidson (Eds.), *Conceptions of giftedness* (pp. 100–111). Cambridge, England: Cambridge University Press.

Gardner, H. (1980). *Artful scribbles*. New York: Basic Books.

Gardner, H. (1983). *Frames of mind. The theory of multiple intelligences*. New York: Basic Books.

Gardner, H. (1995). Why would anyone become an expert? *American Psychologist, 50,* 802–803.

Gardner, H., & Hatch, T. (1989). Multiple intelligences go to school: Educational implications of the theory of multiple intelligences. *Educational Researcher, 18*(8), 4–10.

Globerson, T. (1985). Field dependence/independence and mental capacity: A developmental approach. *Developmental Review, 5,* 261–273.

Globerson, T. (1989). What is the relationship between cognitive style and cognitive development? In T. Globerson & T. Zelniker (Eds.), *Cognitive style and cognitive development* (pp. 71–85). Norwood, NJ: Ablex.

Goldberg-Reitman, J. (1992). Young girls' conception of their mothers' role: A neo-structural analysis. In R. Case (Ed.), *The mind's staircase: Exploring the conceptual underpinnings of children's thought and knowledge* (pp. 135–151). Hillsdale, NJ: Erlbaum.

Goleman, D. (1995). *Emotional intelligence.* New York: Bantam.

Golomb, C. (1992). *The child's creation of a pictorial world.* Berkeley: University of California Press.

Gresham, F. M., & Elliott, S. N. (1990). *Social Skills Rating System.* Circle Pines, MN: American Guidance Service.

Griffin, S. (1992). Young children's awareness of their inner world: A neo-structural analysis of the development of intrapersonal intelligence. In R. Case (Ed.), *The mind's staircase: Exploring the conceptual underpinnings of children's thought and knowledge* (pp. 189–206). Hillsdale, NJ: Erlbaum.

Griffin, S., Case, R., & Siegler, R. (1994). Rightstart: Providing the central conceptual prerequisites for first formal learning of arithmetic to students at risk for failure. In K. McGilly (Ed.), *Classroom lessons: Integrating cognitive theory and classroom practice* (pp. 25–49). Cambridge, MA: MIT/Bradford Books.

Guilford, J. P. (1959). Three faces of intellect. *American Psychologist, 14,* 469–479.

Harter, S. (1985). *Self-perception profile for children.* Unpublished test, University of Denver, Denver, CO.

Hatch, T. (1997). Friends, diplomats, and leaders in kindergarten: Interpersonal intelligence in play. In P. Salovey & D. J. Sluyter (Eds.), *Emotional development and emotional intelligence: Educational implications* (pp. 70–89). New York: Basic Books.

Horowitz, F. D., & O'Brien, M. (1986). Gifted and talented children: State of knowledge and directions for research. *American Psychologist, 41,* 1147–1152.

Hunt, T. (1928). The measurement of social intelligence. *Journal of Applied Psychology, 12,* 317–334.

Jackson, N. E., & Butterfield, E. C. (1986). A conception of giftedness designed to promote research. In R. J. Sternberg & J. E. Davidson (Eds.), *Conceptions of giftedness* (pp. 151–181). Cambridge, England: Cambridge University Press.

Janos, P. M., & Robinson, N. M. (1985). Psychosocial development in intellectually gifted children. In F. D. Horowitz & M. O'Brien (Eds.), *The gifted and talented: Developmental perspectives* (pp. 149–195). Washington, DC: American Psychological Association.

Jarecky, R. K. (1959). Identification of the socially gifted. *Exceptional Children, 25,* 415–419.

Keating, D. P. (1978). A search for social intelligence. *Journal of Educational Psychology, 70,* 218–223.

Keating, D. P. (1980). Four faces of creativity: The continuing plight of the educationally underserved. *Gifted Child Quarterly, 24,* 56–61.

Keating, D. P. (1990). Charting pathways to the development of expertise. *Educational Psychologist, 25,* 243–267.

Keating, D. P. (1991). Curriculum options for the developmentally advanced: A developmental alternative to gifted education. *Exceptionality Education Canada, 1,* 53–84.

Keating, D. P. (1995, June). *Building the learning society: Education's critical role.* Invited address to the annual meeting of the Canadian Society for the Study of Education, University of Quebec, Montreal, Quebec, Canada.

Krechevsky, M. (1994). *Project Spectrum: Preschool assessment handbook.* Cambridge, MA: Harvard Project Zero.

Lickona, T. (1991). Moral development in the elementary school classroom. In W. M. Kurtines & J. L. Gewirtz (Eds.), *Handbook of moral behavior and development: Volume 3. Application* (pp. 143–161). Hillsdale, NJ: Erlbaum.

Lovell, K., & Shields, J. B. (1967). Some aspects of a study of the gifted child. *British Journal of Educational Psychology. 37,* 201–209.

Lupkowski, A. E. (1989). Social behaviors of gifted and typical preschool children in laboratory school programs. *Roeper Review, 11,* 124–127.

Malkus, U. C., Feldman, D. H., & Gardner, H. (1988). Dimensions of mind in early childhood. In A. D. Pellegrini (Ed.), *Psychological bases for early education* (pp. 25–38). New York: Wiley.

Marland, S. P., Jr. (1972). *Education of the gifted and talented.* Washington, DC: U.S. Government Printing Office.

Masten, A. S., & Coatsworth, J. D. (1998). The development of competence in favorable and unfavorable environments: Lessons from research on successful children. *American Psychologist, 53,* 205–220.

Matthews, D. J. (1988). Gardner's multiple intelligence theory: An evaluation of relevant research literature and a consideration of its application to gifted education. *Roeper Review, 11,* 100–104.

Matthews, D. J. (1990). *Patterns of competence in early adolescence: A domain specific approach to gifted education.* Unpublished doctoral dissertation, University of Toronto, Toronto, Ontario, Canada.

Matthews, D. J. (1995, March). *Developmental diversity and giftedness: Identifying giftedness by domains.* Paper presented at the annual meeting of the National Association of School Psychologists' Annual Convention, Chicago, IL.

Matthews, D. J. (1997). Diversity in domains of development: Research findings and their implications for gifted identification and programming. *Roeper Review, 19,* 172–177.

McKeough, A. (1992). Testing for the presence of a central social structure: Use of the transfer paradigm. In R. Case (Ed.), *The mind's staircase: Exploring the conceptual underpinnings of children's thought and knowledge* (pp. 207–225). Hillsdale, NJ: Erlbaum.

Meichenbaum, D., & Biemiller, A. (1998). *Nurturing independent learners. Helping students take charge of their learning.* Cambridge, MA: Brookline Books.

Okagaki, L., & Sternberg, R. J. (1988). Unwrapping giftedness. In G. Kanselaar, J. van der Linden, & A. Pennings (Eds.), *Individual differences in giftedness: Identification and education* (pp. 30–45). Amersfoort, Netherlands: Acco.

Pariser, D. (1987). The juvenile drawings of Klee, Toulouse-Lautrec, and Picasso. *Visual Arts Research, 13,* 53–67.

Parten, M. B. (1932). Social participation among preschool children. *Journal of Abnormal and Social Psychology, 27,* 243–269.

Porath, M. (1991). Educational implications of a developmental perspective on giftedness. *Exceptionality Education Canada, 1,* 61–77.

Porath, M. (1992). Stage and structure in the development of children with various types of "giftedness." In R. Case (Ed.), *The mind's staircase: Exploring the conceptual underpinnings of children's thought and knowledge* (pp. 303–317). Hillsdale, NJ: Erlbaum.

Porath, M. (1993). Gifted young artists: Developmental and individual differences. *Roeper Review, 16,* 29–33.

Porath, M. (1995). Social giftedness in childhood. *Alberta Gifted and Talented Education, 9,* 2–9.

Porath, M. (1996a). Narrative performance in verbally gifted children. *Journal for the Education of the Gifted, 19,* 276–292.

Porath, M. (1996b). Affective and motivational considerations in the assessment of gifted learners. *Roeper Review, 19,* 13–17.

Porath, M. (1997). A developmental model of artistic giftedness in middle childhood. *Journal for the Education of the Gifted, 20,* 201–223.

Porath, M. (1998, June). *Young children's interpersonal understanding: The social map in the first year of school.* Paper presented at the annual meeting of the Canadian Society for the Study of Education, Ottawa, Ontario, Canada.

Rabinowitz, M., & Glaser, R. (1985). Cognitive structure and process in highly competent performance. In F. D. Horowitz & M. O'Brien (Eds.), *The gifted and talented: Developmental perspectives* (pp. 75–98). Washington, DC: American Psychological Association.

Roedell, W., Jackson, N., & Robinson, H. (1980). *Gifted young children.* New York: Teachers College Press.

Roeper, A. (1978). Some thoughts about Piaget and the young gifted child. *Gifted Child Quarterly, 22,* 252–257.

Salovey, P., & Sluyter, D. J. (Eds.). (1997). *Emotional development and emotional intelligence: Educational implications.* New York: Basic Books.

Schneider, B. H. (1993). *Children's social competence in context.* Tarrytown, NY: Pergamon Press.

Strang, R. (1930). Measures of social intelligence. *American Journal of Sociology, 36,* 263–269.

Strauss, S., Globerson, T., & Mintz, R. (1983). The influence of training for the atomistic schema on the development of the density concept among gifted and nongifted children. *Journal of Applied Developmental Psychology, 4,* 125–147.

Taylor, E. H., & Cadet, J. L. (1989). Social intelligence: A neurological system? *Psychological Reports, 64,* 423–444.

Thorndike, E. L. (1920). Intelligence and its use. *Harper's Magazine, 140,* 227–235.

U.S. Department of Education Office of Educational Research and Improvement. (1993). *National excellence: A case for developing America's talent.* Washington, DC: U.S. Government Printing Office.

Walker, R. E., & Foley, J. M. (1973). Social intelligence: Its history and measurement. *Psychological Reports, 33,* 839–864.

Webb, R. A. (1974). Concrete and formal operations in very bright 6- to 11-year-olds. *Human Development, 17,* 292–300.

Zahn-Waxler, C., Radke-Yarrow, M., Wagner, E., & Chapman, M. (1992). Development of concern for others. *Developmental Psychology, 28,* 126–136.

Zins, J. E., Travis, L. F., III, & Freppon, P. A. (1997). Linking research and educational programming to promote social and emotional learning. In P. Salovey & D. J. Sluyter (Eds.), *Emotional development and emotional intelligence: Educational implications* (pp. 257–274). New York: Basic Books.

10

On the Nature of Expertise in Visual Art

Sandra I. Kay

Moore and Murdock (1991) challenged researchers who study problem finding to answer several questions:

> What accounts do we have by problem finders of problem finding? What are their preferences for finding and forming questions and problems, and how do these preferences affect solving? What are the process pathways problem finders take as they explore the parameters of memory and knowledge? What pathways do they choose to arrive at their solutions? (p. 292)

The answers are critical to researchers who study creative thought and, therefore, to researchers interested in people who are gifted. Gleaned from the qualitative data collected during an empirical investigation of the thought processes of artists, some observations on the nature of expertise in these problem finders could offer potential for further investigation. This chapter reports unexpected findings regarding the nature of expertise (Kay, 1994) and explores the implications for explaining and nurturing creative giftedness. A brief description of the original investigation (Kay, 1989) precedes the focus on the qualitative differences that emerged among the various levels of expertise.

Experiment in Problem Definition

The purpose of the original investigation (Kay, 1989) was to explore the relationship between *problem solving* (the process of finding a solution to a stated problem) and *problem finding* (the formulation of a problem prior to the actions taken to solve the problem) in the manipulation of figural symbol systems by professional artists, semiprofessional artists, and nonartists. The possibility that these thought processes are qualitatively different for different people is supported in the literature by comparisons of experts and novices (Chi, Feltovich, & Glaser, 1981; deGroot, 1965; Schoenfeld & Herrmann, 1982). For example, deGroot (1965) concluded that the actual problem-solving process involved in chess mastery differs between expert and novice both quantitatively and qualitatively. Variables that measure the speed of the performance on a task (latency) or the accuracy attained in the performance define the proficiency with which a task is completed. Analysis of these variables measures quantitative differences alone. Differences in the type or quality of the processes used in problem solving (Chi et al., 1981; Kanevsky, 1990) and in problem finding (Beittel & Burkhardt, 1963; Getzels & Csikszentmihalyi, 1976) have been observed through the analysis of dynamic process variables (Kay, 1991, p. 235).

The principal research question was this: Are there differences in the figural problem-solving and problem-finding behaviors of professional artists, semiprofessionals, and nonartists? Five hypotheses were advanced to address differences between the groups in their scores on spatial visualization measures; reaction time on a figural problem-solving task; and the reaction time, number of pauses, and number of completed ideas on a problem-finding task.

Sixty participants were selected for equal distribution into three independent groups. Each group consisted of 10 male and 10 female adults. Twenty visual artists—10 sculptors and 10 painters—who regularly exhibited their work in museums or galleries and earned their living solely through the production of art constituted the group of professional artists. The group of semiprofessional artists—10 painters and 10 sculptors— consisted of individuals who had formal art training beyond high school and produced ideas in art but did not earn their living producing their art work. The nonartists were graduate students who had not had formal art training since high school and who claimed they did not produce ideas in art under any circumstances.

The problem-finding task (the description of only one of the two tasks is necessary here) used a puzzle-type game available on the consumer market. PABLO, manufactured by Fox Spielverlag, is a construction toy that consists of 120 cardboard pieces of various sizes, shapes, colors, and patterns that can be used with small plastic connectors to build structures.

It was believed that a task other than the drawing task used in other studies of artists (Getzels & Csikszentmihalyi, 1976; Patrick, 1937) might offer a direct perspective on differences in cognitive processes without the confounding of extensive previous experience by one or more groups with the specific task. In other words, to compare the drawing procedure of those who draw and those who do not (nonartists) cannot help to address the issue at hand.

The use of play activities for analysis of cognitive behavior is suggested by the work of Welker (1961) in which the behavior mechanisms characteristic of exploratory and play behavior in animals have been theoretically proposed as being responsible for "the variable and dynamic acts which characterize exploration, play, adaptable problem solution and invention" (p. 226) in advanced animals. The playing with ideas often reported in accounts of the creative process within creative individuals (Ghiselin, 1952; Koestler, 1964) or the playful attitude describing noted scientists (Root-Bernstein, 1989) and artists (Klee, 1964) adds strength to the theory advanced by Welker (1961).

Although not a pure form of problem finding, the PABLO instructions required little direction, affording an opportunity for divergent capabilities in a task of figural transformations. The opportunity to define one's own problem was given to the 60 participants.

All participants received the same instructions. Upon arrival, an attempt was made to make the subject feel comfortable and relaxed. The purpose and procedure of the study were stated as follows (Kay, 1989):

> There will be two measures of spatial ability and three different tasks that I will ask you to complete. I will be videotaping so that I can play the tape back for you. At that time I will ask you to tell me what you were thinking about while you were playing. If you want to talk about what you are doing as you are doing it, please feel free to say anything at any time. Anything you say or think will help me to evaluate the usefulness of the two games as learning tools. (p. 115)

The oral instructions for the PABLO task were as follows (Kay, 1989): "This is a game that just came on the market. You can make anything you would like; just have fun with it" (p. 117).

Upon completion, the videotape was reviewed by the participant. Participants were asked to explain what they remembered thinking as they were working. Responses were audiotaped. All participants were unfamiliar with the task.

The identification of dynamic process variables was facilitated by the use of videotape and, in the manner of Kagan, Krathwohl, and Miller (1963), an audiotaped analysis by the participant immediately followed the activity. Based on H. E. Gruber's case-study approach (personal communication, March 7, 1988), protocols were analyzed for thematic structures.

When the three groups were given PABLO and asked to "do whatever you like with it," specific patterns emerged. The use of play activities did produce behaviors most similar to those found in the empirical studies that required drawing (Getzels & Csikszentmihalyi, 1976; Patrick, 1937). Like these other two studies that involved problem finding, two different behaviors were depicted during the process. The first stage, problem defining, resembled Patrick's (1937) "unorganized thought." It began from the moment the participant opened the box and ended when the first two pieces that remained in the final product were constructed. Once that occurred, a different stage was clearly depicted. The second stage, problem solving, began when those first two pieces that remained in the final product were assembled and ended when the participants stated that they were finished.

Within this two-stage structure, the professional artists demonstrated specific preferences when finding or defining their answers to the PABLO task. For example, a sculptor known for monochromatic, geometric forms constructed a form using squares and rectangles and then stated a desire to spray paint the structure black. This behavior was not demonstrated in the other two groups (semiprofessional artists and nonartists).

Expertise in the Visual Arts

According to the expert-versus-novice literature, the initial perception of a problem or the problem space seems to differ depending on the degree of expertise acquired. DeGroot (1965) found that expert chess players perceived the board positions in terms of broad arrangements or patterns; novices did not. DeGroot discussed the probability that the master, afforded a greater depth and breadth of experience, is less likely to make unsuccessful attempts or changes because of his or her knowledge of what will fail. This behavior was depicted in the professional artists engaged in this study (Kay, 1989). A concern for the fact that deGroot observed chess players, and these artists were also involved with a play activity, could lead one to assume that these behaviors are characteristic of play and not of creative thought. However, all of the artists volunteered an unsolicited comparison of this game playing to their own creative work.

In comparing the PABLO task with his creative thought process, Participant 50 offered this analogy:

> In the game PABLO with cardboard basically, by having those shapes that are there, to me they are like letters. Each shape is symbolizing a letter and by putting several of those letters together—it is like creating a word. Create an idea, a concept. Now, the way I work . . . is I will use existing shapes because that's what you are familiar with— that is what is available to us, and then I want to make these shapes into unique shapes—make them my own shapes. So what I am doing, in a sense, is changing a letter and then by having different changed letters, I create a new word that did not exist before, and I feel that is the difference—why I had little harder time with your things—because to me—they are already pre-conceived. Found objects that I put together as a grouping. While to make it more personal—I would rather create my own shapes which are derived—from shapes. So I am just taking these shapes, the potential of these shapes a little further . . . not that they're better . . . but just taking them into another direction and then putting them together and making them into a totally new thing. But I deal, in my sculpture, with very simple, basic form. Very simple dialogue . . . it's like haiku poetry. You use a few words and create a 5-hour movie, with six words. (Kay, 1989, p. 195)

Play and Creative Thought

The spoken protocols show that all of the artists stated that much of what they were doing (the process) was in essence the same approach that they take in their studio work. Each artist described in various degrees of detail the difference between playing with this game and doing their own work. Where the other participants stated that they found the choices (color, shape, size) afforded by the PABLO game to be overwhelming, the professional artists felt hindered by its limitations. Some of the specific limitations cited were as follows:

- The size of the pieces was too small.
- The colors were not to their liking.
- The shapes were considered flat (cardboard art) by sculptors, but painters found them more three-dimensional, so it took less time to mentally imagine the different views because they could manipulate the pieces.
- The shapes were all the same thickness.
- Participants had to use structured, predetermined, rigid forms.
- Participants had to use "found objects" so the technical responsibilities were different from their work.
- The connectors limited one to constructing at right angles, which is static, rather than offering the dynamic possibilities of using different angles.
- The connectors were all the same so there were no variations possible (including ability for movement).

Other than these restrictions, the artists perceived their behaviors, when reviewed on the videotape, and their thought processes to be the same as when they were developing their own art. Participant 3 offered a good example:

> Oh my gosh—there's enough pieces in here. I may have to be a month on this . . . oh, oh, what do we have here . . . [starts humming] the thing is this is more my kind of thing. I don't think this is fair because this is what I'm doing all the time. [What do you mean? You play with puzzles?] Yes—making a sculpture you are taking these things . . . [selects pieces from large pile to build. Sounding disappointed he continues] . . . all of the catches are the same, huh? This isn't fair because this is what I do all the time [Have you seen this before?] No, not this particular puzzle—but I would imagine that a person who is using this . . . [gets back into his work]. The two things that are different from what I do all the time is that these are flat, flat cardboard pieces, and I make my own shapes from clay. I make my own shapes and thicknesses. These are two-dimensional, with the same thickness, and now I am concerned with the selection of the color which I do not normally do. You know, I may get hooked on playing this game all the time. . . . Want to see the way it looks? [Yes. Are you finished?] Yes, well, wait, I want to make it just a little bit better.

It was an elongated figure playing the guitar. His sculptures are elongated forms of action.

Personal Aesthetic Bias

A second phenomenon, not cited in the literature, appears to be supported by clinical observations and oral protocols. Unlike the other two groups, the professional artists exhibited behavior that has been called *personal aesthetic bias* or *personal aesthetic preference* (Kay, 1989, 1991). Based on a personal set of conventions that is the basis of the language used in an artist's body of work, a personal aesthetic seems to evolve. The distinctive aesthetic that guides creative thought processes when producing ideas in art was reflected in the behaviors of a game task that does not purport to have any association with the complexity involved in producing art.

This personal aesthetic bias behaves like the engineering of a bridge, offering tensile strength to the pursuit of an idea. As in steel structures, this tensile strength supports the endeavor, yet it bends or flexes in response to the forces that act on it. The aesthetic appears to guide the search operation, providing a selective criterion within which one explores (Campbell, 1960). The literature describes an aesthetic characteristic of creative thought in determining the correct solution (Campbell, 1960; Perkins, 1981), but the idea of an aesthetic preference that controls the perception of new experiences has not been expressed in the literature.

It appears that this aesthetic preference could have altered the perception of this task into a problem-solving task rather than the problem-finding or problem-defining task it was originally designed to be. This is substantiated by most of the professional artists who, on opening the PABLO box, commented on the "predetermined nature" of the game. Finding no redeeming qualities to "pretty games," one artist wanted to "spray paint the forms black" (his language). Another artist, also involved in performance art, wished to set fire to the pieces to develop a metamorphosis of them. Restricted by my need to reuse the toy, she instead developed a collage (her language) using pearls and sawdust to temper the predetermined nature of the materials. Given that the professional artists began the task by imposing a particular set of conventions that had been a part of their own work, the application of these conventions to the task can be viewed as a problem to solve.

Because the artists brought their personal aesthetic bias to the situation, the qualities of the task affected their response to the situation depending on their personal style. For example, Participant 37, a sculptor whose aesthetic preference is often represented through bronze forms of the human figure, responded to the task as follows:

> [The artist was just opening the box to the PABLO game] Oh, it looks like Frank Stella. . . . Oh, that's a nice shape . . . this isn't fair to artists because their own aesthetics get in the way . . . too bad you can't attach pieces from the middle of the shape . . . that's too red . . . that's too long . . . well, this is a Frank Stella aesthetic so I'm just going to have to work with his aesthetic . . . [and she did]. (Kay, 1989, p. 199)

To see her work is to know that she is involved with subtle shades and not color, that her forms have no flat areas, and that patterns are not intrinsic to her world of ideas. Exhibiting the sine qua non of flexibility, her final comment was "It's a great toy, actually. Let me add to it a little more." Rather than avoid premature closure (Perkins, 1981) or actively pursue fluent or flexible behavior (Guilford, 1967), the opposite characteristic seems to initiate response to the stimuli. Only when the behavior consistent with the inherent process is found to be an unacceptable strategy is flexibility used to resolve to a solution.

The semiprofessional artists, not having had the time to develop their own sets of conventions fully, viewed the multiplicity of choices as a problem-defining or discovered-problem situation (Getzels & Csikszent-mihalyi, 1976), as did the nonartists, who had even more limited experience with transforming figural information.

Selected Perception

The differences detected between the semiprofessional and the professional artists in their response to the stimuli appear to be initiated by the selected perception of the professionals based on personal aesthetic preference. As in deGroot's (1965) study, "the primary task of the problem solver is TO GIVE SHAPE TO THE BOARD PROBLEM through an economically programmed series of questions, that is, to try to classify the position accurately enough to set up the first board goal hypothesis" (p. 406). As Sternberg (1982) hypothesized, classification could be based on the selective encoding of perceptual information.

With professional artists, the problem space, defined by an intrinsic aesthetic that is brought to the situation by the individual, alters the nature of the task. Therefore, the creative thought of artists does not appear to be totally free-spirited and structure-free. Although idiosyncratic, there is a discipline or responsibility based on the artist's individual aesthetic and the technical responsibilities of the materials. This quote from Participant 50 depicts that finding well:

> There are two things to creative art. One is technical responsibilities. Creativity is directly tied with some kind of technical responsibility. There is tremendous order to coming up with something very creative and beautiful.
>
> See, I go back and forth in my work—I actually flow between parts that are responsible, dogmatic, order/structure and then go try to work with that particular ... and then you go back again. I very often do little doodles and then say "can it be done?" on two levels—one, a technical level and one on an emotional or aesthetic level. ... I like the concept of interpretation. When I say green, different feelings are elicited in different people. With art, you have to explore all the options before you make a decision. With only one answer, you eliminate all the deviations, which in art, is the most interesting part.
>
> You want to see the opportunity within the structure.
>
> There is a kind of responsibility, an aesthetic.

The phenomenon appears to transcend personality, differences between male and female, and the medium (painting or sculpture). All of the professionals exhibited a personal aesthetic bias that "guides the product" (F. Gagné, personal communication, February 29, 1992); however, analysis of their working styles (or approach to studio problems) varied tremendously. For example, where one sculptor spends an average of 6 months to design one piece, another sculptor works on several pieces simultaneously, stating that work on one piece informs him on the others. The working style of a particular artist might vary as well. Several artists commented on their belief that as the situation differs, so does their approach to problem finding.

Aesthetics in Creative Thought

A characteristic cited as important to the solving of a creative problem is an aesthetic sensitivity to elegant solutions. Campbell (1960) described an editing talent in creative individuals that includes this sensitivity to the aesthetic. This ability to appreciate the beauty of a solution has been noted in scientists (Gruber, 1978; Mansfield & Busse, 1981; Root-Bernstein, 1985) and mathematicians (Campbell, 1960; Hadamard, 1949; Polya, 1945), as often as in artists (Arnheim, 1969; Gardner, 1982; Perkins, 1981; Winner, 1982). There appears to be a sensitivity to the aesthetic qualities of an elegant solution that serves as a selective criterion in the search operation. Campbell (1960) quoted Poincaré, who eloquently captured a record of this sensitivity as well as a hint of its importance in defining problems:

> The useful combinations are precisely the most beautiful, I mean those best able to charm this special sensibility that all mathematicians know, but of which the profane are so ignorant as often to be tempted to smile at it. . . .
> When a sudden illumination seizes upon the mind of the mathematician, it usually happens that it does not deceive him, but it also sometimes happens, as I have said, that it does not stand the test of verification; well, we almost always notice that this false idea, had it been true, would have gratified our natural feeling for mathematical elegance. Thus, it is this special esthetic sensibility which plays the role of the delicate sieve of which I spoke, and that sufficiently explains why the one lacking it will never be a real creator. (pp. 387–388)

The selective criterion of aesthetic sensibility is suggested by both Poincaré and Campbell.

Responsibility to the Solution

Although not described as a cognitive characteristic, the executive power proposed by Poincaré (cited in Campbell, 1960) tends to support the belief that the emotional response of the individual is a cognitive one (Scheffler, 1977). The feeling of being finished with a task without knowing the qualities of completeness required until it is achieved appears to be a characteristic unique to creative thought. It does appear to be guided by an aesthetic sensing of completion. Every participant in this study (Kay, 1989,

1991) knew when what he or she wanted was achieved. The desire to strive for the correct solution was more intrinsically motivated than expected in a presented task situation. Satisfying the task of the experiment was the original motivating force, but personal interest or concern dominated the processes involved in the game task. This quality is exemplified in the response of a nonartist: "There came a point in time when I was finished with the wall, I finished with the floor, but didn't feel finished and that's when I went into the Art phase. . ." (Kay, 1989, p. 202). An excerpt from the conversation with a professional artist also illustrates this point:

> [Participant 42] You couldn't let go just because of some silly games. It isn't mine and it isn't yours . . . it wasn't mine, it was more your game, but suddenly I found myself taking it seriously, it mattered if I ended up with something good not for you, but for me, because I just needed to know this felt satisfying.
>
> [Researcher] And yet you knew that only you and I were going to see it. . . .
>
> [Participant] Right. But the best pieces I've ever made, I made for me. Actually the first pieces I made after my operation last year were only for me. I never thought about this show and there . . . the first ones I made when I was in pain and could barely move, they are the best. At the time it didn't matter about anyone else. No one else existed. Maybe that's one of the things about artists. . . . I was a maid for a friend of mine, and I was the best maid anybody could have because the same perfection I used in those . . . like in those detail pieces was exactly the same kind of detail I did in cleaning. . . . In life everything matters.

Knowing when a solution is "good" or "right" in an ill-defined problem (J. Wakefield, personal communication, February 28, 1992) or when something is "done" are issues constantly addressed in actions that demand creative thought. Although all of the participants felt the need to arrive at a good solution, the behaviors (Kay, 1989, 1991) and oral protocols imply that different strategies were used by the groups to reach the "right" solution.

Whereas most of the nonartists stated that first they reduced the number of choices by limiting themselves to using only one color or making a flat arrangement, the semiprofessional artists stated their need to explore the possibilities (similar to the discovery-oriented behavior described in the 1976 study by Getzels and Csikszentmihalyi). However, the experts differed from the other two groups in their ability to use a personally defined aesthetic style to efficiently and decidedly arrive at this state of "doneness." In defining their problem-finding procedures by grounding their decisions in their personal set of conventions or personal aesthetic style, the professional artists seemed to have had much less difficulty arriving at a "good" solution.

Contrast to Perkins's Schemata

It might be suspected that this personal aesthetic bias is similar to what Perkins (1981) described as "schemata." Perkins defined *schema* as "a mental structure that allows a person to perceive or act effectively by anticipating the organization of what the person apprehends or does, so the person needn't function as much from scratch" (p. 173). However, the parallel Perkins drew is the way knowing the rules of English grammar guides the spoken language. The rules are the rules of a discipline or field of study. The rules are extrinsic to the creative individual—boundaries to work in or to break, but boundaries outside the individual's personal aesthetic. No doubt, the creative person must be well-informed and well-versed in the discipline in which he or she performs. But within the realm of the discipline it appears that the artist brings a personal, subjective aesthetic—intrinsic to that individual—that works within and often beyond the aesthetic of the field or discipline.

In describing a computer program with an aesthetic, Perkins (1988) claimed the difference between that program and human creative efforts is that humans "from time to time challenge their operating rules as such and revise them" (p. 371). The example given is one of Einstein's observations of the lack of a symmetrical pattern in electrodynamics. The apparent asymmetry of the discipline disturbed him, provoking the search which, according to Perkins, led to his work on relativity. Again, the concept of schemata seems to represent the ability that creative individuals have to be sensitive to the patterns that make up a particular field of study. That aesthetic sense, although perceived by him or her, lies outside of the individual. The intrinsic quality that characterizes the personal aesthetic bias exists in addition to the schemata of a field.

Constraining Effect of Aesthetic Style

The personal aesthetic preferences or style exhibited by the professional artists raises a major issue, namely, the balance between freedom and constraint in the creative process (Johnson-Laird, 1988; Mansfield & Busse, 1981). Instead of establishing rules to organize the given information, artists choose the information to attend to.

> The parameters of the rule are constructed by the objects that you have not eliminated. These are your biased preferences. One does not have to arrange them, for these are your choices and they could essentially form the sides of a road and the road is what allows you to perform. Because you can't be an artist if you don't do anything. (Kay, 1989, pp. 195–196)

The development of an aesthetic style can be seen as the creation of "perceptual templates" (F. Gagné, personal communication, February 29, 1992) that guide artists during the initial problem-defining phase of their creative endeavor. Perceptual templates accelerate the process of defining a first draft or direction to follow, providing a shorter, more efficient procedure to delineate the basic form of the final product. But this increased efficiency also can have a price. It could act as a procrustean bed to the creative process in the same way that well-worn trails reduce the degree of exploration for hikers in the forest: Keeping to the trails requires less effort than heading into the bush. This homeostatic drive could be at work in the creative process through reliance on one's aesthetic style as a guide toward outlining the final work.

This phenomenon does resemble the description given by Cattell (1968) of an "Ideational Inertia or Rigidity Factor" (p. 412). Tentatively describing this factor as an energy directed toward inflexible or consistent behavior, he explained that many examples of rigidity are "operationally simple character stability" (p. 413). He put aside the negative connotations associated with rigidity; indeed, he asserted that the creative process needs such a balance between flexibility and consistency in behavior.

The problem-finding process that is often depicted as one of total freedom is actually constrained by a well-developed aesthetic perception that guides the task-defining process toward realization of the artist's aesthetic style. Perhaps the fondness for children's art mentioned by many professional artists (Klee, 1964) reflects their admiration for the absence of self-imposed constraints in such work.

Developmental Differences

Could the progressive development of artistic expertise generate qualitative differences in process? Before directly answering that question, let me show how the results from my study (Kay, 1989) provide a possible explanation for contradictions found on the creative processes of artists at different levels of expertise. The contradiction concerns especially two studies. In the first, Patrick (1937) watched 50 professional artists and 50 nonartists sketch pictures based on a poem they were given. A detailed analysis of the process, enlisting spoken feedback, formed the core of the research procedure. The major results were as follows: (a) No difference was observed between the artists and the nonartists in the amount of time spent before engaging in the actual drawing or for the total amount of time spent on the entire task (but major differences were seen in the quality of the results); (b) in contrast to the nonartists, the artists did not change the essential structure of their work but revised only the surface structure; and (c) the problem-solving process for both groups was described as consisting of periods of unorganized and organized thought.

In their innovative work on problem finding, Getzels and Csikszent-mihalyi (1976) proposed to 31 male art students an open-ended or discovered problem situation in which 27 objects were provided for consideration for a still-life drawing. Among their results, they found that the more creative art students took more time before engaging in the actual drawing and spent more time on the entire task than did the less creative students. The art students identified as more creative also were more willing to change the entire product. Students who approached the task with a predetermined way of working toward a solution were considered less creative.

The results of the latter study (Kay, 1989, 1991) allow for a possible reconciliation of these apparently conflicting results. This reconciliation requires understanding that the operational definitions for group membership of Patrick's (1937) two groups were used to determine membership for my extreme groups, whereas Getzels and Csikszentmihalyi's (1976) two groups are assumed to be more closely related to the semiprofessional artists. By comparing the problem-defining processes among the three groups with varying degrees of expertise, a more complete picture emerges. I assumed that the semiprofessionals spent less time and practice making art because they had other full-time work commitments. Amount of practice as key to the development of expertise is supported in the literature (Ericsson & Smith, 1991).

Like Patrick (1937), I found no differences between the artists and nonartists in the amount of time spent in the actual building and in the total amount of time taken to complete the entire task (Kay, 1989, 1991). Yet qualitative differences were clearly observed (see Kay, 1989, for a discriminant analysis and discussion). Also in keeping with the behaviors of Patrick's artists, the professionals did not change the essential structure of their work but revised only the surface structure.

Among Getzels and Csikszentmihalyi's (1976) art students, behavioral differences in the approach to the discovered problem situation implied a crucial difference between those students seeking "to maximize the discovered nature of the task" (creative) and those (less creative) students who behaved as though they were in a "presented problem situation" (1976, p. 90). However, semiprofessional artists in the latter study (Kay, 1989) maximized the open nature of the task, as they took almost twice as long as the other two groups did to finish. In fact, the behavior pattern of the semiprofessional artists was most similar to the pattern of behavior describing the more creative art students in the earlier study. For example, the Problem Solution Stage (scored from the time a student began to draw to completion of the task) was marked by three types of observed behavior: "openness of the problem structure, discovery-oriented behavior, and changes in problem structure and content" (Getzels & Csikszentmihalyi, 1976, p. 98). The percentage of total drawing time that elapsed before the final structure of the drawing contained its essential elements was calculated to determine the score for openness to the problem structure. The greater the amount of time, the higher the score. For discovery-oriented behavior, a low score was given if the student drew without interruption. Changes in the medium or paper used or the rearrangement, substitution, or manipulation of objects during the drawing phase were considered reflective of discovery-oriented behavior and consequently received a high score. Changes in the problem structure and content received higher ratings. Indeed, if the student was willing to revise or eliminate elements of the drawing when evaluating the final product, an extra point was given toward the total problem-finding score. A low score was given if the student drew without interruption. Lack of changes or rearrangements also resulted in a low score.

Although the semiprofessionals in my study (Kay, 1989, 1991) took twice as long as the other two groups to complete the task, the final structure was not apparent until they were close to completion. In contrast, the professional artists took the least amount of time, had the fewest pauses, and changed or rearranged their work less than did the other two groups. The professional artists would have scored the lowest in all three behaviors observed in the more creative art students (Getzels & Csikszentmihalyi, 1976).

These findings suggest that expertise in creative problem finding develops along a continuum from the layperson to the expert (Patel & Groen, 1991), but that it elicits qualitatively different behaviors depending on the individual's position on this competence continuum. It is possible that the discovery-oriented behaviors as described by Getzels and Csikszentmihalyi (1976) could be a set of strategies or skills used by those whose performance falls within the middle range of a hypothetical normal distribution of competence (Salthouse, 1991). Various scholars have suggested that different principles or processes operate at different phases in the acquisition of expertise (Charness, 1991; Patel & Groen, 1991; Salthouse, 1991; Subotnik & Moore, 1988). It is possible that the personal aesthetic preferences guiding the behaviors of professional artists constitute a process used at the highest level of competence. Efficiency is key to identifying an expert's approach to problem-solving tasks that have a best or correct solution (deGroot, 1965; Ericsson & Smith, 1991).

It is possible that an efficiency criterion is also important in open-ended, problem-defining tasks. Where the nonartists determined the parameters of the task by eliminating choices, the professional artists selected meaningful possibilities as defined by their aesthetic preferences (Kay, 1989, 1991). The experts seem to rely on internal interests to guide their problem-finding pathways, manipulating or circumventing external constraints when necessary to their internal structure (e.g., spray painting the bright colors on PABLO with black paint). In this way, they use equal time for unequal results.

Implications

From these preliminary findings, it would seem important that researchers look more closely at the role of aesthetic development in creative producers of ideas (Tannenbaum, 1983). These findings suggest that aesthetic development might be critical to the development of creative thought. The fact that all three groups involved in the study (Kay, 1991) sensed a rightness or goodness of fit to their design solutions deserves further investigation.

Although the results of an investigation of an adult population cannot be applied to the behaviors of children, questions can be framed regarding developmental issues surrounding the education of creatively gifted children. The flexibility of working on an intrinsic agenda within a given set of external constraints was inherent in the behaviors and verbal protocols of the professional artists. Is the behavior depicting aesthetic preferences evident as a result of developed expertise as adults, or is it inherent to the creative process, thus also evident in the explorations of creatively gifted children? Are there developmental stages to the creative process? Are some strategies or skills, such as personal-aesthetic-guiding principles, more prominent in decision making at different stages, or does this characteristic generally differentiate the creative from the technically competent?

Perhaps during the expansion of a knowledge base, the proficient or competent producer of ideas experiences a waning period in the aesthetic development of a personal voice. Preferences might recess to explore more possibilities. On the other hand, a well-developed intrinsic agenda can be observed in a precocious 5-year-old (Kay, 1999). The former hypothesis is challenged when one observes a preschooler with strong preferences with regard to subject matter, direction of learning experiences within the variations of theme, and materials (e.g., which of three white pencils provides the correct shade of white). The lack of attending to this need could contribute to the negative associations with elementary art experiences reported in Bloom's (1985) study of sculptors. Attending to this need might have been the catalyst to the recorded memorable moment when one artist's elementary art teacher gave him the keys to the supply room (Brown & Korzsenik, 1993). Perhaps protecting the formation of these personal-aesthetic-guiding principles contributed to the motivation behind the home-tutoring approach adopted by the parents of Pablo Picasso (Rubin, 1980) and Wang Yani (Goldsmith, 1992).

If the development of personal aesthetic preferences or a set of guiding principles is intrinsic to an individual's creative process, recognition and respect for the development of this personal agenda would encourage expertise in creative thought. The sculptor Auguste Rodin pursued his own agenda even though he was rejected by the Academy until he was 62 (Frisch, 1939). If strong preferences for finding and forming problems affect problem solving, then a different understanding of the behaviors of a 10-year-old who refuses to include color in his investigations would provide direction for curriculum modifications (Passow, 1979) that enhance creative talent. Aesthetic development might be integral to all creative thought and not domain specific. Root-Bernstein (1989), in researching creative scientists of the 19th and 20th centuries, listed 180 eminent scientists and inventors with proclivities in the visual arts. Some scientists openly discuss the aesthetic preferences within a particular research facility (Subotnik, 1992). Aesthetic preferences might be a domain-general habit of mind requisite to developed expertise (Pelletier & Shore, 2000). Or the sensitivity to aesthetic considerations might distinguish the creative producer in a field from other experts. Further research in these directions should address some of the questions raised by Moore and Murdock (1991).

References

Arnheim, R. (1969). *Visual thinking*. Berkeley: University of California Press.

Beittel, K. R., & Burkhardt, R. C. (1963). Strategies of spontaneous, divergent, and academic art students. *Studies in Art Education, 5(1)*, 20–41.

Bloom, B. S. (Ed.). (1985). *Developing talent in young people*. New York: Ballantine Books.

Brown, M., & Korzenik, D. (1993). *Art making and education*. Chicago: University of Chicago Press.

Campbell, D. T. (1960). Blind variation and selective retention in creative thought as in other knowledge processes. *Psychological Review, 67*, 380–400.

Cattell, R. B. (1968). Genius and the processes of creative thought. In D. Rosenhan & P. London (Eds.), *Foundations of abnormal psychology* (pp. 406–443). New York: Holt, Rinehart & Winston.

Charness, N. (1991). Expertise in chess: The balance between knowledge and search. In K. A. Ericsson & J. Smith (Eds.), *Toward a general theory of expertise* (pp. 39–63). New York: Cambridge University Press.

Chi, M., Feltovich, P., & Glaser, R. (1981). Categorization and representation of physics problems by experts and novices. *Cognitive Science, 5*, 121–152.

deGroot, A. (1965). *Thought and choice in chess*. New York: Basic Books.

Ericsson, K. A., & Smith, J. (1991). Prospects and limits of the empirical study of expertise: An introduction. In K. A. Ericsson & J. Smith (Eds.), *Toward a general theory of expertise* (pp. 1–38). New York: Cambridge University Press.

Frisch, V. (1939). *Auguste Rodin*. New York: Stokes.

Gardner, H. (1982). *Art, mind, and brain*. New York: Basic Books.

Getzels, J. W., & Csikszentmihalyi, M. (1976). *The creative vision: A longitudinal study of problem finding in art*. New York: Wiley.

Ghiselin, B. (1952). *The creative process*. Berkeley: University of California Press.

Goldsmith, L. T. (1992). Wang Yani: Stylistic development of a gifted child artist. *Creativity Research Journal, 5*, 181–193.

Gruber, H. E. (1978). Emotion and cognition: "Aesthetics and science." In S. S. Madeja (Ed.), *The arts, cognition, and basic skills* (pp. 134–145). St. Louis, MO: CEMREL.

Guilford, J. P. (1967). *Nature of human intelligence*. New York: McGraw-Hill.

Hadamard, J. (1949). *The psychology of invention in the mathematical field*. Princeton, NJ: Princeton University Press.

Johnson-Laird, P. N. (1988). Freedom and constraint in creativity. In R. J. Sternberg (Ed.), *The nature of creativity* (pp. 202–219). Cambridge, England: Cambridge University Press.

Kagan, N., Krathwohl, D. R., & Miller, R. (1963). Stimulated recall in therapy using videotape: A case-study. *Journal of Counseling Psychology, 10*, 237–243.

Kanevsky, L. S. (1990). Pursuing qualitative differences in the flexible use of problem-solving strategy by young children. *Journal for the Education of the Gifted, 13*, 115–140.

Kay, S. (1989). Differences in figural problem-solving and problem-finding behavior among professional, semiprofessional, and non-artists (Doctoral dissertation, Columbia University, 1989). *Dissertation Abstracts International, 50*, 9002552.

Kay, S. (1991). The figural problem solving and problem finding of professional and semiprofessional artists and nonartists. *Creativity Research Journal, 4*, 233–252.

Kay, S. (1994). A method for investigating the creative thought process. In M. A. Runco (Ed.), *Problem finding, problem solving, and creativity* (pp. 116–129). Norwood, NJ: Ablex.

Kay, S. (1999). Assessing qualities of artistic talent. In N. Colangelo & S. Assouline (Eds.), *Talent development III: Proceedings from the 1995 Henry B. and Jocelyn Wallace National Research Symposium on Talent Development* (pp. 379–382). Scotsdale, AZ: Gifted Psychology Press.

Klee, F. (1964). *The diaries of Paul Klee, 1898–1918*. Berkeley: University of California Press.

Koestler, A. (1964). *The act of creation*. New York: Macmillan.

Mansfield, R. S., & Busse, T. V. (1981). *The psychology of creativity and discovery*. Chicago: Nelson-Hall.

Moore, M. T., & Murdock, M. C. (1991). On problems in problem-finding research. *Creativity Research Journal, 4*, 290–292.

Passow, A. H. (1979). A look around and a look ahead. In A. H. Passow (Ed.), *The Gifted and the talented: Their education and development* (78th Yearbook of the National Society for the Study of Education, Part I, pp. 439–456). Chicago: University of Chicago Press.

Patel, V. L., & Groen, G. J. (1991). The general and specific nature of medical expertise: A critical look. In K. A. Ericsson & J. Smith (Eds.), *Toward a general theory of expertise* (pp. 1–38). New York: Cambridge University Press.

Patrick, C. (1937). Creative thought in artists. *Journal of Psychology, 4*, 35–73.

Pelletier, S., & Shore, B. M. (2000). The gifted learner, the novice, and the expert: Sharpening emerging views of giftedness. In A. J. Tannenbaum, L. Cohen, & D. C. Ambrose (Eds.), *Toward a theory of creative intelligence.* Cresskill, NJ: Hampton Press.

Perkins, D. N. (1981). *The mind's best work.* Cambridge, MA: Harvard University Press.

Perkins, D. N. (1988). The possibility of invention. In R. J. Sternberg (Ed.), *The nature of creativity* (pp. 362–385). Cambridge, England: Cambridge University Press.

Polya, G. (1945). *How to solve it.* Princeton, NJ: Princeton University Press.

Root-Bernstein, R. S. (1985). Visual thinking: The art of imagining reality. *Transactions of the American Philosophical Society, 75*, 50–67.

Root-Bernstein, R. S. (1989). *Discovering.* Cambridge, MA: Harvard University Press.

Rubin, W. (Ed.). (1980). *Pablo Picasso: A retrospective.* New York: Museum of Modern Art.

Salthouse, T. A. (1991). Expertise as the circumvention of human processing limitations. In K. A. Ericsson & J. Smith (Eds.), *Toward a general theory of expertise* (pp. 1–38). New York: Cambridge University Press.

Scheffler, I. (1977). In praise of the cognitive emotions. *Teachers College Record, 79*, 171–186.

Schoenfeld, A. H., & Herrmann, D. J. (1982). Problem perception and knowledge structure in expert and novice mathematical problem solvers. *Journal of Experimental Psychology: Learning, Memory, and Cognition, 8*, 484–492.

Sternberg, R. J. (1982). *Handbook of human intelligence.* Cambridge, England: Cambridge University Press.

Sternberg, R. J. (1988). *The nature of creativity.* Cambridge, England: Cambridge University Press.

Subotnik, R. F. (1992). Talent developed—Interview with Dr. Frank Wilczek. *Journal for the Education of the Gifted, 15*(4), 370–381.

Subotnik, R. F., & Moore, M.T. (1988). Literature on problem finding. *Questioning Exchange, 2*, 87–94.

Tannenbaum, A. J. (1983). *Gifted children.* New York: Macmillan.

Welker, W. I. (1961). An analysis of exploratory and play behavior in animals. In D. W. Fiske & S. R. Maddi (Eds.), *Functions of varied experiences* (pp. 175–226). Homewood, IL: Dorsey.

Winner, E. (1982). *Invented worlds: The psychology of the arts.* Cambridge, MA: Harvard University Press.

11

Finding the Problem Finders: Problem Finding and the Identification and Development of Talent

Alane J. Starko

The field of education of gifted and talented individuals has, at its heart, several basic questions. What does it mean to be gifted? In what ways are gifted individuals or gifted behaviors different from other individuals or behaviors? Can we affect giftedness? How do the things we do at home or at school affect the development of children's gifts?

There are almost as many definitions of giftedness as there are theorists in the field (see, for example, Sternberg & Davidson, 1986). Many of these definitions entail the initiation and development of creative ideas (Renzulli, 1978; Siegler & Kotovsky, 1986). From this perspective, the gifted individual is a creator, rather than a consumer, of knowledge, information, or art. He or she goes beyond previous efforts to create the new, the improved, the unexpected. In each case, the individual solves a problem or expresses an idea in new ways. The novelty and appropriateness of the solution constitute a creative product or gifted behavior.

Rarely, in considering such definitions, have theorists asked "How do these individuals decide *which* problems to solve or ideas to express?" This chapter examines the issues and literature surrounding that question. The process of identifying and focusing a problem has been called *problem finding*. Described by Dillon (1982) as "those activities, processes and events which precede the solving of a clearly posed problem" (p. 102), problem finding has been investigated in diverse disciplines. This chapter reviews current literature on problem finding and how it might relate to the identification and development of gifts and talents. It examines the nature of problem finding, studies of problem finding in a variety of disciplines, the assessment of problem finding, and the implications of these studies for the identification and development of talent.

Nature of Problem Finding

The most quoted passage in problem-finding literature is probably from Einstein and Infeld (cited in Dillon, 1982):

> The formulation of a problem is often more important than its solution, which may be merely a matter of mathematical or experimental skill. To raise new questions, new possibilities, to regard old problems from a new angle, requires imagination and marks real advance in science. (p. 98)

A similar argument could be made in nearly any discipline. Progress in any domain is bounded by individuals' ability to identify the problems worthy of solution, the ideas that are important to express.

It is possible to conceptualize problem finding in varied ways, emphasizing different aspects of the process. Problem finding entails sensitivity to needs or an awareness of possibilities in a given situation. It may demand focusing and clarifying a problem or analyzing data to determine a broad issue underlying several seemingly disparate situations. It may also include an evaluative component, selecting which problems are worthy of pursuit. Jay and Perkins (1997) suggested that a comprehensive definition of problem finding must include "(a) conceiving and envisaging problem or question-forming possibilities in a situation, (b) defining and formulating the actual problem statement, (c) periodically assessing the quality of the problem formulation and its solution options, and (d) problem reformulation from time to time" (p. 258).

Any discussion of problem finding must examine the nature of problems, determining what it is that must be "found." Getzels (1964, 1982, 1987) distinguished between presented and discovered problem situations. These differed according to the degree to which the problem, method, and solution are already known. Most school problems are presented problems. Someone, usually a teacher, presents students with a predetermined problem to be solved. In the large majority of cases, the method and solution are already known, at least to the teacher.

Dillon (1982) also distinguished among levels of problems: existent, emergent, or potential. An existent problem is evident. A problematic situation exists, and the appropriate activity is to recognize it and solve it. This type of situation usually is referred to in the commonplace usage of the word "problem." Something is troublesome or standing in the way of a desired state. To resolve the situation, the obstacle must be recognized and a solution found.

An emergent problem is implicit rather than evident. It must be discovered before it can be solved. In this case, the appropriate activity is to probe the data for an unclear, hidden, or incipient problem and elements of a possible solution. Emergent problems are important to persons dealing with complex situations and data sets. A good manager—or car repair person—is able to discover "what the problem is" before setting out to solve it. The "Problem-Finding" stage of the Creative Problem Solving process (Treffinger, 1995) refers to emergent problems. Problem solvers are instructed to examine all the data in a given "mess" to identify problems to address.

A potential problem does not yet exist as a problem. Its elements exist and may strike the discoverer as an unformed problem, interesting situation, or idea worth elaborating. By combining the elements in some way, the observer creates or invents a problem where no problem previously existed. Perhaps potential problems are most clearly seen in the invention process. No one assigned Chester Greenwood to invent earmuffs or Lucy Sawyer to invent the flour sifter. These inventors' sensitivity to the needs around them allowed them to identify a problem whose solution would benefit many. In a parallel manner, an author "finds" a story and a painter "finds" an image that can bring joy or insight to those around them. Problem finding is necessary before problem solving for emergent or potential problems. An existent problem, by definition, needs little or no problem finding. The problem is obvious and demands a solution. For example, there is little need to engage in problem finding when faced with a broken appliance or a spreading fire. Although some redefinition is possible, the general problem is evident; it is the solution that must be found.

This distinction raises one of the core dilemmas in considering problem finding as a potential variable in young people. If we are to identify or study problem finding in students, they must be placed in circumstances in which it is possible to find problems. If the only problems students address in school are the existent problems already defined and solved by teachers, problem-finding behaviors are not likely to emerge there. It is only when students interact with situations that have the potential for emergent or potential problems that problem finding can become a meaningful variable in a school setting.

Problem-Finding Research

Created and Emergent Problems

Studies of problem finding may be divided into two general groups using categories devised by Dillon (1982): (a) those dealing with the creation of new (potential) problems and (b) those concerning the discovery of emergent problems. Key to the development of the first body of research is Getzels and Csikszentmihalyi's (1976) study of problem finding in art. The researchers observed strategies used by college art students creating a problem with various objects for a still-life drawing task. Variables examined included the number of objects examined, the amount of exploration of each object, and the uniqueness of objects used. These variables were used to rank students according to the breadth, depth, and uniqueness of their problem finding. The drawings produced were evaluated by artist–critics on graphic skill or craftsmanship, originality, and overall aesthetic value. The correlation between craftsmanship and problem finding was positive but not statistically significant. However, correlations between problem finding and both originality and overall aesthetic value were significant. Twenty years after the original study, the correlation between problem finding in art school and success of artists at midlife was still positive and significant (Getzels, 1982). After yet another decade, including interviews with scores of eminent creators, Csikszentmihalyi

(1996) described a tendency toward exploration as a hallmark of the creative individual across domains:

> Creative people are constantly surprised. They don't assume that they understand what is happening around them, and they don't assume that anybody else does either. They question the obvious—not out of contrariness but because they see the shortcoming of accepted explanations before the rest of us do. They sense problems before they are generally perceived and are able to define what they are. (p. 363)

Getzels and Csikszentmihalyi's (1976) conclusions emphasize the importance of exploratory behavior in problem finding. The art students who were most successful in developing creative products took more time developing their problem, explored more potential objects and combinations of objects, and considered more unique objects than those who were less successful. The variables of exploratory time and consideration of multiple possibilities continue to underlie research on created problems.

For example, Dudek and Côté (1994) described a variation on Getzels and Csikszentmihalyi's (1976) study using collage, rather than drawing, as the medium. In contrast to the original study, Dudek and Côté found that originality of the product was associated more with the amount of labor and energy expended in the solution phase of the product than with preliminary exploratory behaviors. They suggested that "the term *problem finding* should not be limited to the preparatory phase" (p. 139). Additionally, Dudek and Côté postulated that at least in art, the term *problem expression* may be more accurate than problem finding. They cited evidence of artists' ongoing efforts to find means of expression for personal ideas or vision. In such cases, exploratory efforts may not be focused on identifying the problem per se, but in creating original and appropriate means through which a problem may be expressed.

Other studies of problem finding or problem posing might be more accurately described as studies of problem discovery. In these cases, the problems were not new, as are original works of art or writing, but were, at least in part, embedded in a data set to be found by participants. In some cases the data sets were created by researchers; in other cases, they were part of the individuals' natural environment. Problem-finding tasks spanned a variety of disciplines, including teaching (Moore, 1990; Shulman, 1974), children's simulated experiences in government (Allender, 1969), interpersonal problems in high school students (Getzels & Smilansky, 1983; Schwartz, 1977), school administration (Peterson, 1986), and local government (Shapiro & McPherson, 1987; for a more detailed review of problem-finding studies, see Starko, 1999).

Although no variable is consistent across all studies, differences in problem finding or exploratory behavior were associated with differences in knowledge or experience; time examining potential problem situations; and a flexible, inquiring style of investigation. In addition, individuals' framing of problem situations was sometimes seen to be shaped by ongoing attitudes or points of view: the individual vision described by Peterson

(1986) or the group metaphors studied by Shapiro and McPherson (1987). In each case, a general frame of reference to the entire situation defined the parameters within which problems were identified, understood, and addressed.

Processes Associated With Problem Finding

Whereas the research cited thus far has emphasized the visible exploratory activities of problem finding, other studies have addressed the processes underlying this variable. Kiesler and Sproull (1982) discussed problem sensing in management as a process of noticing, interpreting, and incorporating relevant stimuli. They identified key obstacles to the processes as errors associated with social perception, information processing, and social motivation. The view of problem sensing as a composite of social cognition processes implies that the process of problem sensing is individualistic. "Problemness" is not an innate characteristic of a stimulus waiting to be discovered but arises from an interaction of stimuli with the cognitive structures and processes of the observer.

Like problem solving (Chi, Feltovich, & Glaser, 1981; Leinhardt & Greeno, 1986), the processes of problem finding may be affected by the experiences and expertise of the individual. These experiences shape the individual cognitive structures through which incoming information is processed. It would be difficult, for example, for a nonlinguist to identify or construct a problem if the most relevant cue to the problem was inconsistencies in the usage of early English. Similarly, a student who has spent weeks observing a class aquarium is much more likely to wonder whether fish would be healthier with a mechanical oxygen system or with live plants than a student whose knowledge of fish is limited to a few pages in a science text. A student with long-term interest and expertise in the Civil War would be much more likely to notice inconsistencies in letters from that time period than another without similar expertise. To the first, the letters may represent a puzzling situation, to the other, a collection of old paper and strange spellings.

Evidence to support the importance of expertise in identifying emergent problems was found by Mumford, Baughman, Costanza, Uhlman, and Connelly (1993). They investigated the categories used in the problem finding and problem solving of college marketing majors. Individuals whose category structures were more similar to those of experts were more successful in solving presented problems. Mumford, Reiter-Palmon, and Redmond (1994) presented a model illustrating the way individuals map new, ill-formed problem situations onto representations of problems found in memory. Although direct correlation of new problems with old may not result in finding original or interesting problems, flexible use or combination of problem representations may allow for effective problem finding. Individuals whose expertise includes a large repertoire of previous problem situations may have more resources for problem finding than those with less prior knowledge.

Kay (1991, 1992) suggested that problem-finding processes in art may also vary with degree of expertise. She found that semiprofessional artists were more likely to engage in the kinds of open-ended exploration typically associated with problem finding than professional artists. Professional artists' decisions were more likely to be affected by a "personal aesthetic bias" (1992, p. 8) that guided their problem finding. Whereas semiprofessional artists were seeking problems, professional artists seemed to fit the task at hand into the context of a broad, ongoing problem. Their efforts to find new means of expression within a particular aesthetic direction echo the artists cited by Dudek and Côté (1994). The organizing structure of the personal aesthetic may function in a manner parallel to the content organization of other experts, allowing them to identify powerful problems that fit into their ongoing search for meaningful patterns.

It is possible, however, for expertise to be a two-edged sword. Sternberg and O'Hara (1999) pointed out the danger of clinging too tightly to the known. Whereas identifying the questions that will advance a field requires knowing where the field is, familiarity with a body of knowledge can make it difficult to imagine ideas organized in a different way. At times, problems can be recognized only when individuals are willing to let go of a knowledge base previously thought to be secure. In the same manner, artists unwilling to periodically examine their ongoing aesthetic would be in danger of staleness.

A key question regarding the role of knowledge in problem finding is the generality of problem-finding processes. Just as the domain specificity of creative processes in general is open to debate, so the general or specific nature of problem finding remains to be investigated. Porath and Arlin (1992) used a general measure of problem finding as well as domain-specific tasks in art and science to investigate problem finding in secondary students. Correlations between general and domain-specific measures were significant but not large. The results lend support to a general problem-finding ability while still leaving room for specific problem-finding strategies that may vary by discipline.

Arlin (1975, 1990) considered the processes underlying problem finding in relation to developmental-stage theory. She postulated problem finding as part of a fifth developmental stage, postformal reasoning. Arlin (1975) presented a flow chart model of the problem-solving process that designates the creation of questions as the top of the heap in relation to Guilford's (1959) products, more complex than systems. It represented a type of problem finding that entails abstract representation of the problem before solution, a restriction that may not be justified for all types of problem finding.

Little is known about the relationship of problem finding to motivation and personality variables. Jay and Perkins (1997) suggested that any examination of problem finding must pursue answers both to the how and to the why questions: *How* do people find problems? *Why* do they do so? The very nature of problem finding requires that an individual go beyond the demands of a given situation and seek new challenges. It is a proactive rather than reactive process, demanding not only ability but also motivation. Dudek and Côté (1994) described the "intense involvement" evidenced in creative works, "the great eagerness and desire to 'make it original' . . . to stick to it until it reads that way to them" (p. 140).

Although several authors have identified intrinsic motivation, values, or related variables as essential components of creativity in general (see, for example, Amabile, 1989; Csikszentmihalyi, 1994; Collins & Amabile, 1999; Perkins, 1988; Sternberg & Lubart, 1999), little has been written on the role of motivation in problem finding. Jay and Perkins (1997) cited unpublished research by Jay examining problem finding of secondary students using physical science materials. Little spontaneous problem finding was observed, but changes were noted after problem-finding scaffolding was introduced. It is difficult to assess the results of the brief summary, but the study may provide evidence that ability alone is not sufficient to trigger problem finding; there must be inclination as well. The ability to find problems is of little value if the capable individual does not use that ability. It is also possible that the study provides support for the notion that students may need explicit encouragement and direction before using problem-finding strategies in schools. Only if students feel that such activities are acceptable, and in fact valued, are the activities likely to occur spontaneously. Additional study will be necessary to examine the relative contributions of cognitive and affective factors in problem finding.

Problem Finding in Young People

Few efforts to date have examined developmental changes in problem finding or how problem finding in children may differ from that in adults. A key question in such investigations must be the relationship of problem finding to the development of other cognitive processes. Arlin (1975, 1990) postulated that problem finding can develop only after formal operational reasoning. In a similar vein, Smilansky (1984) asserted that one can become a problem finder only after one is capable of solving similar problems. If problem finding emerges only as postoperational thought, efforts to identify it as a variable in young children may be futile. However, such an assertion is based on a tightly defined view of problem-finding processes. It is still unclear whether problem finding is a single construct or whether it may be multidimensional or domain specific. It is possible that various types of problem finding may develop along different timelines or that individuals may have profiles of problem finding, perhaps paralleling Gardner's (1983) multiple intelligences.

Problem finding has been studied in students of various ages. Some studies have examined students' created problems, using methods paralleling those of Getzels and Csikszentmihalyi (1976). Starko (1989) examined the problem-finding strategies of four groups: (a) professional writers, (b) high school students identified as possessing specific interest and ability in creative writing, (c) students in above-average-ability language arts classes, and (d) students in average-ability language arts classes. In the problem-finding task, participants were presented with a collection of 18 objects and asked to generate ideas for writing that could relate to one or more objects. More able writers were more likely than other groups to deliberately manipulate ideas to generate ideas for writing, and they were more fluent in the number of ideas generated. Less able writers were more likely to wait for ideas to "pop out" without any strategies to enhance that possibility. There were no significant ties between originality of ideas and any of the described strategies.

Moore (1985) followed procedures even more closely paralleling those of Getzels and Csikszentmihalyi (1976). Middle school students identified as creative and less creative were presented with a collection of objects on one table and asked to arrange some of them on a second table and then produce a piece of writing based on the objects. Patterns of scores for problem finding and problem solution in the creative and less creative groups differed in the directions predicted based on the art research, although not always significantly. The relationship between problem-finding strategies and originality of solution was significant and positive.

A series of studies in progress (Starko, 1993) is examining problem-finding behaviors in elementary school students in an art task. In the first study, students in kindergarten and grades 2 and 4 were presented with an assortment of materials and asked to make something. Data analysis provided little evidence of the types of exploratory behaviors found in other studies. Most students plunged immediately into the task (occasionally before the researcher had completed the directions). However, discussions after the task gave clues to emergent problem-finding processes. Some children described beginning the task and discovering midway what the creation was going to be: "I started sticking things together and then it turned into a dog, so I made a dog."

Two subsequent investigations (Starko, 1995b) examined the possibility of problem finding during the construction process. Students in grades 2, 4, and 6 were presented with the same building task and asked to tell the researcher when they first had an idea of what they were going to make, any time they changed their idea, and when they completed the building task. These studies provided evidence that young children continued to define the building problem while pursuing the task at hand. In the first, total number of ideas, time before final idea, total time used, and ratio of time to final idea to total time all increased with one measure of originality, although none significantly.

In the second, exploratory time before selecting a final idea, total time used, and number of items used all increased as originality increased. However, the number of items handled but not used was greatest in the middle group, and the number of ideas generated was the reverse of the expected order, with students whose products were rated lowest in originality generating the greatest number of ideas. These puzzling results brought to light a seeming conflict with Getzels and Csikszentmihalyi's (1976) original study. Some students seem to have explored several ideas but did not select the one most likely to be judged as original. Such choices may reflect the importance of evaluative thinking in problem finding. To be a creative problem finder one must not only generate potential problems, but also must select problems that lend themselves to effective, original solutions (Runco, 1991; Runco & Chand, 1994).

Other studies examined students' problem finding in other types of problems. Hoover and Feldhusen (1990) studied problem finding in natural science by examining the questions of gifted 9th-grade students presented with ill-defined situations. They determined that hypothesis generation was not related to intelligence or attitude toward science. Hoover (1992, 1994) cited similar results with 5th-grade students. In that study, it was also determined that problem finding in science did not correlate with any part of the Torrance Tests of Creative Thinking (Torrance, 1990).

Subotnik (1988) examined the relationship between factors from the Structure of the Intellect model (Guilford, 1959) and problem finding in science. Westinghouse Talent Search winners who, as gifted adolescents, had independently selected their projects (problems) were more likely to name processes of cognition, convergent production, and evaluation as crucial to the selection of their research questions. This lends support to the importance of convergent processes in problem finding in science.

In a longitudinal study of Westinghouse winners 7 years after winning the search, Subotnik and Steiner (1994) found that participants were divided into (a) those currently engaged in research involving recognized, discovered, or invented problems; (b) those involved in researching presented problems; and (c) those not involved in research. When these categories were compared with the processes by which the individuals selected their original talent search problems, it was determined that 50% of those currently involved in research had independently generated their own talent search questions, but that only 20% of those no longer involved with research had done so. In addition, those currently involved in finding and solving problems were more likely to have a mentor taking an active interest in their work than were those no longer involved in research. This evidence suggests that not only could problem-finding behaviors be identified in adolescents but that such behaviors predict problem finding into young adulthood.

Delcourt (1993) also noted problem-finding activity in adolescents identified as creative producers in secondary school. Students were described as "continuously explor[ing] their many interests as they actively sought project ideas through a variety of techniques including reading, sharing information with others, and taking courses both in and out of school" (p. 28). In this study, the opportunities and encouragement for students to identify and pursue individual problems occurred during specialized services for gifted students. Information on the problem-finding processes of students not participating in such services is not available.

One of the most interesting questions regarding the development of problem finding in young people is whether it can be influenced through intervention. Without a comparison group, it is impossible to tell whether Delcourt's students' problem-finding processes were affected by their participation in a program designed to facilitate individual investigations. Burns (1990) examined a similar program for elementary students. Although not writing specifically about problem finding, she investigated the effects of training activities on students' initiation of creative investigations. Students who engaged in a series of lessons on identifying interests and problem focusing initiated significantly more investigations than students not receiving such training. Her results were echoed by Kay (1994), who described the use of a discovery unit in assisting elementary students to conduct original investigations.

Although research continues to be limited, several hypotheses are possible regarding problem finding in young people as a unique, complex variable. Some studies provide support for exploratory factors, such as time spent identifying the problem or consideration of multiple options, as emerging before or during adolescence (Moore, 1985; Starko, 1993, 1995b). There is also evidence that convergent, evaluative thinking is necessary for the selection of an effective problem (Starko, 1995b; Subotnik, 1988). As noted by Starko (1995b), without such processes, individuals may explore options and generate multiple possibilities but select a problem that is unimportant or unoriginal. Some evidence suggests that it may be possible to distinguish problem finding in young people from more conventionally assessed variables, such as intelligence, attitude, or creative thinking (Hoover, 1992, 1994; Hoover & Feldhusen, 1990). There is also evidence to support the idea that problem finding, at least in some areas, may be developed through instruction and practice (Burns, 1990; Kay, 1994). Such a hypothesis could suggest that schools might be involved not just in the identification of problem finding as a trait but in the development of problem finding as a talent. In either case, the study of problem finding by educators and instructors hinges on our ability to identify and assess it reliably.

Assessing Problem Finding

Although problem finding has been identified, and even quantified, in a variety of fields, only limited efforts have been made to standardize measures of problem finding or use them to seek exploratory behavior. In one case an assessment of problem finding was used as part of the identification process for a specialized gifted program (Wagner & Zimmermann, 1986). The authors described devising a new test for mathematical giftedness that stresses six complex mathematical activities including "finding (constructing) related problems" (p. 246).

Wakefield (1985, 1986, 1987, 1992) conducted a series of investigations adapting standardized tests to assess problem finding. For example, Wakefield (1985, 1992) used blank cards inserted into the Pattern Meanings and Line Meanings tests of the Wallach and Kogan (1965) battery. Fifth-grade students were asked to create their own test items on the blank cards and to respond divergently to the original items as well as to the presented (standard) ones. Results were correlated with the Group Inventory for Finding Creative Talent (GIFT; Davis & Rimm, 1980), California Achievement Tests (CAT), and three subtests of the WISC–R (Wechsler, 1974): Vocabulary, Picture Arrangement, and Block Design. A significant positive relationship was found between responses to original items and both the GIFT and the CAT, but not the WISC–R subtests. Three years later, response to the original items was the only reported measure that significantly correlated with expert ratings of student drawings (Wakefield, 1992).

Like Wakefield, Smilansky (1984) adapted existing standardized tests to include the creation of original problems. High school students were tested with Series D and E of the Raven Progressive Matrices (Raven, Court, & Raven, 1985). After completion, participants were asked to create a new problem for the test, one as difficult as possible to solve. The ability to solve matrix problems was determined to be different from the ability to invent the same type of item. There were no participants who scored high on problem invention but low on problem solving, suggesting that problem finding is more difficult than problem solving.

Smilansky and Halberstadt (1986) extended the earlier research by examining participants in extreme groups (high solving–high invention, low solving–low invention, high solving–low invention). Several cognitive and interpersonal measures were administered to each individual. Participants in the three groups did not differ in any school achievement measures, possibly because of the highly selective nature of the high schools studied. Differences were found suggesting that the cognitive style associated with greater field independence contributes to problem invention. There also were significant differences among groups in the number of negative adjectives checked when describing themselves. Those who demonstrated superior problem inventiveness described themselves in a much more positive fashion than others, choosing less than half the negative adjectives of either of the other groups. Finally, there were no significant differences among groups on the four divergent thinking scores of the circles task (Torrance, 1990), lending support to problem invention as a variable distinguishable from divergent thinking.

Okuda, Runco, and Berger (1991) investigated the assessment of problem finding using real-world problems in a divergent thinking task. Elementary students were asked to list problems at home or school and respond divergently to the problems. Response to the discovered problems was a better predictor of creative activities than traditional divergent-thinking measures. Chand and Runco (cited in Runco, 1993) replicated the above study, then asked students to solve one of the problems. Explicit instructions designed to enhance originality improved originality in presented problems and in the solution task, but not in problem generation.

Despite these efforts, the nature of problem finding, like creativity itself, challenges the limits of standardized instruments. It is not clear whether problem finding in one venue transfers to another. If an individual is extraordinarily adept at finding problems in art or in mazes, it is uncertain whether the same individual is capable of finding high-quality problems in mathematics. It is possible that general problem-finding processes may be identified and that differences in problem finding from one domain to another may be explained by differences in expertise. On the other hand, perhaps problem finding in science necessitates very different processes than problem finding in literature. We simply do not know. At this point, even the best assessments can only approach the nature of real-world problem finding: choosing to explore the world, sensing a need or possibility, and selecting a problem worthy of solution.

Problem Finding and the Identification of Talent

If, as it appears, problem finding may be a construct that exists in young people, it may be a useful variable in the identification of talent. For individuals working within a definition of giftedness that entails the pursuit of creative goals, it may be helpful to identify young people with particular aptitude for selecting powerful, original problems. However, here, as in other definitions of giftedness and talent, the trait–behavior paradigm split comes into play. Although some individuals may be interested in identifying those students who are particularly adept at identifying and solving problems, others may be more interested in attempting to develop problem-finding abilities in young people. Whether problem finding is to be addressed as a trait to be sought or a talent or skill to be developed remains for educators and researchers to determine.

Finding Problems in School

Regardless of whether the goal is to identify existent problem-finding talent in a school context or to facilitate its development there, the first step is the same. If problem finding is to be discovered or nurtured in schools, schools must become places that are problem friendly, places in which problems can be found. Such an atmosphere would necessitate considerable change in some school situations. In traditional schools, problems are developed by teachers or texts and solved by students. In a problem-friendly school, students must, at least some of the time, be the ones who are raising questions and determining the direction of their creative endeavors. There are at least two basic approaches that may encourage problem finding in schools: activities to develop student questioning and teaching investigative strategies of the disciplines.

Encouraging student questions. Virtually all problem finding entails asking questions. The ties between question asking and problem finding are clear in science. Individuals developing creative projects in the sciences wonder about things: why things happen, how things happen, what would happen if the individuals intervened to make things happen differently. In parallel ways, the exploratory activities associated with problem finding in other domains seem inextricably tied to the activity of wondering. Historians wonder what people long ago did or thought and what historical documents mean. Writers wonder about people and situations; artists wonder about combinations of shape, about emotion, and about form. If students are to be encouraged as problem finders, they must be encouraged to wonder and to seek answers to their questions.

The most basic strategy to encourage student questioning is to tell students that we hope they will ask questions, then provide multiple opportunities for them to do so. This will mean going beyond the routine, "Are there any questions?" to specific probing about ideas, events, or situations. Students may be asked what they wonder, what they observe that might be puzzling, or what they have not yet learned about a topic. Specific lessons might be planned whose purpose is simply to see how many interesting questions can be generated about a particular topic. Students could consider what kinds of questions different professionals might ask about an object or event and learn how to record intriguing questions for later investigation. The implicit message of all such activities should be unmistakable: It is good to ask questions, and we welcome questions in this classroom.

Problem finding in the disciplines. Although it is not yet clear whether problem finding is a general or domain-specific skill, it is clear that individuals find and solve problems in a variety of domains. Writers decide what to write, historians decide what to study, mathematicians identify puzzling patterns and decide to explore them. Each domain has its own kinds of problems and strategies that are used to identify and investigate them. If students are to ask questions and find problems in particular domains, they must know the methodology of the domains—that is, they must know not just the *what* of a subject but the *how* as well.

Teaching students about problem finding and in a particular area entails teaching them how a domain works. Students who study historical research techniques as well as the content of history are not only better prepared to understand the content they learn but also to begin to ask the kinds of questions historians ask. Students who have learned about how authors search for interesting characters or situations in the world around them seem more likely to use those strategies to create a problem in their own writing. Although there is no clear evidence that teaching and practicing problem-finding strategies in the disciplines will enhance students' problem finding, it seems a common-sense step in the right direction (for a more complete discussion of curriculum structured around problem-finding activities, see Starko, 1995a).

Schools, Research, and Unanswered Questions

Any discussion of problem finding at this point in the research effort raises more questions than it answers. It is not yet clear how problem finding operates, whether it generalizes across disciplines, or how it may emerge developmentally. Relationships between problem finding and other variables, such as intelligence, creativity, learning style, personality factors, or motivation, have yet to be thoroughly explored. Assessment of problem finding is still in its infancy.

When considering problem finding in schools, questions emerge that extend beyond the research dilemmas: For what purpose might schools identify talented problem finders? Is the identification of problem-finding abilities within the mission of education of individuals who are gifted and talented? The answers to such questions depend, of course, on the nature of the mission itself. If the purpose of education of individuals who are gifted and talented is to provide students who show particular strength in academic areas with adapted curriculum experiences, it is possible that problem finding may not be an important part of that agenda. As the field comes to understand problem finding, we may find that the ability to find problems and raise questions may be separate from the abilities to solve problems and find answers. In schools focused on correct answers and accurate content, the question raisers may not display academic advantage. As such, they may demonstrate little need for academic adaptation or special services.

Alternatively, if the role of education of individuals who are gifted and talented is to develop a range of human abilities, different dilemmas are posed. No educational system can possibly undertake the task of developing all the exceptional talents human beings may display. At least in the United States, it is unlikely that schools will attempt to develop the talents of the most outstanding navigators, gardeners, or comedians. Those who suggest a talent development mission for the field of education of those who are gifted and talented must ultimately identify the types of talents we are willing to develop. As schools or as a society, if we are interested in the individuals who raise important questions and those who answer them, the identification and development of problem finding may be an important goal.

References

Allender, J. S. (1969). A study of inquiry activity in elementary school children. *American Education Research Journal, 6,* 543–558.

Amabile, T. M. (1989). *Growing up creative*. New York: Crown.

Arlin, P. K. (1975). A cognitive process model of problem finding. *Educational Horizons, 54*(1), 99–106.

Arlin, P. K. (1990). Wisdom: The art of problem finding. In R. J. Sternberg (Ed.), *Wisdom: Its nature, origins, and development* (pp. 230–243). New York: Cambridge University Press.

Burns, D. E. (1990). The effects of group training activities on students' initiation of creative investigations. *Gifted Child Quarterly, 34,* 31–36.

Chi, M., Feltovich, P., & Glaser, R. (1981). Categorization and representation of physics problems by experts and novices. *Cognitive Science, 5,* 151–152.

Collins, M. A., & Amabile, T. M. (1999). Motivation and creativity. In R. J. Sternberg (Ed.), *Handbook of creativity* (pp. 297–312). New York: Cambridge University Press.

Csikzsentmihalyi, M. (1994). The domain of creativity. In D. H. Feldman, M. Csikszentmihalyi, & H. Gardner (Eds.), *Changing the world: A framework for the study of creativity* (pp. 135–158). Westport, CT: Praeger.

Csikzsentmihalyi, M. (1996). *Creativity: Flow and the psychology of discovery and invention.* New York: HarperCollins.

Davis, G. A., & Rimm, S. (1980). *Group inventory for finding creative talent*. Watertown, WI: Educational Assessment Service.

Delcourt, M. A. B. (1993). Creative productivity among secondary school students: Combining energy, interest and imagination. *Gifted Child Quarterly, 37,* 23–31.

Dillon, J. T. (1982). Problem finding and solving. *Journal of Creative Behavior, 16*, 97–111.

Dudek, S. Z., & Côté, R. (1994). Problem finding revisited. In M. A. Runco (Ed.), *Problem finding, problem solving and creativity* (pp. 130–150). Norwood, NJ: Ablex.

Gardner, H. (1983). *Frames of mind.* New York: Basic Books.

Getzels, J. W. (1964). Creative thinking, problem solving, and instruction. In E. Hilgard (Ed.), *Theories of learning and instruction* (63rd NSSE Yearbook, Part 1, pp. 240–267). Chicago: University of Chicago Press.

Getzels, J. W. (1982). The problem of the problem. In R. Hogarth (Ed.), *New directions for methodology of social and behavioral science: Question framing and response consistency* (pp. 37–49). San Francisco: Jossey-Bass.

Getzels, J. W. (1987). Problem finding and creative achievement. *Gifted Students Institute Quarterly, 12*(4), B1–B4.

Getzels, J. W., & Csikszentmihalyi, M. (1976). *The creative vision: A longitudinal study of problem finding in art.* New York: Wiley.

Getzels, J. W., & Smilansky, J. (1983). Individual differences in pupil perceptions of school problems. *British Journal of Educational Psychology, 53*, 307–316.

Guilford, J. P. (1959). Three faces of intellect. *American Psychologist, 14*, 469–479.

Hoover, S. M. (1992, February). *Constructs and processes of problem finding ability among gifted individuals.* Paper presented at the Second Annual Esther Katz Rosen Symposium on the Psychological Development of Gifted Children, Lawrence, KS.

Hoover, S. M. (1994). Scientific problem-finding in gifted fifth grade students. *Roeper Review, 16*, 156–159.

Hoover, S. M., & Feldhusen, J. F. (1990). The scientific hypothesis formulation ability of gifted ninth-grade students. *Journal of Educational Psychology, 82*(4), 838–848.

Jay, E. S., & Perkins, D. N. (1997). Creativity's compass: A review of problem finding. In M. A. Runco (Ed.), *Creativity research handbook* (Vol. I, pp. 257–293). Cresskill, NJ: Hampton.

Kay, S. I. (1991). The figural problem solving and problem finding of professional and semiprofessional artists and nonartists. *Creativity Research Journal, 4*, 233–252.

Kay, S. I. (1992, February). *On the nature of expertise.* Paper presented at the Second Annual Esther Katz Rosen Symposium on the Psychological Development of Gifted Children, Lawrence, KS.

Kay, S. I. (1994). From theory to practice: Promoting problem finding behavior in children. *Roeper Review, 16*, 195–197.

Kiesler, S., & Sproull, L. (1982). Managerial response to changing environments: Perspectives on problem sensing from social cognition. *Administrative Science Quarterly, 27*, 548–570.

Leinhardt, G., & Greeno, J. G. (1986). The cognitive skill of teaching. *Journal of Educational Psychology, 78*, 75–95.

Moore, M. (1985). The relationship between the originality of essays and variables in the problem-discovery process: A study of creative and noncreative middle school students. *Research in the Teaching of English, 19*, 84–95.

Moore, M. (1990). Problem finding and teacher experience. *Journal of Creative Behavior, 24*, 39–58.

Mumford, M. D., Baughman, W. E., Costanza, D. P., Uhlman, C. E., & Connelly, M. S. (1993). Developing creative capacities: Implications of cognitive processing models. *Roeper Review, 16*, 16–21.

Mumford, M. D., Reiter-Palmon, R., & Redmond, M. R. (1994). Problem construction and cognition: Applying problem representations in ill-defined domains. In M. A. Runco (Ed.), *Problem finding, problem solving and creativity* (pp. 3–39). Norwood, NJ: Ablex.

Okuda, S. M., Runco, M. A., & Berger, D. E. (1991). Creativity and the finding and solving of real-world problems. *Journal of Psychoeducational Assessment, 9*, 45–53.

Perkins, D. N. (1988). The possibility of intervention. In R. J. Sternberg (Ed.), *The name of creativity* (pp. 362–385). New York: Cambridge University Press.

Peterson, K. D. (1986). Vision and problem finding in principals' work: Values and cognition in administration. *Peabody Journal of Education, 63*, 87–106.

Porath, M., & Arlin, P. (1992, February). *Developmental approaches to artistic giftedness*. Paper presented at the Second Annual Esther Katz Rosen Symposium on the Psychological Development of Gifted Children, Lawrence, KS.

Raven, J. C., Court, J. H., & Raven, J. (1985). *Manual for Raven's Progressive Matrices d cabuay cales*. London: H. K. Lewis.

Renzulli, J. S. (1978). What makes giftedness? Reexamining a definition. *Phi Delta Kappan, 60*, 180–184, 261.

Runco, M. A. (1991). The evaluative, valuative, and divergent thinking of children. *Journal of Creative Behavior, 25*, 311–319.

Runco, M. A. (1993). Divergent thinking, creativity and giftedness. *Gifted Child Quarterly, 37*, 16–22.

Runco, M. A., & Chand, I. (1994). Problem finding, evaluative thinking and creativity. In M. A. Runco (Ed.), *Problem finding, problem solving and creativity* (pp. 40–76). Norwood, NJ: Ablex.

Schwartz, D. M. (1977). *A study of interpersonal problem-posing*. Unpublished doctoral dissertation, University of Chicago, Chicago, IL.

Shapiro, J. Z., & McPherson, R. B. (1987). State board desegregation policy: An application of the problem finding model to policy analysis. *Educational Administration Quarterly, 23*(2), 60–77.

Shulman, L. S. (1974). Seeking styles and individual differences in patterns of inquiry. *School Review, 73*, 258–266.

Siegler, R. S., & Kotovsky, K. (1986). Two levels of giftedness: Shall ever the twain meet? In R. J. Sternberg & J. E. Davidson (Eds.), *Conceptions of giftedness* (pp. 417–435). Cambridge, England: Cambridge University Press.

Smilansky, J. (1984). Problem solving and the quality of invention: An empirical investigation. *Journal of Educational Psychology, 76*, 377–386.

Smilansky, J., & Halberstadt, N. (1986). Inventors versus problem solvers: An empirical investigation. *Journal of Creative Behavior, 20*(3), 183–201.

Starko, A. J. (1989). Problem finding in creative writing: An exploratory study. *Journal for the Education of the Gifted, 12*, 172–186.

Starko, A. J. (1993, November). *Problem finding in elementary students: Two explorations*. Paper presented at the annual meeting of the National Association for Gifted Children, Atlanta, GA.

Starko, A. J. (1995a). *Creativity in the classroom: Schools of curious delight*. New York: Longman.

Starko, A. J. (1995b, May). *Problem finding in elementary students: Continuing explorations*. Paper presented at the Henry B. and Jocelyn Wallace National Research Symposium on Talent Development, Iowa City, IA.

Starko, A. J. (1999). Problem finding: A key to creative productivity. In A. S. Fishkin, B. Cramond, & P. Olszewski-Kubilius (Eds.), *Investigating creativity in youth* (pp. 75–96). Cresskill, NJ: Hampton Press.

Sternberg, R. J., & Davidson, J. E. (Eds.). *Conceptions of giftedness*. Cambridge, England: Cambridge University Press.

Sternberg, R. J., & Lubart, T. I. (1999). The concept of creativity: Prospects and paradigms. In R. J. Sternberg (Ed.), *Handbook of creativity* (pp. 3–15). New York: Cambridge University Press.

Sternberg, R. J., & O'Hara, L. A. (1999). Creativity and intelligence. In R. J. Sternberg (Ed.), *Handbook of creativity* (pp. 251–272). New York: Cambridge University Press.

Subotnik, R. F. (1988). Factors from the structure of intellect model associated with gifted adolescents' problem finding in science: Research with Westinghouse Science Talent Search winners. *Journal of Creative Behavior, 22*, 42–54.

Subotnik, R. F., & Steiner, C. L. (1994). Problem identification in academic research: A longitudinal case study from adolescence to early adulthood. In M. A. Runco (Ed.), *Problem finding, problem solving, and creativity* (pp. 88–200). Norwood, NJ: Ablex.

Torrance, E. P. (1990). *Torrance tests of creative thinking*. Bensenville, IL: Scholastic Testing Service.

Treffinger, D. J. (1995). Creative problem solving: Overview and educational implications. *Journal of Educational Psychology, 7*, 301–312.

Wagner, H., & Zimmermann, B. (1986). Identification and fostering of mathematically gifted students. *Educational Studies in Mathematics, 17*, 243–259.

Wakefield, J. F. (1985). Towards creativity: Problem finding in a divergent thinking exercise. *Child Study Journal, 15*, 265–270.

Wakefield, J. F. (1986). Creativity and the TAT blank card. *Journal of Creative Behavior, 20*, 127–133.

Wakefield, J. F. (1987, November). *The outlook for creativity tests*. Paper presented at the Council for Exceptional Children's Topical Conference on the Future of Special Education, Orlando, FL.

Wakefield, J. F. (1992, February). *Creativity tests and artistic talent*. Paper presented at the Second Annual Esther Katz Rosen Symposium on the Psychological Development of Gifted Children, Lawrence, KS.

Wallach, M. A., & Kogan, N. (1965). *Modes of thinking in young children*. New York: Holt, Rinehart & Winston.

Wechsler, D. (1974). *Wechsler intelligence scale for children—Revised*. New York: The Psychological Corporation.

12

Was Mozart at Risk?
A Developmentalist Looks
at Extreme Talent

David Henry Feldman

On February 12, 1778, Wolfgang Amadeus Mozart's father, Leopold, aware of the fact that his son, prize student, and best hope for comfortable retirement, was fast moving out of his control, wrote a letter to the 22-year-old Wolfgang, then in Paris:

> It now depends solely on your good sense and your way of life whether you die as an ordinary musician, utterly forgotten by the world, or as famous Kapellmeister, of whom posterity will read,—whether, captured by some woman you die bedded on straw in an attic, full of starving children, or whether, after a Christian life spent in contentment, honor, and renown, you leave this world with your family well provided for and your name respected by all. (cited in Hildesheimer, 1983, p. 62)

Clearly, Mozart's father, whose role in his development was pervasive and controversial, believed that the promise of Mozart's talent was greatly at risk. Mozart's father saw his own role as that of manager, protector, impresario, and disciplinarian, even when his son was grown and had composed more than a hundred pieces, some of which are treasured today as great works of art. For example, by this time Mozart had written the opera *La finta giardiniera* (K. 196), which premiered in the presence of the Elector Maximilian III in Munich in 1775, and also the Serenade in D ("Haffner," K. 250/248b), the C major Piano Sonata (K. 309/284b), and the E-flat Piano Concerto ("Jeunehomme," K. 271). The theme I wish to pursue in this discussion is the degree to which Mozart, prodigy among prodigies, was at various points in his all-too-short life seriously at risk to lose his place in history, and if he was at risk, what were the critical events and forces that conspired to avoid that risk and make sure that (at least some of) his gifts to the world were received?

We might also consider, for the sake of symmetry if for no other rea-

This chapter was prepared with the assistance of the members of the Developmental Science Group at Tufts University. Support from the Grant Foundation and the Rockefeller Brothers Fund is gratefully acknowledged.

251

son, if Mozart was at promise for more than he accomplished. It is difficult to imagine what more he might have given the world, but as anyone who has seen *Amadeus* (the play or the movie) knows, Mozart died at 36 at the very peak of his musical powers. Had he lived another 10 years, what treasures might have come from this, perhaps the most naturally gifted of all classical composers? Aside from the fictional idea that he was killed by Salieri and aside from the plausible but unproven idea that he composed the *Requiem* (K. 626), his last work, in anticipation of his own death, the possibility of great works beyond the *Requiem* must be at least considered.

The story of the creation and re-creation of Mozart's various images since his death in 1791 is an interesting one (see Ostwald & Zegans, 1993). His work, after a period of about 50 years during which it received less than its deserved recognition, has been placed among the most treasured fruits of Western civilization. The standing of Mozart's music seems more secure at this point than it ever was, leading sometimes to the most extravagant encomiums, as, for example, in this one by the musician and critic Ernst Bloch: "Others may reach heaven with their works. But Mozart, he comes, he comes from there!" (*Geist der Utopie*, Frankfurt, 1964, pp. 68ff., cited in Hildesheimer, 1983, p. 15).

In the two centuries since his death—his works alternately raised to divinity, brought down to Earth, or worse, often declared beyond analysis —Mozart remains an enigma, as much a reflection of cultural preoccupations as the object of disciplined inquiry (Morris, 1994). Rather than try to shed light on the elusive nature of this great prodigy, I pursue a less distant goal, namely, to gauge the likelihood that the wonders that Mozart produced might have been lost to us. In context, then, *at risk* means the likelihood that Mozart's compositional life may have been curtailed or even prevented from occurring. In other words, I examine the probability that the miracle of Mozart might not have occurred.

My premise is that the likelihood of Mozart's doing what he in fact did was very small. In a very real sense it is true that the "miracle" of Mozart is a miracle of timing, circumstance, chance, and what I have elsewhere called *co-incidence* (Feldman, 1986/1991), the favorable and sustained coordination of vital forces of development to achieve a challenging objective. To make the case that Mozart was indeed at risk in the sense of being prevented from fulfilling his potential, I consider several kinds of variables as they played themselves out during his brief time in this world.

Variables Contributing to Mozart's At-Risk Status

When attempting to analyze the course of a person's development, there are almost infinite numbers of variables that might be examined. With prodigies, at least among the most extreme cases, this process is somewhat simplified because of the highly focused nature of the developmental process. It is as if the organism were "canalized" to develop in a certain specific direction, to use Waddington's (1969) term from biology for the resistance of certain physical characteristics (such as height) to disruption from their projected growth targets. Whereas for most people, the setting of a life course and the organizing of resources to achieve it is a major source of concern during the opening decades of life, in the case of true prodigies these decisions seem to have been made largely before the child is born or shortly thereafter (Feldman, 1986/1991; Feldman & Goldsmith, 1986; Goldsmith & Feldman, 1989).

Still, there are numerous issues to consider. Based on our own research with several prodigies and their families (Feldman, 1986/1991), as well as other work on musical prodigies (Kenneson, 1998), there seem to be several prerequisites that are central to the process of the development of full potential, especially in music. These include intellectual and personal qualities of the child, of the rarest sort, particularly great talent, moderate general capability, persistence, and inner confidence; qualities of the parents, including their experience in the target field, degree of devotion to their child's development, and willingness to sacrifice their own achievements for those of their children; the availability of resources specific to the target field, such as appropriate instruction, technologies, technical and logistic support, and access to appropriate challenges and rewards; the state of the target domain itself, particularly its knowledge structures in relation to the talents of the aspiring prodigy, its degree of participation by appropriately prepared individuals, stability or lack of stability of its dominant forms and structures, and its match to the sensibilities of the prodigy. How all of these things (and no doubt more) play themselves out in a given case is a matter of great complexity (Simonton, 1992).

More contextually relevant variables are also of the essence in reckoning the degree of risk in achieving full expression of potential, particularly in prodigies. These include such matters as the opportunities for participation in a field by members of various groups; the existence and accessibility of pedagogical resources such as schools, institutes, guilds, apprenticeships, and the like; sufficient opportunities to participate at all levels, including the highest levels; incentives and rewards for excellence; sufficient material resources to attract and retain the most talented individuals; and a segment of the public sufficiently sophisticated to comprehend and appreciate performances at all levels, including the rarest and most extraordinary (cf. Feldman, Csikszentmihalyi, & Gardner, 1994).

At the more distant peripheries of the process, but essential nonetheless, are such matters as the state of a society's economy; its involvement in wars and its concerns with external threats; its stance toward change and innovation; its degree of sensitivity and acceptance of various groups, such as women, Jews, and others; its traditions in supporting certain fields, such as poetry, music, the military, business, or religious institutions; and its forms of government, trade, spirituality, sexuality, and the like (see Gardner, 1997; Simonton, 1992). For an Irishman to become a gloomy and introspective poet is in keeping with a centuries-old tradition, as is it is for a young Japanese man to devote his life to the crafting of ceremonial bells. Imagine the reverse, a gloomy young Japanese poet and a pious Irish ceremonial bell maker to get a sense of how much the broad context affects the process of talent development.

It is beyond the scope of a brief treatment such as this to fully (or even passingly) consider all of the above variables and issues; there are no doubt others that might be added to the list (Simonton, 1992). But with the complexity and magnitude of the task now more firmly established, let us turn to some of the specific events, issues, and decisions that were critical during Mozart's early years.

As already mentioned, it will be my purpose to show that the odds were very much against Mozart's being provided the opportunity to fully develop his unique talents. Some of the reasons why we might easily have lost Mozart's precious gifts to the world were impossible to anticipate or modify, whereas others represent opportunities and concerns that are well within our power to change, if not for Mozart then for others who face similar sorts of challenges. The justification for an exercise like this one is of course not to try to render judgment (harsh or otherwise) on those who were responsible for Mozart's development. It is rather to try to learn from this and other cases what the critical issues are in bringing out extremely high potential, in developing that potential to its fullest in the context of a rich and satisfying life, and in passing on such knowledge to others who find themselves confronted with the often lonely and daunting responsibility for making decisions that might make all the difference to a uniquely gifted child—and thus to the world (Bloom, 1985; Horowitz & O'Brien, 1985).

Birth and Early Experience

We know little of Wolfgang Amadeus Mozart's early experience, but we do know that he was the sixth child born (of 7) and the second surviving child of Leopold and Anna Maria Mozart. Mozart's sister, Nannerl, 5 years his senior, was the other surviving child. Although it was not unusual for children to die in the 1700s, it is not difficult to see that, on sheer probability grounds alone, the odds of *the* Mozart surviving in this particular family were a slim 2 of 7, or 1 of 7 if we assume (also correctly) that a girl would have had no real opportunity to become a professional composer in Mozart's time. Very likely 1 out of 7 children of Leopold and Anna Maria had the potential for works of genius, and that one survived.

It could be argued that it was not a unique blend of genetic material and fortunate pre- and postnatal experience that led to Mozart's unique potential, but rather the special environment created by his parents and family in Salzburg. This is quite unlikely, because, however salubrious that environment might have been, Mozart's talents were without doubt also of the rarest and most extraordinary sort. They appear perhaps once in a generation, possibly once in a century. Leopold and Anna Maria would have to have been fecund to a degree unprecedented in human affairs to have raised the probability more than a few points of another Wolfgang appearing in their midst. And because the overt history of the family's participation in music was no more than a single generation in duration (in contrast with, for example, the Bach family, with several generations of musicians), the probabilities point dramatically to an event so rare that it can be seen only as a fortunate accident of birth and survival against very high odds indeed.

The Mozart now recognized all over the world might very well never have been born. This is a chance aspect of being at risk, because there is very little that Mozart's parents could have done that might have increased the odds of their producing *the* Mozart. Medical practice has improved infant mortality rates (although differentially among various groups), making the odds greater for any given family, but they are small in the best of circumstances (Simonton, 1992).

It is safe to say, in other words, that none of the other children of Leopold and Anna Maria had even the remotest chance of reaching the heights of musical creation that characterized the mature Wolfgang (Marshall, 1985, 1991). Nannerl was, to be sure, a very talented musician, but without a trace of the restless need to transform, generate, and extend the musical experience that was the hallmark of the composer Mozart from age 7 or 8 until his death at 36.

As already mentioned, we know almost nothing of the first months and years of Mozart's childhood experience, making it impossible to raise or lower the estimate of the odds of his having survived those critical early periods. We do know that less than half of all children during that century survived beyond age 5 (Aries, 1962; Kessen, 1965), but that tells us little about this one child. What we do know is that, by age 3, Wolfgang was picking out thirds on the clavier, an early keyboard instrument that his sister was being introduced to under the direction of Leopold, himself a music teacher of some repute in his native Salzburg (Kenneson, 1998).

Early Opportunities in Music

In research on prodigies, a striking pattern emerges of early exposure to the domain in question, particularly in chess and music. The same tends to be true of world-class performers in several fields who were not prodigies (Bloom, 1985). For Mozart, the existence of an intensely musical environment was already in place when he arrived on the scene on January 27, 1756. Leopold Mozart was a music teacher in the Salzburg cathedral school and had developed some well-respected (then and now) techniques for teaching, especially the violin; his book on violin teaching was published in the year of Wolfgang's birth.

There was a clavier in the household, and Leopold was already teaching Nannerl to play while Wolfgang was still in diapers. By age 3, Wolfgang took an interest in the clavier and began to learn how to play, so that by 5, he was playing pieces and composing simple tunes. He was quickly taken under his father's devoted (some would say too devoted) tutelage, the only sustained instruction he ever had. Wolfgang never went to school.

There are two points about family history to be emphasized: one having to do with music, the other having to do with prodigies. It is rare for a family having little history in music to produce a great musician. Mozart did not come from a long-standing musical family. His father's family were artisans, bookbinders, and bricklayers for several generations. His mother's family also had little musical history. His family was not musical until Mozart's father broke with family tradition and studied the violin several years before Wolfgang was born. Had this not occurred, the probability of Mozart's critical early experience being appropriately musical would have been greatly reduced.

The second point is that certain families tend to be prodigy-producing families. The ancestors of violinist Yehudi Menuhin, for example, have been producing prodigies since the 15th Century (Feldman & Goldsmith, 1986; Rolfe, 1978), although not musical prodigies until the current generation. In music, most if not all of the great musicians have been prodigies, particularly the composers (Kenneson, 1998; Ostwald & Zegans, 1993; Simonton, 1992). There is no evidence of early precocity in Mozart's family before (or after) Wolfgang. Again, the probability of this particular combination of potential and environment seems extremely small.

This makes Mozart's exceptional music gifts even more astounding, produced as they were in only the second generation of musical preoccupations in a family with no known history of producing prodigies. Mozart's two surviving children were not exceptional in music, and neither produced their own children. Whatever was unique about Mozart's genetics, it ceased with his children (one of whom may not have been his). His sister's children were not to become major musicians either, suggesting that some unique combination of traits and qualities, perhaps appearing at only one moment in time, occurred in the mix of material that set down the genetic program for Wolfgang Amadeus Mozart. It is abundantly clear that great talent is both rare and influential in the course of development (Milbrath, 1998).

What is interesting, then, aside from genetics, is how well-timed the creation and development of a highly refined musical environment was for Mozart. Because his father was a first-generation musician, it was not at all likely that the essential musical environment would be present during the critical periods of Wolfgang's experience. Had he been born first (the usual assumption is of course that firstborns receive more of the family's resources), it is less likely that he would have received the quality and quantity of musical experience made available to him. In fact, his older sister Nannerl's lessons on clavier proved to be a catalytic element in Mozart's development. It is unlikely that systematic exposure to music would have occurred otherwise, because in those days children were not believed to be sentient beings until they had survived the first half decade (Kessen, 1965), but Mozart got vital experience before he was 3.

Leopold Mozart, the looming, overbearing, meddlesome, and ultimately destructive character of the film and play, is almost certainly overdrawn for dramatic effect in those works. What is true is that, as parents of prodigies have done for centuries (including those of Pablo Picasso and

Menuhin), the Mozarts' decision to devote their lives to the realization of a child's potential was both crucial to the process and complicated it greatly (Kenneson, 1998). For Leopold, a comfortable and respectable career as a teacher in the service of the church was sacrificed for a chance at greater respectability and affluence at court through his brilliant children. Again, had the children been born earlier or later, it is less likely that the course taken would have been chosen, for at least two reasons (Feldman & Goldsmith, 1986; Gardner, 1997).

First, as already mentioned, Leopold's career in music began late. If the children had been born earlier, he would not have had the teaching skills or the secure place as an established musician that would have provided the techniques that were used in teaching his children. Had they been born later, Leopold's own career may have been sufficiently successful and lucrative, his commitments so deep, that he would have achieved too much to give it up.

Perhaps more important than the timing of Leopold's musical career was the fact that the opportunities for achieving a better station through nobility and high church auspices were still seen as sufficiently promising to put his own career aside. It was, after all, near the end of the *ancien régime*, only a decade or so before the French Revolution, the beginning of which preceded Mozart's death by only 2 years. Later, the so-called Turkish War led to a substantial decline in theatrical and musical opportunities. The American Declaration of Independence was framed when Mozart was 20. In other words, the kind of effort made to place Mozart among the nobility was rapidly becoming an anachronistic, futile enterprise. The structure of European culture was about to change forever, but Leopold (and Wolfgang) were for the most part unaware of how profoundly the world they aspired to participate in was about to change (Gardner, 1997).

The duration of the period when a career like Mozart's could be achieved was therefore very short. Fifty years earlier the infrastructure of music was insufficiently evolved to support child prodigy performers and composers (a point I return to later), and 50 years later Ludwig van Beethoven had begun to move beyond the forms that proved so appropriate for Mozart's astonishing variations and transformations (Morris, 1994). Had Mozart entered the scene at almost any other period (except perhaps our own, and even this is not at all clear), it is unlikely that the unique quality of his compositional record would have been achieved (Gardner, 1997).

The notions of "critical periods" or "sensitive periods" are used to describe moments when maturational and developmental milestones must be achieved or the opportunity is lost forever, such as the first decade of life for a native language or the first year for establishing certain visual pathways; these would also seem to be good metaphors for critical periods in the evolution of a culture or a domain of knowledge (Bornstein and Krasnegor, 1989).

In Mozart's case, it is clear that his compositional career benefited from the by-then-established pattern among noble and high church personages to commission compositions or to hire full-time court or church musicians (although their status was not high, being in the same category as kitchen staff). A good deal of Mozart's work was done specifically for one or another royal or church patron in countries from England to Italy in his official capacity as church organist and Konzertmeister to Archbishop Colloredo of Salzburg, or (more briefly) for other personages. Indeed, one contributing factor to Mozart's chronic financial difficulties, especially during his last years, was the incipient breakdown of this loosely organized system, along with and hastened by a war that took even noblemen occasionally to the front, rendering them (sometimes permanently) unavailable as patrons (Morris, 1994). It also must be added that Mozart hated parochial Salzburg and being in the service of the church and much preferred the life of an independent composer, a much more difficult and insecure life, particularly in a declining market (Gardner, 1997).

Mozart's "Midlife Crisis"

It is widely believed (and probably true) that Mozart's last years were increasingly stressful and not successful financially. Much has been written about this period of his life, but I would like to focus on an earlier period, the time when the letter with which this discussion opened was written—when Wolfgang was reaching young adulthood. From a reading of well-documented evidence from the years 1774 to 1778, when Mozart was 18 to 22 years old, it appears that he went through a crisis that might have changed his life course and that could well have deprived the world of Mozart's most prized works. The letter from his father admonishing him to attend to his career, written in 1778, was not without justification.

Wolfgang was prepared to put his career at risk for the sake of true love, in this case, the love of 16-year-old singer Aloysia Weber. Having begun the critical process of establishing his independence from Leopold by traveling to Paris (not alone, but with his mother), Wolfgang fell madly in love and began an ultimately unsuccessful courtship of his student Aloysia. There is little evidence that Aloysia was ever attracted to her smitten suitor, although she greatly appreciated his talents as a teacher and mentor. Had Aloysia felt differently, we might have had a different Wolfgang Amadeus Mozart. A somewhat similar and even more dramatic example of filial loyalty versus love and marriage was played out in the lives of Clara and Robert Schumann (Kenneson, 1998) and may have contributed to the demise of Robert.

Mozart married Aloysia's older sister Constanze 4 years later, a match much better suited to a career (although his father vehemently opposed it). Again, much has been written about this episode and its aftermath (cf. Hildesheimer, 1983; Marshall, 1991).

In relation to the theme of Mozart's being at risk for not fulfilling his potential, what is interesting is how the events of these years conform to what Jeanne Bamberger, herself a former piano prodigy and now one who studies music prodigies, has called a "midlife crisis" (Bamberger, 1982). Bamberger has documented a period, usually during adolescence or young adulthood, when prodigies are highly at risk. The reasons are that their musical skills deteriorate in the face of an increasing ability to reflect and analyze their own capabilities and that they must establish an independent life from the people who have brought them to their current place.

There is little evidence that Mozart ever actually lost his musical skills or had to face a sharp diminution in them, but the issue of his becoming independent from his father was perhaps the major turning point in his life. Had things gone differently, had he been a successful suitor of Aloysia, it is not at all clear that the Mozart we now honor would have ever emerged. There is some evidence that he composed less during this period than either before or after, although there are problems with trying to get an accurate estimate because he did not begin keeping records of his compositions until several years later (Gardner, 1997). Still the reality of this crisis seems hard to escape, particularly when viewed in comparison with other prodigies. The case would need to be stronger if there were better evidence of diminished capacity in performing or composing music, but the need to work free from Leopold's suffocating grip seems well-established.

Mozart had, after all, spent most of his childhood years traveling around Europe with his sister and father; one journey lasted more than 3 years and began when he was 7. There is no evidence that Mozart disliked this life, but for his music to mature it became increasingly necessary to achieve an independent stance apart from his father. These are issues that all children face, but they are intensified and made more complicated with prodigies (Feldman, 1986/1991). That Mozart succeeded in struggling free from his father's control was only partially attributable to his own efforts, and even these efforts might have rendered him independent but unable to reach the compositional heights he was to reach over the next decade. Had Aloysia accepted his proposal of marriage, it is possible he would have been even greater, but the odds are against it.

Mozart's marriage to Constanze seems to have been a happy enough one, and it almost certainly contributed toward the most productive and (from all accounts) most satisfying period of his life as a composer and performer. It appears that Mozart had to work fairly hard to convince himself that he loved Constanze, and her mother very likely engineered the whole affair, but the marriage was a positive contributor to the probability that Mozart was able to do his work. During the years between 1782 and 1788, Mozart was very busy and productive. Hildesheimer (1983) described these years as follows:

> Actually, Mozart's creativity reached a high point both qualitatively and quantitatively in the four years from the beginning of 1784 to the end of 1787. In this period he wrote twelve (more than half) of his piano concerti; a horn concerto; a symphony; five quintets for various combinations of instruments, among the E-flat, K. 452 . . . for piano, oboe, clarinet, horn, and bassoon, which he himself at the time of composition, held to the best work he ever wrote. . . . Also written during this four-year period were five string quartets, two piano quartets, three trios, five sonatas, *Figaro*, *Don Giovanni*, the short opera *Der Schaus-*

pieldirektor (K. 486, February 3, 1786), various Masonic pieces, nearly all his lieder, plus—we are still talking about the same four years!—several important miscellaneous works like *Einmusikalischer Spass*, K. 522, *Eine kleine Nachtmusik*, K. 525, the A minor Rondo for piano, K. 511, and, of course many numbers to be inserted into the operas of other composers. (pp. 175–176)

This period of successful composing, teaching, performing, and socializing with other musicians—a period of relative contentment—began to unravel about 1789, 2 years before Mozart's death. It is beyond the scope of this discussion to try to analyze those final 2 years, but the evidence is by no means conclusive that the decline was unrelenting and almost inevitable, as it is portrayed in *Amadeus*. Mozart was in good health up until 2 months before his death on December 5, 1791, and his powers as a composer remained strong until the day he died. Some scholars of Mozart's life believe he was increasingly isolated and alienated from Viennese society, that a cruel and indifferent world ignored his greatness and callously hastened his death (e.g., Hildesheimer, 1983). Others see this as too pat a story and believe that Mozart's reverses could easily have been temporary; with a war going on and a changing social scene, subsequent events might have rather quickly led to restored success (e.g., Gardner, 1997; Salomon, 1983).

Whatever was true of Mozart's last few years, it is clear that his life was one that brought with it perhaps the greatest promise of its time for musical genius, at least a good portion of which was expressed in the more than 600 works we now cherish (Morris, 1994). The point of this discussion has been to demonstrate that the probabilities of our receiving any of these gifts was small, and there were several crucial points along the way where the fruits of Mozart's unique potential might have been distorted, diminished, or lost altogether, as ultimately occurred in December 1791 (Feldman, 1986/1991; Simonton, 1992).

Lessons Learned From Mozart

To be sure, we should be grateful for the tangible gifts of Mozart and for the priceless contribution to Western culture. It may help us to appreciate just how much of a treasure we have been given if we reflect a bit, as I have tried to do here, on just how unlikely we ever are to be able to enjoy the full benefits of a natural miracle like Mozart and recognize just how complex and delicate a process it is when potential of any sort has been given full voice.

Given what we have learned from the extreme case of Mozart, are there lessons that might help us have a better chance of finding and developing talent in youngsters of unusual promise? Although a talent of Mozart's quality is rare, perhaps one a century, it appears that many of the same issues and challenges that confronted Mozart's family and Mozart himself face anyone trying to find full expression for extraordinary potential. There seem to be at least three conclusions about the development of talent that emerge from studying cases at the extremes.

The first of these is how much more readily talent is recognized, engaged early, and launched toward high levels of mastery when there is a familial history or valuing in the same field as the child's talent domain. In Mozart's case there was almost a near miss; only one generation separated him from being born into a family with no musical preoccupations and perhaps little musical talent in its other members. In study after study (e.g., Bloom, 1985), it is clear that having parents and other family members involved in the same talent area (or a closely related one) confers a distinct advantage on the young child new to the world. A corollary of this lesson is that parents and others close to the young child are advised to be vigilant to their own strengths as well as to areas not present in the family milieu. A challenging situation indeed is one in which the talent of the child is in a domain in which no one else in the family is either talented or interested. Awareness of the possibility of mismatches of children's and parents' talents can help raise awareness of the need to be watchful for the appearance of talents outside of one's own areas of strength and resourceful in accessing expertise to respond to such talents. In certain fields like music, early detection of musical talent appears to be crucial to optimal development of that talent, almost like a critical period in biology (Bornstein & Krasnegor, 1989).

A second lesson to be gleaned from a case like Mozart's is that a central issue for all people growing up is to find and sustain a productive direction for the expression of one's talents. In Mozart's case, his talent was so overwhelming in one area (music) that the identity of his path was relatively easy (pursuing it successfully was another matter, of course). For the most extreme cases, finding a direction to go or a path to follow is not difficult. Doing anything else is difficult, perhaps impossible. The concert violinist MiDori once said in a television interview that she could not live without her violin (CNN "Future Watch," July 7, 1990). The more extreme the talent (assuming it is a single one and that a field exists to respond to it), the easier is the choice of which direction to go. But the issue is one that all children and all people face. It is a reasonable speculation based on the study of extreme cases that each of us yearns to find fulfillment of our unique potential (see Feldman, 1986/1991). Seeing how the process unfolds in an extreme case helps frame the issue for those of us who must find our path without such clear maps and markers as were manifest in a case like Mozart's.

On the other hand, Mozart's case also alerts us to the difficulties caused when there is no appropriate role in society to match the best expression of one's talents. Mozart had to invent his role as independent composer, concertizer, instructor, a free agent not affiliated with any institution (Marshall, 1985, 1991; Ostwald & Zegans, 1993). These challenges may have affected Mozart's productivity, satisfaction, and even possibly his longevity. His efforts, however, almost certainly opened up possibilities for those who followed his lead, helping establish and clear the way for the many succeeding independent composers, performers, teachers, and conductors. Indeed, the current scene in professional music turns on the viability of roles like the one Mozart pioneered, leading us to the third lesson we have learned from studying this case.

Just when and where a talent appears can be crucial. Domains and fields evolve (Feldman, Csikszentmihalyi, & Gardner, 1994; Gardner, 1993, 1997), providing various opportunities and curtailing others. To understand how talent can be optimally developed requires not only the study of cases, extreme and otherwise, but also studies of the domains in which potential is released and unfolds and how they change, as well as studies of the broader contexts of these domains—the fields that preserve, value, select, support, and promote the forms of talent that are its preoccupation. Families of children of extreme talent in music and occasionally in other areas are sometimes willing to place their children within what they perceive to be the optimal circumstances. Families have been known to move to the other side of the world if it is clear (to them) that doing so is crucial for their child's optimal development. A related conclusion is the realization that at a given moment, there may be talents for which the necessary resources simply do not exist. Even a willingness to relocate anywhere in the world is insufficient when the world is simply without the crucial needed resources. If a talent appears for which there has not yet developed an appropriate cultural expression, knowledge system, technology, symbol system, or the like, no amount of searching will produce them.

And so we must accept the reality that it is not possible to respond optimally to all forms of talent in all children at all times. We can hope that, as we come to understand the processes of optimal talent development better, we will be in a position to lose less of the available talent than in previous eras through ignorance, inattention, lack of commitment to optimal development, or misguided notions of egalitarianism or other ideas that diminish the likelihood of optimal development of valued potential. To reflect on these sorts of developmental processes and the conditions under which great potential is realized through them may, it is hoped, equip us better to raise the probabilities that, if and when a child of the potential of a Mozart again appears in our midst, the fruits of that potential will not be forever lost. The last one was a close call.

References

Aries, P. (1962). *Centuries of childhood*. New York: Vintage Books.

Bamberger, J. (1982). Growing up prodigies: The midlife crisis. In D. H. Feldman (Ed.), *Developmental approaches to giftedness and creativity* (pp. 61–77). San Francisco: Jossey-Bass.

Bloom, B. (Ed.). (1985). *Developing talent in young children*. New York: Ballantine.

Bornstein, M., & Krasnegor, N. (Eds.). (1989). *Stability and continuity in mental development: Behavioral and biological perspectives*. Hillsdale, NJ: Erlbaum.

Feldman, D. H. (1991). *Nature's gambit: Child prodigies and the development of human potential*. New York: Teachers College Press. (Original work published 1986)

Feldman, D. H., & Goldsmith, L. T. (1986). Transgenerational influences on the development of early prodigious behavior: A case study approach. In W. Fowler (Ed.), *Early experience and competence development* (pp. 67–85). San Francisco: Jossey-Bass.

Feldman, D. H., Csikszentmihalyi, M., & Gardner, H. (1994). *Changing the world: A framework for the study of creativity*. Westport, CT: Greenwood Press/Praeger.

Gardner, H. (1993). *Creating minds*. New York: Basic Books.

Gardner, H. (1997). *Extraordinary minds*. New York: Basic Books.

Goldsmith, L. T., & Feldman, D. H. (1989). Wang Yani: Gifts well given. In W. Ho (Ed.), *Yani: The brush of innocence* (pp. 51–62). New York: Hudson Hills Press.

Hildesheimer, W. (1983). *Mozart*. New York: Vintage Books.

Horowitz, F. D., & O'Brien, M. (Eds.). (1985). *The gifted and talented: Developmental perspectives*. Washington, DC: American Psychological Association.

Kenneson, C. (1998). *Musical prodigies: Perilous journeys, remarkable lives*. Portland, OR: Amadeus Press.

Kessen, W. (1965). *The child*. New York: Wiley.

Marshall, R. (1985). Wolfgang\Amadeus: Amadeus/Wolfgang. *Brandeis Review, 5,* 9–16.

Marshall, R. (1991). *Mozart speaks*. New York: Schirmer Books.

Milbrath, C. (1998). *Patterns of artistic development in children: Comparative studies of talent*. Cambridge, England: Cambridge University Press.

Morris, J. (Ed.). (1994). *On Mozart*. Cambridge, England: Cambridge University Press.

Ostwald, P., & Zegans, L. S. (Eds.). (1993). *The pleasures and perils of genius: Mostly Mozart*. Madison, WI: International Universities Press.

Rolfe, L. (1978). *The Menuhins: A family odyssey*. San Francisco: Panjandrum Books.

Salomon, M. (1983). Review of W. Hildesheimer's *Mozart. Musical Quarterly, 69,* 270–279.

Simonton, D. (1992). The child parents the adult: On getting genius from giftedness. In N. Colangelo, S. Assouline, & D. Ambroson (Eds.), *Talent development: Proceedings from the 1991 Henry B. and Jocelyn Wallace National Research Symposium on Talent Development* (pp. 278–297). Unionville, NY: Trillium Press.

Waddington, C. (1969). Paradigm for an evolutionary process. In C. Waddington (Ed.), *Towards a theoretic biology II* (pp. 106–128). Edinburgh, Scotland: Edinburgh University Press.

Author Index

Numbers in italics refer to listings in the reference sections.

Dweck, C. S., 17, 18, 20, *22*
Dyk, R. B., 177, *187*

Ebner, F. F., 65, *73*
Eccles, J., 32, 40, 49, *51*
Edelman, G., 138, *143*
Eisenberg, N., 197, 201, 209, 210, *212*
Elliott, E. S., 17, 18, 20, *22*
Elliott, S. N., 202, 205, 209, *213*
Elman, J. L., 138, *143*
Embretson, S. E., 128, *145*
Ericsson, A., 79, *87*
Ericsson, K. A., 169, 181, *185,* 228, 229, *231*
Erwin, T. D., 152, *163*

Fagan, J. F., 125, 126, *143, 146*
Fagan, J. F., III, 11, *22,* 29, 40, *51*
Fagen, J. W., 125, *142, 143*
Falbo, T., *22*
Farber, E. A., 43, *54,* 123, *147*
Faterson, H. F., 177, *187*
Fein, D., 123, 129, 140, 141, *143, 145*
Fein, G. G., 127, *144*
Feiring, C., 8, *24*
Feldhusen, J. F., xvi, *xix,* 3, *5,* 71, *73,* 129, *144,* 184, *185,* 241, 242, *247*
Feldman, D., 78, *87*
Feldman, D. H., 4, *5,* 10, *22,* 31, 33, 36, 38, 41, 43, *51, 52,* 64, 69, 71, *73, 74,* 78, 79, *87,* 89–91, 97–99, 101, 104, 109, 114, *116, 117,* 197, 199, 200, *212, 214,* 252, 253, 256, 257, 259–262, *262, 263*
Feldman, J. F., 11, *25,* 29, 40, *53,* 125, 127, *145*
Feltovich, P., 217, *231,* 237, *246*
Feuerstein, R., 170, *185*
Fiedler, M. F., 12, *25,* 34, *54,* 131, 132, 134, *146*
Field, T. M., 16, *22*
Fiscella, J., 11, *21*
Fischer, K. W., 197–199, 201–203, 208, 210, *212*
Fischoff, B., 129, *143*
Flavell, J. H., 168, 170, *185*
Fletcher, J. M., 45, *51*
Fletcher-Flinn, C., 45, 46, *51*
Flett, G. L., 18, *22*
Foley, J. M., 195, 196, *215*
Folsom, C., 154, *163*
Ford, M. E., 196, 197, 207, 209, *212*
Forsberg, 42, *53*
Forsythe, D. R., 152, *164*
Fosberg, H., *53*
Fosnot, C. T., 114, *117*
Fowler, W., 17, *22,* 64, *73,* 137, *143*
Francis, D. J., 45, *51*

Frankowski, J. J., *144*
Fredericksen, N., 197, *212*
Freeburg, N. E., 17, *22*
Freeman, J., 19, *22,* 136, *143*
Freppon, P. A., 210, *215*
Frick, J. E., 125, 127, 128, *142, 145*
Friedman, R. C., ix, *ix,* xi, xii, *xiv,* xvi, *xix,* 3, 4, *5,* 192, *193*
Friedrich, G., 129, *144*
Frisch, V., *231*
Frye, D., 14, *24*
Fu, V. R., 19, *24*

Gagné, F., 72, *73*
Gallagher, J. J., 7, *22,* 197, *212*
Galton, F., 10, 16, *22,* 169, *185*
Gardner, H., 30, *51,* 71, *73,* 77–86, *87, 88,* 123, 136, *143,* 196, 197, 199, 200, 204, 205, 208, 209, 211, *212, 214,* 224, *231,* 239, *247,* 253, 257–260, 262, *263*
Gardner, J., 86, *87*
Gardner, M. K., 150, *163*
Gazzaniga, M. S., 56 n.3, *73*
Genesee, F., 184, *185*
Geppert, U., 17, *22*
Gerrig, R. J., 156, *163*
Gesell, A., 125, *143*
Getzels, J. W., 177, *185,* 192, *193,* 218, 219, 223, 225, 228, 229, *231,* 234, 236, 239, 240, *247*
Ghiselin, B., 218, *231*
Glaser, R., 168, 169, *185, 186,* 200, *214,* 217, *231,* 237, *246*
Globerson, T., 197, 198, 200, *212, 213, 215*
Goertzel, M., 10, 16, *22*
Goertzel, T., 10, *22*
Goertzel, V., 10, *22*
Gohl, E., 127, *145*
Goldberg, J., 198, *212*
Goldberger, N. R., 149, *163*
Goldberg-Reitman, J., 200, 201, *213*
Golden, M., 18, *21*
Goldsmith, L., 10, *22, 51, 87,* 253, *263*
Goldsmith, L. T., *5,* 47, *51, 73,* 91, 114, 115, *117,* 230, *231,* 253, 256, 257, *263*
Goleman, D., 205, *213*
Golin, J., 11, *21*
Gollin, J. B., 196, 197, 208, *211*
Golomb, C., 201, *213*
Gonzalez, V., 129, *147*
Goodenough, D. R., 177, *187*
Goswami, A., 183, *185*
Gottesman, I. I., 28, *54*
Gottfried, A. E., 16, 18, *22,* 63, *73,* 123, *143*
Gottfried, A. W., 16, *22,* 63–65, *73,* 123, 132–134, 136, 139–141, *143*
Gottleib, G., 138, *144*

Subject Index

Acceleration, 183
Achievement motivation, 17–18
Adolescence, 83–84, 107–108
Adult achievement, potential for, 30, 31
Adults, 168
Advanced development (as term), 8
Aesthetic bias, personal, 221–223, 225–226
Aesthetic style, 226–227
Age
    and changes in giftedness, 31–32
    and giftedness matrix, 82–85
Art, expertise in visual. *See* Visual art, expertise in
Artificial intelligence, xviii
Ashkenazy, Vladimir, 95
Aspirations, 18
Assessment
    of intelligence in infants, 127–128
    of precocity, 11–12
    of problem finding, 242–244
    of social giftedness, 209
At risk, 259
Attention (in infants), 11

Bayley Scales of Infant Development, 131, 132
Behavior genetics, 28–29
Binet, Alfred, xv
Biopsychological potential, 78–79
Bloch, Ernst, 252
Bloom, Benjamin S., xv
Bruner, Jerome S., xi

California Achievement Tests (CAT), 242, 243
Campbell, D. T., 224
Case, R., 198
Case studies
    of development of giftedness, 36–37
    of exceptionally high-IQ children, 60–70
CAT. *See* California Achievement Tests
China, 86
Cognitive development, 16–17
    and development of gifted performance, 40–42
    and emotion, 58
    in gifted preschoolers, 11
    infants, detection of cognitive precocity in, 124–134
    and revolutionary shifts, 59

Cognitive leap, 65–70
Cognitive process models, 39
Cognitive risk taking, 19
Cognitive studies, 13–15
College students, qualitative differences in thinking among, 177–180
Columbus Group, 70–71
Constructivism, 30, 149
Contextualism, 150
Continuity, in development, 13, 29, 59, 63, 70, 125, 168, 170
Continuity, heterotypic, 10, 29
Creativity, 19, 79, 82–83
    and aesthetics, 224
    and play, 220–221
Cross-modal transfer (in infants), 11
Cry counts, 10
Crystallizing experiences, 82
Csikszentmihalyi, M., 31, 78, 115, 227–228, 235–236, 239, 240
Cultural-Historical theory, 55
Culture, and development of gifted performance, 40–42

Darwin, Charles, 85
Development. *See also* Cognitive development
    advanced, 8
    case studies focusing on, 36–37
    early, of young gifted children, 10–15
    and expression of giftedness, 31–32
    individual differences in, 28–30
    integration of giftedness with, 33–34
    propitious influences on, 8
    prospective studies on, 37–44
    and qualitative differences in thinking, 182–183
    as revolutionary shifts in cognition, 59
    as sequence of bidirectional transactions, 28–29
    of social giftedness, 198–199, 202–205
    and visual art expertise, 227–229
Developmental psychology, 8–9
Developmental-systems approaches, 138–139
Devlin, Billy, 106
Differentiation of abilities, 33
Disabilities (in prodigies), 10
Dittersdorf, Karl Ditters von, 77
Domain(s), 78, 109–111
    and age, 31–32

273

Sensitivity, 204
Sesame Street, 184
Shakespeare, William, 79, 85
Sidis, William James, 90
Slenczynski, Ruth, 91
Social Ability, 195–196
Social behavior, in gifted preschoolers, 11
Social cognition, in gifted preschoolers, 11
Social context (of individual development),
  29
Social giftedness, 195–211
  and advanced social abilities, 205–208
  definition of, 197–198
  developmental perspective on, 198–199,
    202–205
  integrated theoretical perspective on,
    200–201
  modular perspective on, 199–200
  preliminary research on, 201–202
  and social intelligence, 195–197
Social intelligence, 195–197
Social Skills Rating System, 202, 205
Sociohistorical theory, 56
Stern, Issac, 91
Stoker, Bram, 89
Stoner, Winifred, 91
Stravinsky, Igor, 77, 85
Study of Mathematically Precocious Youth
  Mathematics Talent Search, 35–36
Symbol systems, 42–43

Talent and talent development, xvii, 81,
  115
Teachers (of prodigies), 111–112, 114
Terman, Lewis, 7
Terminology, xv–xvi
Testing. *See* Assessment
Test taking, 18
Thinking
  qualitative differences in. *See* Qualitative
    differences in thinking
  relativistic. *See* Relativistic thinking
Torrance Tests of Creative Thinking, 241

Values, 86–87
Variance, sample, 9–10

Velasquez, Diego Rodríguez de Silva y, 77
Velazquez, Ricky, 103–106
Verbal intelligence, 43, 47
Verbal precocity, in preschoolers, 12
Very young children, giftedness in, 7–21
  cognitive studies of, 13–15
  creativity, 82–83
  domain-specific abilities in, 12–13
  first signs of precocity, 10–11
  future research, directions for, 19–20
  identification of, 11–12
  prodigies, 10
  and qualitative differences in thinking,
    170–172
  reasons for studying, 8–9
  and role of parent, 15–19
Visual art, expertise in, 217–230
  and aesthetic sensing of completion,
    224–225
  and aesthetic sensitivity to elegant solu-
    tions, 224
  and constraints of aesthetic style, 226–
    227
  and developmental differences, 227–229
  and personal aesthetic bias, 221–223
  and personal aesthetic sense, 225–226
  and selected perception, 223–224
Visual habituation–memory (in infants),
  10–12
Visual memory (in infants), 12
Vygotskian theory, 55–60, 67–70
Vygotsky, Lev S., 55–56, 60, 63, 64, 67–72

Wagner, Richard, 77
Weber, Aloysia, 258
Weber, Constanze, 258, 259
Wechsler Intelligence Scale for Children–
  Revised (WISC–R), 132, 177–178, 242,
  243
Weiner, Norbert, 90
Westinghouse Talent Search, 241
WISC–R. *See* Wechsler Intelligence Scale
  for Children–Revised

Yani, 10
"Young Archimedes" (Aldous Huxley), 43

About the Editors

Reva C. Friedman, PhD, is an associate professor in the Department of Teaching and Leadership at the University of Kansas, where she is responsible for degree and graduate certificate programs in gifted child education. She is codirector of the American Psychological Foundation's Esther Katz Symposium on the Psychological Development of Gifted Children. She has completed 15 years of service on the Board of Directors for the National Association for Gifted Children, and she has served as the secretary and governor-at-large of the Association for the Gifted. Most recently, she earned the University of Kansas School of Education Distinguished Faculty Award for Teaching and completed a master's degree in social work. Her research interests center on the psychological factors that have an impact on talent development, particularly self-perceptions and motivation, and on inclusive education models that emphasize students' talents and strengths. She publishes and presents papers and workshops on these topics regularly at international, national, regional, state, and local meetings of professional associations and various community and consumer groups. Her most recent book, *Talents in Context: Historical and Social Perspectives on Giftedness*, coedited with Karen B. Rogers, was published by the American Psychological Association in 1998.

Bruce M. Shore, PhD, is a professor of education and chair of the Department of Educational and Counselling Psychology at McGill University in Montreal, Quebec, Canada, where he is also director of the School/Applied Child Psychology Program. He has served as secretary of the World Council for Gifted and Talented Children and on the governing boards of the National Association for Gifted and Talented Children (NAGC) and the Association for the Gifted. In 1997, he was awarded the NAGC Distinguished Scholar Award. His research interests focus on the cognitive nature of high ability in relation to adult expertise, including creative expertise; the pedagogical relationship among inquiry-rich learning, teaching, and high ability; and the potential of gifted education, as seen through these perspectives, to contribute to the improvement of education for all children. His most recent book, coauthored with Catherine Clark, *Educating Students With High Ability,* was published by the United Nations Educational, Scientific, and Cultural Organization (UNESCO) in 1998.